THE MYSTERY OF
THE CRYSTAL SKULLS

THE MYSTERY OF
THE CRYSTAL SKULLS

A Real Life Detective Story of the Ancient World

CHRIS MORTON AND CERI LOUISE THOMAS

BEAR & COMPANY
PUBLISHING
SANTA FE, NEW MEXICO

Library of Congress Cataloging-in-Publication Data

Morton, Chris, 1963-

The mystery of the crystal skulls : a real-life detective story of the ancient world / Chris Morton and Ceri Louise Thomas.

p.   cm.

Originally published : London ; San Francisco : Thorsons, 1997

Includes bibliographical references and index.

ISBN 1-879181-54-1

1. Crystal skulls.   I. Thomas, Ceri Louise, 1962-   II. Title.

BF1442.C76M67   1998

001.94--dc21   98-23740

                                                                        CIP

Published 1998 in the United States & Canada by

BEAR & COMPANY

P.O. Box 2860

Santa Fe, NM 87504-2860

First published in 1997

by Thorsons, London, England

An Imprint of Harper Collins Publishers

Text illustrations by Peter Cox and John Gilkes

Cover photo by Frank Dorland

Cover design by Lightbourne Images

Printed and bound in the United States of America

by R.R. Donnelley

TO THE EARTH, AND ALL HER CHILDREN

There are more things in Heaven and Earth, Horatio,
Than are dreamt of in our philosophy.

William Shakespeare, *Hamlet*

CONTENTS

ACKNOWLEDGEMENTS

In addition to all those mentioned in the book, we would like to thank the following people and organizations, without whose help this book would not have been possible:

Our commissioning editors at the BBC's Religious Programmes Department for their commitment to fresh ideas, and to all our hard-working film crew and production staff. We also appreciate the co-operation of Hewlett-Packard, the British Museum, the Smithsonian Institution and the Instituto Nacional de Archaeologia y Historia (Mexico). In Guatemala we would like to thank Rolando Urutia and all those who attended the Gathering of the Indigenous Elders of the Americas. In Mexico, we would like to acknowledge the assistance given by Bertina Olmedo, Arturo Oliveros and Michel Vetter. In the USA, we are grateful for the additional advice given by archaeologists Dr Karl Taube and Dr John Pohl. In Britain, our thanks go to Simon Buxton of the Sacred Trust, writer Kenneth Meadows and our translator Georgina Ochoa de Blausten. A special thank you also to Leo Rutherford for encouraging us to pursue our dreams.

We would also like to thank all the staff at HarperCollins, especially Michelle Pilley, our commissioning editor, for her enthusiastic support throughout, and Lizzie Hutchins, our desk editor, for her skill and patience.

And finally, a big thank you to our friends, relatives, brothers and sisters for their vital encouragement and feedback – and especially to our parents Marion and Andrew Morton, and Madeleine and Peter Thomas, and Ceri's grandmother Joan Hallett, for their invaluable support.

PICTURE CREDITS

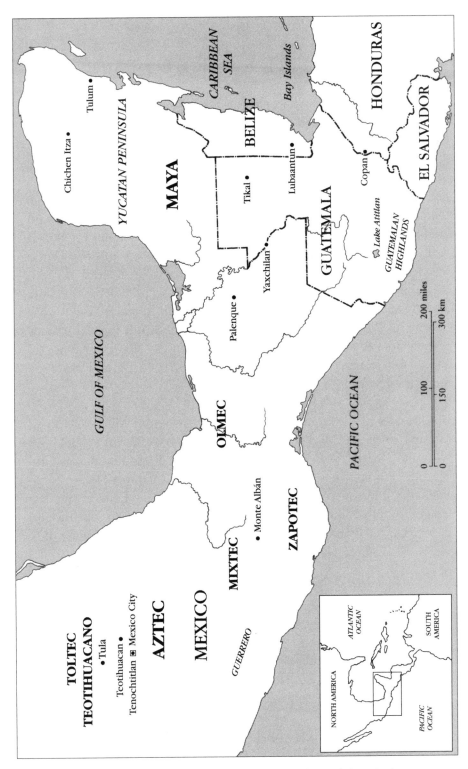

Figure 1: Map of Mesoamerica (ancient Central America)

1. THE LEGEND

It was just before dawn and we were deep in the jungle, trekking through the dense undergrowth to get to the ruins of the once great Mayan city buried somewhere deep within. In the darkness of the rainforest your mind starts to play tricks on you. You start to see and hear all manner of strange things – creatures, spirits, shadows of the unknown. It was then we heard the terrifying roar of a jaguar. In one split second that sound, cutting through the background of jungle noises, and all too close at hand, shattered our illusions of self-confidence, suddenly reminding us of our own delicate mortality. We stopped, for an instant frozen with fear, before turning in our tracks and stumbling off, as fast as we could, into the vast darkness of the unknown.

We were in one of the most beautiful places in the world, Central America, on the holiday of a lifetime, visiting the ancient Mayan ruins of Tikal in Guatemala. We were trying to reach the crumbling temples, palaces and pyramids before dawn. There we would wait for the sun to rise slowly from the surrounding greenery to cast whispers of yellow-golden light over the crumbling remains of this once great civilization, as if bringing it back to life. The jungle canopy is over 200 ft (60 m) high and yet the crumbling pyramids, some still covered in creepers and vines, reach right up through it to the heavens above. From atop one of these great mountains of human endeavour, whichever way you turn, the rainforest stretches as far as the eye can see. It could be a blanket of clouds or a vast ocean below, a beautiful ocean of green, where bright-coloured macaw and toucans sweep across golden pyramids that rise like rocks from the shore.

It was in this forgotten city that we saw our first skull, that symbol of death which normally strikes fear into the heart of modern man. It was a stone skull, carved into the side of one of the pyramids. To us this was a monstrous image. But our guide, Carlos, explained that to the ancients who had carved it, the skull had quite a different meaning. The Mayans and other ancient tribes of Central America had a different understanding of death from our own. To them death was not a full stop. It was not something to be afraid of, but rather something to look forward to, a great opportunity to pass into another dimension, a chance to join with the world of the spirits and the ancestors. To these ancient people death was part of the balance of nature, part of giving back to Mother Earth the life she had given. The skull, it seemed, was symbolic of this view. And then Carlos told us the legend of the crystal skulls...

According to an old Native American legend, there are 13 ancient crystal skulls, the size of human skulls, with movable jaws, that are said to speak or sing. These skulls are said to contain important information about the origins, purpose and destiny of mankind and answers to some of the greatest mysteries of life and the universe. It is said that this information is not only important to the future of this planet, but vital to the very survival of the human race. According to these ancient teachings, one day all of the crystal skulls will be rediscovered and brought together for their collective wisdom to be made available, but the human race must first be sufficiently evolved, both morally and spiritually, so as not to abuse this great knowledge.

This legend, said Carlos, had been handed down by generations of Native Americans over thousands of years. Indeed, as we were to discover, variations on this legend are found amongst several Native American tribes, from the Mayan and Aztec descendants of Central America to the Pueblo and Navajo Indians of what is now the south-western United States, right up even to the Cherokee and Seneca Indians in the north-eastern USA. The Cherokee version of the legend, for example, says that there are 12 planets in the cosmos inhabited by human beings and that there is one skull for each of these planets, plus a thirteenth skull vital to each of these worlds.

Of course, when we first heard Carlos' brief words, standing on the steps of one of the pyramids of Tikal, we thought the legend was a fascinating story – a snippet of ancient mythology, a wonderful, colourful tale, but a story, just a story, nothing more than that. It was an interesting curiosity that we might just recount to friends when we got back home.

What we didn't know then was that we were about to discover something that would change our view of the legend quite dramatically, something that would lead us on an adventure, on a journey of mystery, intrigue and wonder. It was to be a quest that would take us right across two continents, from the jungles and ancient ruins of Central America to the remote palm-fringed islands of Belize, and from the cold snows of Canada to the deserts of the United States. It would be a journey that would take us from the corridors of the British Museum in London and the laboratories of one of the world's leading computer companies in California to a sacred gathering in a secret location deep in the mountains of Guatemala. Along the way we would meet some of the world's leading scientists and archaeologists, encounter UFO investigators, psychics and mystics, and hear words of great wisdom from native elders, shamans and medicine men. We would uncover strange facts, hear ground-breaking new scientific theories and learn of ancient teachings kept secret for thousands of years. It was to be a journey where we would learn that things are not always as they seem and that truth can be stranger than fiction. It was also a personal voyage of discovery where we would explore our own attitudes to life and death and our place in the universe, an inner journey that would take us into the darkest reaches of the human soul.

In the meantime, before leaving the ruins of Tikal, Carlos told us a little more about the ancient Mayan civilization that had built the great city that now lay in ruins before us. It was a civilization which stretched across a vast area of Central America, from what is now southern Mexico in the north to Honduras in the south, and from the Pacific coast of Guatemala in the west to the Atlantic and Caribbean coast of Belize in the east. This area spanned the tropical forests of Chiapas, the highlands and steaming lowlands of Guatemala, and the huge expanse of low-lying savanna stretching out into the Atlantic Ocean known as the Yucatán Peninsula.

As Carlos explained, the ancient Maya built one of the most advanced and sophisticated civilizations the world has ever known. The cities that remain include the large, bold and militaristic Chichen Itzá; Uxmal, with its monumental architecture, carved snakes and weird 'chac-mool' figurines; the deeply aesthetic and beautifully proportioned Palenque; Tulum, set against the white sandy beaches and azure waters of the Caribbean Sea; and the once thriving metropolis of Tikal, which now stood crumbling before us, but which had once housed over 50,000 inhabitants.

We were still wandering in the ruins of Tikal just before nightfall, contemplating the achievements of this now almost forgotten people. Our guide and the handful of other tourists had gradually drifted away through the rainforest back to their temporary jungle lodge homes and we found ourselves alone in the Great Plaza of the old city just as the sun was going down. The plaza is a striking and somewhat eerie place tucked away in a small jungle clearing. To its north lie the 12 ruined temples of the North Acropolis, to the south the palace of the Central Acropolis. To the east and the west rise two great pyramids, known as the Temple of the Jaguar and the Temple of the Masks (*see colour plate no. 3*).

What struck me first about these pyramids is just how steep they really are. In concept they are similar to the pyramids everyone knows from Egypt, but they are smaller than the famous pyramids of Giza, far steeper and do not have smooth sides. Instead they are built in huge layers, or giant steps, and each pyramid has a crowning temple on top.

Every aspect of the pyramids' design was sacred to their ancient builders. The first nine large steps represent the 'lower world' and the walls and crown of the temple on top bring the total to 13, precisely the number of gods in the Mayan 'upper world'. The crowning stone carvings on top of each temple represent the thirteenth and ultimate layer. People can only ascend to these great temples by one route and on one side, where far smaller steps are provided. The number of human-sized steps is always significant. In this case there were 52. Like 13, this number is also important in the complex, sacred and divinatory Mayan calendar.

As we looked at these great temples in the fast fading light I suddenly felt compelled to make the steep climb up the eastern face of the Temple of the Jaguar. While Ceri wandered around taking photos in the plaza below, I reached the top of the pyramid, quite out of breath, just as the evening sunlight was turning to gold. Looking out from the doorway of the temple, just below the thirteenth layer, the towering pyramid of the Temple of the Masks looked straight back at me across the plaza as if mirroring my gaze. Its face was illuminated sun-coloured gold and behind it lay a deep sea of green against the background of the fast darkening sky. It was the most beautiful view I had ever seen.

And then another vision entered my mind. It seemed to seep in from around me as if entering my veins. Of course it was just my imagination, but it seemed under no conscious control. Though there was no one else there I distinctly felt the strange sensation of other people coming up the steps behind me then turning to stand at my side. I felt as though I was surrounded by a group of ancient priests in full ceremonial dress, with long flowing robes and elaborate head-dresses of feathers. They appeared to be performing some kind of ceremony, as they had done many times before. It seemed to be about celebrating and respecting some greater power, but there was also an air of foreboding about what might be to come. It was almost as if I could hear two notes, a high and a low. Then, as suddenly as it had appeared, it was gone.

Of course this all seemed quite crazy in the cold light of day, but this strange figment of the imagination remained with me as we went on our way.

The following morning we climbed aboard a clapped out old school bus and headed for Belize, the neighbouring country to Guatemala, amidst warnings we might get robbed by bandits *en route* to the coast.

Belize is a small country sandwiched between Guatemala and the Caribbean Sea, but it has great natural variety, ranging from a turquoise coral reef lined coast strewn with small islands or atolls to mangrove swamp and palm-covered shores to an interior of jungle-clad mountains. Belize is also home to a great variety of people of different races, many of them refugees from one difficult period of history or another. Until recently it was also home to many pirates.

As we sat in one of the many bars on the small island of Caye Caulker, our host behind the counter seemed to be getting immense pleasure out of recounting this part of the country's grisly history to us. Not only did he know all about pirates, he even looked like one as he proceeded to explain that Belize had once been a veritable haven for them. The old trade routes between Africa and the New World lay close by, but the coastline had another advantage. In the old days of seafaring, the coral reef had been a great navigational hazard. Many ships had been wrecked there quite naturally and so become easy prey to the pirates. It was possible to navigate past the reef safely to the shore, but only if you knew the way 'like the back of your tattooed hand'. This meant the pirates could make themselves quite at home along the coast, protected by the reef, and live without much fear of ever being caught by the naval authorities.

Many of the pirates became familiar with the native Mayans and even took to adopting some of their customs. The most obvious example of this was the famous pirates' flag, the skull and crossed bones. Apparently this was a very positive and religious symbol to the Mayans. Of course it became a symbol of fear to the average seafarer, but it is by no means clear that this was the pirates' original intention, although it was certainly the result of their actions.

Back in the bar, our conversation inevitably drifted towards the subject of buried treasure. Had any ever been found? Our barman was not aware of a treasure chest ever having been washed up on the shore, but there was something that might be considered buried treasure that had been found on an archaeological dig in the interior way back in the 1920s. To our amazement, it transpired that this treasure was an actual crystal skull. The barman told us that the skull had been found in the lost city of Lubaantun, a Mayan name meaning 'the City of Fallen Stones', which lay in the jungles of Belize. We were stunned. We had thought little more about the legend of the skulls. That a real crystal skull had actually been found seemed unbelievable. We had to know more.

I asked our host if the skull had anything to do with the legend. He didn't know. But what he did know was that ever since the skull had been discovered, truly incredible claims had been made about it. Apparently many people who had spent time alone with it claimed to have seen or heard things in its presence. The skull was said to have a distinctive glow, like an aura, extending around it, and those who had gazed deep into its interior claimed to have seen images there. Many said they were able to see the past or the future inside the skull and even that it had the ability to influence future events.

Others claimed they had heard noises, like the soft chanting of human voices, emanating from the skull. In fact, so many people had heard the skull 'talking' or 'singing' to them that it was now quite widely known as 'the talking skull' or 'singing skull', just as in the old legend.

The origins of the skull were, it seemed, a mystery. There were all kinds of theories about where it had originally come from, our barman said, including that it had initially been brought by extra-terrestrials. He had heard that some incredible photos had even been taken to 'prove' it. Whether or not it really had anything to do with the ancient legend he didn't know. But he had also heard that it was one of the world's largest gemstones. As a piece of jewellery alone, it was said to have been valued at millions of dollars!

We were fascinated – and as film-makers, we certainly thought that a real crystal skull would make a great subject for a documentary. So we asked the barman if he knew any more. Who had found the crystal skull? Where was it now? Might we be able to film it?

He said that the skull had been found by a young woman during archaeological excavations back in the 1920s, but that it was now somewhere in Canada. That was pretty much all he could tell us. But he did add, perhaps rather inevitably, that he could arrange for us to visit the site of the skull's discovery if we were really interested in finding out more. He just happened to 'know a man' who knew a man who could take us there. But it would obviously cost us 'a dollar or two'.

Although some of the claims about the crystal skull did sound a little far-fetched, at least it seemed as though a real crystal skull had been found, and it was certainly intriguing. So we haggled a little over the price and finally asked the barman to make all the necessary arrangements for a trip the following day.

And so began our journey of discovery, our quest to find out the truth about the crystal skulls. Though we didn't know it then, our investigations would take us from the cutting edge of modern science to an exploration of ancient traditions that stretch back deep into the mists of time. We would gradually uncover ideas that would challenge many of our basic assumptions about the past history of this planet and the evolution of mankind. What we learned would lead us to question how we currently think about the world, the universe and our place within it. We would think again about where we as individuals and as a society have come from, where we belong in the world and where we are going. Our whole way of looking at the world would be dramatically altered. Finally we would hear of startling prophecies about mankind's immediate future on this small planet and be told by native elders that now we had 'the keys to the future' we would 'tell the world about it'.

But in the meantime, we set off on the first leg of our journey to explore the mystery of the crystal skulls...

2. THE DISCOVERY

At sunrise the following morning we set off for the lost city of Lubaan-tun. We found ourselves in a small motor boat snaking our way through the swampy waterways which dominate the coastline of Belize. After the inevitable two-hour wait for our four-wheel drive vehicle to turn up at a banana plantation jetty, we were off on a bumpy ride over rough jungle track deep into the interior. There was a timeless quality about the Mayan villages we passed along the way – the wooden huts, the sound of chickens, the children laughing and playing, and the women washing their clothes in the river. It felt as if we had entered a different world.

We finally reached our destination in the early afternoon, only to find a very sorry-looking archaeological site. But there was a guide who still manned this almost forgotten place. He was a local Mayan named Catari-no Cal. Dressed in regulation park-keeper's beige uniform and Welling-ton boots, he came over and greeted us warmly in excellent English. It turned out that we were the only tourists to have ventured to this remote setting in days.

Catarino proceeded to show Chris and I round the site. He explained that it had originally been excavated by a British explorer called Frederick Mitchell-Hedges back in 1924. Although it had been cleared then, after decades of neglect the jungle had crept back in to try to reclaim its former captive and by now the ancient pyramids were only just about dis-cernible. But we couldn't help noticing that the individual stones from which each of the structures was made were not the simple rectangular blocks of stone used at Tikal. Instead each stone was quite unique and slightly rounded or curved to fit in with all the other stones around it. So there were no simple and uniform straight lines, no horizontal or vertical layers. Instead each building was curving and flowing, almost a living work of art, with areas that bulged and receded almost as if the structure were actually breathing. Indeed, each one was constructed so carefully in this almost organic fashion that it seems the builders had no need for cement or any other type of binding material.

Now, however, these beautiful pyramids were very dilapidated. As Catarino explained, this was due to the fact that a later party of explorers in the 1930s had tried to discover what was still inside them using the fastest and most modern technique available to them – dynamite – at the same time giving a whole new meaning to the name 'the City of Fallen Stones'!

As a result, Catarino explained, the city was no longer one of the best examples of the achievements of the ancient Maya, about whom he proceeded to tell us a little more. Theirs had, it seemed, been a highly developed civilization. Although considered Stone Age people, living on peasant agriculture close to the land, with few material possessions or technical instruments, they were expert architects, astronomers, scientists and mathematicians. They possessed a complex system of hieroglyphic writing and numbering. They also built up a vast network of independent city states, linked by roads and boasting some of the most magnificent cities the world has ever seen, with towering pyramids, exquisite palaces, temples and shrines, all decorated with the most elaborately carved stone 'stelae'. Each city was a distinctive work of art, expertly planned, designed and executed, with many buildings, including astronomical observatories, carefully aligned with the sun, the moon, the planets and the stars.

The whole system came complete with its own form of government, politics and administration, its own science based on the movements of the planets and the stars, and a whole religion based on the rhythms of the natural world. The ancient Maya believed in a complete pantheon of gods and super-heroes who demanded regular tribute of ceremony, religious ritual and the occasional human sacrifice. They were also great believers in clairvoyance and divination. They were avid watchers of the skies and the movements of the heavenly bodies and placed great emphasis on their own powers of prophecy and prediction. Through their complex system of calendrics they were even able to predict eclipses accurately.

The Mayan civilization flourished for over 1,000 years from around 300 BC. Dynasties grew, royal leaders were adorned with elaborate costumes, priests gave guidance and performed strange esoteric rituals, local wars were fought and peace was brokered. And then suddenly the cities were abandoned. Around AD 830, well before the arrival of the Europeans in the Americas, the 'Classic' Maya simply left their great cities to be taken over by the jungle and slowly crumble to dust. As far as anyone could tell from the evidence left behind, no famine or drought had taken place, no disease and no great war had broken out. It was a mystery – over 1,000 years of development, of growth and refinement, and a culture that reached extraordinary spiritual, scientific and artistic heights ... and then nothing, with no explanation at all.

In fact nobody really knew where the Maya had originally come from or, for that matter, where they had got the advanced knowledge necessary to build their great civilization in such a short space of time. There remained many mysteries about the ancient Maya.

As we wandered around the crumbling pyramids pondering why the ancient Mayan civilization had simply disappeared, Catarino spoke again. 'One of the strangest things the Maya left behind was found right here at Lubaantun.'

He reached in and pulled something out of his pocket. It was an old black-and-white photograph that had definitely seen better days.

'This was discovered in the 1920s by Mr Mitchell-Hedges' daughter Anna when she was 17 years old.'

He handed us the dog-eared photo. My eyes were immediately drawn to the image. It was unmistakably a photograph of a real crystal skull. It was an extraordinary object, at once horrifying and yet beautiful. Even in that tattered old photo, the skull had a strange, mesmerizing quality. As I stared into those hollow crystal eyes, I was captivated.

As Chris handed back the photo, I wanted to know more. The image of the skull had drawn us in, raising questions that demanded answers. Who had made such an object and why? Where was it now? Were there any others like it and if so, where? Was this one of the 13 skulls of legend? The questions raced through my mind. Now we knew for sure that a real crystal skull did exist we felt compelled to find out more.

The first question was, where had Catarino got this photo? We were a little surprised when he said it was Anna Mitchell-Hedges herself who had given it to him. After all, this was the woman he said had originally discovered the crystal skull way back in the 1920s. How could this be?

Catarino explained that Anna Mitchell-Hedges had subsequently returned several times to visit the place of the skull's discovery and her last visit had been in 1987. We worked out that if Anna had discovered the skull as a teenager in the 1920s, she would probably now be in her late eighties. But was she still alive?

According to Catarino, when Anna had made her last trip back she had been a very elderly woman. He had got the impression that she had come back to see the site one last time before she died. Given these words, it now seemed very unlikely that she was still around to tell the tale.

As Catarino was speaking, the shadows started lengthening across the ancient ruins and we realized it was time to leave. We thanked Catarino for his patience with our questions and wandered back to our vehicle, wondering how we could ever track down this old lady. We were just climbing into the truck when Catarino came rushing over.

'Wait, wait,' he said. 'I remember. Anna Mitchell-Hedges did give me her address, but it was a long time ago and I don't know if I've still got it.'

But we had to leave there and then. Our driver was getting impatient. So we swapped addresses with Catarino and he assured us he would look for Anna's address and send it on to us if he found it.

As we made our way back to the coast for the last few days of our holiday, the whole story began to seem somehow unreal. A young girl on an archaeological dig finding an ancient artefact known only in legend seemed so unlikely, so impossibly romantic. In any case, we didn't really expect to hear anything more from Catarino and it was soon time to put the whole idea of crystal skulls out of our minds as we returned to the everyday realities of life in Britain.

But we had only been home for a few weeks when a letter did arrive from Belize. It was from Catarino. He had found Anna Mitchell-Hedges' address. It was in Canada. We were delighted and wrote to her, albeit with some trepidation. We were unsure we would get any answer and half expected that if we did it would only be to inform us that Anna had now passed away. So when a letter did arrive back from Canada, we opened it nervously. As we read its contents, we were thrilled to find that Anna Mitchell-Hedges, now aged 88, was still living happily and healthily – and complete with her crystal skull. Not only that, but she would be only too pleased to tell us the story of the skull's discovery.

Anna had enclosed a copy of her father's autobiography, *Danger, My Ally*,[1] and from this, together with subsequent telephone calls to Anna, we were able to piece together the remarkable tale.

The story began in the Britain of the 1920s, with Anna's father, Frederick Albert, or 'Mike', Mitchell-Hedges (1882–1959), a real Indiana Jones-type figure, who had adopted Anna when she was a young orphan. For many years Anna's life remained inextricably linked to that of her father. She had never married and had accompanied him on many of his overseas voyages.

'My father's great love was ancient archaeology,' she explained. 'He had a very enquiring mind. He wanted to know more about the past and was the sort of person who liked to find things out for himself. He questioned the way things were and didn't like to accept what other people told him.'

Indeed, according to Anna, Frederick Mitchell-Hedges had been something of a legend in his own lifetime. He was your archetypal British adventurer-explorer, determined to make his mark in the twilight years of the British Empire. He was a flamboyant, charismatic and somewhat unconventional character who had no time for the petty niceties of suburban English middle-class life, and certainly no time for what he considered the boring nine-to-five existence of the various office jobs, in banking and the stock market, he had tried during his early career.

Instead he had turned to a life of adventure and exploration. His motto, 'Life which is lived without zest and adventure is not life at all', spurred him on in his various overseas missions 'to see parts of the world no white man had ever seen before'. He funded his trips largely through silver-trading and lecturing. He enjoyed gambling and always allowed time to indulge his great love of deep sea fishing along the way. He was a man who seemed almost deliberately to court danger, at one stage apparently even finding himself taken prisoner by the famous Mexican bandit turned national hero Pancho Villa, unwillingly caught up in his border raids against the United States. He travelled extensively and his passion for adventure found its greatest fulfilment in organizing great voyages of exploration and discovery to far-flung places, all the while fuelled by his obsession with the idea of finding the treasures of lost civilizations.

For Frederick Mitchell-Hedges was a member of the Maya Committee of the British Museum. He believed that the cradle of civilization was not in the Middle East, as was commonly supposed, but was the legendary lost continent of Atlantis. He was convinced this was a real civilization which had disappeared after some natural catastrophe and that its remnants were to be found in Central America. Moreover, he was determined to prove it.

To this end he gathered together a party of explorers who set sail from Liverpool in 1924[2] bound for British Honduras (now Belize). On reaching the Americas they docked at the small port of Punta Gorda, from where rumours had emanated of a lost city hidden deep in the jungle. They tried, at first unsuccessfully, to penetrate the interior via the crocodile infested Rio Grande, a trip which ended in disaster with the loss of all their medical supplies aboard a dug-out canoe which capsized and sank. As a result, one member of the team contracted malaria and later died. Only with the help of the local Kekchi Maya tribespeople, direct descendants of the ancient Maya, was the party finally able to penetrate the dense tropical rainforest and continue their search.

One day, deep in the jungle, they stumbled across some mounds of stone, overgrown with moss and foliage and suffocated by roots and vines. This was the sign they had been looking for. Frederick Mitchell-Hedges was heard to cry out, 'We can't be very far from this lost city!'

Work began in earnest as the party and local Mayan helpers toiled in the jungle heat to clear the site. It was back-breaking, seemingly relentless work, hacking away at the undergrowth and felling huge trees which piled themselves high on top of the ancient stones below. It took over a year to clear most of the undergrowth. When they had finished, the trees lay fallen before them in a great mountain of twisted branches. It was time to set fire to the what was left of the forest. The fire raged hot and high for days beneath the blistering sun. It burned 'like a mighty blast furnace', spewing out white hot ash and burning red embers all around. It dried the lips, reddened the eyes and almost choked the very life breath from the party of explorers. But as the flames subsided the ruins of a once great city slowly emerged from amidst the smoke and burning ashes. As Frederick Mitchell-Hedges recounts in his autobiography, published in 1954:

> 'We were amazed at the immensity of the ruins. Walls, terraces and mounds came into view as the holocaust swept onwards ... in its centre had stood a mighty Citadel.
>
> ... The Citadel was raised above the level of the surrounding countryside and when it was first built it must have stood out like a glittering snow-white island, one hundred and fifty feet high. Around it spread the lesser dwellings and burial mounds of the common people and, further out, the thousands of acres of green, waving maize that must have been necessary to feed and support the large population.'[3]

When the blaze had died away Mitchell-Hedges and his team were able to explore the great city:

> 'It covered ... a total area of six square miles with pyramids, palaces, terraces, mounds, walls, houses, subterranean chambers, [even] a huge

amphitheatre designed to hold more than 10,000 people and approached by two great stairways. The Citadel was built over seven and a half acres and originally every foot had been covered with cut white stone...'[4]

Mitchell-Hedges was amazed at the workmanship that had gone into the construction:

'The magnitude of the labour required is almost beyond computation for their only tools were flint axes and chisels. I tried to square a similar block of stone with one of these implements, of which we found many. The task took an entire day.'[5]

Frederick Mitchell-Hedges was to spend several years uncovering the secrets of the past that lay hidden in this lost city. During the long excavation of the site he was joined by Anna, or 'Sammy' as she was affectionately known to her father (*see black-and-white plates 32 and 33*). She settled instantly to life in the jungle, as if she had been born to it. Anna shared something of the same rebellious spirit of adventure as her father and had a strong, inquisitive nature. It was this that led her to make her dramatic discovery.

It was a particularly hot day, an afternoon when the air itself seemed to stand still in the drowsy heat. The archaeological site, which was usually very busy, was strangely silent. 'Everyone had gone to sleep. They had been worn out by the heat,' remembers Anna. It was a few weeks before her seventeenth birthday. She was alone in her hut and feeling restless. Suddenly it occurred to her there was something she had been wanting to do for a while.

'I thought this was my chance to go up and see how far I could see from the top of the highest building. Of course, I was strictly forbidden to climb up there because the stones were very loose and dangerous. But I had heard that you could see for miles around from the top of one of the pyramids and that intrigued me.'

So Anna headed towards the site, knowing that the excavation team were sleeping soundly in their beds.

She began to climb the tallest pyramid. Monkeys chattered in the distant trees and insects buzzed noisily around her as she picked her way carefully over the loose stones until, at last, she reached the top. It had been worth it:

'Once I was up there I could see for miles around and it was very beautiful. I felt that I could have stayed there for a very long time. But the sun was very, very strong and there was something shining in my face. Way way down below through a crack I could see something shining back at me and I got very, very excited. How I got down from that building so quickly I don't know, but when I got back I woke my father up and told him I'd seen something. Then, of course, I got a very bad scolding because I shouldn't have gone up there.'

Anna's father was disinclined to believe she had seen anything at all:

' "You imagined it," he said.
'But the following morning my father got all his men together. Before I got up he had everybody moving the stones from the top of the pyramid, because there was no way we could get in from the bottom. It took several weeks of carefully removing stones before a big enough hole was created.'

It was the day of Anna's birthday when she volunteered to go down. She was lowered slowly by her father and his helpers into the narrow gap between the stones:

'I had two ropes tied around my body and a light strapped to my head and I was let down into the opening. As I descended into the dark, I became very nervous, because there could be snakes and scorpions down there. When I got down I could still see something shining, reflecting the light on my head back at me. So I picked it up and I wrapped it in my shirt so it wouldn't be hurt and I told them to pull me up as fast as they could.'

As Anna emerged from the temple into the bright daylight she wiped the dirt from the surface of the object and stared at it in wonder. 'It was the most beautiful thing I had ever seen.' The object was truly remarkable. It was life-size and looked almost exactly the same as a real human skull, and yet it was almost completely transparent. It was a real crystal skull. She held it up to the light. It was carved from a magnificent piece of clear rock crystal and caught and reflected the light in devastatingly beautiful, captivating and complex ways. And, miraculously, it appeared to have survived completely unscathed.

There was a moment of stunned silence as the small crowd of excavators gazed at this strange object, mesmerized by the way in which it captured and reflected the sunlight, sending it forth in a dazzle of light. Anna's father took the skull from her and held it high for all to see. Then all at once everyone went wild with joy. 'All the Maya helpers on the dig started laughing and crying. They kissed the ground and started hugging each other,' Anna said. It was a magical moment, she recalled, perhaps the greatest moment in her long life. It was 'as if an ancient and powerful force had returned to the lives of those present'.

As evening fell and the first stars appeared in the skies, Frederick Mitchell-Hedges placed the skull with great ceremony upon a makeshift altar the Mayans had built. As he and Anna looked on, fires were lit all around the skull and in the light of the blaze they could see the Mayans blessing it. Then the sound of drumming began. Mayan dancers appeared from the shadows, decorated with the plumes of jungle birds and the skins of jaguars. They moved with agility and grace to the rhythm of the drum. There was chanting and singing. It was a night of celebration, as Anna recalls. 'They performed ceremonies, rituals and dances in front of the skull in the firelight.'

From the depths of the jungle people appeared, as if something had called to them across the forest.

'It was as though a message of joy had been sent out across the Mayan lands. A lot of Maya came that we never even knew, and they came so quickly and from so far afield that I don't know how they could possibly have heard of the skull in such a short space of time. But they knew.'

The celebrations around the skull continued for several days and amongst those who came to see it was a very old Mayan from a neighbouring village. He looked at the skull and told Anna and her father that it was 'very, very ancient'.

'The Mayan priests say it is over 100,000 years old. The Mayans told us the skull was made after the head of a great high priest many, many thousands of years ago because this priest was loved very much and they wanted to preserve their truth and wisdom forever. The old man said that the skull could be made to talk, but how it was done he wouldn't say.'

Both Anna and her father were puzzled by the discovery. What they did-n't know at the time was that the object would prove to be one of the most mysterious ever found, that it would come to change Anna's life and the lives of many others who have since come into contact with it. For, as we had heard, many have claimed that the skull has magical and myste-rious powers. Some maintain, as the legend had said, that it is encoded with sacred knowledge that can enable us to tap into the secrets of the distant past and possibly even the future. Many others simply believe that the skull can profoundly influence the way people think and feel.

Although Frederick Mitchell-Hedges had no idea of the incredible claims that would come to surround the skull, he seemed to have been deeply affected by the reverence the local people showed for it. He was also concerned that, since the discovery, the Mayan workers had been considerably less willing to spend their days toiling on the dig. He gave it much thought and discussed it with Dr Thomas Gann, the consultant anthropologist on the expedition. Anna said, 'My father decided that the skull was obviously so sacred and so important to the Mayan people that we couldn't possibly keep it. He said, "We cannot possibly take this skull away from these poor people." '

So, with characteristic flourish, he gave it to the Maya. 'They were very, very glad,' recalls Anna, who was not so pleased by her father's gen-erosity, after the danger she had gone through to retrieve the skull. 'I was very angry because I had risked my life to go down there and get it.'

But, following the gift, excavations were resumed. The pyramid where Anna had found the skull was part of the further explorations and three months later, the separate lower jaw of the skull was found buried beneath an altar in the main chamber of the pyramid. Anna had originally found only the upper cranium. When the Maya added the lower jaw to the skull, the masterpiece was complete. After this, as Anna remembers, 'They had it for nearly three years and they had fires burning all around it.'

By 1927 the excavations at Lubaantun were drawing to a close. The final items were catalogued and sent off to museums. Mitchell-Hedges and his team had unearthed hundreds of rare and beautiful artefacts, but none could match the beauty of the crystal skull.

As the party prepared to depart, it was a sad moment for Anna. She had lived with a Mayan family who had treated her 'as well as their own daugh-ter' and she had 'shared in their joys and sorrows over the years'. As Anna and her father bade farewell to their Mayan friends, the Mayan chieftain stepped forward and pressed a bundle into Frederick Mitchell-Hedges' hands. As he unwrapped the bundle, Anna was delighted to find that it was the crystal skull:

> *'The Maya presented my father with the skull for all the good work he had done for their people, giving them medical supplies and work and tools and everything. And that's why they gave it back to us. It was a gift from the Mayan people.'*

So fate had it that the crystal skull should accompany Frederick Mitchell-Hedges as he left Lubaantun for England.

Putting his overseas adventures behind him, Mitchell-Hedges was eventually to settle in England. In 1951 he took up residence in the impressive seventeenth-century Farley Castle in Berkshire. There he would lecture guests from overseas about his expeditions and his wonderful antique collection, and show the crystal skull to members of the British aristocracy who were invited to elegant dinner parties in his grand candlelit dining-room.

Frederick Mitchell-Hedges used to delight in telling his guests that it was called 'the Skull of Doom'. He said, 'It has been described as the embodiment of all evil' and that 'according to legend [it] was used by the High Priest of the Maya' to will death. 'It is said that when [the Mayan priest] willed death with the help of the skull, death invariably followed.'[6] According to Anna, much of this description could actually be put down to her father's sense of humour, but he had been told by the high priest of the Maya that if the skull were to fall into the wrong hands, it could be used for evil purposes.

Mitchell-Hedges was no doubt fascinated as lords and ladies gazed upon the awesome image of the skull. Their initially fearful reaction was so very different from that of the Maya who had helped to bring the skull up from the darkness of its tomb. The rich sophisticated Europeans saw only fear where the 'poor' 'uneducated' Mayans had seen cause for celebration and joy. Was it that in those dying days of the British Empire the skull was a stark reminder that none could escape their fate? No grand titles, no worldly riches could overcome the inevitability of death.

But whatever their initial reaction, the crystal skull soon held Mitchell-Hedges' guests entranced. They marvelled at its craftsmanship and became seduced by its beauty. They admired the perfectly chiselled beauty of its teeth, the smooth contours of its cheekbones and the way the jaw fitted faultlessly into the cranium. The question on everyone's lips was, how could such 'simple', 'primitive' people, living deep in the jungle all those years ago, have created something so accomplished, so perfect?

Over the years many have been particularly captivated by the way the skull seems to hold, channel and reflect light. For it is made in such a way that any source of light from beneath it is refracted into the prisms at the front of the skull. So if the skull is placed in a darkened room and a fire or candle lit beneath it, the light appears shining right out through the eye sockets.

Others have also observed that the skull has two small holes carved into its base, one on either side of the main cranium. These are just the right size and shape for two narrow sticks to be inserted from below, enabling the skull to be suspended over any fire or light source, and allowing the top part of the skull to be moved in relation to the separate lower jaw. In this way, or with the attachment of the lower jaw by string or animal gut, it is possible to move the skull around in such a manner that it gives the impression that it is talking.[7]

Taking very literally what Mitchell-Hedges had been told about the skull being 'made to talk', some have suggested that it may have been used in this way by the ancient Mayans. They have speculated that the skull could have been placed on an altar at the top of the steps of one of the great pyramids, suspended over a fire concealed from view beneath the altar. The skull's eyes would have blazed fire red as its jaw moved in precise synchronization with the booming voice of a mighty high priest, whose cohorts would have controlled the skull's movements. The priest might have made a series of oracular announcements, perhaps announcing the names of the next victims for human sacrifice. This would indeed have been a terrifying spectacle to the masses of ordinary people gathered in the plaza below. Thus, some have concluded, the skull appeared thousands of years ago as a terrifying animated talking god-head, used by the priestly class to wield power over their frightened subjects.[8]

But this is assuming that when the old Mayan said the skull could be 'made to talk', he meant it literally. And the idea that it was a tool the Mayan priests used to fool and terrify their subjects is hardly in keeping with the joy the Mayans are said to have demonstrated on seeing it.

One person who became particularly fascinated by the skull was the author Sibley Morrill. He thought it had been 'made to talk' in quite a different way. He was struck by the skull's incredible anatomical accuracy and noted that it almost faultlessly compared with a real human skull. But one feature was strangely missing. Real human skulls have a series of marks which run across them, known as suture marks. These are the seams that are left when the different plates of the skull have grown together. Morrill pointed out that these markings would have been very easy to add and would have given the skull even greater realism. The fact that they were missing indicated to him that the skull was not made simply to serve as a memorial to any particular individual.

Morrill puzzled over the absence of these marks and reached the rather dramatic conclusion that the only reason they could have been so obviously and intentionally left out was that the maker of the skull was forbidden to add them, or that 'such an easily carved feature would be completely unacceptable'.[9]

The reason for this, he thought, was that to have suture marks would interfere with the true purpose of the skull. Morrill believed its primary purpose was for 'foreseeing the future and affecting the outcome of events'. He said, 'Suture marks ... would be as out of place as engravings on the surface of a crystal ball.'[10] His view was that:

'The foreseeing of the future would be handled by ... the priest, [who,] after preliminaries that might include fasting, the use of drugs, or both, and after other prescribed rites, would peer down into the crystal in an effort to see in its depths and striations ... what the future held.[11]

'[Morrill concluded:] How effective an aid the crystal skull was in foretelling the future is unknowable. All that can be said with certainty ... is that it was probably the most effective crystal ball ever devised, and ... it is highly probable that in some cases over the centuries the skull served that purpose well.'[12]

So, what had the skull really been used for? Had it been an animated godhead, a sort of talking oracle? Was it an elaborate crystal ball, used for seeing into the past, present and future, or was it the head of some ancient priest? What was meant by it being 'made to talk'? What clues to its ancient role lay hidden in those polished prismatic surfaces? What secrets lay behind its penetrating crystal gaze? There had been an enormous amount of speculation but as yet no firm evidence or definitive answers.

In 1959 Frederick Mitchell-Hedges died and left his devoted daughter Anna in sole possession of the skull. Anna has looked after it in her own home ever since, although she has allowed more than the occasional visitor to come and experience 'the power of the skull' for themselves. This turned out to be our next step.

3. THE KEEPER OF THE SKULL

Through our telephone conversations with Anna it was now becoming increasingly clear that the incredible claims about the crystal skull's paranormal powers had continued unabated ever since its original discovery. From the moment that the skull had been recovered from deep in the jungle, it had been widely recognized that there was something very strange, extraordinary and powerful about this object. But, over the years, it seemed to have escaped being labelled or categorized. In fact, from what we could tell, it seemed quite simply to have defied explanation altogether.

By now, Ceri and I were quite convinced that the skull would make an excellent subject for a documentary investigation. We mentioned this to Anna and explained that we would need a lot more information. All Anna was prepared to say, however, was that if we wanted to know more about the skull then we would have to 'come and meet him' for ourselves.

The strangest thing was that in speaking to Anna on the telephone we kept getting the impression that when she was talking about the skull she was actually talking about a real person. She spoke about the crystal skull as 'he' or 'him' and used the same affectionate tone that people often use when talking about their children, grandchildren or even a much-loved pet.

We were intrigued, but it seemed that the only way for us to find out more was to take Anna up on her kind offer and make the trip out to Canada. This would not only give us the chance to see the crystal skull for ourselves, but also to make the necessary arrangements for our documentary. This was a bit of a risk, as we had just blown all our money on the trip to Central America and at this stage had no guarantee whatsoever that the film we intended to make would be commissioned at all. But, in what must have been a temporary fit of madness, we decided to make the trip to Canada all the same.

It was during the cold snows of the Canadian winter that we arrived at Anna's neat modern house in the quiet little town of Kitchener, near Toronto, Ontario. A greater contrast to the steaming tropical jungles of Belize we could hardly imagine. But Anna, looking much younger than her years, greeted us warmly and she and her nephew Jimmy, who was in his late thirties and also visiting, were wonderfully hospitable during our short stay.

As soon as we arrived, Anna led us into her small sitting-room to 'meet' the crystal skull. As we entered the room, our eyes were immediately drawn to the skull, which was placed on a black velvet cushion on the coffee table. It was absolutely flawless, remarkably anatomically accurate and exactly the same size and shape as a small adult's head, yet it was almost totally transparent. It really was magnificent, the most exquisitely carved and beautiful object that either of us had ever seen. It was like gazing on perfection (*see colour plates 1 and 2*).

'I'm only the caretaker,' Anna began. 'The skull really belongs to everyone. He has brought lots of happiness to people. I show him all over the world. I'm asked to go here, there and everywhere – Australia, New Zealand and even Japan. But I particularly like people to come here so that I can see their joy and happiness in my own home.'

As she was speaking, I found myself staring at the skull, captivated. The way the light seemed to be captured, channelled and played around deep in its interior and reflected back off its silky smooth surface was totally mesmerizing. There was some strange, almost indefinable quality about looking at the skull, but I couldn't figure out quite what it was. It was as though the skull was holding me there, somehow communicating with my unconscious mind. It was as if some part of my mind was stirred in a subtle, almost incomprehensible way. I was totally absorbed.

Anna spoke to me, but I didn't hear. She had to tap me on the shoulder before I realized that she was saying something. 'I don't normally allow people to do this, but you can pick him up if you like.'

'I'm sorry, I wasn't with you,' I replied.

'Oh, that's perfectly normal,' chuckled Anna. 'The skull usually casts a spell over people when they meet him. They often seem to go into a trance for a few moments.'

I lifted up the crystal skull. I was surprised at how heavy it felt. 'It weighs almost 12 lbs [5 kg],' said Anna.

I handed the skull to Ceri, who commented that it was 'deathly cold' to the touch and quickly placed it back on the table.

'There's nothing to be frightened of,' said Anna. 'People are often frightened when they first see the skull,' she added.

'It's not surprising, really,' said Jimmy. 'Just look at how the skull has become a symbol to be feared. It's either in horror movies, *Friday the Thirteenth* and all that, or it's a warning on a bottle of poison.'

It was true, the skull did always seem to be a fearful image in our culture. Its primary purpose always appeared to be to terrify people or warn them of danger.

Anna continued, 'People usually come to see the skull in twos and threes and often one of them is nervous about seeing him. But the next thing you know they are sitting right near to the skull. They say, "It's not what I thought it would be. It's beautiful." And the joy comes into their faces and they are happy.'

This struck me as rather curious. Here was an image of death that Anna claimed actually made people feel happy. At first I didn't understand it. But I have to admit that, after a while, I started to feel sort of warm, almost cosy, in the skull's presence. I began to think about it. Perhaps meeting the skull was a way of overcoming our fear of death, of meeting the very image of our future selves. We normally try to push all thoughts of death away. And yet here I was staring the very image of death in the face.

As I was sitting there looking at the beautiful, pristine, clear nature of the crystal, it occurred to me that perhaps the very reason why the skull had been carved out of a transparent material was so that it did not represent any one person. It could be anyone's skull. Perhaps that was it – the skull was meant to represent each and every one of us. After all, each of us has a skull within us, buried under our skin, and one day that will be all that will be left of us. So, of all the symbols available to humanity, what could be more universal than a skull? For it is a symbol that speaks to every living person.

As I examined the skull, its smooth contours and hollow eye sockets, I thought about how I would one day die and that I too would be little more than an empty skull. Not only me, but everyone I knew and cared about would go the same sad way. I wondered if perhaps that was the purpose of the crystal skull, to remind each of us of our own mortality and of the very short time that each of us has as a living being on this Earth.

But there seemed to be more to it than that. In any case, who needs a reminder that they are going to die? Surely that couldn't be the only reason for making the skull. If it was, then it was a bizarre and macabre one.

I held up the separate jaw-bone. It was beautifully crafted, with each tooth picked out in fine detail. Perhaps the skull only seemed macabre to me because of the attitude I had towards death, because it was something that I didn't want to acknowledge. As I slotted the separate jaw-bone carefully back on to the skull, it suddenly struck me that that stark, cold image of death actually concealed a powerful message: it reminds us that we are alive! I remembered something I had heard somewhere – that it is often only when people are closest to death, when they are in a sense staring death right in the face, that they feel fully alive and able to truly appreciate life. Could it be that the crystal skull was also here to help us appreciate life?

I moved the skull around, watching the way in which it caught the light. Had it been designed so that as we look upon its cool chiselled contours we are reminded of the feel of the soft skin on our own faces and the warm pulse than runs through our veins?

But there was still something further, something about the skull's transparent nature. For this was an image of death that you could almost see through, right to the other side. It was as if this death's head was telling us that death is actually something that we can transcend, something we can go through and come out the other side.

I put the crystal skull back on its velvet cushion on the coffee table, next to a framed black-and-white photograph of Frederick Mitchell-Hedges. Anna was just beginning to tell Ceri that her own good health and longevity were all thanks to the crystal skull. I had to admit, she was a very spritely 88-year-old with unusual amounts of energy. 'The skull gives you health, happiness and joy of life,' she explained. 'He is always in my room, even when I am sleeping. I know the skull protects me. All through my life he has protected me.'

Ceri drew my attention to the tiny bubbles she had noticed deep inside the crystal skull. They were laid out in softly curving planes, glittering within the body of the crystal like tiny stars within a distant solar system on a very clear starry night. It was amazing to think that these tiny bubbles must have been trapped in the crystal as it was being formed many millions of years ago.

As I gazed on, I couldn't help getting the feeling that there was still far more to the crystal skull than I had so far been able to fathom. It was more than just a reminder of our own mortality. There was something else, something beyond that. But it seemed that the real significance of the crystal skull was as yet intangible to me.

Anna was discussing the visitors who came to see the skull. 'The skull brings people together in many, many ways. It's always a happiness for me to show it to people, to see the joy it brings them. So many people come, sometimes as many as 14 people, sometimes 18. I have a lot of Indian people. American Indians and Canadian Indians stay with the skull for hours and I can't tell them, "Well, it's time for you to go." The skull is loved very much by everyone who comes to see it. I've even had the actress Shirley Maclaine come to work with the skull.

'I welcome people because it's a way of giving a little happiness and really, it's the skull that does that. I call it "the Skull of Love", just as the Mayans would think of it.'

'The sun has come out,' said Jimmy. We looked out through the windows to see pale wintry sunshine on the road outside. Jimmy offered to show us how the skull responded to sunlight so we followed him out into the garden.

I was fascinated by the way that the skull reacted to light. It appeared completely different depending on how it was lit, almost as if its face were changing, and as it was changing so too were the patterns and refractions of the light inside. I held it up to the sunlight. Although the sun was not particularly bright, the effects on the skull were none the less beautiful. The prismatic qualities of the crystal created a display of reflections that showed quite clearly all the different colours of the rainbow. It was stunningly beautiful.

I was interested to know how the skull looked in really bright sunshine. 'Well, it gave me a shock,' said Anna, as we settled back down with a pot of tea. She told us how she had been showing the skull to a group of schoolchildren. She had put it on its cushion and then turned her back to talk for a few minutes, only to hear the children shrieking, 'It's smoking, madam!' Anna turned around to see that the cushion was beginning to catch fire.

Jimmy explained that the prismatic qualities of the crystal are such that if the sun's rays are very strong and fall at a particular angle onto the back of the skull, they are focused and condensed and appear as a bright, sharp beam of light out of the skull's eyes, nose and mouth. 'If this happens for more than a few minutes then the skull can actually start a fire,' he added.

'This was one of the things that the Mayans used the skull for,' said Anna.

We were interested to know exactly what the skull's uses had been.

'The Mayans used the skull for many things, but particularly for healing,' said Anna. 'If you are ever worried or not feeling well or anything like that, you just go to the skull and it gives you health, happiness and joy of life.' She continued, 'I have a tremendous amount of letters. I love to read those letters from people who are being healed by it.'

'Remember Melissa,' said Jimmy.

'Oh, that little girl who had the bone marrow trouble,' replied Anna. 'She came to stay with us for a few weeks, and I gave her a photograph of the skull and she carries that photograph with her everywhere. Anyway, she came back to tell me that her bone marrow is fine and she can walk now. That's the biggest joy of my life really. Another lady, only last month, she had an operation but she wasn't doing very well. So she came and she saw the skull and sat with him for a very long time. She sent me a letter the other day to say that she is now healed.'

I was puzzled. If the skull really had the power to heal, why had Anna's father even in his written account referred to it as 'the Skull of Doom' and claimed that the ancient Maya had used it 'to will death'?

Anna explained, 'The Maya told us that it was a healing skull. It was actually used for many, many things, but particularly for healing. But, you see, for the Maya, death itself was sometimes seen as a form of healing.'

'The way I understand it,' added Jimmy, 'is that for the Maya death was the ultimate way to access the other dimensions they believed in and the skull was used to help this final transition to the other world.'

'I can tell you exactly how the Maya used it during the willing death ceremony,' said Anna. 'This came about when an old medicine man or priest was getting too old to carry on their work and a young person was chosen to carry on the work of the elder. When the day came, the old one would lie down and the young one would kneel down beside them and they would both put their hands on the crystal skull. Then a high priest would perform a ceremony and during the ceremony all the knowledge and wisdom of the old one would pass on into the young one through the skull and the old one would pass away during the ceremony and go to sleep forever. And that was the willing death ceremony.'

Anna went on to explain that she had been looking after the skull for many years now and letting people come to her house and experience its power for themselves. She said the Mayan people knew what she was doing with the skull and that they were very happy about it. She said that before she died she wanted to ensure that the work she had been doing would be carried on. 'This is what my father would have wished and it is the wish of the Maya people too.' She added, 'I think I have someone in mind already to take over the care of the skull when I'm gone.' She said she was also planning a final visit to Lubaantun. We wondered whether Anna was planning to give the skull back to the Mayan people, but she said the skull would not be going with her.

In Anna's opinion, the crystal skull was bequeathed to her and her father for a reason, a reason whose time would come. 'The Mayans told me that the skull is important to mankind. It is a gift from the Mayan people to the rest of the world.' She added, 'The Mayans have a lot of knowledge. They gave us the skull for a definite reason and a purpose. I am not exactly sure what that reason is, but I know that this skull is part of something very, very important.'

We of course wanted to know more, but all Anna would say was, 'You will just have to ask the Mayans.'

4. THE MYSTERY

Every now and then in the history of mankind there comes a discovery so unique and so incredible that it cannot be explained according to our normal set of beliefs and everyday assumptions, a discovery so remarkable that it challenges our normal view of history, and therefore our whole view of the world today. Could it be that the crystal skull was just such a discovery?

After all, we had always assumed that we were more advanced and developed than our simple and primitive ancestors. Everything we had learned about human history seemed to have shown that civilization had logically evolved in a constantly improving fashion over the millennia, so that we now found ourselves, almost by definition, living at the very pinnacle of mankind's evolutionary development.

The crystal skull appeared to challenge this view. For how could such ancient and 'primitive' people have made something so accomplished? Indeed, where exactly did the Maya, with their elaborate cities, their complex hieroglyphics, their mathematics and calendrics, and their knowledge of astronomy, fit in with our simple model of a constantly evolving and improving human history?

The skull was a mystery. Not only was it beautiful to look at, but it seemed that nearly everyone who had come into contact with it had some strange tale to tell of unusual experiences or inexplicable phenomena. Whatever its real powers, the skull certainly seemed to have us entranced.

Now we knew crystal skulls were not just the stuff of legend, there were other questions to consider. Were there any other skulls like Anna's? What did her skull have to do with the ancient legend? Why did some people, including Anna's own father, consider it evil, whilst for others, such as Anna, it was a force for good? And had the ancient Maya really made such a beautiful and sophisticated object themselves?

After our visit to Anna Mitchell-Hedges, these questions remained unanswered. But our desire to find the answers was now even more pressing. We began by trying to find out more about the ancient Mayan civilization. From the books we were now reading it seemed that archaeologists had managed to reconstruct quite a vivid picture of it from the detailed inscriptions, monuments and artwork the Maya had left behind. They had a pretty good idea of many of their ancient customs, rituals, knowledge and beliefs, and in some cases very specific information, such as the birth dates of kings and the names of their ancestors for up to seven generations.

So we now began talking to various Mayan experts and archaeologists, hoping that they might be able to tell us more about the crystal skull. Did the Mayans make it at the same time as they built their great cities, only to abandon it and perhaps others like it on their sudden departure? Could the crystal skull perhaps give us some clues as to why they left? How had it come to remain in the temple ruins?

We also wanted to see whether there were any other clues as to how the Mayans might have made the skull or how they might have used it, or even, as Frederick Mitchell-Hedges had suspected, whether it in fact dated back to some even more mysterious pre-Mayan civilization.

But as we began our further investigations it soon became apparent that these were questions to which there would be no easy answers. Despite the details archaeologists had uncovered about some aspects of Mayan history, whole chunks of knowledge seemed to be missing.

Indeed, as we continued our investigations we realized that we had unwittingly stumbled into a veritable minefield of great archaeological controversy. For not only was there heated debate about who the Maya were, where they had come from and where they had disappeared to, but one question in particular seemed to divide the archaeological establishment perhaps more than any other, and that was, where had the Mitchell-Hedges crystal skull really come from?

As we were to discover, the controversy began even with the site of the skull's original discovery – Lubaantun. Mitchell-Hedges himself was of the view that the site was really pre-Mayan in origin. He felt the evidence from the site suggested that pre-Mayan peoples were involved in its construction and that it actually dated back to a much earlier period.

What had made Mitchell-Hedges suspect that Lubaantun might have been pre-Mayan was that, as we ourselves had noticed, the building techniques used there were so very different from those used at every other Mayan site. In their recent book *The Mayan Prophecies*¹ author-historians Adrian Gilbert and Maurice Cotterell point out that the style of construction was remarkably similar to the techniques used by the even more ancient Incas of what is now Peru in South America. There are certain similarities between Lubaantun and the famous ancient Inca sites such as Machu Pichu, hidden high up thousands of miles away in the Andes. Gilbert and Cotterell suggest that whoever built Lubaantun might have enlisted the help of or learnt construction techniques from the ancient Incas of South America. Or perhaps both the ancient Maya and Inca had learned their construction techniques from some other civilization even more ancient than their own. This raised the question, had the crystal skull originally come from this same mysterious pre-Mayan civilization?

Mitchell-Hedges believed this civilization to have been the legendary Atlantis. Though this struck us as rather unlikely, he did in fact later find evidence that there had been some sort of pre-Mayan civilization in this part of the world during his later excavations of the Bay Islands off the nearby coast of Honduras. He donated several specimens from these digs to the British Museum in London and the Museum of the American Indian in New York, and Captain James Joyce of the British Museum wrote to comment:

> '*It is my opinion that [the samples] represent a very early type of Central American culture; probably pre-Maya. The fact that they appear to bear relations with the pre-Conquest civilisations of Costa Rica, early Maya, and archaic Mexico, suggests that this is an early centre from which various forms of culture were diffused over Central America...*
>
> '*The results [of further research] are likely to shed new light on the current ideas of the origin and development of the American aboriginal civilisations...*
>
> '*I consider that your discovery is of great importance.*'²

George G. Heye, then Chairman and Director of the Museum of the American Indian, had also written:

'In every way we concur with the findings of the British Museum in regard to your amazing discoveries made on a chain of islands off the coast of Central America... The specimens ... are of a hitherto unknown culture...

'[They] open up a new era in scientific thought relative to the age and history of the original inhabitants of the American continent...

'Your discoveries open up an entirely new vista in regard to the ancient civilisations of the American continent, and must compel archaeologists to reconstruct their present scientific theories in regard to the riddle which has existed for so many years in Central and South America. In fact as further work is done and more knowledge gained, in my judgment it will make fresh history, and open up a reconstruction of thought on the antiquity of cultural civilisations of a world-wide character.'[3]

We managed to track down an archaeologist, Dr Norman Hammond of Boston University, who had spent some time at Lubaantun during the 1970s carrying out further excavations of the site. Chris called Dr Hammond to ask him who he thought had really built the city. Dr Hammond was quite happy to talk about this and said that he believed it was the Mayans and the Mayans alone, without any external assistance, who had built Lubaantun. In his opinion the site had been built around AD 700 and abandoned around AD 850. It did not bother him at all that the buildings were constructed so differently from those at most other Mayan sites, as there were even examples of sites in the Mayan area that were built from red bricks and mortar like many modern homes, instead of from the usual blocks of cut white limestone. In Dr Hammond's opinion, Lubaantun, like these other sites, was entirely Mayan and he would not countenance the view that any other people, whether Incas, Atlanteans or whoever, had been in any way involved.

But it was when we turned to the question of the crystal skull itself that we discovered that Dr Hammond's views were about to drop a real bombshell onto our investigations. The minute Chris raised the subject of the skull Dr Hammond stated quite clearly and categorically that in his opinion, the crystal skull was irrelevant to Lubaantun, that it had never really been found there at all! He said that there was no evidence that Anna Mitchell-Hedges had ever even been to Lubaantun in the first place and that the story of the skull having been found there had only surfaced after her father died. He said that Anna Mitchell-Hedges' own claim was the only evidence of the find.

By now we knew the crystal skull's discovery had been controversial, but we didn't know it had been quite as controversial as that. Norman Hammond said, in no uncertain terms, that he didn't want anything more to do with the subject. We were horrified. We were about to make a film telling Anna Mitchell-Hedges' fascinating story, when a respected archaeologist suddenly claimed the whole thing was pure invention. What were we to do?

As we were fast finding out, it was one thing trying to get our film off the ground but quite another trying to determine the truth about the Mitchell-Hedges crystal skull. The truth seemed to be slipping through our fingers like grains of sand on a beach. If Anna Mitchell-Hedges had never really been to Lubaantun, how was it that she appeared to have all the photos to prove it? If the party had not really found the crystal skull there at all, why would Anna have invented such an incredible story?

It seemed that what had really got people wondering about the true origins of the skull was a series of puzzling discrepancies that appeared to exist between Anna's detailed account of the skull's discovery and her own father's virtual silence on the issue. Even in his own autobiography, Frederick Mitchell-Hedges said very little about the skull. In fact, in a later American edition, published in 1955, he makes no mention of it at all. In the original edition he refers to it only briefly and somewhat enigmatically as follows, in a section of his autobiography mostly devoted to a later trip to Africa:

'We took with us the sinister Skull of Doom of which much has been written...'[4]

If much had been written on the skull we certainly hadn't been able to find it. But the plot thickened further when we read the remaining scant details Frederick Mitchell-Hedges offered about the skull:

'How it came into my possession I have reason for not revealing.
...It is at least 3,600 years old and according to legend was used by the High Priest of the Maya when performing esoteric rites. It is said that when he willed death with the help of the skull, death invariably followed. It has been described as the embodiment of all evil. I do not wish to try and explain this phenomena.'[5]

However, he did add, at the end of the same chapter, 'Much more of what we discovered [is] to be told in a book which Sammy will write.'[6]

This lack of information in Frederick Mitchell-Hedges' own account of the discovery, perhaps more than anything else, perhaps more even than the incredible claims made about the skull's magical and healing powers, was why it had stirred up such incredible controversy, particularly amongst those in the archaeological establishment. In the light of his secrecy, some degree of scepticism was now completely understandable. But it had led to some pretty wild speculation.

Dr David Pendergast, Mayan specialist at the Royal Ontario Museum in Toronto, wondered whether it was perhaps possible that Frederick Mitchell-Hedges had even planted the crystal skull himself for Anna to discover. The fact that she had found the skull on her seventeenth birthday made him slightly suspicious. Could it really have been an incredible present from her father, which he had painstakingly planted with the intention that she might discover it apparently quite by accident on her birthday?

The problem was that even if this were the case, it still begged the question as to where Frederick Mitchell-Hedges got the crystal skull from himself. David wondered whether it was possible that he might have found the skull somewhere else or bought it previously, presumably at vast expense. But the question then would be, how had he managed to transport it without anyone knowing all the way to Lubaantun through the rainforest?

A possible origin for the skull emerged when we took another look at the writings of Sibley Morrill. It appeared from his account[7] that Morrill also had some doubts about the Lubaantun discovery story. He had his own theory as to how Mitchell-Hedges might have obtained the crystal skull.

It was apparently widely rumoured towards the end of the nineteenth century that the Mexican President, at the time Porfirio Díaz, owned a secret cache of treasures thought to include one or more crystal skulls. These treasures were said to have been handed down from one Emperor to the next and to have given the owner the powers necessary to rule.

The end of the nineteenth century and the beginning of the twentieth was a time of great turmoil, citizen unrest and civil war in Mexico, and ultimately the President was deposed. It was rumoured that his treasures were ransacked and divided up amongst the rebels as their spoils of war. One of these rebels was none other than the bandit turned national hero Pancho Villa, at whose side Frederick Mitchell-Hedges claimed to have been forced to fight back in 1913–14. This led some to speculate that Mitchell-Hedges' crystal skull might actually be one that originally belonged to the line of Mexican Emperors and that Mitchell-Hedges might have obtained it from Pancho Villa's men, who in turn may have stolen it from the Mexican President.

Certainly Sibley Morrill was keen to point out:

> *'It is important to know that some high officials of the Mexican Government are of the unofficial opinion that the skull was acquired by Mitchell-Hedges in Mexico, and that it, like countless thousands of other artefacts ... was illegally removed from the country.'* [8]

Indeed, Sibley Morrill devotes virtually an entire book to the elaborate theory that Mitchell-Hedges was actually acting as a spy for the British government in the period before the First World War and that he was fighting alongside Pancho Villa accompanied by the legendary literary figure Ambrose Bierce, who mysteriously disappeared in Mexico at around the same time. Morrill believed Bierce was there spying on behalf of the US government. Both Britain and the United States did have valuable oil, gas and mineral interests in the area at the time. In 1913 Mexican oilfields were the main source of oil for the British naval fleet, and the US government was concerned at rumours that both the Japanese and the Germans were providing arms and training to the Mexican rebels with a view to helping them ultimately invade the United States. Morrill believes Mitchell-Hedges' and Bierce's job was to infiltrate Pancho Villa's army to obtain vital information in what was then considered the likely event that Pancho Villa would become President of Mexico.

If it were the case that Mitchell-Hedges bought or obtained the crystal skull on some sort of spying mission, he would certainly have had good reason for not revealing how he came by it. But if he had come by the crystal skull on some previous visit to Mexico, how on Earth could he have managed to hide it in the intervening years? Furthermore, is it not likely that a crystal skull would be so expensive that no one would possibly buy one just for their daughter's birthday, particularly given the unusual risks, such as capsized boats and the like, faced by Mitchell-Hedges along the way? Indeed, Anna's response to the suggestion that her father had planted the skull for her to find was 'Absolute nonsense.' She said he would not have spent thousands of pounds on an expedition just 'so that he could bury a crystal skull'. [9]

So where exactly had the crystal skull come from? Was it Mayan, as Anna believed? Was it a relic of a pre-Mayan civilization? Was it the prized but stolen possession of a Mexican Emperor?

But now we made another interesting discovery, a discovery that would lead us even further into the enigma of the legendary crystal skulls. In an attempt to find out more about the Mitchell-Hedges skull we put in a call to Elizabeth Carmichael, assistant keeper at the British Museum's Museum of Mankind in London. To our great surprise she informed us that there really was more than one crystal skull, just as the original legend had suggested, and that in fact the British Museum had one of their own!

Chris and I set off without further delay to find out more. The British Museum's Museum of Mankind is tucked away behind Piccadilly Circus in central London. The second mysterious crystal skull was housed in a glass case at the top of the stairs on the first floor of the museum, looking somewhat out of place amidst the totem poles and wooden artefacts of Papua New Guinea.

This skull too looked incredibly clear and anatomically accurate. Again it seemed to be around the same size and shape as a small adult's head, but the quality of the crystal was a little more cloudy and the way it was carved appeared to be more stylized than the Mitchell-Hedges skull. Though this skull also appeared to be cut from a single piece of crystal, it was not nearly as life-like as the Mitchell-Hedges skull. Though in many ways similar in overall size and shape, the eye sockets were merely indicated by deep, totally circular holes, the teeth had little detail and there was no detachable jaw-bone. None the less this skull was also very attractive to look at (*see colour plate no. 8*).

Underneath the skull's glass case was a small label which read:

'*Aztec Sculpture.*
  '*Skull of rock crystal. Mexico. Probably Aztec.*
  '*c. AD 1300–1500. The style of this piece suggests that it dates from the Aztec period. If, however, as one line of the carving suggests, a jeweller's wheel was used to make the cut, the piece would date from after the Spanish Conquest.*
  '*Length 21cm. 1898.1.*'

There was no hint of any possibility that this skull might be Mayan. Indeed, it might not even be ancient.

After examining the skull we went down to the oak-panelled research library to meet Elizabeth Carmichael. She had a professional, brisk, no nonsense manner. She explained that she often came out of her office to find all sorts of people staring at the skull for hours on end. She said she could not understand why people came in to the museum just to gaze at the skull when there were so many beautiful objects there, adding she personally did not find the skull aesthetically pleasing at all.

But she also explained that this all probably had something to do with the rumours that had once been reported in the tabloid press. Much to her distaste, some staff were supposed to have claimed that the skull had started moving around by itself in its sealed glass case! The papers had even said that there were cleaners in the museum who insisted that the skull was covered with a cloth at night because they were so scared of it.

I asked if there were any truth in these rumours. Elizabeth Carmichael simply said that if the skull really had been moving around by itself then it was probably due to the vibrations of lorries passing on the road outside or some equally normal phenomenon. She went on to comment that there were an awful lot of ridiculous superstitious beliefs surrounding the skull and all kinds of incredible claims had been made about it, but in her opinion it was all nonsense. She did, however, confess that she herself would not want to be left alone in a room with it.

It soon became clear that the origins of the British Museum crystal skull were almost as mysterious and controversial as those of the Mitchell-Hedges. The museum records showed only that the skull had been purchased from Tiffany's in New York in 1898. It was said to have been brought by a Spanish soldier of fortune from Mexico and had always been considered Aztec. The Aztecs, who lived several hundreds of miles further north-west than the Mayans, and several centuries later, in what is now central Mexico, were known to have been even more obsessed with the image of the skull than the Mayans.

Elizabeth Carmichael, however, explained that there was no real evidence as to exactly where the British Museum skull had come from. She said that whilst it was indeed possible that it might really be Aztec, there was also a strong possibility that it was actually a modern fake.

She also informed us that the British Museum skull had in fact once been examined alongside the Mitchell-Hedges skull back in 1936 and that an article had been published about this comparative study in *Man*, the journal of the Royal Anthropological Institute of Great Britain and Northern Ireland.[10] She even had a copy of this article in her office.

As we read through the details of this comparison it seemed that there had been some debate at the time about the marked similarity between the two artefacts. One of the experts carrying out the study suggested that the British Museum skull was a copy of the original Mitchell-Hedges skull, which is more detailed and anatomically accurate, whilst the other believed the reverse to be the case. Either way, the article reached the conclusion that the two skulls had probably come from the same source.

But this article could not answer the question of how old the skulls really were, stating simply:

'The technique will not help us to settle their relative ages for in neither case is there any trace of identifiable tool marks, and it is certain that neither specimen was made with steel [i.e. modern] tools.' [11]

I asked Elizabeth Carmichael how we could find out whether either of the skulls was really a 'modern fake' or not. She told us there were scientific tests which could now be done, which might prove the matter once and for all. When we asked whether we might be able to film such tests, she offered to suggest this to her head of department. She explained that it might take some time to get official approval, but in the meantime we might like to look through the other records the British Museum had in their files about their own skull or the Mitchell-Hedges skull as an aid to our investigations.

As we went through the records, it transpired that there was another problem with Anna Mitchell-Hedges' story of her discovery. For there was apparently no written record of the discovery of the Mitchell-Hedges skull in the British Museum files relating to Lubaantun, although these files contained detailed records of all the other thousands of artefacts found there. We also discovered that when Captain James Joyce of the British Museum had visited Mitchell-Hedges' party in Lubaantun to inspect their excavations, back in the twenties, it appeared that no mention had been made to him about the discovery of the crystal skull. Neither had the other members of the Mitchell-Hedges expedition, notably Dr Thomas Gann or Lady Richmond Brown, ever spoken publicly or written about the skull's discovery. [12]

Anna Mitchell-Hedges, however, explained, 'My father allocated the account of the various finds and incidents at Lubaantun to the member of the team that found the object, and was scrupulous in observing their right to give the facts first.' [13]

Hence the comment in his autobiography that Anna herself would explain 'much more of what we discovered'.

We went back and had another look at Frederick Mitchell-Hedges' autobiography. In it we found one very strong hint of a particularly straightforward explanation as to why Mitchell-Hedges had been reluctant to reveal exactly how he got the skull, an explanation which would account for why the skull's discovery did not appear in the records of the dig held at the British Museum, as well as why Captain Joyce never saw it and why no member of the team ever publicly spoke or wrote about the find either at the time or afterwards. For Frederick Mitchell-Hedges quite clearly explained that, upon discovering the lost city of Lubaantun,

> 'Our immediate purpose was to inform the Governor of our discovery, and, at a meeting of the Legislative Council of British Honduras, an act was passed granting us a sole concession valid for twenty years, to excavate over an area of seventy square miles around the ruins.' [14]

Quite how Mitchell-Hedges was able to negotiate such an agreement was revealed in George G. Heye's press release on behalf of the Museum of the American Indian, in which he explained:

> '[Mitchell-Hedges] conducted his own expedition under an agreement that his finds were to go to the New York Institution [the Museum of the American Indian] and to The British Museum.' [15]

Given this agreement that all finds would automatically go to one or other of the museums, is it any wonder that no mention was made of the crystal skull at the time? As Anna was also keen to point out to us, 'If we had kept the crystal skull when we first found it, it would have gone to a museum automatically like all the other things we found,' and, 'If Captain Joyce had seen the skull the British Museum would have got it.' But in the actual event and whatever the real reason, by the time Captain Joyce came to inspect the dig the skull had already been given back to the Mayans. So it never did end up in the British Museum. Anna was also keen to say that if the crystal skull had not really been found at Lubaantun, then why do the Belizean government, and the British Museum on some occasions, still claim to this day that the skull is really their property and should be returned to them?

But there was one other problem for academics and archaeologists such as Elizabeth Carmichael. It was that there were two written records of a crystal skull in the British Museum's archives from the first part of the twentieth century and neither was specifically related to Lubaantun. The first of these was the article we had already read, which appeared in the July 1936 issue of *Man*. This article specifically referred to the skull the British Museum themselves did not own as being 'in the possession of Mr Sydney Burney' and made no mention of Mitchell-Hedges. It also noted that the skull had 'the character almost of an anatomical study in a scientific age', though no sign of any tool markings could be found on it.

The other record was a note handwritten by one of the former museum keepers which said that a rock crystal skull had come up for auction at Sotheby's of London on 15 September 1943, listed as 'Lot 54'. The surprising thing about this entry was that it too referred to the skull as apparently having been sent for sale by London art dealer W. Sydney Burney, not Frederick Mitchell-Hedges. In fact the note implied that the British Museum had tried to buy the skull but in vain as it was then 'bought in by Mr Burney' and 'sold subsequently by Mr Burney' to none other than a 'Mr Mitchell-Hedges for [only] £400'! This apparently private transaction is thought to have occurred in 1944.[16]

These, the oldest written records of what one can only assume to be the Mitchell-Hedges crystal skull, had led some archaeologists, Elizabeth Carmichael now among them, to speculate that Frederick Mitchell-Hedges did not really find the crystal skull at Lubaantun at all but simply bought it in London in 1944 from a man called Mr Burney, who, it is assumed, was an antique dealer. Indeed, these two written records have led many to speculate that the skull is in fact not ancient at all but of far more modern, possibly European, origin, being made some time towards the end of the nineteenth century or at the beginning of the twentieth.

By now we were obviously beginning to have grave doubts about Anna Mitchell-Hedges' story. But Anna had a simple answer even to these apparent problems. According to her, Mr Burney was a family friend who loaned her father money and the skull had actually been used as collateral. When Mr Burney proceeded to put it up for sale, her father paid him back and got his crystal skull back. This explains why the mysterious Mr Burney should have withdrawn the skull from auction and sold it privately to Mitchell-Hedges rather than simply selling it off to the highest bidder. Another interesting, perhaps coincidental, consequence of this sale, however, is that legally no one can now dispute that the Mitchell-Hedges family are the rightful and legal owners of the skull.

But was the Mitchell-Hedges crystal skull a modern fake or could it really be one of the ancient skulls of legend? The suggestion that it might be modern, and possibly European, had been made by several of the archaeologists we had spoken to, and was now strongly supported by the British Museum files, whatever Anna Mitchell-Hedges might say.

So we asked Anna if she would be willing to let her skull undergo tests so that we could get an answer to this question once and for all. We were somewhat surprised when she explained that 'he' had already been scientifically tested. Rigorous tests had been carried out several years before by the world famous computer company and crystal experts Hewlett-Packard. Anna said we would find the results of these tests 'most interesting' but that if we wanted full chapter and verse on what the scientists had discovered we had better go and talk to them for ourselves.

That was it, we were off to talk to the scientists at Hewlett-Packard without further delay.

5. THE SCIENTISTS

The crystal skull had not only attracted the attention of archaeologists. Scientists too had been fascinated, intrigued by the skull's mysterious history and all the incredible possibilities it seemed to represent. When Anna Mitchell-Hedges agreed to loan her skull to a team of scientists at state-of-the-art computer and electronics company Hewlett-Packard, they had the chance to examine the skull in detail.

Hewlett-Packard is one of the world's leading manufacturers of computers and other electronic equipment. They use crystals in a whole range of electronic devices. Their scientists therefore are experts not only on computers but also on the physical, technical and scientific properties of crystal.

The tests on the crystal skull took place in late 1970 in Hewlett-Packard's crystal laboratories in Santa Clara, California (*see black-and-white plates 34–6*). We visited these laboratories, deep in the heart of California's Silicon Valley, to try to find out what the scientists had discovered.

The tests had been overseen by Jim Pruett, components manager of the frequency standards team. By the time we arrived in California, he was long gone, but Ceri and I were able to speak to the current principal scientist at the lab, Jack Kusters, and the former engineering manager for quartz devices, Charles Adams, who had been present during the tests. Between them these two men have over 50 years' experience of working with crystal.

As Jack and Charles explained, initially the team was not even convinced that the crystal skull was really made of proper quartz. There are in fact several other materials that look almost exactly the same as quartz crystal to the naked eye, including various types of plastics and glass. Even lead crystal, the material from which most glasses, decanters and other decorative objects are now made, is actually a type of glass and not crystal at all. Also, there is a lot of artificially manufactured or 'synthetic' quartz crystal around today.

Natural quartz, or rock crystal, on the other hand, is entirely a product of Mother Nature. It actually grows in the ground, taking sometimes billions of years to form. Crystals grow deep within the Earth's crust, usually around volcanic and earthquake activity. The process requires immense heat and pressure and always a 'seed' crystal is needed to start it off. This seed is created when a single silicon atom, under intense heat and pressure, fuses with two oxygen atoms from superheated water or steam trapped in the same space. The atoms fuse to form a single crystalline cell of silicon dioxide, the substance from which all quartz crystal is made. (The by-product is hydrogen.) Over the millennia, if conditions are right, this seed starts to grow. But the surrounding fluid must contain just the right proportions of silicon and water, or pressurized steam, maintained at a phenomenal intensity of heat and pressure for a sufficiently long period of time. As the primordial fluid oozes over the first cell of silicon dioxide, the cell starts to replicate itself, laying down its complex crystalline structure one atom at a time. Every cell in the crystal repeats the same pattern. Each cell is a tiny little crystal in and of itself, and each cell repeats the same pattern as the one before. In this way the crystal builds up a complex three-dimensional network structure, known as a 'crystal lattice', with absolute geometric regularity, where every cell is exactly symmetrical and precisely repeated throughout the whole. And so little by little, over the years, a piece of pure, transparent natural quartz crystal comes into being. In its natural state it is highly angular in shape, always with six sides, tapering at either end to a fine point.

Of course, not every piece of natural quartz crystal is perfect. Impurities can creep in, traces of iron or aluminium or any number of other substances can get trapped in the network. Such traces of other elements show up as discoloration, aluminium for example turning the crystal smoky grey, known as 'smoky quartz', or iron adding a tint of pink, known as 'rose quartz', to name but two. High levels of radioactivity can also affect growth and cause discoloration. Only if there is no radioactivity and there are no other trace elements in the area is a totally pure and transparent crystal formed.

Quartz, however, is one of the most common naturally occurring materials. As Jack told us, current estimates are that around 80 per cent of the Earth's crust contains quartz. But much of this is too full of impurities or too small to be of any practical use, other than as sand. And, whilst some of the less pure varieties of quartz are still beautiful, they are of relatively little use to the electronics industry. In fact a problem for the industry has been that large and pure pieces of natural quartz are actually very rare.

Recently this problem has been solved to some extent by the manufacture, or rather growth, of man-made or synthetic quartz. The first experiments in manufacturing or growing synthetic quartz began in 1851, but it was not until the latter part of the twentieth century that the technique was sufficiently perfected for manufactured quartz to be of practical use in electronics. In fact at the time that the tests on the crystal skull were performed at Hewlett-Packard, carefully selected natural quartz was still the main source of crystal for electronic devices, but since then scientists have become so successful at growing their own quartz that synthetic quartz has now all but completely replaced natural quartz as the essential ingredient for most electronic equipment.

The point about manufactured quartz is that the purity and size of the crystal can be absolutely guaranteed. But this is not to say that the process no longer requires the help of Mother Nature. On the contrary, it is only possible to manufacture quartz by growing it from natural pieces. What the scientists do is to speed up a process that would naturally take an eternity, so that it now only takes a matter of weeks. This is done by artificially creating the optimum environment for growth. In a vast 'autoclave', a highly sophisticated type of furnace, natural pieces of quartz scraps or 'lascas' are dissolved in water at highly elevated temperature and pressure. But the essential ingredient is still a natural piece of high quality quartz; without it the process cannot even begin. This carefully selected piece of natural crystal is simply suspended in the autoclave and the rest of the process is left to nature itself. The surrounding fluid quite simply grows onto the original crystal and the results are removed from the autoclave, or harvested, when the resulting crystals reach the required size. But these new crystals, even over generations and generations of man-made manufacture, can only ever be as pure as the original piece of natural quartz crystal supplied by Mother Earth.

Given all the different types of material that look exactly the same to the naked eye as natural quartz, the first task for the Hewlett-Packard scientists was to determine exactly what the crystal skull was really made of.

In one of the tests the skull was submersed in a glass chamber containing Benzyl alcohol of exactly the same density and refractive index as pure quartz. As the skull was lowered into the tank it seemed to disappear (*see plate 36*). This proved that it was made of the most incredibly pure type of quartz. But not only was it pure, it was also natural. Polarized light was directed at the skull in its chamber and vague shadows or 'veils' then appeared, which showed that the skull was of natural origin. These shadows, tiny variations in the growth pattern of the crystal, somewhat akin to the rings on a tree, are removed in the precisely controlled environment of manufactured quartz. So the skull was not made from any type of plastic or glass, nor was it made from modern synthetic crystal. It was definitely natural rock crystal supplied by the Earth.

The presence of the veils also revealed something else quite remarkable about the crystal skull. Given its size, unusually large for a natural piece of quartz, some had suspected that the skull had been made from several pieces of crystal carefully pieced together. But the polarized light test proved beyond doubt not only that the main cranium was made from only one piece of crystal, but also that the detachable jaw-bone was carved from exactly the same piece of rock. At some stage the crystal skull had been one solid block of rock crystal.

The investigating team was absolutely astonished by this. For pure quartz crystal is one of the hardest materials in the world. On the Mohs scale of hardness, used by gemologists, it is only slightly softer than diamond. This makes rock crystal an incredibly difficult material to carve, particularly given that it is also somewhat brittle and has a tendency to shatter. The workmanship on the skull was so exquisite the team estimated that even if the carvers had used today's electrically powered tools with diamond tips, it would have taken at least a year to carve such an incredible object. But the team concluded something even more surprising than this. They felt that it would have been almost impossible to make such an exquisitely carved object using any known type of modern diamond-tipped power tool. This is because the vibration, heat and friction produced by such tools on such a delicate object as the lower jaw would actually have caused the skull to shatter – a fact which apparently led one member of the team to comment, 'This skull shouldn't even exist!'

But the original investigating team's belief that the skull had not been made with modern tools was more than just a hunch. It was borne out by further tests. Even under extreme magnification of the surface of the skull there was no evidence of modern tool markings, no evidence of the usual tool 'chatter' or of the tell-tale pattern of repetitive parallel scratch marks. Given that any such markings would have been extremely difficult to remove, these findings seemed to confirm what the team had already begun to suspect – that the crystal skull had actually been made by hand!

This was phenomenal, as the only hand-carving techniques for crystal currently known take an incredible length of time. The scientists could only assume that the skull had been carved by slowly and patiently rubbing the original block of quartz down by hand, probably using a mixture of river sand and water. Even with the use of copper rods or hand-held carving 'bows', the team concluded that the crystal skull must have taken several generations of effort to carve! Whilst the precise length of time this had taken was impossible to confirm, the Hewlett-Packard staff magazine *Measure* put the nearest estimate at '300 man-years of effort'![1]

As Jack and Charles explained, whoever made the skull would have had to have started with a huge chunk of angular quartz crystal around three times the size of the finished skull, and when they first started carving they would have had no way of knowing whether the inside was pure or full of fractures and holes. They would have had to carefully grade the sand by the size of each of its grains, starting with the largest grains to rough out the overall shape and gradually reducing their size as the work became more detailed, right down to a microscopically fine grain size, like powder, to finish off the final smooth polish. What is more, if they had made a mistake at any point, they would have had to start again from scratch. If even a single grain that was too large had fallen onto the surface on which they were working as they neared completion of the skull, they would have had to start again. This must have been a truly formidable task.

I explained that I had heard the rather outlandish theory, suggested by the ancient legend and also by many of those who had spent considerable time with the skull, that the skull might actually have been made by extra-terrestrials. After all, if it could not even have been made with modern tools, then how could it possibly have been made by hand? But the scientists from Hewlett-Packard, perhaps understandably, dismissed this theory. As Jack Kusters said:

'Being a scientist, I find it very hard to believe that people, pardon me, creatures, from other universes came and dropped things off here and then disappeared and never bothered us again. These other alternatives are simply not within the realm of possibility. I do not believe in the existence of aliens, so I have to conclude that it was made by human hand.'

This finding was of course incredible enough itself. But it was one that Frederick Mitchell-Hedges had already suspected:

'It must have taken over 150 years, generation after generation working all the days of their lives, patiently rubbing down with sand an immense block of rock crystal until finally the perfect skull emerged.' [2]

Likewise, in the 1936 study in *Man*, Adrian Digby of the British Museum had already observed that 'Mr Burney's [presumably Mr Mitchell-Hedges'] skull bears no traces of recent (metal age) workmanship.'[3]

Here, though, was what appeared to be proof positive, using the latest scientific techniques, that the skull had been made entirely by hand and without the use of any kind of modern metal age tools.

However, it was absolutely impossible for the scientists to tell exactly when this had been done. For, as Jack and Charles explained, quartz crystal does not age. It does not corrode, erode, decay or change in any way with time. This is actually one of the many unusual properties of quartz that makes it so vital to the modern electronics industry, but it also makes it impossible even to carbon date. With other materials, even if there are no visible signs of ageing, as in the case of the crystal skull, scientists can usually work out very accurately both the age of the original material and any workmanship thereon by measuring the degree of radioactive decay in the carbon atoms of which it is comprised. When you are dealing with quartz crystal, however, this is just not possible.

So, for all the team's scientific knowledge, up-to-the-minute technology and specialist expertise, there was absolutely no way of knowing how old the crystal skull really was. It could have been hundreds or even billions of years old. For all the scientists knew it could be as old as the Earth itself, or even older. It could even date back to the very beginning of time.

But the scientists at Hewlett-Packard were able to uncover one more potential clue to the mystery of the crystal skull. Other tests showed that the skull was not only made from a single piece of natural quartz, but from 'piezo-electric' silicon dioxide, precisely the type of naturally occurring quartz that is so widely used in modern electronics.

As Jack explained, the piezo-electric properties of some kinds of quartz were only discovered towards the end of the nineteenth century by Marie Curie's husband and brother-in-law, Pierre and Jacques Curie. *Piezo* is Greek, meaning 'to squeeze', and *electrose* means 'to get a charge from'. The fact that the crystal skull is made from this type of quartz means that it actually has a positive and negative polarity, just like a battery. It also means that if you apply pressure to the skull, or 'squeeze' it, it is actually capable of generating electricity! Alternatively, if you apply an electric charge to the crystal skull it actually changes its shape, without in any way affecting its mass or density.

But, like all piezo-electric quartz, the crystal skull is anisotropic in this as well as every other respect, which is to say that all of its properties, other than its mass, are different in every direction. In the case of its electrical properties, its precise orientation is defined by its X–Y axis, in other words, it can carry an electric current, but only in six particular directions relative to this X–Y axis. In any other direction it acts as an insulator.

In the case of the crystal skull, the scientists found that it was 'vertically piezo-electrically oriented', which is to say that its X–Y axis runs directly through the centre of the skull, from top to bottom. This means that if you apply an electric charge to the top of the crystal skull, not only does its shape change in the process, but also the electric current passes from the very top of the skull's head straight down to the Earth below. In the case of squeezing the skull to generate electricity, strangely enough, if you reverse the direction of pressure, the direction of electrical polarity in the crystal also reverses.

The Hewlett-Packard team also examined the skull's unusual optical properties, such as its ability to channel light from below, so that it is focused out through the eye sockets. Apparently, this is only possible on account of the orientation of the skull's optical axis, as quartz crystal has an optical as well as an electronic axis. What this means is that light actually travels quicker through the skull in one direction than another. Jack explained that not only was the skull able to perform these incredible tricks with normal multi-directional light, but also that if you shine directional, or polarized, light at the skull, not only does the light pass along its optical axis quicker than in any other direction, but the skull also actually rotates that light as it travels along its axis!

Another characteristic of the skull is that it is incredibly environmentally stable. This is another of the properties of piezo-electric silicon dioxide that makes it so invaluable for use in modern electronics. What it means is that the crystal skull is highly resistant to changes in the environment. It is particularly resistant to chemical changes. Most similar natural materials are slowly attacked by various chemicals, whether acids or even just plain water. The crystal skull, on the other hand, is resistant to chemicals. As Jack explained,

'Quartz crystal is highly stable, physically, chemically and temperately, and whilst it does respond to light and to electricity, this is precisely what makes it so useful in electronics.'

For modern science has also established that one of the particularly unusual properties of piezo-electric quartz is that it can function as an excellent oscillator or resonator. Jack explained this as follows:

'If a thin slice of crystal is cut parallel to its electronic axis and subjected to an alternating current, the crystal can be made to vibrate. The dimensions of the cut crystal are such that it will vibrate most strongly at the a.c. frequency that corresponds most closely to its own natural frequency. At this frequency, the mechanical motion of the crystal will reinforce the a.c. voltage.'

In other words, crystal, unlike other materials, has an amazing ability to hold electrical energy under control and to oscillate at a constant and precise frequency. This means that, in theory at least, the crystal skull may actually be able to hold electrical energy, potentially a form of information, and send out electrical impulses, or vibrating waves of information.

This ability to oscillate is yet another of the many unusual properties of this type of quartz that makes it so invaluable to the modern electronics industry. Its use in oscillator circuits for example, makes it vital to any piece of equipment where extremely accurate control of electronic frequencies is required. It is particularly important in precision electronics, especially in those instruments used for time-keeping. Indeed, quartz crystal is now found in almost every piece of precision time-keeping equipment from wristwatches to clocks. It is even used in the atomic clock, which is the most accurate clock in the world, the one by which all others are now measured. It is accurate to three seconds every million years (although its manufacturers only guarantee it for the first three years). Quartz crystal is at the very forefront of scientific advance in this and every other respect. The atomic clock, for example, has been used to test Einstein's theory that time actually travels more slowly as the speed of light is approached. This clock is also vital to research into measuring seismic (or earthquake) activity on distant planets. And the whole device is based on a simple quartz crystal.

But quartz is not only found in the most advanced time-keeping instrumentation, it is also vital to the fields of information technology, telecommunications and mass communication, not to mention navigational equipment, radar and sonar systems, and the latest medical and ultrasonic technology. Its incredible electrical properties mean that it is now found in all manner of electronic devices, from radios to computers, from terrestrial television systems to even the most advanced telecommunication satellites that now orbit the Earth in space. All of these use quartz crystals in one form or another. Even the vast information superhighway has only been possible thanks to recent developments in the field of crystal research and technology.

So crystal today is at the very forefront of scientific advance. It lies at the very heart of the modern computer, electronics, telecommunications and mass communications industries. Indeed, the power of crystal has quite literally changed the face of society. We now live in a world where electronically-based information and communications are an everyday part of life, a world where even the time of day is determined electronically. We are able to communicate instantaneously with people maybe thousands of miles away and to store and retrieve vast quantities of information from all over the world quite literally at the touch of a button. Crystal has been at the core of probably one of the greatest technological revolutions the world has ever seen. We have become so dependent on all the devices containing quartz crystals that it is now even vital to our civilization.

Why had the crystal skull been made from precisely the type of quartz whose properties and potential we have only just begun to recognize?

6. THE ANCIENT COMPUTER

Only since the beginning of the twentieth century have scientists begun to harness the incredible power of quartz crystal. So how was it that our 'simple' and 'primitive' ancestors had known to make the skull from precisely this type of material? Was it mere coincidence or could it be that they knew something we didn't?

Could it be that the crystal skull really was some sort of store of information, just as the ancient legend had said? Could it really contain an important message from our ancestors? At first, this seemed very far-fetched. It was almost unbelievable that a simple lump of rock could contain the great secrets of our forefathers from way back in the mists of time. But, despite our initial scepticism, after our trip to Hewlett-Packard we began to take this idea more seriously.

We spoke to Dr John Pohl, Mesoamerican specialist at UCLA, who explained that on his various trips to Central America he had heard that descendants of the ancient Maya today recognize the distinctive qualities of quartz crystal and 'liken crystal to some sort of ancient radio, television or computer device, a device for communicating "between the worlds", a sort of doorway into other dimensions, a means of communicating with the world of the spirits and the ancestors'.

We were also struck by the words of Dr Joseph Alioto in a book he had contributed to, *Holy Ice*, written by crystal researcher Frank Dorland, following the Hewlett-Packard tests. Dr Alioto pointed out that, less than 100 years ago, if you had described to anyone:

'...an invisible energy force that pervades all their surroundings, an energy force that would allow them to see and hear other people all over the world instantaneously, they [would have thought] you were either a great sorcerer or a great liar. Furthermore, if you were to suggest that they could capture these sounds and images through the use of a specially constructed box containing an assemblage of various pieces of metal and crystals, you would probably create quite a stir.

'Well, of course, what has just been described is something we [now] take for granted in our daily lives – television. Yet, it was only a few short decades ago that this idea was relegated to the category of fantasy and science fiction.' [1]

This had been our initial reaction to the idea that the crystal skulls might contain information. But, as we had just discovered from Charles Adams and Jack Kusters at Hewlett-Packard, the heart of the modern computer, where all the information is stored, is actually a tiny silicon crystal chip. The cells of this chip, or 'silicon integrated circuit', are effectively the brain cells, or memory, of the computer. This tiny crystalline chip, with its incredible storage capacity, now lies at the very heart of our information age. This chip uses the unique properties of crystal to store information. So it now occurred to us that if a silicon crystal chip can store vast amounts of information inside our modern computers, then why not the natural quartz crystal inside a crystal skull?

Indeed, as Charles Adams had informed us, in theory at least, a piece of raw quartz such as a crystal skull is perfectly capable of storing information. Due to the unique properties of crystal, a natural piece of piezo-electric silicon dioxide has information storage capacities, just like a silicon crystal chip. In fact it transpired that some early experiments had been done in this area. So, after our meeting with the scientists at Hewlett-Packard the idea that a raw quartz crystal skull might be capable of storing information began to seem more plausible. The problem, as Charles put it, is that no scientist has yet been able to figure out a way of successfully inputting information and retrieving it again from a piece of raw quartz. But, as he was also quick to point out, this was not to say it could never be done.

Indeed, there are many who believe it can already be done. Some, such as crystal researcher Frank Dorland, believe that the way to extract information from a piece of natural quartz such as the crystal skull actually lies in some form of direct communication with the human mind. Whilst this idea, too, at first struck us as rather far-fetched, we discovered that some early experiments had also been done in this area, using computers.[2] Professor Giles Brindley of the Royal National Orthopaedic Hospital in Middlesex saw the potential for physically paralysed subjects to be able to communicate directly with a computer by means of direct electronic links to their brains. Early results indicate that it might well be possible for subjects to use the power of their thoughts alone to communicate directly with a computer. These experiments suggest that one day it may be possible to have direct communication between the human mind and the computer without the need for bulky keyboards and other electronic paraphernalia in between. Whether or not this is what the future really holds, these early experiments certainly suggest that it is possible for the human mind to communicate more directly with a silicon crystal chip than at present. So could similar possibilities exist for direct mental communication with a crystal skull?

But if there really is information stored inside the crystal skulls, what might that information be, how might it be stored and how might we be able to retrieve it? In an attempt to find out we began to look at how information is stored inside our modern computers. What we discovered was that 'information' as it is spoken of today, is not a 'thing', but a 'process'. It is neither solid nor static, nor literally 'stored' in a tangible form; it is not lying around in a filing cabinet somewhere. Whilst we may talk about information being 'stored on a silicon chip inside a computer', the information itself has no obvious physical form. You cannot touch, see or hear it except through the process of retrieving it from the system electronically.

In the case of the computer we have managed to work out a way of inputting and retrieving the information 'stored within it' through the process of electronics. But what of any information inside a crystal skull? We may not yet know the correct way to input and retrieve any information stored within it, but that does not necessarily mean that the information is not there. The analogy that comes to mind is of a Stone Age man or woman finding a computer and being told that it contains great knowledge and information. Without the necessary understanding of electronics and the appropriate passwords and commands, they would simply not believe it. Could we be in a similar situation with the crystal skulls? It may be that the information they contain is in a form that we simply do not yet comprehend. For it is only when we are able to interact properly with any information storage system that the knowledge stored within it comes into a form of existence that we can understand.

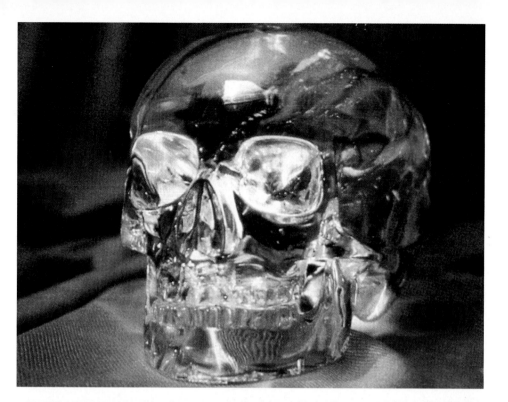

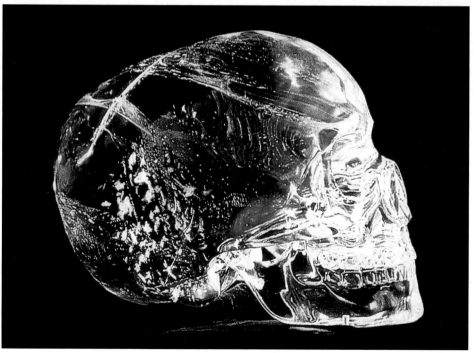

PLATES 1 & 2 The Mitchell-Hedges crystal skull

PLATE 3 (TOP LEFT) The Temple of the Jaguar at Tikal, Guatemala

PLATES 4 (TOP RIGHT) & 5 (ABOVE) The Temple of the Inscriptions
at Palenque, Mexico

PLATE 6 (TOP) Anna Mitchell-Hedges with her crystal skull

PLATE 7 (ABOVE) Carole Wilson 'channelling' information from the
Mitchell-Hedges crystal skull

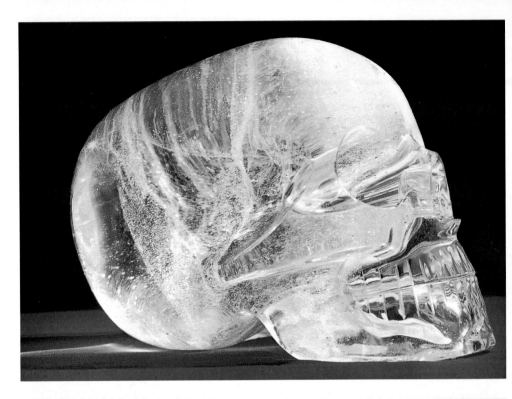

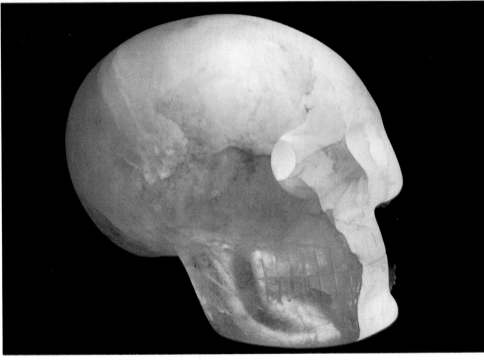

PLATE 8 (TOP) The British Museum crystal skull

PLATE 9 (ABOVE) The 'cursed' Smithsonian Institution crystal skull

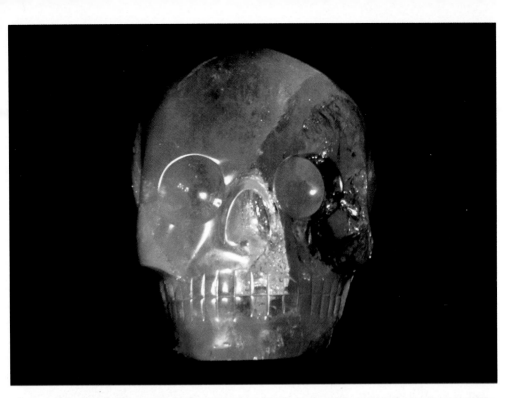

PLATE 10 (TOP) 'Max', the crystal skull belonging to JoAnn and Carl Parks
in Houston, Texas

PLATE 11 (ABOVE) Nick Nocerino with his crystal skull 'Sha Na Ra'

PLATE 12 (RIGHT)
Real skull-mask with obsidian blade nose and shell eyes (found during the Templo Mayor excavations and thought to have been used during human sacrifice ceremonies and/or skewered on a *tzompantli*, or skull-rack)

PLATE 13 (BELOW)
Sixteenth-century Spanish illustration of the Aztec practice of human sacrifice

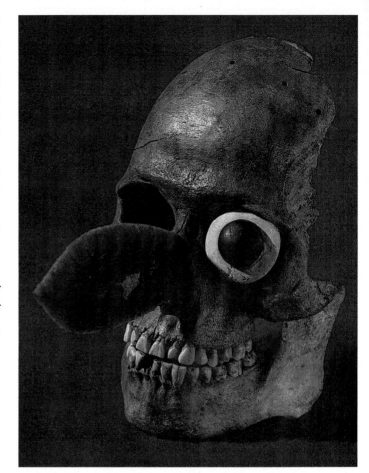

PLATE 16 (TOP LEFT)
The Pyramid of the Sun
and the Avenue of the Dead
at Teotihuacan

PLATE 17 (FAR LEFT)
The stone skull found at the
entrance to the mysterious cave
beneath the Pyramid of the Sun
at Teotihuacan

PLATE 18 (TOP) The stone
skull at Palenque, Mexico

PLATE 19 (LEFT) The
entrance to the tomb of Pacal
Votan inside the Temple of the
Inscriptions at Palenque

PLATE 20 (TOP) The astronomical observatory or 'Caracol' at Chichén Itza, Yucatan Peninsula, southern Mexico

PLATE 21 (ABOVE) Stone skull platform or *tzompantli* at Chichén Itza

PLATE 22 (TOP RIGHT) The ancient Mayan ruins of Tulum on the Caribbean coast

PLATE 23 (RIGHT) Stone carved skulls (combined with the symbol of Quetzalcoatl) on the building of the Atlantes at Tula, the Toltec capital near Mexico City

PLATE 24 (ABOVE) The skull at the centre of the Mayan universe (taken from the ancient manuscript *The Codex Borgia*)

PLATE 25 (ABOVE RIGHT) Some of the crystal skulls gathered for scientific tests at the British Museum's research laboratory in London

PLATE 26 (RIGHT) From left to right: the British Museum crystal skull, Max the Texas crystal skull, the crystal goblet from Monte Alban, the Smithsonian crystal skull, the modern German crystal skull, the reliquary cross crystal skull, the British Museum's tiny crystal skull, Sha Na Ra

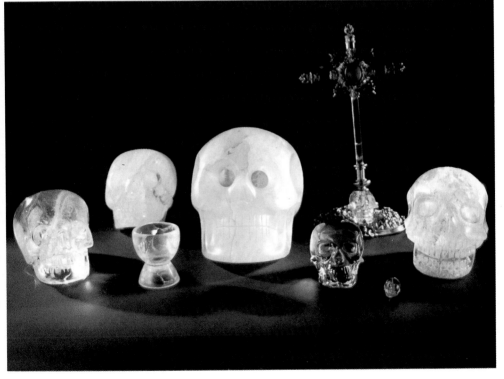

PLATE 27 (TOP) Mayan priest/shaman Don Alejandro Cirilo Oxlaj Peres (right) and colleague at the tribal gathering in Guatemala

PLATE 28 (ABOVE) Contemporary Mayan tribespeople performing the stela ceremony at the tribal gathering in Guatemala

PLATE 29 (TOP) Representatives of various tribes perform a ceremony to the sun with the crystal skulls Max and Sha Na Ra. From left to right: Don Alejandro Cirilo Oxlaj Peres, Mayan priest from Guatemala; Maestro Tlakaeletl, contemporary Aztec priest from Mexico; Florademayo, tribal representative from Nicaragua; Mary Thunder, representative from North America

PLATE 30 (ABOVE) Florademayo (Nicaragua) and Mary Thunder (Texas) in ceremony with crystal skulls

PLATE 31 The chac-mool figurine inside the Temple of the Warriors at Chichén Itza

I know this from first-hand experience. When I first started working with computers there were many occasions when I found it almost impossible to retrieve information. There was many a time when I began to doubt that what I was looking for really existed at all – that is, until I was lucky enough to stumble upon the proper way of retrieving it from the system. So it may be with the crystal skulls.

Some, such as Frank Dorland, do believe that direct communication between quartz crystal and the human mind is already possible and that we can in fact retrieve the information stored within a crystal skull. The mechanism through which this works is both complex and remarkably subtle. Dorland suggests that a piece of raw piezo-electric quartz crystal, such as a crystal skull, is already capable of interacting with the human body and mind, but in a way of which we are not normally consciously aware.

Frank Dorland spent over six years researching the Mitchell-Hedges skull and even accompanied it to the Hewlett-Packard laboratories for its scientific testing. Though he was now too old and infirm for us to meet him, we were able to read about his controversial theories in his book, *Holy Ice*, written as a result of the original discoveries about the crystal skull which were made at Hewlett-Packard.

Frank Dorland believes that 'the Communication Age' in which we now live ought really to be called 'the Crystal Age' and that we are really just at the dawning of this new era. He is of the view that there is more to the electronic properties of crystal, and to the crystal skull, than we currently understand, and that more great discoveries are yet to come. In his opinion, natural quartz crystal has the ability to affect our own state of consciousness, to bring our own subconscious or unconscious thoughts to full conscious awareness, to boost vague intuitions and to enable us to recover forgotten knowledge from the distant past. He also believes quartz crystal can help us to heal our own bodies.

Dorland's theory is based on the idea that both the human body and natural quartz are constantly broadcasting electro-magnetic signals on an unheard wavelength. Here Dorland asks us to bear in mind that there is more going on in the invisible world around us than we usually imagine. At all times, we are surrounded by a 'sea of electronic energy waves', constantly bombarded by naturally occurring electro-magnetic rays that we are simply unable to detect. The sun, for example, produces a complex range of radiant energies of which we humans are only aware of two parts: the infra-red, which produces warmth, and normal light, which is visible to the eye. Likewise most man-made electro-magnetic energy waves, such as radio, television and microwave signals, cannot be detected by our normal senses. In fact, as Dorland points out:

> *'Human detection capabilities in the average person are currently esti-mated to be less than 2 per cent of the known wavelength spectrum. This means that most of us are not aware of over 98 per cent of the currently known events that surround us at all times.'*[3]

Indeed, it is likely that there are many other energy frequencies around us, as yet undiscovered by science.

Dorland suggests that we think of the human body and mind as a radio system that can both transmit and receive these as yet undetected electro-magnetic energy waves:

> *'The body, with its complex electrical and chemical network of nerves and high moisture content, is [not only] the power source [and transmit-ter but also] a sensitive antenna system capable of receiving signals from an uncountable variety of sources.'*[4]

What happens, he says, when we come into contact with a piezo-electric quartz crystal such as the crystal skull is that the electro-magnetic energy waves we produce are received by the quartz. The crystal then starts oscillating and amplifying these signals and rebroadcasts them, in modified form, back out into the atmosphere, where they are picked up again by the cells of the body. In effect, the quartz crystal modifies and amplifies our own electro-magnetic energy waves and relays them back to us. So, in the process, these waves of 'energy information' be-come stronger and clearer. As we had just discovered, raw piezo-electric quartz is certainly renowned as a natural electronic oscillator, or res-onator, and amplifier.

Dorland suggests that this process will only occur, however, when a crystal has been 'switched on'. Like any electronic instrument, it has to be activated by a source of electrical energy, which in this case is the human body and mind. Whilst a crystal can receive some energy through the air, he believes the most effective way to energize it is to touch it or hold it in the hand. Then the crystal reacts to the energies it receives by vibrating on a frequency compatible and in harmony with the body and the brain.

Dorland believes our body and subconscious mind can pick up a vast array of electro-magnetic messages from a piece of piezo-electric quartz, but we are not normally consciously aware of much of the information we actually receive, just as we are not normally aware of, say, micro-wave signals.

This is also the case with the radiant energy of the sun. Much of this we are unaware of, but it is known to be received by the cells of the body and to stimulate the pineal gland. Likewise, Dorland believes that in the case of the energies radiated by crystal the hypothalamus is the key gland involved. This gland, situated in the lower mid-brain, in one of the most protected spots inside our skulls, plays an important part in regulating the day-to-day functioning of the electrical and chemical processes of the body. It is known to be influenced by the tiniest electronic impulse and, according to Dorland, is capable of receiving and filtering the oscillating energies radiated by electronic quartz crystals. These messages are then sent throughout the body, but they are rarely, if ever, brought to the attention of our conscious minds.

This interaction with quartz, Dorland claims, can help balance the neuro-endocrine system of the body and keep us in good health. He also believes the natural amplifying qualities of crystal help to boost commu-nication between the cells of the body. The theory is that this increased communication can also assist the conscious mind in making contact with various levels of the unconscious and help bring subconscious thoughts to full conscious awareness.

Certainly improved communications between the conscious and unconscious levels of the mind have recently been shown to have benefi-cial effects on health. In the not too distant past, many body functions such as heart rate were thought to be outside the control of the conscious mind. However, recent experiments in the use of 'bio-feedback', a tech-nique of using electronic equipment to feed back information to patients about their internal physiology, have shown that people can modify their own autonomic nervous systems, helping to control conditions such as high blood pressure, which were previously thought to be under no con-scious control.

Frank Dorland uses the term 'bio-crystal feedback' to describe the pos-sibility of similar types of feedback between a natural quartz crystal and the human mind. He recognizes the mind as one of the keys to the health of our bodies and claims that piezo-electric quartz can boost communica-tion between the different cells of the body and between body and mind. Dorland believes that these enhanced levels of communication are impor-tant for health in ways that we do not yet fully realize. According to him, a whole new science is being born of these studies, known as 'bio-crystal-lography', the study of the interchange of energies between quartz crystal and the human mind.

But, he claims, bio-crystal feedback can be used not only to heal the body but also to 'make conscious many things an individual already knows and is capable of accomplishing while not consciously aware of this untapped knowledge'.[5] By improving communications between deeper levels of the human mind, piezo-electric quartz can release knowledge held deep within the subconscious and unconscious mind and bring it to full conscious awareness.

As Dorland puts it:

'The crystal cells transmit these radio-like waves through the nervous system to the cortex cells in the ... brain. [There] they are unscrambled and composed into meaningful signals which may be recognizable as pictures, words or perhaps just a sense of knowing in the conscious mind. These messages may be received from many sources but, primarily, they seem to come from the subconscious memory bank and super-conscious sources.'[6]

According to Dorland, this knowledge may come not only from a person's own subconscious mind, but also from the 'collective unconscious'. The collective unconscious was first identified by the eminent Swiss psychiatrist Carl Jung. He pointed out that at the conscious level we are all separate, discrete, unique and individual human beings, but if you dig down a little deeper, what you find is a level of the unconscious at which we all share roughly the same set of thoughts, ideas and emotions. It is almost as if these archetypal concepts have a life of their own, an independent form of existence outside the mind of any individual. So this level is a 'collective' unconscious.

At first the idea that some thoughts and ideas might exist outside of the mind of any one particular individual struck me as rather odd, even illogical. After all, our thoughts always appear to be happening *within* our own minds and we certainly all need our individual brains in order to think. Therefore I had always assumed that our thoughts came from *within* our own brains, originating *inside* our own minds.

But it now occurred to me that this might be a bit like assuming that because we see pictures on and hear sounds coming from a television, and need the individual TV set in order to receive them, the pictures or sounds must originate *within* the television set itself. However, we all know that in fact these sounds and images are picked up from the mass of broadcast signals in the air that we are not normally consciously aware of or able to receive without the aid of the appropriate technology. I wondered whether some of our thoughts might come to us through a similar process.

Whilst there can be no denying that we do need the circuitry of our own individual brains in order to think, this does not necessarily mean that all our thoughts and ideas originate there. Perhaps we receive some, if not all of them, from some other source, some great body of thoughts and ideas that has its own independent form of existence somewhere outside ourselves as individuals, perhaps somewhere in the ether around us – just like TV signals. Just because we may not be consciously aware of this body of thought or always 'receiving' signals from it does not mean that it does not exist, any more than TV signals cease to exist when nobody happens to be receiving them.

The thought occurred to me that perhaps the crystal skull might be the most effective piece of equipment, just like a TV set, for picking up information from this source?

Certainly Dorland suggests that the crystal skulls may somehow enable us to tap into this collective unconscious more effectively. For he refers to something similar when he states that:

> 'A universal communication network is believed to exist on the subconscious level of which few are aware … [and crystal may be used] to contact the memory banks of other individuals who may have the desired information in their files … which means that a tremendous store of information is available from this source.'[7]

But this is not the only source of information that Frank Dorland believes piezo-electric quartz crystal can help us to tap into. He claims it can also help us to contact the 'inherited subconscious memory bank' of our species, containing genetically inherited information dating back even to our earliest ancestors. Dorland points out that dated fossil skulls from 500,000 years ago apparently indicate that there was a sudden increase in the size and capacity of the 'brain box', or skull, at this time, and this is what set the stage for the introduction of *Homo sapiens*. The implication is that this increase may well have had something to do with providing enough space in the brain for this inherited subconscious memory bank.

Apparently we currently only use a tiny fraction of our mental capacities. Dorland suggests that the reason for this is that we are actually carrying around inherited memories of the past history of humanity, but because this is all neatly tucked away in our subconscious we are normally completely unaware of it.

As he points out, it is already widely accepted that our inherited DNA is responsible for determining our physical characteristics, but science has so far failed to recognize that our subconscious memories may also be inherited from our ancestors. In Dorland's opinion, a piece of quartz crystal such as a crystal skull could play a key role in activating these genetic memories.

So perhaps the natural amplifying qualities of quartz crystal could be used not only for enhancing communication with our own memories, subconscious thoughts and the 'collective unconscious', but also with our 'ancestral memories'.

Frank Dorland also suggests that it may somehow be possible to 'programme' a crystal skull with a set of thoughts, memories, messages or instructions. The mechanism involved here is unclear, though he suggests this may have been done in the past by the ancients. According to him:

> 'Natural quartz crystal is believed to have been in use during the last 12,000 to 15,000 years by a great many of our leaders for this and other purposes ...[8]
>
> 'The ancients secretly reserved the crystal for use by the religious hierarchy, royalty, military leaders and, of course, the secret brotherhoods.[9]
>
> 'Modern scientists have experimented with lasers and quartz crystals, adapting them as a permanent memory bank of factual data to be safely stored away inside a crystal and recovered at a later date on command ...Since crystal is a permanent material which neither ages nor decays, [perhaps] the data fed into a crystal [skull in this way] could remain active for thousands of years?'[10]

While Frank Dorland's theories are open to debate, they certainly raised many fascinating possibilities. Could the piezo-electric properties of the crystal skulls really improve inner communication, not only helping to heal the body but also bringing to awareness unexplored information from the unconscious? Had we now discovered the reason why the crystal was fashioned into the shape of a skull? Was it to symbolize the ancestors, whose memories are stored deep within our own minds? Could the crystal skull help bring forth our own 'ancestral memories'?

Whether the crystal skull could be used to access information actually stored within it, in the ether or deep within our own psyches, Dorland's theory certainly implied that the crystal skulls might hold the key to accessing vast areas of ancient knowledge.

7. THE TALKING SKULL

Just like the ancient legend, Dorland's theory suggested that the crystal skull may really be able to provide us with important information from the past. Mayans today apparently also believe this to be the case. Even the scientists at Hewlett-Packard recognized that natural quartz crystal has information storage capacities and so were not entirely closed to the possibility that the crystal skull might have information programmed into it. But what sort of information might that be and how might we be able to access it?

When Chris and I were visiting Anna Mitchell-Hedges, we had already met a woman who said she knew how to access the information inside the skull. Like Frank Dorland, she claimed conventional scientists had failed because they were using the wrong approach. She said the secrets of the skull could only be uncovered using 'the technology of the mind'. We were somewhat sceptical, but curious none the less. If this were really possible, what might we find? Perhaps secret knowledge that had been buried in this crystal store-house for thousands of years. Perhaps the hidden wisdom of esoteric societies that had long since vanished from the surface of the Earth, or some ancient formula, now long forgotten, left behind by the mathematical geniuses of Mesoamerica, or even the secrets of the Mayan cosmos, the knowledge of the ancients who understood the movements of the planets and the stars.

As we sat in Anna's small living-room gazing at the skull, with its smooth transparent surface, it felt as if we were sitting in front of some strange computer but without the right password to log on. Would we ever be able to plug into this ancient Internet, let alone surf its multiple worlds? How could we extract the secrets said to lie hidden deep within its quartz crystalline structure? We awaited with interest the arrival of Carole Wilson, the woman who claimed to actually be able to do this. Then Anna revealed that Carole was in fact one of Canada's best-known psychics.

Initially I was sceptical. I have always had grave reservations about psychics. The notion had always conjured up in me the image of an old woman dressed in gypsy-style clothing sitting in a small tent, gazing into a glass ball and making up any old rubbish. A stereotype, obviously, but it was my belief that all such people really did was to tell people what they wanted to hear and then charge them for the privilege of being so easily duped. I wondered whether we were about to meet such a charlatan.

When Carole arrived she turned out to be a quiet, well-dressed woman in her fifties with a very professional manner. I was somewhat surprised to find that she was accompanied by the former head of the Toronto police homicide department. It soon transpired that there had been many occasions when the local police had been investigating unsolved murder cases and where insufficient evidence or an absence of any leads had frustrated them. Once they had become so desperate that they had called on Carole. With the help of her psychic powers, in almost no time at all the case was solved and the murderer brought to justice. Since then the police had used Carole's services many a time and had managed to successfully solve a whole string of murder and missing persons cases.

As Carole explained, 'Dead people do a lot of talking,' and she either hears them directly or can pick up information about them by working with objects which once belonged to them. This gives her psychic information about murder victims, which has almost without fail proved successful in explaining otherwise unsolved crimes.

Carole now works closely with police forces throughout the United States, Canada and Britain. Indeed, her work proved so invaluable to the Toronto police force that she was now married to the chief detective who had been responsible for homicide investigations and missing persons cases. This was John Gordon Wilson, the man who was now accompanying her.

Carole went on to describe her first encounter with the Mitchell-Hedges skull. She had first seen it during the 1980s while on a visit to Anna's house with two friends who were planning to try to date the skull, although they were ultimately unsuccessful in their attempts. She had also heard some outlandish claims about the skull:

'Before I first saw the skull, I was half expecting something amazing to happen. Yet when I actually saw it, nothing did, or at least nothing seemed to. It felt such a disappointment. All the people I was with were saying, "Look at the light, look at what's inside it!" and I could see nothing. I thought it was a question of the emperor's new clothes and that there was really nothing extraordinary about the skull at all. But as I sat there I found myself drifting off. My eyes were closing and I felt very sleepy. And the next thing I knew everyone was saying to me, "That was fantastic. How amazing!" Only afterwards did I discover that I had gone into a trance and had spent the last two hours conveying information from the skull, the message of the skull if you like, and I couldn't remember a word of it.'

After that, Carole had continued to work with the skull on a regular basis. She was somehow able to access what Anna's nephew Jimmy described as 'incredible information'.

'Once Carole had logged on to the system,' he said, 'the material seemed almost unending, reams and reams of data. But the information was of such a peculiar and awesome nature that we were pretty convinced that most people were probably not ready to hear such phenomenal material at that time.'

Carole explained that for several years she had not been willing to make any of her findings public, although much of the material had been carefully transcribed and recorded. She had felt most people would simply find it just too unusual, too hard to accept or too 'out of this world'. Then she had started to make her work known by writing and self-publishing a book, *The Skull Speaks*.[1] Now she, Anna, Jimmy and her husband John all felt the time was right to start to share some of this information with a wider audience.

The work Carole was about to perform with the crystal skull is known as 'channelling'. As she explained, this is a technique commonly used by psychics and mediums, whereby the psychic individual allows themselves to be used as a 'channel' for 'spirit entities' or 'souls' from 'other dimensions' to communicate.

Carole told us that these other dimensions are not physical in the same way as the dimension that we call 'normal reality', but exist in parallel to our everyday world. These other realms are usually invisible to us during normal waking consciousness, but in an altered state of consciousness, through meditation, hypnotism or a trance, a channel can gain access to them. Through this process the channel can communicate with the beings that exist in these other dimensions – the spirits, the ancestors and the dead. These spirit entities can be from the past or the future, for in the other dimensions our normal physical rules such as linear time do not apply.

The technique of channelling involves the channel or medium putting themselves into an altered state of consciousness or trance-like state in order to become a bridge between these worlds and our own. The channel has to suppress their own normal waking state of consciousness, their own ego, their own sense of identity or self, sufficiently to allow the consciousness of the non-physical being or spirit entity to enter their body and mind. The 'visiting' spirit entity is then able to use the channel's body, movements and voice to communicate. Both during and after channelling, the channel is usually completely unaware of what they have said and done when they have been in this altered state, much like a person who has been under the influence of hypnotism. But Carole explained that there is nothing morbid about what she does: 'What I do is not "paranormal" or "supernatural". In fact, this whole process is actually quite natural and was used on an almost everyday basis by many societies prior to our own.'

As I sat listening to this extraordinary woman describing this strange process, I thought about the fact that police departments took her work so seriously that she was now working on cases on an international basis. It struck me as rather peculiar that those involved in solving criminal cases of the most distressing kind should act upon her advice. For this was a woman who believed she could communicate with a chunk of crystal! I couldn't quite come to terms with it.

As these thoughts were going through my mind, Carole looked across at me and said, 'Belief is a curious thing. Belief functions to maintain the status quo in your mind. It helps you to feel more secure. It's the same for everybody. But belief can be very narrow. It likes the here and the now. It doesn't like change.' She added, 'You don't have to believe in what I do. Because whether you believe it or not, the crystal skull is a subtle and very powerful teacher.'

The plan was that Carole was going to channel the 'entity' of the crystal skull and we would be able to ask it questions. Carole requested that any questions we asked were very specific. She explained that the skull did behave a bit like a computer in that you had to give it very specific instructions and to be very clear about what you were asking, otherwise you might not get a very helpful answer. For example, someone once before had asked the skull what a skull was and had received the answer that it was 'a bony structure'! She also warned that sometimes the skull anticipated the questions in advance and told us not to be put off by this.

Anna then placed the crystal skull on a small turntable so that Carole would be able to touch it from all angles and manipulate it as she wished during the channelling session. Carole sat down and the crystal skull was placed directly in front of her, where it glimmered softly in the lamplight (*see colour plate no. 7*).

Carole closed her eyes. She began altering her style of breathing and used a low hum to ease herself into the appropriate mental state. The whole room began to take on a somewhat eerie atmosphere of the kind you might expect during a séance, as Carole's gestures and posture changed. Suddenly tense, she began to emit an incredibly high-pitched humming sound. Before I was even able to ask the first question she began speaking in a strange, somewhat staccato voice, with a very stilted use of the English language. I remember being struck by the fact that you could actually hear this new voice echoing strangely around the room.

'You seek to know the origins of this receptacle which you call "the crystal skull"... I tell you that it was made many, many thousands of years ago by beings of a higher intelligence... It was formed by a civilization before those you call "the Maya". Our level of civilization was, as you say, "at that time" far in advance of that which you now have by many factors...'

The speech was interrupted by high-pitched humming and then continued:

'This receptacle contains the minds of many and the minds of one... It was not made using what you call the "physical". It was moulded into its present form by thought. The thoughts and knowledge are crystallized into this receptacle ... this receptacle is thought process crystallized ... thus the information was crystallized into this receptacle...

'We have put thought form into pure language within that which you call "the crystal skull"...

'Much of the world that we created, we created with mind. Mind creates matter. You will understand this and crystal technology will be given to those who understand it in more detail ... that crystal is a living substance and you can infuse mind with matter...'

So it seemed that the crystal skull had been made by an advanced civilization using thought. But it was all a little confusing, to say the least. I was about to ask why the crystal had been shaped into the form of a skull when the voice continued, in the same manner:

'This receptacle is crystallized because you, within the third dimension, need to see, to hear and to touch... Its form makes it easier for mind to attach to mind, without what you call personality... But you respect the personality, the head, the enclosure of your brain ... so this form of the receptacle has been guarded and guided for many an age... The Earth life of this receptacle is 17,000 years... It has been handed down from generation to generation, polished with sand and hair ... and no harm will come to it.'

So the reason the crystal had been made into the shape of a skull was so that it would be respected and cared for over the years. I was about to ask if there were any other crystal skulls, as the legend had said, but once more the voice spoke before I was even able to open my mouth:

'You are seeking information as to the other receptacles of mind... There will be other receptacles found ... for there are many ... for no one man and no one mind were given all knowledge... Each of the receptacles contains the information of where the others are...

'We would give you one where we left markings upon the Earth [some have since suggested this may be the area of the Nazca Lines of Peru, although there are obviously many other alternative possibilities] ... and high in the mountains... There will be one of blue in the region you call "South America"... There will be another found when the lost civilization that you call "Atlantis" rises to you ... and we would urge you to explore the ocean bed ... we would urge you to explore the discoveries in the area you call "Bimini"... But we will direct you... we will show you that which you call a "temple"... This was an area of communication between the Earth and other systems... When all receptacles are placed together you will be keepers of wondrous knowledge... Light and sound will be the key, when the right vibration is produced you will have the information you require... But the time is not yet... There are still some that have not yet been given form ... and others which remain safely under your ocean bed... But you shall not find them all, as you say "at this time"... It would be too dangerous

for man to have this information ... too early in his evolution ...
because mankind still seeks to better all the original destruction of
our time.'

I did not really understand all of this somewhat cryptic information, but
I was curious as to why the crystal skulls had been made in the first place.
Yet again, the voice anticipated my question:

'The receptacle has been given this form to encourage the mind of
oneness and to reduce your desire for separation... Your mind seeks
separation... We sought to leave you with the concept of oneness, but
your mind seeks only separation. As you say, "As you seek so shall ye
find." And already the process of separation has begun. You have
already begun the separation but there will be more. You have a desire
to separate that will lead to your own destruction... Separation causes
annihilation and death. We can already feel the influence of this
separation as violence... There is much violence occurring within
your planet. Violence against men, violence against nature ... violence
against the Earth.'

Again, I didn't really understand these rather cryptic remarks and I was
more interested in whether the crystal skull could tell us anything about
mankind's history. The answer came:

'We understand that you come seeking in quest of the beginnings of
man. We wish to tell you that your own origins were thought in form,
and that you have to cast your eyes up and not down. There will be
many discoveries pointing to this acknowledgement within the next
5, 10, 15 years... And the beginnings of what you call your civiliza-
tion are over 15,000 years before the acknowledgement of that which
you call Atlantis. For there is also much evidence of our civilization
still beneath your oceans. Already there are discoveries near Bimini.
But there will be many more discoveries over the next 5, 10, 15 years,
which will point you towards the right direction... There will be more
discoveries in South America, in Australia and in Egypt. In that which
you call your deserts you will find much knowledge. But you will find
traces of our civilization through most parts of your land masses and
there is much beneath your seas, especially beneath the oceans which
you call "the Atlantic", "the Indian" and that which you call "the Dead

Sea". There, closest to your Earth's surface, and soon to be discovered, are remnants of our civilization... These discoveries will confuse and cause much disharmony, but they will be needed to reduce the mind of separation.

'But many of these discoveries will not be permitted at this time. We can only permit that which will not cause too much havoc for your minds. We came to your Earth from a different world. From other dimensions we came into this dimension. We came to experience, needing to experience density. That which we first heralded had nothing of the density of what you call a "body". The life on this Earth plane was primitive in form, but we took upon ourselves the physical form which is recognizable to you. We sought only to experience material density and to bring knowledge and enlightenment. But we did not confine ourselves to any one what you call "geographical location". There were many, and many of our relics and of our teachings are still to be found scattered amidst your land masses and your sea masses.'

I was keen to know exactly who these 'we' were that the voice of the skull seemed to be talking about when it continued:

'But there are still many among you who seek to find where in your universe we are to be found. But still you cling to the idea that we are of the third dimension and you still cannot grasp the idea that we are of the other dimensions, beyond your rudimentary space-time relativity.'

The voice then proceeded to divulge some rather cryptic information about space and time:

'We would tell you that the essence of time is an illusion. Time has been created, in fact, by a higher intelligence as a form of control upon the brain and function of the body image. This is a safeguard against corruption of matter but, in essence, is non-existent. Thought exists independently of the body and brain, but time is the creation of matter. Thought is without time. Time, as a mechanism, was introduced to material and current mind only, not to thought or spirit, to keep you bound within the third dimension, and within the perimeters of the small planet you call "Earth". We would urge you to explore with truth and understanding that which the mind is capable of understanding and not that which the brain is restricted to.

'Time is related to you as numbers. We offer to you that number and time have no depth. These are merely programmed into the current mind as safeguards, to keep you in time and space. They are a function not really of mind, but of brain. And they are really a dysfunction of brain, to keep you tied to the physical dimensions of the three-dimensional world. The relativities you call "number", "time" and "space" are a function of the brain related only to the third dimension. This current mind keeps you a prisoner in time and space, in the material, physical world you call reality. But the delusion of time must remain for a period. Do you understand?'

I was not at all sure that I did. Instead I was still trying to work out whose voice this really was and why the crystal skulls had been created in the first place. The voice went on:

'We have come now to warn you, because the separation has already begun. The destruction is already beginning to take place. The mind of separation has taken hold and some serious things have already taken place. For you, with your primitive knowledge, have already started something which now cannot be reversed. It was started through your scientists playing with and bending sound and light waves and that which you call "particles" into your atmosphere. You will have noticed that there are many destructive waves now hitting your planet. There will be more destruction brought about by atmosphere intervention, unusual weather patterns and rapid climatic change, and there will be movement of your land masses also.

'We wish to tell you that your civilization has grossly misunderstood the use of light and sound and matter. That is why you have only uncovered that which is closest to you.

'But, even now your scientists and your governments play with toys that they do not understand. They play with light and sound and that which you call "particles" and "radiation", and they will rain havoc. But because the reaction is not immediate and not obviously near to yourselves, you continue and you continue until this very planet will erupt and destroy.

'As we have said, your current mind seeks only separation. You have a desire to separate that will lead only to your own destruction. For this is the same mind that caused the Great Flood and caused the previous destruction of many a land mass. But this destruction has begun to

happen again already. And we can already feel the influence of this sepa-
ration in our world. But, at present, you are unaware of this separation
because it is of your own making. But we tell you that your Earth will
undertake great changes…

'Even the body of your planet will change, as with your weather, as
with all to do with your Earth as you now know it. There will be
changes upon this Earth in the form of the human, the animal and that
form you know as "vegetation" and that form which you know as "land
mass" and that which you know as "atmosphere".

'There will be a disaster that is of great consequence. But, in essence,
your "disaster", as you would term it, has already begun. You will find
much death amongst your life upon the planet. You will find that which
is grown in the ground will cause much change and you will see that
which feeds upon the ground will end up with much death. You will see
much destruction due to what you call "radiation" and you will find
much pestilence in that which now flies upon your planet. There will be
eruptions and disruptions of weather patterns, and much separating of
atmospheres. You will have much wind … and your livestock will die in
great numbers. Your waters will rise where they should not rise and your
land will be sinking underneath the waves. Land masses will disappear
and seas and oceans will rise.

'There will be a great splitting of the Earth … from within the Earth.
The magnetic field will shift and is already shifting now. The Earth will
be split asunder and the discharge will wander through the Earth and
into the atmosphere. The atmosphere is already entering a state of nega-
tive pollution. This is what you are doing with your negative energies on
the Earth.

'And this is why we left these receptacles for you to find, in your time
"long ago" when we realized that so many had forgotten their original
purpose of incarnation into this physical dimension. When we realized
that the mind of separation would take hold and that there would be a
great catastrophe on this Earth, we chose to return to our own original
dimension, but we left behind the legacy of our minds. We knew there
would be those whose knowledge and seeking and spiritual progression
would turn them towards this path. We knew that because of the disas-
ter that would befall this planet, there would be those who would be
needed to call upon their reincarnational memories to heal, to counsel
and to love a world gone mad, a world without knowledge, a world
without hope, where the fires of destruction would reign.

'But when the time comes it will be the duty of all those who seek spiritual knowledge to instruct others when the Earth moves from its axis. Within this receptacle, and the others we have left you, lies that which you will need. Our knowledge, here crystallized, will be imparted when the right time arrives. It was determined that through these receptacles the minds of one would be activated and would present themselves when your Earth was in need. And this is now beginning to happen, as you say "at this time" and "in this place". We are here to tell you that there is ... will be ... and has already begun, a great change within your Mother Earth. We urge you to make known to mankind the things which we are to give you, in the hope that the holocaust can be reduced. For although what is given cannot now be changed, its effects can be much diffused.'

At this point the voice explained that it was going to leave us now because it could sense that the physical body it was using, presumably meaning Carole, was getting very tired and so it would have to go. A long humming sound began again and as it faded away Carole slumped into her chair, completely exhausted and unable to speak for some minutes. It took a few glasses of water to get her to speak again, in a long drawl, like someone drunk. When she eventually came round she seemed completely unaware of the events that had just passed and was unable to answer any more questions.

We were completely baffled as to what to make of the information Carole had channelled. We had originally been sceptical enough about the idea of psychic communication with spirit beings, let alone beings from another planet or 'dimension', whatever that meant, warning us about imminent disaster on a global scale. But our cynicism had already been tempered by what we had heard about Carole's valuable police work and by the fact that Carole herself seemed genuine and honest.

Everyone around us treated the information we heard with a great degree of seriousness and respect, and there was something about the predictions made that had an alarming but still undeniable ring of truth. Indeed, these became even more unnerving when John showed us transcripts of Carole's channelling sessions with the skull from the 1980s. The channelled information always seemed to have been quite consistent. In a session recorded in 1987 the voice had predicted, 'Livestock will die in great numbers.' This seemed to have particular relevance for us now, having just come from Britain, where the BSE crisis had now led to the slaughter of tens of thousands of cattle.

Around nine months later, the prediction about the Earth's magnetic field shifting also took on a sobering degree of truth when we read in an issue of *New Scientist* that it had just been discovered that the magnetic field is indeed beginning to shift. There are even some scientists who now predict that the whole axis of the Earth might be about to do a complete flip.[2]

At the time, however, we didn't know what to make of everything we had heard. Was this really 'the voice of the skull' speaking through Carole? We just couldn't say. But these strange words remained in our minds as we resumed our more everyday approach to the mystery of where the crystal skulls had really come from.

8. THE CURSE OF THE SKULL

The debate over the true origins of the crystal skulls was to take a new turn when one of the world's most powerful museums became embroiled in the controversy.

After our trip to Anna Mitchell-Hedges, we put in a call to the British Museum back in London. We wanted to see how their plans for testing their skull were progressing. But Elizabeth Carmichael now put us in touch with Dr Jane Walsh, Mesoamerican specialist at the Smithsonian Institution in Washington, DC, because she had become interested in crystal skulls when one had turned up at her office unexpectedly. We were intrigued. It seemed that Carole Wilson's channelled prediction that some of the other crystal skulls would soon be rediscovered was coming true.

The Smithsonian's crystal skull had come into their possession only very recently, and under very sad and mysterious circumstances. It had just arrived one day at the Smithsonian's National Museum of American History, having been sent through the post by an anonymous donor. Dr Walsh told us the story:

'I got a call one afternoon from Richard Ahlborn, who is the curator over at American History. He said, "I've got something here the Department of Anthropology might be interested in."

'At first he didn't say what it was but I got the impression from the tone of his voice that whatever it was he seemed very keen to get it off his hands. Then he explained that he had received in the mail a box, which had a crystal skull inside it.

'*The skull had arrived accompanied by an unsigned handwritten note which read simply: "Dear Sir, This Aztec crystal skull, purported to be part of the [Mexican President] Porfirio Díaz collection, was purchased in Mexico City in 1960... I am offering it to the Smithsonian without any consideration. Naturally, I wish to remain anonymous..."*

'*Richard asked me if I would be interested in taking it. Unaware of the pitfalls that lay ahead, I said, "Yes, by all means, I'll come right over and pick it up."*

'*But Richard said, 'No, no, it's too heavy. I'll deliver it."*

'*So he called me and said he was downstairs. On the way down I stopped off at one of the technician's offices and asked for a cart to pick it up. The technician wanted to know what I needed the cart for. So I explained that I needed it to pick up a crystal skull and I received the rather ominous warning, "Don't look it in the eye – they're cursed!"* '

Undeterred, Dr Walsh wheeled the skull back to her office. And so it was that she found herself the caretaker of the world's largest, and probably the ugliest, known crystal skull. We looked with interest at the photographs she sent us. Larger than life, the skull is about 10" (25.5 cm) high, 8.25" (22.8 cm) wide and weighs a phenomenal 31 lb (14 kg). Unlike the Mitchell-Hedges and British Museum skulls, it is not clear, but very cloudy. Also unlike the Mitchell-Hedges' skull, but like the British Museum one, this skull has no separate jaw-bone.

One particularly curious feature of the skull is the fact that despite its massive weight it is actually completely hollow, so that you can look right through its eye sockets deep into its empty interior. It looks almost like a peculiar Halloween lantern, as if a candle might once have been placed within it which could be glimpsed only through the eye sockets. The skull has a smooth finish but is lacking in detail and its features are only crudely represented. But, whatever the quality of its craftsmanship, this skull is by no means a beautiful object. To me it looked rather ugly, whilst Ceri said she found it 'positively disturbing', 'like looking at the mere shell of a human being'. The overall impression it gives is of a strange, almost non-human face. Ceri said it looked as though it were the image of some earlier period of human development and certainly from one particular angle it does look almost Neanderthal (*see colour plate no.9*). But is this skull really cursed? Could we really not look it in the eye? And where had it come from?

Jane Walsh said she had had the skull in her office for quite a while now and had looked it in the eye many a time. 'Nothing's happened so far. I haven't experienced any curses or anything,' she said lightly.

But there was something about the arrival of the skull which some considered evidence of it being cursed. For why did its mysterious donor wish to remain anonymous?

Investigations in this area had uncovered some rather disturbing information. Attempts to track down the anonymous donor had led instead to his lawyer. The reason for this, as the lawyer explained, was that the donor himself, whose name he could not reveal, was now dead. After sending in the skull he had committed suicide. His lawyer explained that since coming into possession of the crystal skull this man had experienced a whole series of awful tragedies – his wife had died, his son had a terrible accident that left him brain dead and he had gone bankrupt. Finally, he had decided to end it all.

The question was, did all this have anything to do with the curse of the skull? Dr Walsh seemed quite convinced that the anonymous donor had simply decided to take his own life as a result of the tragedies that had befallen him and that these tragedies had nothing to do with the crystal skull.

However, Dr Walsh had noticed something rather strange that had been happening ever since the skull had come into her possession:

'I don't believe the skull is cursed... But, since I've had it in the office it seems to attract other skulls because I've gotten calls and had people bring in several other skulls and I keep hearing of new ones.'

The surprising thing was that what Jane Walsh had been experiencing was very similar to what had been happening to us. As we continued our investigations we kept finding that each time we heard about a crystal skull, its owner or someone associated with it would put us in touch with someone else who would know of another one.

After all this, Dr Walsh too had become very interested in finding out where her own and the other crystal skulls had really come from. Was her skull really Aztec and once the property of the Mexican President, as the handwritten note accompanying it had stated? Dr Walsh, it seemed, was not at all convinced that this was necessarily the case, particularly given that its anonymous donor also claimed that it was purchased in Mexico City, as recently as 1960. So, like us, she had set about investigating crystal skulls and had even started writing a research paper about them in an attempt to determine where they had come from.[1]

Dr Walsh had been investigating the subject for some time now, but she had not yet reached any firm conclusions. However, having done so much apparently inconclusive research, she was getting more and more determined to solve the mystery. She had decided that the only way to get to the bottom of it was to carry out more rigorous scientific testing. That is why the British Museum had put us in touch with her. For it was now her plan to try to bring the crystal skulls together in order to carry out a series of tests. The idea was that by having as many of the crystal skulls as practically possible gathered in one place it would be possible to compare their artistic styles and do comparative scientific tests in order to finally establish their authenticity. Dr Walsh hoped also to mount an exhibition for the public.

We were amazed when we heard of Jane Walsh's plan. The ancient legend itself had said that one day all of the crystal skulls would be rediscovered and brought together, and at that time they would reveal their important and sacred information for the good of all humankind. Could it be that now was the time for their information to be made available? Were the skulls coming together for the start of the new millennium? It was beginning to look as though all was about to be revealed.

But the problems were many. For one thing Dr Walsh seemed not at all convinced that any of the crystal skulls were genuinely ancient. She tried to explain the depth and complexity of the problem by telling us about some of the other crystal skulls she had now come across.

Dr Walsh had looked first to other museums around the world and had soon found yet another near life-size crystal skull. This one, she explained, was housed in the Trocadero Museum, or Musée de l'Homme, in Paris. The Parisian skull, though smaller than the Mitchell-Hedges, the Smithsonian and the British Museum skulls, is still of a reasonable size. Made from clear quartz, it is around 4.5" (11 cm) high, weighs only 6 lb (2.75 kg) and has no separate jaw-bone. But the interesting thing about this skull is that it is very stylized in its features, with very rounded eyes and chiselled teeth, very much in the style attributed to the ancient Aztecs and their close neighbours the Mixtecs.

This skull also has a vertical hole drilled right through it from top to bottom. As Jane Walsh explained, a horizontal hole would mean that it was in the same style as the real human skulls the Aztecs used to skewer onto skull racks, which in her opinion would indicate 'an almost certain pre-Columbian provenance', in other words, that it was genuinely ancient or at least dated to before the arrival of Christopher Columbus and the Europeans in the Americas. But a vertical hole indicated that it might have been used by the early Spanish conquerors, perhaps as the base for a crucifix. However, the hole on the Parisian skull was known to be 'bi-conical' in shape, indicating that it was definitely made by hand, not machine tools, and was therefore probably made before the arrival of the Spanish.

We spoke to the curator of the American collection at the Trocadero Museum, Daniel Levine, who is convinced that the skull they have is genuinely ancient and, he believes, Aztec. Monsieur Levine told us that French experts have already agreed that it was made by the Aztecs in the fourteenth or fifteenth century and that it may have been an ornament on a sceptre carried by an Aztec priest. Apparently 'the style of the piece is characteristically Aztec' and 'the Aztecs are known to have done a lot of carvings of this type in rock crystal'. He indicated that the museum had also already carried out their own scientific tests on the skull. The bi-conical drill hole meant that the skull had definitely been made by hand and they had even found traces of copper tools like those used by the Aztecs on the skull's surface. So the Trocadero Museum was quite convinced this skull, at least, was genuinely ancient and could see no need for further scientific testing.

But was there any evidence of exactly where it had really come from or when it had first been discovered? All Daniel Levine could tell us was that it had originally been given to the museum and had already been part of the Collection Française when proper records began back in the late 1800s.

So we spoke again to Dr Walsh, who pointed out that this was hardly sufficient evidence of a genuinely ancient origin. Indeed, one of Dr Walsh's scientific colleagues had apparently pointed out to her that any traces of copper on the skull's surface might not necessarily have been there right from the time the skull was made. Apparently some types of crystal polish, including those used today, contain copper compounds. So the traces of copper might be the result of someone polishing the skull only yesterday! Therefore, the copper traces and the fact that the skull was made by hand didn't prove a thing.

Indeed, it seemed that Dr Walsh was gradually moving towards the view that perhaps *none* of the crystal skulls was genuinely ancient. Like most archaeologists, she seemed particularly concerned that, to her knowledge, none had been found on any official or properly recorded archaeological dig. There were no official records to prove the Mitchell-Hedges crystal skull had been found at Lubaantun, while the British Museum crystal skull, bought from Tiffany's, was said to have been brought from Mexico by a Spanish soldier of fortune, but again there were no records of where he had got it, or even anything to show that this was really anything more than a story. The Smithsonian's own skull could have come from just about anywhere, and so for that matter could the Parisian skull.

Dr Walsh had now also come across some other skulls that were of equally mysterious, and therefore potentially dubious, origin and she put us in touch with their owners. These included two small skulls, less than 5" (12 cm) high, one clear, one cloudy, with fixed jaws, brought to her office by an antique dealer called Kirk Landauer from Maryland, near Washington. Judging by the photos he sent us, the clear one looked almost like a monkey's head, the other one like no creature ever known. The cloudy skull had apparently been found in 1916 in the Yucatán area of southern Mexico; the clear skull was bought from an antique dealer in Mexico during the 1920s. But no exact details of either find were available.

Yet another small skull was brought to Dr Walsh's office by the son of another antique dealer, who lived in Altadena, California. This man, Larry Hughes, told us he had bought it around seven years previously from a wealthy man who said it had originally been collected in the 1880s or '90s, but he didn't know where from and there were no documents accompanying it. Again this skull was only about 4" high (10 cm), cloudy and with a fixed jaw. It also looked a bit like a monkey's head, but it had circles, like goggles, around its eyes. As Dr Walsh explained, this was a symbol traditionally associated with the Mesoamerican rain god, Tlaloc. The skull also had what looked like an ancient hieroglyph carved across the top. Dr Walsh said she had shown a photo of this skull to two Mexican archaeologists, who immediately identified it as being in the style of the ancient Mesoamerican town of Xochicalco. As she later confirmed in her research report:

'Two Mexican archaeologists, to whom I showed the glyph, instantly recognized it as Xochicalco in style... A Xochicalco-style glyph, if authentic, would date this particular artifact to somewhere between 800 and 950 AD, predating by several centuries the work of [both] Aztec and Mixtec lapidaries [or stone carvers]'[2]

Another interesting thing about this little skull was that it also fitted the description of one we later heard about from a crystal skull researcher named Joshua Shapiro. He had seen such a skull in 1989. It apparently belonged to an old Mexican named José Iníquez, who claimed to have found it in 1942 during a field trip to some ancient Mayan ruins in the Yucatán with his school party. He also said that after this skull came into his possession every dream and desire he had ever had in his life had been fulfilled. But he had died in 1993 and the whereabouts of his skull thereafter remained unknown.

Suddenly tiny crystal skulls seemed to be turning up just about everywhere we looked, even in leading museums. Jane Walsh said she thought these little skulls were actually more likely to be ancient than the larger ones. But the ancient legend Ceri and I had heard specifically said that there were 13 *life-size* crystal skulls, so we were only interested in testing the larger ones.

Dr Walsh had, however, come across one other life-size crystal skull. It belonged, she said, to a woman named JoAnn Parks who lived in Houston, Texas. Like all the other skulls, it was of mysterious origin and surrounded by claims of miraculous powers. Whilst Jane Walsh herself did not believe any of these claims, she was keen to get hold of this skull for the scientific tests so, while she continued with her research paper, we set off for Texas.

9. THE HEALING SKULL

It was a warm winter's day when we arrived in Houston. The Parks lived in a typical suburban home with one of those street numbers running into the thousands which always surprises us British, whose street numbers never get nearly that far. JoAnn had told us that the day we planned to visit an 'activation ceremony' with the skull had been scheduled, which we would be welcome to join, and as we arrived we found the suburban Saturday afternoon calm disturbed by a steady drumbeat emanating from the Parks' home.

JoAnn Parks came to the door to greet us with a big smile. Petite, with bouffant white-blonde hair and dressed in a bright green shiny trouser suit, she welcomed us into her home and invited us to join her and a group of about six other women, presumably friends and neighbours who had gathered for the occasion. Pictures of JoAnn's family adorned the walls, along with a dramatic print of a jaguar stalking through the forest, alongside assorted pictures of JoAnn's crystal skull.

The sofas in the Parks' comfortable living-room had been pushed back, the curtains were drawn and the women were sitting silently on the floor in a circle, eyes closed, with one woman in the centre. She was in her mid-40s, wearing a colourful poncho and clutching two large crystals. She had large intense eyes and a peaceful expression on her face. As we later discovered, her name was 'Star' Johnsen-Moser. JoAnn sat down and joined in the drumming. The crystal skull was at the centre of the circle, facing Star, so at first I couldn't see its features. I could see that it was bigger than the Mitchell-Hedges skull and that the crystal was both cloudy and clear, with a white patch on the top of the head.

We quietly joined the circle. The drumbeat was steady and hypnotic. After a few minutes Star started to breathe very strangely, with very short, gasping intakes of breath. Beginning slowly at first, she started to talk in a strange language I did not recognize, becoming quicker and more fluent as she went on. Her face contorted and she started to writhe around, gesticulating. In a sudden unexpected movement she thrust the two crystals upwards, stabbing at the air with them in all directions. She began chanting, joined by the other women, who vigorously repeated the sounds.

There was something slightly surreal about witnessing this extraordinary ceremony. What were Chris and I doing, watching this strange chanting and crystal waving being performed in front of a crystal skull? Had these people taken leave of their senses? Star was now waving the crystals around directly above the skull and the chanting was becoming louder and louder. Star then put her hands on the crystal skull, slumped forward and stopped.

I had not been sure what to make of Carole Wilson channelling, but this crystal-waving 'activation ceremony' seemed even stranger still. Trying to make sense of it as Star recovered her composure, I asked her about her relationship with the crystal skull. Star, who lived on a remote farm in Missouri, explained that she wasn't even 'interested in crystal' until she met the crystal skull in 1987 and since then her life had 'totally changed':

'As soon as JoAnn brought the skull out I could hardly understand my feelings, because I had never seen a crystal skull before... But as soon as she brought the skull out, something stirred in my heart. It was like meeting a long-lost friend and I just felt this overwhelming degree of love for this rock, for this skull. It was on a very basic emotional level... A little while later I spontaneously found myself speaking in this strange language and I thought, What the hell is going on? What would my friends think? What would my family think? But something told me the crystal skull would understand this language.

'So I went to see it again and I began speaking in this language. And then I could see what looked like things beginning to happen and things beginning to quicken inside the skull. And then, all of a sudden, this "presence" seemed literally to emerge from right out of the skull, with such a force that it almost knocked me off my feet.

'I felt almost paralysed by this immense degree of pain. But it wasn't like a physical pain. I couldn't move and I thought, What's happening to me? But then, just when the intensity of the energy was becoming almost *intolerable, what looked like an intense beam of light, almost like a laser beam, seemed to come right out of the skull and went straight into my heart and then down to the Earth below. I felt a tremendous amount of energy and power flowing through me, almost as if I might be about to burst into flames or something. But then the presence in the skull began speaking in this same language that I could now recognize and understand. And it was just so beautiful, such a wonderful experience.'*

As Star spoke tears started to well in her eyes. She explained that ever since that time she had been having 'telepathic communications with the presence in the skull'. She went on to tell me that the language in which the presence communicated with her was an ancient Tibetan language named Tak. This language was named after an ancient civilization that had existed over 36,000 years ago, before the continents of the world drifted apart, in an area of the world that is now known as the Takla Makan desert in Central Asia.¹ She pointed out that Tak was also the ancient Tibetan name for the constellation of Orion. Indeed, it seemed this was no coincidence as, according to Star, there was some connection between the crystal skulls, we human beings and the stars. As she explained it:

'We all came through the star cluster of the Pleiades and Orion ... we all came through that same source and we are now on our journey back where we came from.'

These stars apparently also had something to do with our own bone structure and our DNA, although Star said she could not be too specific yet about the detail of these points. She did add, however, that she had also contacted the 'presence' inside the Mitchell-Hedges skull on a visit to Anna Mitchell-Hedges' home. Through this contact she had also experienced the total destruction of a whole planet called Maldeck, which had once existed within our own solar system. Star said this planet had been completely blown apart due to an 'abuse of the power of the word' which had led its inhabitants to abuse the power of technology. As Star recalled this experience, she stopped speaking, she was visibly shaken and tears started to fall from her eyes.

I asked how she felt about her experiences in working with the skull.

'I've found it very difficult to put into words what I've learned and experienced. It's almost more like a feeling or an emotion. What I began

feeling is that this presence is like our "oversoul". It is like the part of us that is above and beyond each of us as separate individuals. But I have been given the distinct impression that this oversoul somehow came into this, our own physical dimension and split into separate bodies in making its original expression on its descent into matter. And at one time our civilizations, such as Tak, were in complete communication with this higher evolution, with this higher source, but then over the course of our time on this Earth we have forgotten how to communicate properly with each other and with this original source.

'It is as though in working with the crystal skull it is like tracing a thread of light, which is our connection with our original source. In working with the skull it feels as though you are moving along that thread of light back to the source and passing through various other dimensions en route.*'*

Star also explained that it was now time to awaken to our full consciousness and to reawaken the memory of our connections to our source. This was what the activation ceremony had been about. The skull had told her 'to gather together a Family of Light for the purpose of remembering' and to start to create the right energies on Earth. Those present, it transpired, were her 'fellow lightworkers' who had come together with the skull for this purpose. She said we needed 'to open ourselves up again to connect our own pathways with the pathways of the stars, so that we can allow ourselves again to receive the light from the stars that we have all come through'.

She said she had received some very detailed and specific information from the skull but had been told that the time was not yet right to share much of this information with others, as people would have enough trouble in accepting even the most basic information from the skull at this time.

I was certainly having enough trouble accepting it all. All this talk of stars, bones and an exploding planet was a little too much for me. Luckily JoAnn Parks came over and saved me by handing me the crystal skull. It was heavy, weighing 18 lb (8 kg), although a lot smaller than the Smithsonian skull. I noticed that half of the face was cloudy and the other half clear, giving it quite an unusual visage that some may consider ugly alongside the clear chiselled beauty of the Mitchell-Hedges skull. There was none of the fine workmanship to be seen on the Mitchell-Hedges skull, no real attempt at the accurate rendering of a skull and no separate jaw-bone. Compared with the Mitchell-Hedges skull, the Houston skull looked more like a rough draft, almost hastily produced, with thinly drawn teeth and crude round eyes (*see colour plate no. 10*).

As I looked at the skull at close range, I wondered whether it was really possible that the type of 'light being' or 'presence' Star had spoken about might really exist inside this skull? Somehow, I couldn't imagine it. It all seemed ridiculous. But then there was something appealing about this odd-looking rock.

Looking at the crystal, I noticed thin cracks dividing the cloudy areas from the clear. These imperfections travel deep within the skull, giving the appearance that it had been made up of different pieces of crystal stuck together, although it is actually made up of one single chunk of quartz.

'I had a crystal carver examine it,' said JoAnn. 'He said that those cracks do in fact make this type of crystal very difficult to carve. The structure gets weakened and it could split apart under the pressure of a carver's tools. Most carvers would prefer not to risk working with these flawed materials, particularly if they were using modern machine-powered tools.'

The carver had described the material from which the crystal skull is carved simply as 'junk crystal', the stuff that most carvers would throw in the bin. As I looked at the skull, I could appreciate that great delicacy and care would have to have been taken not to shatter the poor quality quartz. One clumsy move and the skull would have been in pieces.

The fact that the crystal looks as if it is made of different pieces is because, according to JoAnn, it was formed under conditions of great geological instability. Over a period of thousands of years, a section of crystal was laid down and then dramatic changes in the geological environment led it to crack. The crystal continued to grow but in the next section of growth it changed as a result of the changed geological conditions, leading to these interesting variations in colour. JoAnn claimed that the rock the skull was carved from had been 'through five major Earth changes, which created these imperfections or inclusions, then it healed itself over again'.

So where had this strange 'junk crystal' skull come from? JoAnn explained that it was a chance encounter that originally brought her and her husband into contact with the crystal skull and that since then it had changed their lives forever.

As JoAnn started talking her face saddened as she recalled the terrible series of events that had led her to the skull. JoAnn and Carl had two children. But in 1973, their elder daughter, Diana, who was only 12 years old at the time, was diagnosed as having bone cancer.

Around the time that his daughter became ill, Carl, a carpenter by trade, found himself doing some work for a quiet self-contained man, Norbu Chen. The work was almost complete when Carl happened to notice an article in a magazine: 'Norbu Chen the Tibetan healer'. He showed it to JoAnn, who was anxious to work with anyone who might be able to help her child, as the doctors had given Diana only three more months to live.

JoAnn recalled her meeting with Norbu: 'When I met him he was completely quiet and polite but I knew instantly that there was something out of the ordinary about this man.'

Norbu was a red-hat Tibetan lama who had undergone many years of arduous training in India before moving to Houston and setting up his healing practice, the Chakpori Ling Healing Foundation. He led JoAnn down red-carpeted stairs into a small room that had red carpets on the floors, walls and ceiling. She had never seen anything like it before. Her eyes were immediately drawn towards the red altar at one end of the room, 'where in the flickering candlelight was the most awesome sight I had ever seen. In the centre of the altar was a crystal skull. Nothing in my God-fearing Christian upbringing had prepared me for anything like the sight of that skull.'

Despite the unorthodox appearance of Norbu Chen's 'doctor's surgery', something inspired JoAnn's trust and she took her daughter to see him. With the help of Norbu and the crystal skull, she says, 'My daughter lived very well for three years before she finally did pass on.'

Sometime after Diana died, Norbu Chen told JoAnn that he was looking for a secretary and so she offered to help out. She worked for Norbu for several years, but during this time learned little about the crystal skull. All Norbu told her was that the skull had been given to him as a gift from a Guatemalan shaman. However, as JoAnn explained:

'I saw many Tibetan monks. They lived in a small building behind Norbu's house. They studied from ancient Tibetan books, conducting healing ceremonies and prayer sessions every morning in the healing room. They burned incense, chanted and rang bells.

'The monks honoured the crystal skull reverently. They would chant and talk Tibetan to it. It was used by the monks to direct energy into the bodies of the people who came to be healed. They would tap into the

*energy of the skull and run it through the meridian of the patient's body
to assist their healings.'*

During her time at the foundation JoAnn says she 'witnessed many miracles emerging from that healing room', including the help it gave to her
daughter, and over the years Norbu Chen became a close friend of the
Parks. In 1980, he too died, but just before his death he gave JoAnn and
Carl the crystal skull, telling them nothing more about it 'except "One
day you will know what it is for." ' Norbu explained that when he died it
was the Tibetan belief that he would have another body waiting for him
to move into and that he would begin another life. The crystal skull, he
said, was part of his life, but it too needed to reach its next stage and that
was why he was giving it to JoAnn and Carl.

JoAnn and Carl took the skull home, but they had no idea what to do
with it, so it ended up at the bottom of their bedroom closet.

About a year later the crystal skull started to come to JoAnn in her
dreams. At first its image would appear just occasionally. Then, about two
years further on, it started 'talking' to her. 'It wasn't an actual voice,' she
explained. 'It was telepathic.'

JoAnn had never experienced anything like it before. She had always
considered herself a rational person 'with both feet planted firmly on the
ground'. At first, the telepathic communication was infrequent enough
just to dismiss it, but gradually it started to happen more often and at
odd times of day, when JoAnn would be fixing lunch for her grandchildren, for instance, or doing the books for Carl's business. The skull
would even come and speak to her while she was out driving the car. It
kept saying, 'I want out of this closet.'

As JoAnn explained, 'I began to wonder if I was losing my mind. I even
thought about visiting our family doctor.' But things got even more bizarre
when the skull started repeatedly telling her that she had to 'contact the
man' without giving any details of who 'the man' was. Finally, one afternoon, 'I found myself sitting in my bedroom closet having conversations
with this rock.' She told it firmly, 'Leave me alone, I don't want anything
more to do with you, just get out of my life!' She slammed shut the vanity
case in which it was stored and pushed it to the back of the bedroom closet,
covering it with other boxes and cases and shutting the closet door.

*'But the skull was persistent. He was not about to give up. As I ran down
the stairs he continued, "The world is going to know about me. I am*

important to mankind. And, by the way, my name isn't 'Skull', it's 'Max'!"
'Well, now we were on first name terms, we could really talk!'

Some time later JoAnn was to see a TV programme about UFOs that showed a photograph of the Mitchell-Hedges skull. The only information that she had had on crystal skulls prior to this had been Chen's brief parting words over seven years previously. Now she was thrilled to discover that there were other people with 'these extraordinary talking rocks'.

When JoAnn rang the TV station for more information, they gave her the number of a man called Nick Nocerino, who they thought might be able to help. Max, who was as conversational as ever, assured JoAnn that this was the man he had been talking about, the man he had wanted JoAnn to contact.

JoAnn called Nick, who, in gravelly tones, assured her that he had been looking for Max since 1949. He 'tuned into' him and was surprised to see Tibetan monks. JoAnn was amazed. She had only given Nick the description of the skull over the telephone and here he was telling her some of its history! She quickly arranged to meet Nick at Houston airport the following week.

Cutting a mysterious figure in a black beret and trenchcoat, Nick Nocerino turned out to be the world's foremost expert on crystal skulls, a man who had spent a lifetime researching the subject and director of the Society of Crystal Skulls International. After the Second World War he had been sent to Central America to carry out intelligence work on behalf of the US government. It was in a remote village in Guatemala that he had seen a rose quartz crystal skull with a detachable jaw-bone and heard of another fitting Max's description. He was told that this other skull was used for healing, was not as beautiful as the rose quartz skull and didn't have a separate jaw. It was made of crystal that was both cloudy and clear and had a white patch, like a cap, on the top of its head. This skull was believed to have been found in a Mayan tomb in Guatemala in 1924 and to have been given away by a local shaman for unknown reasons.

Nick was delighted to have finally tracked Max down and JoAnn was flabbergasted to find that the man that Max had been telling her to find was not just a figment of her imagination. In fact, it was a great relief to her to finally get confirmation that she had not gone completely mad.

Nick Nocerino assured JoAnn that the crystal skulls did have the ability to communicate telepathically with people they were close to. He explained that during the course of his research he discovered that the skulls did have many attributes that did not seem to make rational sense and that seeing visions in the skull or hearing the skull 'speak' was perfectly normal. He said he knew how frightened people were by the idea of psychic experiences, or any interior, non-rational experiences. But he believed that psychic phenomena had actually been experienced by the vast majority of the population. For instance, many people often 'get a feeling' that something may be about to happen just before it does. As Nick explained, such experiences often frighten people, who usually dismiss them for fear of going mad or being thought 'abnormal'. But such experiences were very normal to Nick and he was not afraid to say so.

Nick suggested that perhaps the best way for JoAnn to realize that she was not crazy was to see other people with the skull, to see what their experiences were. He assured her that Max talking to her was nothing besides what other people would experience with him. Nick himself was something of a veteran when it came to weird experiences with the skulls, as we were to find out for ourselves. So JoAnn opened her home to people who were curious about crystal skulls. First of all, only one or two came, then over time, more and more arrived, until people were coming from all over the world to see Max, just as with Anna Mitchell-Hedges' crystal skull.

'Max has brought me such joy,' says JoAnn, 'and he also brings happiness and laughter to others.' JoAnn now regularly tours around the USA taking Max to different cities to 'meet the people', which she says he 'absolutely adores', adding, 'You could say that he has become a bit of a star.' She has heard many people say that they have extraordinary experiences with him. What is most often reported back to her by people who have sat with Max is the feeling of well-being that he gives them. JoAnn feels that at last she understands the words Norbu Chen spoke to her just before he died. Now she says she thinks she has found out what Max is for and, 'He is doing what he should be doing.'

So, was healing the real purpose of the crystal skulls? Was this why they were created? After all, JoAnn claimed that the crystal skull had helped her daughter and both JoAnn and Anna Mitchell-Hedges had many letters claiming that their crystal skulls had had healing effects on those who had spent time with them. JoAnn feels that this is primarily spiritual healing, while Anna Mitchell-Hedges believes her skull works directly on physical ailments. She is sure that it has not only kept her in good health but has also healed others.

We were somewhat sceptical about the skulls' healing powers, but one thing we did notice was that we came away from JoAnn's house in an exceptionally good mood. Was it something to do with the healing power of the skull or simply the power of suggestion? We just couldn't tell.

Either way, it was now time to make a trip to the outskirts of San Francisco to meet Nick Nocerino in person.

10. VISIONS IN THE SKULL

'I didn't go looking for skulls,' said Nick Nocerino. 'I didn't start off with any interest in skulls. They just had a habit of finding me.'

We had to admit that where crystal skulls were involved, one did seem to lead to another, as Dr Jane Walsh at the Smithsonian Institution had also noticed.

We were at Nick Nocerino's house, drinking hot coffee which his wife Khrys had prepared for us, as she does for the many inquisitive visitors who turn up at the Nocerino home. She is used to her husband's rather strange activities now, but when she married him 49 years ago, she didn't know anything about his extraordinary psychic gifts. 'He was just a regular guy,' she says.

Today, Nick, a swarthy Italian American with an off-beat sense of humour, is considered an authority on crystal skulls and when he is not researching them, he, like Carole Wilson, often uses his psychic skills to help the local police force with murder inquiries. He said that on one investigation he knew so much about the murder, its circumstances and the whereabouts of the body that the police arrested and questioned him!

About crystal skulls, he said simply:

'People dream about 'em, have visions where they see 'em. People are called to the skulls, they are fascinated by them. I don't understand why this happens.

'I have been researching crystal skulls for around 50 years and they are still as much of a mystery to me as the first day I saw one.'

We were sitting in the dimly lit beige and brown living-room, hoping that Nick could shed some light on the strange things that we had been hearing about the crystal skulls. JoAnn had already told us about his ability to psychically 'see' the history of a crystal skull and he had promised to give us a demonstration of his techniques.

Nick said all he could really do was to report his own experiences with the skulls, which began during his boyhood, growing up in Queens, New York, during the Great Depression. One day, aged about eight, he glanced in the bathroom mirror to see a skull reflected back at him. He felt that it was looking right at him, then, 'Suddenly a snake slithered out of one eye socket, and a jaguar crept out of the other.'

The nightmarish image terrified the young boy. He took solace with his grandmother, who practised hands-on healing. She saw in the boy unusual psychic abilities and spent time helping him to develop his skills, in spite of the fact that such talents were not looked on kindly by the Catholic community in which they lived.

It was in Europe, torn apart by the Second World War, that Nick was to encounter his first crystal skull. He joined the navy and during the occupation of the southern coast of France got a couple of days off ship, together with some friends from the French Foreign Legion. The group was sleeping rough and travelling on foot. One day they reached a farm. It had been several days since they had had a chance to wash so, on seeing a well in the farmyard, they went over, hauled up a pail of water and started washing. The farmer came over and told them they must leave immediately. One of Nick's companions, Alex, who spoke French, told him they only wanted to wash. Then the farmer caught sight of the crystal that Nick wore around his neck, one which had been given to him by his grandmother. He became very agitated and ran back to the farmhouse.

'What is all that about?' Nick asked, worried that the old man might have gone off to get his shotgun.

'He told us to wait, not to go anywhere,' Alex replied.

The lads continued washing. Twenty minutes later the farmer came rushing out into the yard carrying a bundle. He ushered the young men into the dark low-ceilinged farmhouse, cleared a space in the middle of the old wooden kitchen table and placed the bundle carefully on it. He then proceeded to untie it, his hands trembling as he did so. Slowly the grubby layers of cloth were peeled back to reveal a life-size, clear quartz crystal skull.

Nick was captivated. He had never seen anything like it before. He held the skull in his hands and, as he explained it, 'My energy started doing strange things.'

The farmer told Nick that he must take the skull as soon as possible. Nick said that he couldn't. The man replied, 'But you are the courier.' The crystal Nick wore around his neck was apparently the sign he had been looking for, the sign that would identify the courier. He told him he had to take the skull and get out of there, because the Gestapo were coming.

But Nick didn't want anything to do with the skull. It was enough trying to keep himself alive without the burden of carrying a skull around. He said it was just as well, because within a week the ship he was on was torpedoed by the French by mistake. Although the crew was able to evacuate safely, everything on board was sunk without trace.

Nick said he was never to see the French crystal skull again, although some think it now belongs to a secret society in France, after whom Nick has named it 'the Blood of Christ skull'. Nick had heard from a 'good source' that secret and masonic societies have long been interested in crystal skulls, although he would not disclose exactly where he had got this information. Certainly the Knights Templar are known to have worshipped a mysterious head. Could this have been a crystal skull? Nick also said, 'Without a doubt, the Gestapo were after psychic artefacts. Both Hitler and Himmler, head of the Gestapo, had an obsessive interest in the occult and collected objects of power. Some believe that it was Hitler's manipulation of the power of the occult that greatly assisted him in his reign.' Nick had even heard rumours from army sources after the war that Hitler did in fact have a crystal skull in his possession and some thought that was the reason he was able to wield so much power.

Nick was to come by his own crystal skull in 1959, using his 'psychic archaeology' skills. Psychic archaeology is the practice of trying to find ancient treasures and artefacts using very finely tuned intuition about where they might be buried. We asked Nick how this worked, but he just replied: 'Don't ask me how I find the crystal skulls psychically. I just know where they are. Like they're finding me.'

So instead we asked Nick where he found his crystal skull. All he would reveal about the place was that it was 'down Mexico way'. He explained, 'I can't be too specific, except to say it was in Guerrero state, in the mountains up the Rio Bravo river.'

The party of four men had apparently been walking for over an hour when suddenly Nick reached down and touched the earth. This was the place, he was convinced of it. He grabbed a shovel and set to work, digging at the hard ground with his Mexican companions. It was not until five or six hours later that they struck large flat stones that had once been part of a building. It was to take several days of digging before they were to unearth a hidden tomb.

The team found a crystal skull that was now sitting on the table right in front of us. Like Max, this skull also had a name that had been given to its owner psychically, in this case 'Sha Na Ra'. And, again like Max, this skull was now sitting amongst the ornaments of a suburban American sitting-room.

Sha Na Ra is a clear quartz crystal skull, although the crystal has a slightly dirty, yellow tinge. The slightly grubby appearance of the skull made me think it needed a good clean, but Nick said he likes to present the skull in the condition in which it was found, and so he had not spent much time polishing the piece. 'Besides which, I've got better things to do,' he said.

Sha Na Ra lacks Max's charm. There is something harsher, more severe about the modelling of this skull, with its prominent cheekbones and slanting eyes. It is generally more angular, sharper and less rounded in appearance than Max (*see colour plate no. 11*).

Like JoAnn with Max, however, Nick said he would be more than happy for the Smithsonian Institution or the British Museum to scientifically analyse Sha Na Ra. He explained that archaeologists don't like to accept the idea that the crystal skulls really come from Central America. In his opinion, this is simply because they have never found any there themselves. 'And they are not about to find any,' he added.

The problem, as Nick sees it, is that archaeologists put enormous trust in what they find on archaeological digs. This is their touchstone. They record exactly where an object was found, measuring at what depth from the surface and making notes of what other objects were found nearby. Nick says that this narrow focus means that they often miss the bigger picture and while they are busy dusting and cataloguing their finds, vital clues may be passing them by. He believes archaeological digs can be a very unreliable source of information and dismisses official archaeological sites with a wave of the hand. It is his belief that the best sites have often been cleared well before the archaeologists start work and that the best finds have already taken place well away from the eyes of officials.

This is because cash-starved local people have found a lucrative trade in selling antiquities illegally removed from archaeological sites. The way they see it is that these items belong to them. The artefacts are their heritage, left by their ancestors, and it is for them to decide what they will do with them, not the archaeological establishment. Illegally obtained archaeological items offer a means of survival. Nick claims that he knows of cases where a whole village has survived on the money they have received from selling artefacts 'illegally' removed from archaeological digs. These items are in hot demand and are sold onto the black market which operates out of San Diego, San José in California and Miami, Florida. Nick even believes that some archaeologists are making a lot of money out of illegally trading antiquities. He claims to have seen 'a lot of things over the years', some of which have made him quite cynical.

But Nick's real interest is not the economics of the antiquities business, but in actually working with the crystal skulls. He said he had had the opportunity to study several in the past. As well as the most beautiful rose quartz skull, he had also seen and worked with 'the amethyst skull', made from purple quartz, and the 'Mayan skull', as he had named them. Apparently the amethyst skull had been found in Guatemala in 1912 and the Mayan skull had belonged to a Mayan priest. Nick had seen both put up for sale in California in 1988 but had no idea where they had ended up since.

Nick feels that the crystal skulls contain important knowledge, if only we could tap into it. This was, of course, the problem we had come up against earlier. As we helped ourselves to coffee, Nick explained the technique he used, which was called 'scrying', also known as 'crystal gazing'. This, he said, was a psychic technique which has been practised for thousands of years. It is essentially a process of 'seeing into the other dimensions', usually with the help of a polished surface. Most often a crystal is used, but other stones such as shiny black obsidian or even a brass plate could be employed for the same purpose. Famous seers such as Nostradamus even gazed into water. According to Nick, the 'scryer' or 'seer' looks into the surface and by clearing their minds in the right way can see things going on in other dimensions. Then the only problem is in trying to determine whether the information they have seen is about the past, present or future. According to Nick:

'Information is available inside the crystal skulls. The information I usually get is not about the future but about the past, specifically the skull's past. Don't ask me how it does it, but it records it. Maybe it's like the human mind – you can't see memories anywhere objectively, in a tangible, physical form, but there is no denying that memories do exist.

Perhaps it is like that with the skull – the memories are there even if we can't see them easily as something physical and tangible. Some say they work the way a computer works. In a sense, they are like computers, loaded with information, which I believe is for the benefit of the whole of mankind. The information they contain may be all kinds of stuff, but I always seem to get images about their past.'

I asked Nick what he thought about the crystal skull communicating in the forgotten language of Tak. Although he himself had no experience of foreign languages with the skulls, he said that they affect different people in different ways, so, 'Who knows? With these things anything seems to be possible.'

Nick was now going to demonstrate scrying for us. We watched as he moved close to the skull, put his hands on it and gazed deep into the top of it. He explained that scrying involves looking deep within the crystal skull. Instead of simply staring at it, the scryer projects their mind deep inside:

'Reflections on the surface of the skull get distracting. It's like you have to see through it. You have to see through what is on the surface to get to the deeper levels which are below. This requires a very deep level of concentration. Not everyone can do this. It's like being hypnotized.

'The weird thing is that the crystal skull becomes cloudy, you are looking at it, feeling like you will never be able to see anything at all, but this clouding over comes before clarity and then, slowly, the information will start to appear in the form of pictures deep within the surface of the skull.'

We sat in a silence broken only by the ticking of a clock on the wall as Nick stared in the half-light into the skull. What was going to happen next? After Star's activation ceremony we were not sure what to expect. After about five minutes, Nick started to describe the extraordinary scenes he saw, which appeared dream-like before him:

'I can see warriors of some sort. They are dressed in elaborate animal costumes, some as eagles, some as jaguars. They are fighting on a hillside. The images are layered … one upon another. It's hard to see clearly… I can see a woman, she has just had a baby. Someone is putting a crystal skull between her legs then they are taking it away. I don't know what it means… It is clouding over again.

'There is something else. I think they must be soldiers, they look like Spanish soldiers from hundreds of years ago. They are on horseback... They are slaughtering people, women and children... They are screaming and crying. Some flee, scattering in all directions. The Spaniards don't seem to notice them now, they are too busy stripping the dead and wounded of their gold.'

As Nick finished speaking I noticed that his eyes were filled with tears. I was taken aback. Could it be that such a tough war veteran had been that moved by images in the skull? Or had he really just imagined them? There was an awkward silence. Nick was staring into the distance, as if still in a trance.

'That is what I saw,' he began slowly. 'I don't understand it. I don't know why I see these things, but that's what I saw.' He sighed. 'I guess there's no way of knowing for sure that what I saw wasn't created by my own imagination.'

We asked him what other images he had seen in the skull. He said that he and many other scryers had often seen what looked like ancient pyramids and sacred sites where religious sacrificial ceremonies were taking place. One was a 'heart-ripping' ceremony in which a crystal skull had been placed inside the chest cavity of the victims once the heart had been removed.

We asked him if he knew what these images might be and he replied, 'Hell, I don't know, but Sha Na Ra dates back to at least the Aztec period, so I guess it's got something to do with that.'

Nick has used the technique of scrying extensively with other crystal skulls, including the Mitchell-Hedges skull. He said, however, that many people won't accept his findings, they simply dismiss them. He recalled how he had met a scientist in Toronto who was researching the history of the planet. Nick had drawn maps of previous land masses that he had seen in the skull. He showed these to the scientist, who was very interested until Nick told him that he had got the information from a crystal skull.

Nick explained that there are other images that emerge from the skulls, dream-like, but with frequent regularity. For him, one of these scenes is of the ocean. Strange aquatic animals appear, moving their large fish-like bodies across the skull's interior. The other is scenes of people moving into caves within the Earth and living there, with their own supply of light. After seeing these people in caves Nick had done some research and discovered that the idea of an 'inner Earth' exists in many legends. A lot of Native American tribes say that their origins lie in the Earth, that after a great deluge their ancestors lived in caves that had their own light source. Although the idea of an inner Earth sounded quite crazy to me, Nick had discovered that both the Nazis and the Soviets had taken the idea seriously, although neither had produced any concrete proof that such a society could or had really existed.

Nick said that another image that has reoccurred many times during his scrying is something which looks like an unidentified aircraft. Such craft appear hovering in the skull, often seeming to disappear underwater or under the surface of the Earth. Their shape varies, sometimes triangular, sometimes the shape of two saucers hovering over each other or a saucer shape with a protruding apparatus which Nick had even managed to capture on film *(see black-and-white plate no.37)*. Nick says:

> *'The images that I have seen are my truth. They are what I have seen. They may be hallucinations, but what puzzles me is that many of these are exactly the same images that have been seen by others who have worked with the crystal skulls.'*

One particularly curious phenomenon is that, according to Nick, nearly everyone who works with a crystal skull for the first time reports seeing almost exactly the same thing. He himself had also experienced this particular set of images with every crystal skull he has ever worked with. They are of 'the whole world in motion, the whole world changing':

> *'I see huge volcanoes, blasting lava that flows in great molten floods down mountainsides, the air choking with black smoke and dust, creating darkness all around, huge earthquakes destroying whole cities, the sea rising up in huge waves, water cascading down, crashing down on forests and temples and smashing everything under its weight, the Earth ripped apart, countries that had been one land mass severed from each other and set adrift across the sea like unmoored boats. It is nature, unleashed as it is in our worst nightmares.'*

Nick added:

'When working with the skulls you don't just see their history from when they were first carved. Remember, crystal is very ancient and it shows you stuff which I believe comes from the dawn of history. I believe that the skulls have lived through immense periods of history and during this time the Earth has changed many times.'

Nick said these dramatic global changes are shown either three or four times, depending on which skull he is working with.

I was stunned by what Nick had said. It sounded totally crazy. Surely the Earth was formed and that was it? I had certainly never heard anything about countries being ripped apart as Nick had described.

But could it be that the crystal skulls really do contain a record of the very real changes that have actually previously affected this Earth? Perhaps such information really is programmed into the skulls? Or could these visions be something to do with our own future? Or are they only in the imagination of the beholder?

Before we left, Nick told us why he thought the crystal skulls had been created in the first place:

'I believe that the skulls are here to help us communicate with our past, with civilizations that have now disappeared. I am talking about prehistory, about societies that existed on Earth long before society as it exists today. I believe that the crystal skulls are telling us that the Earth changes every 20,000, 30,000 or 40,000 years and a new Earth begins to form. I believe that within these skulls is so much vital knowledge that everyone should be made aware of it. Wherever this knowledge came from, I believe that it can help bring peace to the world, and help man to better understand his beginnings, where he really came from and where he may be going.

'I can't prove any of this, any more than I can prove that I have a soul, but I believe I have a soul and I believe that these skulls can help all of mankind. They are messengers of the knowledge. And this is knowledge we vitally need. Through the crystal skulls we can see those catastrophes that have already taken place on this Earth and we can learn not to let those same catastrophes happen again.'

11. THE BOBAN CONNECTION

After Nick Nocerino, the crystal skull expert, JoAnn Parks and Max the healing skull, we weren't sure what to think. We had heard how the skulls were 'ancient' with 'special powers'. But were these beliefs truth or total fantasy?

Hoping to get some fresh insights, we flew to Washington for an update on how Jane Walsh's research was progressing. *En route* to the Smithsonian, however, we stopped off in a small crystal gallery to meet a man who had at one time co-written a book about crystal skulls[1] and who described himself as a 'crystal skull explorer and UFO investigator'.

Joshua Shapiro was small and deadly serious, a computer programmer by trade and an avid advocate of the belief that the ancient crystal skulls are really extra-terrestrial in origin. Joshua is absolutely convinced that the strange image recurrently seen within the Mitchell-Hedges crystal skull is actually a UFO or some form of alien spacecraft. He said he had also had similar experiences with some of the other crystal skulls he had come across. Josh argued that if the Mitchell-Hedges crystal skull could not even have been made with modern machine tools, what alternative was there other than that it had been made by extra-terrestrials?

> '*I believe that the genuinely ancient crystal skulls have some sort of extra-terrestrial connection. As a result of my own and other people's experiences with crystal skulls such as the Mitchell-Hedges, I believe we now have strong evidence to suggest that ancient people had some kind of direct contact with extra-terrestrials and that these skulls are like gifts given by the gods, if you will, that they are here now to help mankind*

and to awaken our own sense of spirituality, in preparation for the coming Earth changes.'

According to Josh there was no denying that 'these genuinely ancient skulls were programmed to be given to the people of the Earth to help us with vital information that is about to become very important to us all'. We had been surprised enough at what we had heard already and here was yet another outrageous theory. Josh continued:

'The crystal skulls are like a catalyst which can help show humanity the other parts of who we really are. They can help us to awaken that part of ourselves, that part of our own consciousness that has now been dormant for a long time. They are here to help us with an accelerated programme of human development, to help us survive and help us towards achieving our own final destiny.

'Most scientists and archaeologists are very unhappy to admit the unusual phenomena surrounding the crystal skulls and the images of an alternative reality which they present to us. I've spoken to many archaeologists and scientists and generally, because of the strange phenomena that occur in the presence of the crystal skulls, they are a little bit wary about putting their reputations on the line. But ultimately there will be no denying where the skulls really came from and what they are really here for.'

Nick Nocerino, however, had been sceptical of the belief that the crystal skulls were extra-terrestrial in origin:

'People are making up all kinds of stories about the crystal skulls, that one of them is the head of some ancient princess, that they came from Mu, Lemuria or Atlantis or something, or even that they were brought by extra-terrestrials. But I've been researching these things for nearly 50 years, and the truth is … we just don't know.'

But when we arrived at Dr Jane Walsh's office, situated at the end of a maze of corridors high up in the Smithsonian Institution building, we got the distinct impression that she was getting close to an answer as to where some, if not all, of the crystal skulls had really come from. It was perfectly clear she did not believe that any of the crystal skulls were extra-terrestrial in origin, nor that they had any kind of supernatural or paranormal powers. For Dr Walsh was approaching the mystery from a standard archaeological perspective and carrying out a serious scientific investigation into the crystal skulls as museum-type objects only. According to this approach it seemed to go without saying that the skulls were neither the product of some mythical civilization of legend nor brought by extraterrestrials. Indeed, from the detailed research Dr Walsh had been doing, it seemed there was reason to believe that the crystal skulls might not even be genuinely ancient.

Dr Walsh was particularly interested in those large skulls which were housed in respected museums: the Smithsonian's own large skull, the British Museum skull and the Parisian skull. What she found curious was that, whatever the source of the privately owned skulls, or even the Smithsonian's skull, both the Parisian skull and the British Museum skull appeared to have turned up at roughly the same time – during the latter part of the nineteenth century.

This had been a great museum-building era in the Western world, a time when Western nations were symbolically asserting their dominance over the rest of the world by building up great institutions such as the Smithsonian and the British Museum. They were busy collecting as many historical valuables from around the world as they could and storing them up in glass cases and corridors for their scientists to study and for their citizens to view at their leisure. During this period it was almost as if the more ancient and exotic the items these museums could acquire, the better.

This was also a time of great interest in pre-Columbian art from Central America. The first few wealthy tourists were arriving in Central America, spurred on by a sort of morbid fascination with the bloodthirsty Aztec culture and the long-forgotten ancient Mayan civilization that had only recently been discovered. Most of these tourists bought inexpensive items such as small clay figurines, but the area was also visited by wealthier buyers and collectors for the great museums. These buyers had the funds necessary to purchase more expensive items and finer objects made from the most exquisite materials.

The problem was that very few properly controlled archaeological excavations had yet been carried out in that part of the world, so there was an incredible degree of ignorance about where any item had really come from. This did not, however, reduce the level of interest in such artefacts. In fact the new museums managed to build up impressive collections in a very short period of time. But the new museums' and new tourists' almost insatiable desire for exotic ancient artefacts had at least one undesirable side-effect: a lucrative market for good fakes and forgeries. As Dr Walsh put it:

'A lot of things were sold as pre-Columbian objects that didn't bear any resemblance whatsoever to real pre-Columbian items, but people had no way of knowing, because very little had been excavated in controlled excavations, so they had very little to judge their authenticity against.'

The question was, with so many good fakes and forgeries around, did these include the crystal skulls? The absence of official archaeological records for the discovery of any of the known crystal skulls had certainly led Dr Walsh to wonder whether some, if not all, of the crystal skulls now residing in leading museums might fall into this category.

Something that had made Dr Walsh particularly suspicious about the origins of the large skulls was that she had been trawling through museum archives and poring over all the old documents she could find relating to crystal skulls, and one name seemed to keep coming up time and again – that of Eugène Boban. This man was a leading French collector and antiquarian who had worked in Mexico during the French occupation of the country (1862/4–7). He had been appointed by Napoleon III to work in the French Scientific Commission to Mexico alongside the French imposed Emperor Maximilian. Boban was known to have owned some genuinely ancient artefacts as well as a collection of rare books and early Mexican manuscripts, and he had written a highly respected work on ancient Mexico, *Documents pour servir a l'histoire du Mexique*, published in 1891. But he also owned antique shops in both Paris and Mexico City.

In one of his sales catalogues, published in 1881, Boban had warned of the abundance of fakes and forgeries which he said were made mostly in the suburbs of Mexico City. As an aid to both private collectors and museum directors he was keen to point out that there was a range of peculiar forgeries about which were not even copies of originals but instead:

'…pure fantasy … a type of bizarre caricature, whose inspiration evades us but whose principal purpose is to delude the public … unfortunately, as they are very easy to obtain and very cheap … many of these monsters strut about in the beautiful glass cases of our museums in Europe.'[2]

Ironically, these fine words of warning were written by the very man that Dr Walsh was now beginning to suspect of peddling just such fakes himself. For she had come across a connection between this man and the Parisian crystal skull, and also quite possibly the British Museum skull. Records in the Trocadero Museum, for example, showed that the Parisian skull had in fact been donated by an Alphonse Pinart in 1878, but that he in turn had bought it from Eugène Boban, who had claimed the skull was pre-Hispanic Aztec in origin.

Only three years after Boban had successfully sold this skull to Pinart, his sales catalogue carried an advert for yet another crystal skull, 'in rock crystal of natural human size', described as 'a masterpiece of lapidary art'. At 3,500 French francs it was the most expensive item listed in the 1881 catalogue. What surprised Jane Walsh was not only that Boban had another crystal skull in his possession so soon after the last one, but also that it was not even listed as Central American in origin. Interestingly enough, Boban also included in this same catalogue the known fakes he had mentioned earlier 'with the intention of unmasking them', although they too had price tags attached!

The life-size crystal skull apparently did not sell at the auction in question, but it was Jane Walsh's belief that it may be the one that ultimately ended up in the British Museum. From the few documents and old letters she had been able to find, she pieced together the theory that when this skull failed to sell in Paris, Boban had taken it back with him to Mexico. There he had tried, again unsuccessfully, to sell the skull to the National Museum of Mexico. This very same skull, Dr Walsh believed, Boban had then tried to sell to the Smithsonian Institution in Washington.

Dr Walsh had found a copy of Eugène Boban's 1886 sales catalogue, which had been sent to the then Director of the Smithsonian Institution, a William Henry Holmes. The skull in this catalogue was described as a:

'...human skull, natural size, dolicephalous in shape, deep eye-sockets, nose cavity, uper [sic] and lower jaws, cut from a large and solid block of hyaline rock-crystal. Smooth, polished surface. A magnificent, perfect and unique specimen...'[3]

The catalogue also stated:

'The human skull played an important part in the religious ceremonial of the Ancient Mexicans, and small specimens in ... rock crystal are not

infrequently found ... but the Boban specimen is by far the largest and finest one known.'[4]

Jane Walsh thought it likely that this was the same skull that Boban had put up for sale in Paris in 1881 and was rumoured to have tried to sell to the National Museum of Mexico. She also believed it very telling that it was only now that it was listed as coming from Mexico. When it had been on sale in Paris, no mention had been made of a Central American origin.

Whether Holmes at the Smithsonian was considering purchasing this skull or not, he could well have been put off by a letter he received from one of Eugène Boban's business competitors, antique dealer Wilson Wilberforce Blake. In a letter dated 29 March 1886 [5] Blake had written to warn Holmes not to buy ancient artefacts from Boban, instead suggesting he buy them from him. This letter described Eugène Boban as 'not honest' and claimed: 'He has some valuable antiquities, but his ownership of them gives them a suspicious character.' It told how Boban had been involved in 'a partnership to defraud the National Museum' of Mexico by trying to sell 'a glass skull made to imitate rock crystal' and 'from Germany' 'as a genuine rock crystal ... for $3,000'. The Mexican museum had apparently been 'on the point of buying it' before they detected the fraud, whereupon Boban had effectively been forced to close his 'museum' in Mexico City and move to New York 'under a cloud'.

Whether or not this was the same skull that appeared in Boban's 1886 sales catalogue, the Smithsonian's Holmes had certainly been interested enough in this skull to note on his copy of the catalogue that it had 'sold for $950 to someone named Ellis'. Dr Walsh had discovered a *New York Times* article from December 1886 which reported a 'Mr Ellis' as the purchaser of 'the highest priced object' in the 'largest sale ever held in this country'. Jane Walsh believes that this Mr Ellis was actually a partner at Tiffany & Co. in New York, who then sold the skull to the British Museum.[6]

Dr Walsh found other evidence for a connection between Eugène Boban and the British Museum skull in a book written by a man whom she believed had actually assisted the British Museum in their purchase. George Frederick Kunz was a well-known mineralogist and occasional Smithsonian adviser who had also written a standard reference book on the subject, *Precious Stones of Mexico*, in which he noted that:

'...rock crystal was used by ancient Mexicans, who fashioned the material into ornaments and skulls...The largest one ... is now in the Archaeological Department of the British Museum, for which it was secured by Sir John Evans, during his visit to the United States in 1897, by purchase from Messrs. Tiffany & Co.'[7]

So it seemed that Boban had sold a skull to a Mr Ellis and this skull was then bought by Sir John Evans and ended up with the British Museum, entering the British Museum records in 1898.

Certainly Kunz' book does suggest a connection between the British Museum skull and Eugène Boban. After expressing his opinion that the skull in question was very characteristic of Mexican work, Kunz discusses its already mysterious origins:

'Little is known of its history and nothing of its origin. It was brought from Mexico by a Spanish officer, some time before the French occupation of Mexico [which began between 1862 and 1864], and was sold to an English collector, at whose death it passed into the hands of E. Boban, of Paris, and then became the property of Tiffany & Co.'[8]

So it appeared there could be little doubt that both the British Museum and Parisian skulls had at one time belonged to Eugène Boban. Indeed, Dr Walsh was also struck by the similarity between Boban's claim that his life-size skull had belonged to the Emperor Maximilian and the claim made about the Smithsonian's own skull, that it had belonged to the Mexican President. She felt that if this were the case, 'It would place [the Smithsonian skull] in the same approximate time period as [the Parisian skull and the British Museum skull].'[9] This appeared to raise the possibility that the Smithsonian skull may also once have been in the hands of Eugène Boban, whose rumoured departure from Mexico on account of his fraudulent activities cast doubt on the authenticity of all of these skulls.

Dr Walsh's arguments sounded quite compelling. But the evidence for what appeared to be her theory, that at least the British Museum and Parisian skulls were therefore probably fake, was rather anecdotal. Most of the information she could find about the character and whereabouts of Eugène Boban came from the letter sent to the Smithsonian by Blake, who would appear to have been one of Boban's main competitors, if not his arch-rival. As Dr Walsh herself admits, this letter was probably Blake's attempt to discredit Boban and thereby successfully secure what was to be his own lucrative deal with the Smithsonian. For in 1886 the Smithsonian did buy hundreds of pre-Columbian artefacts from Blake, including a tiny crystal skull which Blake claimed had belonged to the Emperor's spiritual adviser and was 'the only rock crystal skull of any value'. (This tiny crystal skull could no longer be traced.)[10]

Indeed, the case even for the British Museum skull being a Boban 'fake' is by no means proven. For there are several puzzling discrepancies between the various accounts given of the skull that Boban was trying to sell, which means we cannot assume that they were all descriptions of the same skull. Boban's 1886 sales catalogue, for example, seemed to imply that the skull he was selling was from the collection of the Emperor Maximilian and yet Kunz describes the British Museum skull as having been brought from Mexico by a Spanish soldier some time *before* the French occupied Mexico and imposed Maximilian. So perhaps each of these were actually references to different skulls?

Likewise we cannot assume that the life-size skull in Boban's 1881 catalogue is the same skull that was later included as pre-Columbian in his 1886 catalogue and the same one that finally ended up in the British Museum. For why was this skull not described as being of Central American origin in 1881? Given the possibility that Boban was not entirely honest, as his rival Blake had claimed, this seems rather odd. After all, if Boban had successfully managed to sell a crystal skull labelled as Aztec – the one that ended up in the Parisian museum – why would he not try the same sales technique again three years later, particularly given the strong demand for Central American artefacts?

There also appears to have been little connection between the skull Boban was reported to have tried to sell in Mexico and any of the other skulls he was selling. If, as Blake claimed, the skull Boban had tried to sell to the National Museum of Mexico was from Germany and made of glass, it could not possibly be the same skull that ended up in the British Museum, as that skull is definitely known to be made from rock crystal. We obviously have to bear in mind here that Blake's story may well have been pure invention, designed only to discredit Boban in the eyes of the Smithsonian Institution.

Still another discrepancy emerges, however, when we look at the measurements given for the skull in Eugène Boban's 1886 catalogue and the actual British Museum skull. Whilst close, these measurements do not quite match. Length, breadth and height are all out by about half an inch

(1 to 1.5 cm). Though this may of course be due to a difference of measuring techniques, there is actually no firm evidence that the British Museum skull is in fact the same skull that was included in either of Boban's sales catalogues, never mind the glass skull he purportedly tried to sell in Mexico.

The real question was whether Dr Walsh was correct in her suspicion that Boban was peddling modern fakes, rather than selling genuinely ancient artefacts. Aside from Blake's seemingly unreliable letter about a glass skull, Dr Walsh appeared to have discovered little in the way of hard evidence to suggest that the skulls Boban was selling were anything other than genuine artefacts. The skull listed in Boban's 1886 sales catalogue may really have belonged to the Mexican Emperor or even come from a genuine archaeological dig.

One interesting twist in the tale is that around the time that Boban was selling his skulls the mysterious pre-Aztec city of Teotihuacán had just been discovered. Teotihuacán is a stunning ancient ruined city that lies just to the north of Mexico City. It was centred around three great pyramids, very like the pyramids of Egypt, had always been greatly revered in Aztec mythology and was known to the Aztecs as 'the place where the sun was born' or 'the place where the heavens meet the Earth' or 'the place of the men who knew the road of the gods'. To this day little is known about the city's original inhabitants, the Teotihuacános.

As Dr Walsh discovered, in late 1885 a Mexican newspaper reported that Eugène Boban had been in Teotihuacán touring the site of the great Pyramids of the Sun and the Moon in the company of Leopoldo Batres, the newly appointed Inspector of Monuments, whose job was to oversee the excavations. Then, apparently sometime between January and March of 1886, Boban contacted Holmes, offering to sell the Smithsonian much of his pre-Columbian Mexican collection, including the crystal skull mentioned previously. The letter from Boban himself has now been lost and so Dr Walsh had been forced to reconstruct its contents from Blake's letter. Blake had also been out to the pyramids and was particularly keen to point out that Batres, like Boban, was 'not only a fraud but a swindler'.[11] But could Blake's contempt for Boban and Batres actually have had something to do with the fact that Boban might really have obtained his crystal skull from proper archaeological excavations, perhaps at Teotihuacán, excavations to which Batres may have denied Blake access? Blake does seem to have been correct in his claim that Boban left Mexico just after visiting the Teotihuacán excavations and auctioned off most, if not all, of his collection in New York.

But the vital historical evidence that would prove that the crystal skulls were actually nineteenth-century fakes could not be found and Dr Walsh was left to sum up in her research paper:

'Despite the fact that I am reasonably convinced that the Smithsonian skull [at least] is a nineteenth century fake ... I may, of course, be entirely wrong about this.' [12]

Certainly Nick Nocerino, JoAnn Parks and Anna Mitchell-Hedges were all convinced that their crystal skulls were genuinely ancient, and the crystal skulls that Boban was selling may have also been genuine. But we had to agree with Jane Walsh's research report that it was indeed possible that Boban had also sold fakes of some kind and those fakes may well have included crystal skulls. Still, we had no means of knowing for sure. We hoped the scientific tests would now solve this mystery once and for all. But the question was, if Boban had been selling fake crystal skulls, where had he got them from? So in the meantime we were curious to know who might have been making crystal skulls in the nineteenth century.

Dr Walsh explained that what had continued to niggle away at the back of her mind was that Blake had mentioned a German connection. If the skull in question really was the British Museum one then Blake was completely wrong about its being made of glass, but might it really have been originally 'brought from Germany'? Jane Walsh had spoken to her colleagues in the mineralogy department and asked them if it was feasible that something like a crystal skull could have been made in Germany during the nineteenth century. Her colleagues told her that there was a small town in Germany that was world-renowned as a centre for crystal carving. This town was Idar-Oberstein.

When we looked further into the possibility that at least some of the skulls might have come quite recently from Germany, we discovered that Idar-Oberstein had been a major stone-carving centre of Europe ever since the Middle Ages. Since the fifteenth century it had been famous for carving beautiful objects out of locally mined agate, jasper and quartz, but by the beginning of the nineteenth century the local deposits had run out and the town had gone into decline. Many of its citizens had emigrated to Brazil – but there they found some of the best supplies of raw quartz crystal in the world. They shipped this quartz back to Idar-Oberstein in vast quantities and the town went through a new boom period.

Today there were still several crystal carving workshops in the town. We spoke to the head of one of these ateliers, a man named Hans-Jürgen Henn. As he explained:

> 'Really important Idar-Oberstein became when we got the new import material from the New World, particularly from Brazil, which opened a totally new horizon. The cutters and carvers improved their own knowledge and they really carved items they'd never seen before. The dealers came from all the major cities in the world during last century. Of course, Paris was a very important city for these kinds of objects, where rich people go and purchase such luxury items.'

Apprentices from nineteenth-century Idar-Oberstein usually travelled to Paris to study engraving and had produced many beautiful and intricate pieces of work. Was it possible that while Eugène Boban was in Paris he had bought what is now the British Museum crystal skull from one of these carvers or dealers from Idar-Oberstein? Perhaps the British Museum skull, and the Parisian, Smithsonian and Mitchell-Hedges skulls, had really been carved in Germany by craftsmen trained in Paris, using quartz crystal originally from Brazil.

But there was no proof. After all, Idar-Oberstein dealers generally protected their trade by keeping their clients away from their carvers. The artists' names were never mentioned and no records were ever kept. But we did find something else in Idar-Oberstein which suggested that this may well have been the case. For Hans-Jürgen Henn explained that he himself had a crystal skull.

This skull, he said, had been made in his crystal carvery in Idar-Oberstein as recently as 1993. It was smaller than life-size, about 4.5" (11 cm) high, but was incredibly anatomically accurate. At first sight it looked as though it had a separate lower jaw, as it had such carefully carved features and realistic teeth, but on further examination the jaw was fixed, part of the same piece of crystal as the rest of the skull. The skull was made from the most incredibly pure and transparent piece of quartz, but to the trained eye it was clearly made with the assistance of modern machinery. It had in fact been carved over a period of nearly a year with diamond-tipped power tools – and was currently on sale to whoever could afford to pay over $50,000 (or £33,000) for it!

However modern the skull, we were curious to know what had inspired its creation. The answer revealed that even here, in efficient and rational modern Germany, crystal carvers had a deep sense of the spiritual dimension within rock crystal itself. As Hans-Jürgen explained:

> *'The stones tell us how they want to be carved and cut, and this can make things a little difficult. You see this stone, I guess, was sleeping for a while before he told us what he wanted to be.'*

So the crystal itself had told the carver it wanted to be turned into a crystal skull!

Whilst Hans-Jürgen said he did not know of any other crystal skulls ever having been carved in Idar-Oberstein, it was clear that the town had been carving crystal in the late 1800s, at exactly the same time as Eugène Boban was selling his 'Mexican' crystal skulls around the world. So was it possible that the museums and skull owners had actually been prey to the malicious tricks of rogue antique dealers who had had crystal skulls carved in Germany then shipped them out to Mexico to fool prospective buyers?

But one other aspect of this latest research had not initially occurred to us. For now a crystal skull had been discovered that was definitely modern and that had been carved, albeit very recently, in Europe using imported crystal from Brazil. So it was Jane Walsh's intention that the German skull should now provide the modern template against which to test all the other crystal skulls.

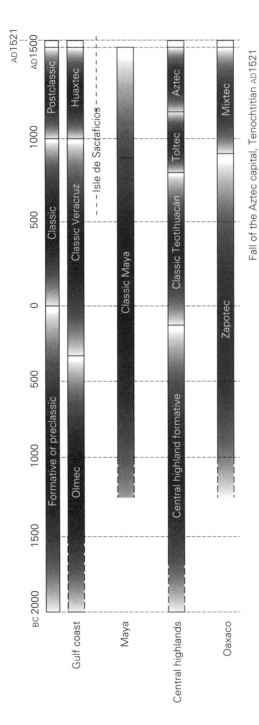

Figure 2: Table showing the rise and fall of the ancient Mesoamerican civilizations

12. THE AZTECS
AND THE CRYSTAL SKULL

Although the German connection now threatened to change all that was known about the crystal skulls, the keeper of the Parisian skull had resolutely maintained that his skull was 'definitely Aztec'. The British Museum skull was labelled 'probably Aztec' and Nick Nocerino was unyielding in his opinion that his skull was at least as old as the Aztecs. Until the tests, we would not know for sure. But we were still waiting for confirmation that they would take place. In the meantime, we wanted to find out more from any archaeological evidence left by the Aztecs and to explore the mysterious ruins of Teotihuacán. Despite Eugène Boban's dubious reputation, we wondered whether his visit to this site might turn out to have some connection with the crystal skulls he had been selling.

The Aztec civilization arose in the early thirteenth century AD around what is now Mexico City, so we decided to go there first. Mexico City today is a huge sprawling urban metropolis housing nearly 20 million people. From the air it looks like a vast ocean of concrete stretching right across a high mountain plateau, surrounded on all sides by the peaks of various volcanoes. Most of these are now extinct, but some, such as Popacatapetl, still occasionally threaten to erupt. As we arrived on the ground, however, these volcanoes became invisible, due to the thick smog that now chokes this vast sprawling city. The pollution is said to be equivalent to smoking 40 cigarettes per day and is known to shorten life expectancy by several years.

As soon as we had recovered from our jet lag we set off through the choking streets for the National Museum of Anthropology. From the outside, the low earthquake-proof concrete building looked more like a nuclear bunker than the veritable treasure chest of ancient wonders that it turned out to be. We were very fortunate that our guide around the museum was a remarkable man by the name of Professor José Salomez Sanchez, a visiting professor of archaeology from the nearby National University. José, like countless other Mexican academics, was these days forced to supplement his meagre academic income through the more lucrative trade of being a tour guide, in order to properly feed and support the two of his four children who were still living at home.

As Ceri and I wandered through the corridors of the museum and gazed in wonder at the many ancient artefacts, José built up a vibrant and dramatic picture of the ancient Aztecs and their predecessors. It seemed the Aztecs had based an entire civilization on the cult and worship of death. They were renowned for ritual human sacrifice and were also absolutely obsessed with the image of the human skull. The museum was lined to the gunnels with varied and exotic artefacts, and many of the ancient objects depicted the image of the human skull.

At its height the Aztec empire spanned a vast area of Central America from the Pacific Ocean in the west to the Atlantic in the east and from the deserts of the north to the jungles of the south. It had an estimated 10 million inhabitants, but was completely destroyed by the Spanish, who arrived in 1519.

The dramatic rise and fall of the Aztec empire is a story of drama, violence, tragedy and betrayal. It tells how a small group of vagrant peasants managed to transform themselves, in less than 200 years, into one of the largest and most powerful civilizations of all the Americas. It is also the story of how a 33-year-old man, with only 600 men and 16 horses, managed to conquer a magnificent empire that was far larger than his home country of Spain. The story of the Aztecs' meteoric rise and fall is also a testament to the power of prophecy and prediction. And, as we were to discover, one or more crystal skulls may have been involved.

The Teotihuacános, the Aztecs' predecessors in this part of central Mexico, are often considered the original founders of Aztec culture. Their civilization is thought to have arisen before the time of Christ and reached its zenith at around the same time as the Roman Empire in Europe. But all that remains of it today is the ruined city of Teotihuacán, which lies just to the north of present-day Mexico City.

The Teotihuacános were followed by the Toltecs, who were renowned as the founders of the city of Tula, a few remnants of which still lie not

far from Mexico City (*see Figure 1*). They were also considered the originators of much of Aztec thought and belief. Tula was mythologized by
the Aztecs as a magnificent and prosperous place where painters, sculp-
tors and carvers of precious stones worked. According to later Aztec
accounts, the Toltecs were 'truly wise' people. They worshipped many
deities, but particularly the great god of all Central American civilizations, the 'feathered serpent' Quetzalcoatl. He was said to have taught
religious practices that emphasized light and learning, and creating harmony and balance between humankind and nature.

The Aztecs believed that Quetzalcoatl had greatly helped their ancestors' artistic and cultural development. He was said to have constructed
spectacular palaces oriented towards the four directions and to have
taught people about religion, agriculture and law. He also taught mathematics and the written language, music and song, arts and crafts, and, in
particular, how to work with precious metals and stones. As the early
Spanish chronicler de Sahagún wrote,

*'In his time, Quetzalcoatl discovered the great riches ... the genuine
turquoises, and gold and silver, coral and conches ... [and] the precious
stones.'* [1]

It therefore remains a distinct possibility that this great leader taught the
Aztecs' ancestors how to create and work with precious stone objects such
as the crystal skulls.

It has always been unclear whether the original Quetzalcoatl was purely
a god or also a real human being. He was described as 'pale of skin and
bearded' and it is thought that there was once a great high priest called
Quetzalcoatl who ran a religious cult and governed a small empire from
Tula. Whether god or human, the story goes that Quetzalcoatl, representing the forces of light, struggled against the forces of darkness in Tula.
These were represented by gods such as Tezcatlipoca, or 'Smoking Mirror',
and Huitzilopochtli, the patron god of the Aztecs, who was also the god of
the sun and the god of war. Human sacrifice was apparently already being
practised in Central America – the Toltecs are thought to have been
almost as obsessed with death and ritual human sacrifice as the Aztecs –
but it was not part of Quetzalcoatl's teachings and it was on this issue that
he is said to have fallen into dispute with many of those around him. He
apparently finally lost the struggle against the forces of darkness, in particular Huitzilopochtli, and was forced to flee from Tula. Legends say that he

'buried his treasure' and 'sailed off across the seas to the East' on a raft of serpents. But he promised to return once again, according to some accounts only when the practice of human sacrifice had ceased, although others said it would be in the year One Reed of the ancient calendar.

Hearing the story of Quetzalcoatl and his battle against the dark forces of Huitzilopochtli, I wondered whether a crystal skull might well have been associated with this great and wise teacher who knew about gems, precious stones and carving. Could crystal skulls have been some of the objects of beauty that this mysterious teacher had taught the people to make? Or had crystal skulls been created to represent the darker forces of Huitzilopochtli?

Some time after Quetzalcoatl had fled, at around the beginning of the thirteenth century, a group of nomads started to appear in central Mexico. First referred to as 'the people whose face nobody knew',[2] they later became known as the mighty Aztecs. As José Salomez Sanchez explained, their real origins are now lost in myth and legend. According to some accounts they came from the legendary Chicomoztoc, or 'the place of the seven caves', often thought to correspond to the high mountainous region they took so long to cross *en route* from their original 'womb'. This common origin, often said to be shared by people who split into seven different tribes along the way, was a place called 'Aztlan'. This was said to be a 'country located beyond the sea', or 'a magnificent town or city built on an island' that had disappeared, somewhere to the east. Many accounts say the Aztecs originally arrived from the north, but it is believed that the people who originally came from Aztlan had been on a long migration, lasting over several centuries, wandering over the plains and mountains of Mexico in search of a land to make their new home. Some versions of the migration story also say that the Aztec people came across Michoacán, 'the land of those who possess fish', and thus perhaps the Atlantic Ocean, before they reached their final home.[3]

It is said that this migration was guided by the tribal prophets, who had told the people that they would build a great city at the place where they saw an eagle clasping a snake in its claws. In the early thirteenth century the Aztecs arrived on the vast plateau, over 7,000 feet (2,240 metres) above sea level, which still forms the Valley of Mexico. This valley is now quite arid and dry, but then held two vast lakes and was a perfect place to support a large population. Indeed, it was already well populated when the Aztecs arrived and the original inhabitants were somewhat displaced at the arrival of these newcomers. Finding the Aztecs were searching for somewhere to settle, the locals directed them towards the very edge of the lake, an area infested with poisonous snakes, which they hoped would soon finish the migrants off.

But in 1325, on a tiny island just off the coast of the lake, the Aztecs apparently saw the sign they had been looking for – an eagle sitting on a cactus plant clasping a snake in its claws. So they settled down quite happily, began eating the snakes and apparently even thanked the locals for suggesting such a wonderful place stocked with one of their own favourite foodstuffs. They built a humble temple of reeds and sticks to pay tribute to their rain god Tlaloc, the god of water and fertility, set about draining the swamps and digging irrigation channels around the island and settled to successful agriculture, particularly growing maize.

But the Aztecs also became a powerful military force. They hired themselves out as mercenaries to all the other small tribes in the area, becoming their brute-force diplomats and advisers, and ultimately usurping each of them in turn. They fast gained a reputation as a shrewd and ruthless people, using a strange combination of friendly overtones followed by attack, without apparently showing any scruples at all. In one particularly horrifying example, José Salomez explained that the Aztecs are said to have invited a neighbouring king to present his daughter to them so that they could 'honour' her at a feast. The king sent his daughter ahead and was then invited to join the celebrations himself. When it was time for his daughter to appear at the banquet, the king was horrified to see an Aztec warrior dancing in, wearing her freshly flayed skin.

In this way the Aztecs quickly established a huge empire. As their fortunes improved, they built two great cities of gold and stone. The one on the lake was known as Tenochtitlan and is now Mexico City, and the other, Tlatelco, somewhat to the north, is now part of the great urban sprawl. Each city was built on an interlocking system of canals and waterways and served by aqueducts supplying fresh water from the nearby mountains. At the centre of each were vast temple and palace complexes housing the new kings, nobles and holy men and serving as sites for the ultimate tribute to the Aztecs' many gods, who demanded regular human sacrifice. At the centre of Tenochtitlan the Aztecs built their mightiest temple, now known as the Templo Mayor (Main Temple).

Under a succession of emperors and shrewd warrior-kings, the Aztecs began to view themselves as a chosen people. They rewrote history, glorifying past victories and destroying all the historical documents of the people they had conquered, so that no evidence should remain to contradict the supremacy of Aztec rule. They were also responsible for the reform of local religion, giving new prominence to the fearful god of war and the sun, Huitzilopochtli, at the expense of Quetzalcoatl.

But the period of Aztec supremacy in Mexico was to last less than a century, for the foundations of the empire were soon to be shaken by the arrival of the Spanish at the start of the sixteenth century. This had apparently been foreseen by the Aztec holy men and some members of the nobility. One of their military leaders, Nezahualpilli, who also had a reputation as a sorcerer and magician, is said to have prophesied the arrival of the 'sons of the sun' (the term by which the Spanish became known) in the early 1500s and to have warned the emperor, Moctezuma II, of 'strange and marvellous things which must come about during your reign'.[4] Nezahualpilli is then rumoured to have escaped death by withdrawing to a secret cave before the Spaniards arrived.[5]

Moctezuma II had a reputation as a scrupulous observer of religious ritual and the esoteric omens of the priestly class, and is said to have become increasingly distressed by what he saw as a number of ill omens. Around 10 years before the Spanish arrived a dazzling comet suddenly appeared in the skies. De Sahagún reported its significance to the Aztecs:

'…an evil omen first appeared in the heavens. It was like a tongue of fire, a flame [or] the light of dawn. It seemed to rain down in small droplets, as if it were piercing the sky.'[6]

Following this, the sanctuary of one of the Aztec goddesses mysteriously caught fire and the water on the lake formed gigantic waves, despite the fact that there was no wind.[7]

It is also said that a mysterious stone 'began to speak' and proclaimed the fall of Moctezuma's empire. Little is known about this stone except that it was referred to as 'the stone of sacrifice' and was kept in a place called Azcapotzalco. According to the early accounts of the Spaniard Diego Durán:

'The stone … again spoke, "Go and tell Moctezuma that there is no more time… Warn him that his power and his rule are ending, that he will soon see and experience for himself the end that awaits him for having wished to be greater than the god himself who determines things." '[8]

PLATE 32 (TOP) Frederick and Anna Mitchell-Hedges (on the right, aged 20) in the jungles of Central America in the late 1920s

PLATE 33 (ABOVE) Frederick Mitchell-Hedges, Lady Richmond-Brown and Dr Thomas Gann in the ruins of Lubaantun (circa 1925)

PLATES 34, 35 & 36 The
Mitchell-Hedges skull
undergoing scientific tests
at the Hewlett-Packard
crystal laboratories

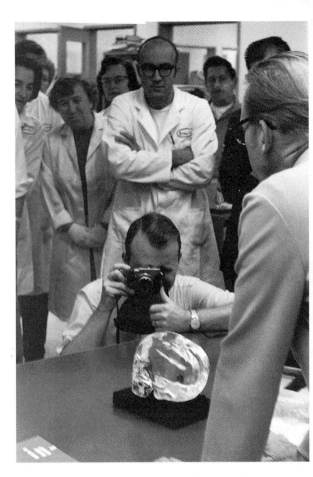

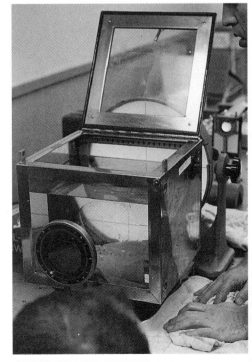

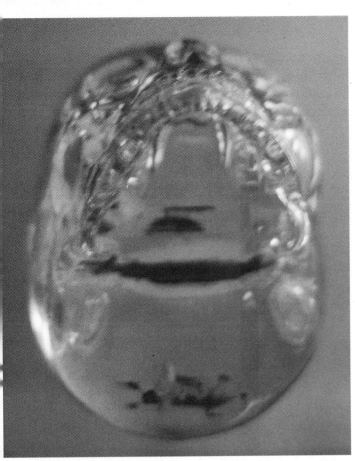

PLATE 37 (LEFT)
A 'holographic image of a UFO' appearing within the Mitchell-Hedges crystal skull

PLATE 38 (BELOW)
'Offering No. 4' excavated from La Venta (on the Gulf coast of Mexico) showing 'alien-like' Olmec pottery figurines (dated to 'several centuries BC')

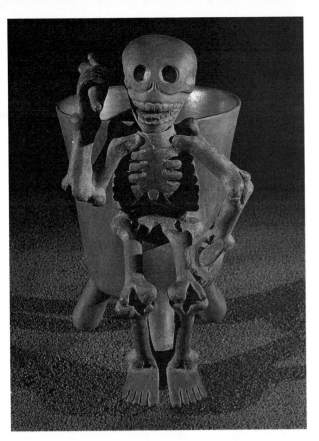

PLATE 39 (FAR LEFT) Clay head from Tlatilco, Mexico, representing the concept of life-death duality in pre-Aztec Mexican culture as early as 1000 BC

PLATE 40 (BOTTOM LEFT) Necklace of 12 small bone-carved skulls (with the 13th missing?) found in the Guerrero state of Mexico and dated to AD 1000

PLATE 41 (LEFT) Mixtec pottery figurine of the ancient Mesoamerican god of death – Mictlantecuhtli

PLATE 42 (BELOW) Aztec statue of Mictlancihuatl, the wife of Mictlantecuhtli and the goddess of the world of the dead

PLATE 43 (RIGHT) Realistic stucco head found at Palenque, Mexico

PLATE 43 (RIGHT) Realistic stucco head found at Palenque, Mexico

PLATE 44 (TOP LEFT) Gargantuan Olmec stone head found at La Venta on the Gulf coast of Mexico (dated to many centuries BC)

PLATE 45 (ABOVE) The ancient Mayan god of all gods and god of the Earth's axis, Itzamna, shown sitting opposite a skull in a sacred bundle

Forensic reconstruction of the face on the Mitchell-Hedges crystal skull:

PLATE 46 (RIGHT) Drawing by Richard Neave of the University of Manchester's Department of Art & Medicine

PLATE 47 (BELOW) Drawing by Detective Frank J. Domingo of the New York Police Homicide Department

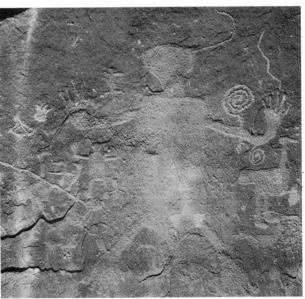

PLATE 48 (TOP LEFT) Patricio Dominguez, Pueblo spiritual adviser

PLATE 49 (TOP RIGHT) Kivas at the ancient Anasazi ruins in Chaco Canyon, New Mexico

PLATE 50 (ABOVE LEFT) Petroglyphs on the wall of the canyon at the Navajo gathering which depict their belief in the alien origins of mankind and the crystal skulls

PLATE 51 (ABOVE RIGHT) Leon Secatero, Navajo spiritual leader

Moctezuma himself also had a magical mirror, made from obsidian, which he used for foreseeing future events. He is said to have looked in this mirror and seen 'armed men borne on the backs of deer'[9] – presumably a reference to the Spaniards' horses, which were at that time unknown in the Americas.

Moctezuma called his holy men and soothsayers together to interpret his fate, saying:

'You know the future … you know everything that happens in the universe … you have access to what is locked in the heart of the mountains and at the centre of the earth … you see what is under the water, in caves and the fissures of the soil, in holes and in the gushing of fountains … I beg you to hide nothing from me, and to speak to me openly.'[10]

But they refused to speak. Enraged, Moctezuma threw them in prison. But when he heard that his priests were not despairing in their cages but 'were full of joy and happiness, and they continually laughed among themselves' he went to see them again and this time offered them their freedom if they would speak.

'They replied that, since he was so insistent on knowing his misfortune, they would tell him what they had learned from the stars in heaven and all the sciences in their power; that he was to be the victim of so astonishing a wonder that no man had ever known a similar fate.'[11]

Some accounts say Moctezuma was so displeased with what he heard that he then left his priests and seers to starve to death.

In April 1519 the first Spanish conqueror Hernando Cortés and his small army arrived at Veracruz on the Mexican coast. The local people saw their ships sailing along the Gulf coast and reported to Moctezuma that 'a mountain has been seen moving around on the waters of the Gulf'. It is also reported that the ruthless Cortés ordered all his own boats to be burned and scuttled in the ocean to prevent his army from being tempted to try and flee. For they were outnumbered by the natives by thousands to one.[12]

But Cortés was a wily politician and diplomat and he managed to persuade the local Tlaxcalans and several other tribes who were already displeased by their subjugation at the hands of the Aztecs to join forces with him against the mighty Aztec empire. Unbeknown to him, however, he already had destiny on his side.

It was the year One Reed when Moctezuma heard that strangers with 'white hands and faces and long beards' who were 'riding on the backs of deer' had arrived on the coast from the east and their leader was demanding a meeting with him. Little wonder that he mistook Hernando Cortés for the great god Quetzalcoatl returning, as prophesied, to reclaim the power that was rightfully his. It was a mistake that would prove fatal not only to Moctezuma himself but also to the Aztec empire.

At first Moctezuma wasn't sure quite what to do. Should he receive Cortés as the god of all gods or treat him as a mortal enemy? But it was said that the worshippers of Huitzilopochtli would be unable to retain their power once Quetzalcoatl himself returned to reclaim it. So Moctezuma welcomed Cortés and his army. He placed a necklace of precious stones and flowers around his neck, offered him his crown of quetzal bird feathers, and indicated to him that he would humbly offer him back the rulership of the whole empire if he so desired. Cortés and his army were escorted into the very heart of Tenochtitlan, where crowds gathered to meet and cheer them, and offered the luxurious surroundings of the imperial palace itself as their home.

The Spanish could scarcely believe what they saw. The Aztec capital was far grander than the Rome and Constantinople with which they were familiar. With a population of around 300,000 it was about five times the size of London at that time. Many of the soldiers compared it to Venice or thought they had stumbled upon some enchanted city of legend such as Atlantis. As one of Cortés' soldiers, Bernal Díaz, wrote in his diary:

'We were amazed and said that it was like the enchantments they tell of in the legend of Amadís, on account of the great towers and cues and buildings rising from the water, and all built of masonry. And some of our soldiers asked whether the things that we saw were not a dream.' [13]

There were floating gardens and extensive orderly markets abundant with gold, silver, jade and foodstuffs of every kind. The royal palace even had its own private aviary and zoo, where jaguars, pumas and crocodiles were tended by trained veterinary staff. The city was of a beauty, order and cleanliness that the Spaniards had never seen before.

But, just as the soldiers were overwhelmed by the beauty and orderliness of the city, they were equally horrified by what they saw when they reached the Templo Mayor at the very heart of the magnificent metropolis. Here they were to find the two main pyramid sanctuaries. One was dedicated to Tlaloc, the god of water and fertility, and the other to Huitzilopochtli, the god of the sun and war. Over 100 steps led up to the top of the pyramids. These were apparently stained black, thick with the clotted blood of ritual human sacrifice. The very air itself hung heavy with the dank stench and putrefying odour of death.

The Aztecs invited the Spanish to attend the celebrations to mark the feast of Huitzilopochtli. As the ritual dances began and the Aztecs were totally engrossed in the festivities, the Spanish seized their moment to attack. They killed the most eminent members of the Aztec nobility and are said to have massacred at least 10,000 people on that night alone. Some of the Aztecs tried to stop them, driving them from the city, but they returned with more of their local allies and, having built 13 great barges, laid siege to the city. On 13 August 1521 Tenochtitlan finally fell. Moctezuma himself was taken prisoner and killed, thousands were murdered and the streets were awash with the fresh blood of the victims of the new Spanish rule.

In the years that were to follow many of those who were not killed by the invaders died instead of pestilence and disease. For the smallpox, cholera, measles and yellow fever the Spanish brought with them were unknown in the Americas and so the locals had no immunity at all. Between war and disease the native population was decimated, falling from 10 million to little more than 2 million in less than 20 years.

Back in the museum, we gazed at scale models of the Aztec capital the Spaniards had destroyed and looked at a huge slab of stone covered in detailed carvings of people in positions that looked like the throes of death. José explained that this was a sacrificial stone of the kind positioned at the top of the Aztec pyramids for use during sacrificial ceremonies. We wanted to hear more about the Aztec practice of human sacrifice, on the assumption that crystal skulls might somehow have been involved.

José explained that the Aztecs had effectively built their whole empire on the blood of human sacrifice. The main victims were enemy soldiers who had been captured in battle and a whole military machine had been created to provide the capital with a constant supply of sacrifices. So the two driving principles of war and human sacrifice each fed off the other, causing the empire constantly to expand.

Nobody knows exactly how many victims were sacrificed by the Aztecs. The early Spanish apparently got some indication of the numbers

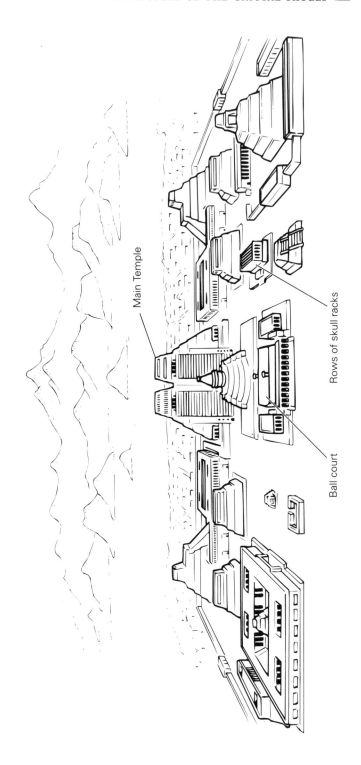

Main Temple

Rows of skull racks

Ball court

Figure 3: A view of the Aztec capital of Tenochtitlan (now Mexico City) as it looked when the Spanish first arrived

involved by looking at Aztec skull racks, or *tzompantli*, some examples of which were still carefully preserved in the museum. After the sacrifice, where the heart was ripped out and held high in the air, the victims were usually decapitated. The disembodied head was skewered on a stake and hung in parallel rows along a skull rack. The racks were then prominently displayed in the heart of the city, alongside the main pyramids and the ballcourt.

Bernal Díaz tried to count the number of human skulls on display when the Spaniards first arrived and estimated there to be at least 100,000. Two of his colleagues claimed to have done an accurate count and came up with the figure of 136,000, all at varying stages of decomposition and decay.[14]

We were later, however, to meet a contemporary 'Aztec priest' by the name of Maestro Tlakaeletl who claimed that the stories of ancient Aztec sacrifice were greatly exaggerated. He told us that the Spanish conquerors had to portray the local people as brutal savages in order to justify their own actions, which amounted to the near total genocide of the peoples of Central America. The skull racks, he claimed, were actually part of ancient Aztec calendrical practices and the heads were those of people who had died quite naturally. The rack was apparently used somewhat like an abacus, to help record the passage of time.

Whatever the truth of the matter, the further details that José told us certainly seemed to show that the ancient Aztecs had a very different view of human sacrifice from the total revulsion we have today in the West.

In order to ensure a supply of captives for sacrifice, the Aztecs had carried out a whole series of ritualized battles against neighbouring states, known as 'the War of the Flowers'. Led by 'jaguar-knights', who wore jaguar skins, 'eagle-warriors', whose helmet was an eagle-head, and others who wore simply the lower jaw of a human skull on top of their own, Aztec warriors rarely killed enemies on the battlefield, but saved them for ritual slaughter instead. Strangely, once captured, the sacrificial prisoner was no longer seen as an enemy being killed but as a messenger being sent to the gods. When a warrior took a prisoner captive he always proclaimed, 'Here is my beloved son,' and the prisoner ritually replied, 'Here is my revered father.' For to the Aztecs and many of their neighbours, it was considered a great honour to be sacrificed and the victim was invested with a great dignity bordering almost on the divine.[15]

Indeed, it seems that sacrifice was such an honourable way to die that it was not only reserved for enemies; the Aztecs also chose victims from within their own ranks. Most often a male child born on a certain day, with the correct astrological alignment, was selected at birth and handed over to another family to be raised until the time of sacrifice. To such a child, dying at the temple was quite simply his true and total purpose in life.

Just after puberty, a few months before the big day, the sacrificial victim would be given four beautiful young brides to live with and would be taught to play beautiful songs on a pipe. Then, when the day came, he would be dressed in richly coloured robes, with bells around his ankles and flowers around his neck. Crowds would gather in the marketplace to cheer him as he walked towards the sacrificial pyramid. As he climbed the up the pyramid he would play his sweet music, stopping to smash his clay pipe on the steps near the top. Reaching the summit he would be given a drink called *dolowachi*, a painkiller and sedative, as the priests assembled for the ceremony. In the words of Friar de Landa:

'They conducted him with great display ... and placed him on the sacrifice stone. Four of them took hold of his arms and legs, spreading them out...'[16]

The drink also helped the victim's chest to relax and open up against the curvature of the sacrifice stone to ease the entry of a knife (*see colour plate no. 13*):

'Then the executioner came, with a flint knife (or obsidian blade) in his hand, and with great skill made an incision between the ribs on the left side, below the nipple; then he plunged in his hand and like a ravenous tiger tore out the living heart.'[17]

Still beating, the heart was held up to the sky in offering to the sun god Huitzilopochtli. The blood, or 'divine water', flowed from the body as the heart, the *cuauhnochtli* or 'eagle cactus', was put in an eagle dish and then burned. The body was thrown down the side of the pyramid, in re-enactment of the mythical struggle between Huitzilopochtli and his elder sister god Coyolxauhqui, whom he was said to have killed. The body was decapitated and the head was impaled on a skull rack (*see colour plate no. 12*). The rest of the body was then severed into parts and the flesh divided up among the nobles for ritual cannibalistic meals; they feasted on the symbolic parts of Coyolxauhqui.

We later came across a stone carving of Coyolxauhqui in the museum of the Templo Mayor. It showed the moment when she had tumbled to her death at the hands of her brother god. Coyolxauhqui's head and limbs had been severed, and a huge skull was attached to her waist. Most archaeologists believe this skull represents the moment of her death and all that would remain of her in this everyday dimension of the 'middleworld'. I must confess, I wondered whether it might instead have been an image of a crystal skull which she carried around her waist (*see Figure 4, overleaf*).

Like being sacrificed at the temple, dying in battle was also an honourable death to the Aztecs. After all, many Aztec warriors died trying to capture victims for sacrifice, so a similar degree of dignity was also attached to the death of a warrior on the battlefield. One old Aztec song captures this sentiment succinctly:

There is nothing like death in war,
Nothing like the flowery death.
So precious to him who gives life.
Far off I see it.
My heart yearns for it![18]

Exactly how you died was very important. As José explained, 'It determined the way you were buried, whether in a foetal position in a clay jar, or spread out flat-eagled on the floor of someone else's tomb.'

But, far more important than that, the Aztecs believed that how you died determined your afterlife, rather than how you lived, as in our usual Christian belief. To die as a warrior or in sacrifice, the most noble of deaths, would assure you of a place in paradise. After death, the soul of the warrior would journey to the house of the sun where, for the next four years, it would accompany the sun on its daily journey across the sky, firing arrows at the sun to drive it on in its celestial journey. After they had completed this task, warriors' souls would be turned into butterflies and hummingbirds and they would live in peace in a garden paradise full of flowers. There they would spend their days feeding from the nectar, singing songs and telling stories about the splendours of the ever-shining sun.

Women who died during the 'battle' of childbirth would also make the same journey as the warriors to a sun-filled paradise. If you died by drowning or were struck by lightning then a similar fate awaited, except that it was in the watery paradise governed by the rain god Tlaloc.

However, if you experienced the natural death of an ordinary mortal, then only after death would your real battles begin. Your soul would have

Figure 4: Stone carving of the Aztec goddess of the moon Coyolxauhqui with a skull round her waist

to undergo a long and arduous journey through the underworld, known as 'Mictlan', before reaching its final resting-place. Mictlan was a place of darkness, fear and trembling, filled with a sickening, putrefying stench. This Aztec version of hell was lorded over by Mictlantecuhtli the Great Lord of Death and his wife Mictlancihuatl.

In the museum we could see many statues and other, mostly pottery, artefacts showing these the two great gods of death. Mictlantecuhtli seemed to take many forms, sometimes with a proper human body, but most often his body was made up of nothing but skeletal remains. The only thing that seemed to remain consistent about this character was that his face was always shown as a fleshless human skull, usually with goggle eyes. Likewise, his wife always had a skull for a face and in many of her statues she wore a skull around her neck and was crowned with a whole garland of smaller skulls (*see black-and-white plates 41 and 42*).

I asked José whether these gods might have had anything to do with the crystal skulls. He explained that before reaching such a conclusion we should bear in mind that the skull image was almost everywhere in Aztec art and was also associated with many other gods.

One of Quetzalcoatl's opponents, the black Tezcatlipoca, or 'Smoking Mirror', was also depicted with a skull for a head. Like Huitzilopochtli, he represented the forces of conflict and change and was believed to have had an ominous dark power. Tezcatlipoca was said to have a dark obsidian mirror in place of his left foot, a magical 'smoking mirror' which enabled him to witness the activities of gods and of men wherever they were. The fact that he was depicted with a skull for a head and was able to see into the other dimensions might equally imply a link between this god and crystal skulls. But, as we had already seen in the British Museum, Tezcatlipoca's skull was usually shown covered in red and black stripes.

By now we had arrived at a huge statue over 15 feet (4 metres) tall and weighing over 10 tons (10 tonnes). This had originally been discovered at the beginning of the nineteenth century, but the Mexican authorities apparently deemed it just too frightening to look upon and promptly reburied it. Though it has also been said that the real reason for the reburial was to avoid the embarrassment of having to admit that they could not explain how the 'primitive' and barbaric Aztecs could have made such a thing, or that it was a political move, designed to avoid stirring up Aztec descendants' memories of the original destruction of their culture under the Spanish.

The statue was of the original Aztec goddess known as Coatlicue, or 'she of the serpent skirt'. Coatlicue was the mother of all the Aztec gods, the goddess of the Earth, and therefore the goddess of life and death. The statue was truly a disturbing image. The head was simply not depicted – seemingly the goddess's face was just too horrific for mortal contemplation – and instead twin serpents indicated blood spurting from the place where it should have been. The goddess's skirt was made of snakes, who, by shedding their skins, indicate the ongoing process of death and renewal, and she had claws to show the destructive side of her nature. Around her neck she wore a garland of severed hands and human hearts, and at her waist another fleshless skull stared out at us. Like Mictlantecuhtli, this skull had goggle eyes, apparently a sign that the goddess watched over

Figure 5: Massive stone statue of the Aztec goddess of creation Coatlicue with severed hands, gouged out hearts and a skull round her neck and waist

both life and death, although again I wondered whether this image might really have been a crystal skull.

What seemed so fascinating about this great statue was that, although Coatlicue was the goddess of the Earth and therefore of life, she was represented with all the paraphernalia of death. José explained that throughout Mesoamerican culture a curious duality had always been seen to exist between the forces of life and death. The goddess of the Earth had the power to create new life, but also to take it away. For it is Mother Earth that gives us life, but she also takes it away again when we die.

This was all part of the ancients' view that both life and death are inseparable sides of the same coin, that you just cannot have one without the other. So, for the native peoples of Central America, there was no real need to be afraid of death, or to try to brush the whole subject under the carpet, as we tend to do today in the West. Death was simply a transition to another place and was usually something to look forward to.

This different attitude to life and death could even be seen in the Aztecs' version of hell. Although most people went to the underworld, it was not some perpetual inferno, as in the Christian view. Like the original journey through the womb at the start of life, the journey through the underworld was dark and restricting, but ultimately, when you reached your final resting-place, even the underworld was not really that bad at all.

As we were gazing at the great statue of Coatlicue, mulling over life and death, José said there was something else he wanted to show us. He led us into a little side-room off the main Aztec Hall of the museum and showed us what was inside one of the cabinets. There hung a small necklace of 12 tiny skulls carved of bone, with what looked like a space for a thirteenth. This necklace was clearly labelled as having been found in Guerrero state and dated to around AD 1000 (*see black-and-white plate no. 40*).

José led us over to another cabinet and asked us to take a close look inside. Peering through the glass, we were somewhat surprised to see two tiny crystal skulls. These skulls were only about 2" (5 cm) high and each had a vertical hole running through from top to bottom. They seemed quite roughly carved but each was beautifully transparent. One was labelled 'Aztec' and the other simply 'Mixtec' (a neighbouring civilization the Aztecs had defeated). No further details were given.

We were amazed. I exclaimed, 'So the crystal skulls really are Aztec after all!'

But José almost immediately explained that it wasn't quite that straight-forward. He said that nobody really knew quite what these crystal skulls represented or what they had been used for, or, for that matter, where they had really come from. He said the skulls had been labelled Aztec and Mixtec because this was all that the museum records actually said about them. The records apparently went back at least as far as the middle of the nineteenth century, but contained no precise details of exactly which archaeological dig the skulls had been found on. They might not even have come from a dig at all. None the less the museum authorities were pretty convinced that these little skulls were genuinely ancient.

José said there would be several problems, however, even in making such an assumption. Whilst it was known from the early Spanish accounts that the Aztecs and Mixtecs were experts at carving precious stones, and although these accounts did specifically mention crystal, it was a very rare material in Mexico in those days. José could not think of any examples of truly large ancient pieces of crystal ever having been found. Of course, the possibility that the large skulls really were ancient could not be ruled out, particularly given the importance of the skull image itself to the Aztecs, but the real problem with all Mesoamerican archaeology was that the early European settlers had destroyed so much of the evidence.

As soon as the Spanish had taken control of the Aztec empire they had begun the systematic destruction not only of most of its people, but also of the whole culture – all in the name of Christianity. No doubt the practice of human sacrifice fired the Spanish with the belief that they were totally justified in imposing Christianity on these 'barbaric' people. But the choice for the indigenous people was convert or be killed. Like the Nazis over 400 years later, the early Spanish settlers even used children to spy on their parents and report them to the new authorities if they were suspected of trying to carry on the old religious ways.[19]

Almost all previous books and records were seized and burned, the finest works of Mesoamerican culture reduced to ashes in a frenzy of bookburning and the destruction of 'idols'. The soldiers were joined in these activities by the early Franciscan and Dominican monks. One friar described his activities:

> 'We found great numbers of books ... but as they contained nothing but superstitions and falsehoods of the devil we burned them all, which the natives took most grievously, and which gave them great pain.'[20]

Few of these now priceless manuscripts escaped destruction as the unique testimony of a whole culture was almost completely wiped from the face of the Earth. Indeed, it is a source of some irony that the main source of information we have about the ancient Aztecs today are the writings of the zealous monks and friars who needed to record the 'pagan' and 'un-Christian' rituals, ceremonies and beliefs in order to identify quite what it was they were hoping to eradicate. Others secretly preserved some record, albeit in a much reduced and impoverished form, of the culture they originally intended to obliterate completely, as they gradually became aware of the tragic loss to humanity that was unfolding before them.

None the less, nearly all of the Aztec artwork and sculpture, and even the architecture, was destroyed. Cortés ordered Tenochtitlan to be totally levelled and then built a huge cathedral, much of which still stands today, on top of the main temple in the city square. All forms of native artistic expression were smashed and burned. The friars looked upon the art and culture of the Aztecs, their painted scrolls and fine sculptures, as 'works of the Devil, designed by the evil one to delude the Indians and to prevent them from accepting Christianity'.[21] Precious metals were also hunted out, to be melted down and sent back to Spain to swell the coffers of the Spanish empire. The Aztecs were apparently appalled at the greed of the Spanish for the 'yellow metal'. I was reminded of some of the visions Nick Nocerino had seen inside his crystal skull.

The early Spanish settler Father Burgoa described the destruction of one particular 'idol' that was held in a sanctuary in a place called Achiotlan:

'The material was of marvellous value ... engraved with the greatest skill...

'The stone was so transparent that it shone from its interior with the brightness of a candle flame. It was a very old jewel, and there is no tra- dition extant concerning the origin of its veneration and worship.'[22]

Father Burgoa also reported that this stone was seized by the first mission- ary, Father Benito, who 'had it ground up, although another Spaniard offered three thousand ducats for it, stirred the powder in water, poured it upon the earth and trod upon it'.[23]

It is certainly hard to imagine that crystal skulls could have survived such ravages, although, as Dr John Pohl of the University of California had already said to us, 'The crystal skulls would have been considered so precious by the Indian people that they would have done their best not to let the Spanish get hold of them.'

Some of the relatively few objects that did remain were the monumen- tal stone statues and carvings, such as Coatlicue, which were so large and made of such hard and enduring igneous rock that they could not be smashed, burned or otherwise destroyed. What the Spanish did with these was to bury them; many have only recently been rediscovered. But, apart from these massive stone monoliths, little remains of Aztec art.

But there was one other piece of evidence, said José, that we might be interested in and which implied that the crystal skulls might really be Aztec. We accompanied him to the nearby Museo Templo Mayor, the Museum of the Main Temple, situated in the centre of the Zócalo Square in the heart of Mexico City. The square was surrounded by colonial buildings on all sides and suggested former colonial might. I found something depressing about the grey drabness of the buildings and the relentless flow of cars that passed in front of them. On the approach to this museum, right beside the cathedral, which is now covered in scaffolding to support it as it gradually sinks lower into the soft subsoil, we could still see the original foundations of the temple, which had only recently been excavated.

As we entered the museum we were greeted by the sight of row upon row upon row of carved stone skulls, a version of the skull rack or *tzompantli*, but permanently preserved in stone, which had been found buried beneath the cathedral. We were also taken aback to see a rack on which real human skulls were displayed. We wondered what had created this fascination with death. Had the Aztecs lined up these skulls simply as trophies of war, as a statement of power, or were there other reasons? Certainly many believe the stone versions of the *tzompantli* did have something to do with the ancient calendar.

José took us on, past rows of real skull racks and various statues of ancient gods, many decorated with skulls, to another small glass cabinet. Inside were some of the few pieces of crystal definitely known to be at least as old as the Aztecs. They had been found in the 1970s during the excavation of the Templo Mayor site. As was common Aztec practice, the pyramids at this site had been built up in several layers, being added to at regular intervals as the empire expanded. Rebuilding is thought to have occurred every 52 years, in accordance with the cycles of the ancient calendar. A basalt funerary casket lay inside the innermost layer, beneath a chac-mool statue often thought to represent the great god Quetzalcoatl. This is where the crystal artefacts had been found – several crystal cylinders, thought to represent the feathered 'tail' of Quetzalcoatl, crystal lip-plugs, crystal ear-spools and, perhaps most interesting of all, a row of 13 small crystal beads, thought to have been worn as part of a necklace. Given their position in the innermost layer of the pyramid, these pieces of crystal dated back to at least AD 1390.

The practice had been to bury and burn important people inside such caskets, and the original inhabitant of this particular one had been incinerated completely. Only the small crystals had survived the flames of cremation. Archaeologists have been somewhat puzzled by these finds because crystal was such a rare material to the Aztecs and so was reserved only for those of the highest nobility. The most likely explanation is that these crystal artefacts were originally worn by one of the 'watchers of the skies', the astronomers, who were the highest strata of society. Crystal, it seems, was seen as the sacred material of the heavens and associated with the ability to see clearly, so it was reserved for the astronomer class.

Astronomers were very important for the Aztecs, who very much based their lives around the observation of the skies. Though materially they had little, 'only stones and soft metals', as José put it, they 'elevated themselves to the position of the skies' and acquired great skills in astronomy. On their original migration they had oriented themselves using the position of the polar star, as did later navigators across the Atlantic, and when they settled in Mexico they oriented all their sacred buildings to the four cardinal points of the compass. Furthermore, most of their deities were placed among the sky forces. Their daily lives and all their rituals and ceremonies were guided by the movement of the heavenly bodies.

Even the practice of human sacrifice was believed to have astrological significance. For, to the Aztecs, the sun was a mortal being. They believed it had to be fed, almost daily, if it was to continue to shine. This was why they always placed the heart of the sacrificial victim in an offering pot or receptacle, burned it and held it up to the sky. They believed that when they did this the spirit of an eagle would fly down from the sky and snatch up the spirit of the person's heart in its claws, carrying it back up from the Earth to the heavens to feed the sun. In this way, they believed the soul of the sacrificial victim joined the sun and kept it fed.

The Aztecs' views on human sacrifice were related to their beliefs about the calendar and the end of time. José had already shown us the famous Aztec Calendar Stone, a huge circular slab unearthed in 1791 from the remains of the Main Temple. At first this was thought to be simply an ornate sacrificial stone, but in fact it held the key to the Aztecs' beliefs about the history of the world and the end of time.

This stone showed at its centre a human face with its tongue hanging out, representing the sun god Tonatiuh demanding offerings of blood and human sacrifice. Radiating out from this were several sub-sections. Some of these sections represented the eight divisions of the day, the Aztecs' equivalent of our hours, while others represented their months, which were each 20 days long. There were 13 months in all in each of their sacred years, or *tonalamatl*. One of these sections was even represented by the image of a human skull.

The four outermost layers of this cyclical calendar represented the four previous 'Suns'. These Suns related to the different eras of the Earth. For, like all Mesoamerican peoples, the Aztecs believed that the world had

Figure 6: The Aztec Calendar Stone

been created and destroyed several times before now, four times in fact. The Aztec Calendar Stone, as well as many of their other stone monuments and surviving manuscripts, showed that the Aztecs believed they lived in the age of the 'Fifth Sun', the age we are still in today. Each of the four previous worlds, or Suns, lasted thousands of years, but each also ended in a great cataclysm. There is some disagreement over the precise order in which each of these worlds ended, but the Calendar Stone itself, probably the most reliable guide, gives the following order:

1 The first age, or First Sun, was the age of 'giants' who 'ate our nourishment', which many have taken to mean dinosaurs. Certainly scientists now believe that the Earth was once hit by a massive meteorite, which effectively wiped out the dinosaurs. Although this was thought to have been around 65 million years ago, this meteorite created what is now known as the Chicxulub crater in southern Mexico. The impact of this meteorite was so great that it is believed to have thrown up a huge cloud

of dust and debris that blocked out the sun's rays and led to great climate change which wiped out all life on Earth. Some believe this meteorite may even have penetrated right through the Earth's crust and disappeared into the centre of the Earth. According to the Aztecs, the first age ended when the giants were eaten by 'tigers' or 'ocelots', presumably meaning that they were replaced by mammals. Though some sources say that this world was destroyed by flood, and others that 'this Sun ended in cold and darkness, following an eclipse', all accounts agree that, as with the end of all the previous worlds, the sun stopped shining, in this case 'in the year known as 13'.[24]

2 The second world, or Second Sun, was the time when 'they became monkeys' and lived in the trees. Quite who 'they' were is unknown, but presumed to be mankind's ancestors. Almost all accounts agree here that this Second Sun was destroyed by a ferocious wind, which swept everything away, the debris blocking out the sun, and even 'this Sun itself was also swept away by the wind'.[25] One famous set of manuscripts, the *Vaticano-Latin Codex* ('codex' meaning a book of hieroglyphs and pictographs), adds, however, that, 'One man and one woman standing on a rock were saved from this destruction.'

3 The third world, or Third Sun, began on the day One Flint of the ancient calendar and was said to have been ruled over by the god of fire. Many have taken this to be the era during which mankind learned how to start and use fire. Rather ironically, though, nearly all sources agree that this world was destroyed by a 'rain of fire'. According to Léon-Portilla, 'It rained fire upon them' and 'This Sun was consumed by fire',[26] perhaps meaning that the sun's rays were blocked from the Earth by smoke and flames, perhaps as a result of volcanic – or mankind's – activity.

4 The Fourth Sun was often known as the Tzontlilac or the time of the 'black hair'. Though the *Vaticano-Latin Codex* says that at the end of this world men died of starvation after a rain of blood and fire from the skies, nearly all other accounts agree with the Calendar Stone that this was the world that was destroyed by water, in a great flood. Near permanent rain resulted in a deluge and 'men were turned into fish'.

Léon-Portilla gave a detailed account of what he heard about the end of this world: 'Thus they perished, they were swallowed by the waters and they became fish ... the water lasted 52 years and with this ended their years ... the heavens collapsed upon them and ... they perished' and 'all the mountains perished',[27] too, swallowed up by the waters that flooded the Earth. The *Vaticano-Latin Codex* again adds, however, that one couple survived the flood, because 'they were protected by a tree', in an account with remarkable similarities to the Biblical story of Noah's Ark.

5 The Fifth Sun began in the year Thirteen Acatl and continues to this day. But the Aztecs also believed that this Sun was to be the final one.

According to Léon-Portilla's account, 'This Fifth Sun, its sign 4-Movement, is called the Sun of Movement because it moves and follows its path.'[28] But in the Aztec language, Nahuatl, the word *ollin* means not only 'movement' but also 'earthquake' and so Léon-Portilla's account continues, '... as the elders continue to say, under this Sun there will be earthquakes and hunger, and then our end shall come.'[29] As the *Vaticano-Latin Codex* puts it, 'There will be a movement of the Earth and from this we shall all perish.'[30] Other accounts, however, suggest that the cataclysm which will end the current and final world will be a combination of all the destructive forces of nature, the earth, the air and the water, in a final conflagration of immense heat and drought and of 'fire from the skies' followed by darkness and cold, with hurricane winds and torrential rain, and featuring a combination of earthquakes, volcanic activity and devastating floods. Again I was reminded of the visions Nick Nocerino had seen inside his skull, also of the information Carole Wilson had channelled from the Mitchell-Hedges skull.

According to Léon-Portilla, 'The Aztec myth of the Five Suns explains man's destiny and his unavoidable end.'[31] This reflects the Aztecs' belief that our world is perishable and that time consists of a chain of cycles doomed to lead to annihilation.

But the Aztecs did not appear to know exactly when the current Sun was due to end. They believed that it was already very old and was likely to end soon. But they also thought that their own actions could have an effect on how long it would last. They believed that they had a duty to try to prevent the sun from dying, and that this could be done through human beings making personal sacrifices in order to keep the sun shining and the Earth in good health. In their case this involved feeding the sun on a diet of human hearts and blood.

This is why, for the Aztecs, ritual human sacrifice was absolutely essential. They believed that at the beginning of this Fifth Sun the only way to persuade the sun to shine again had been to give it the most precious gift, the gift of life itself. And so they continued offering their own lives. It was the only way of keeping the sun alive and avoiding the great cataclysm that otherwise threatened to engulf the entire Earth.

José believed that the sacrificial practices of the Aztecs had been motivated by a corruption of the idea of sacrificing oneself for the benefit of others, putting aside the concerns of the ego in order to serve the good of all people and the divine. So, he suggested, the root of Aztec sacrificial practice was actually a central tenet of many of the world's religions, the idea of offering yourself up to God. Evangelical Christians today speak of 'giving your heart to Jesus' or 'giving your heart to God'. The Aztecs had taken this quite literally, offering their still beating hearts up to the god of the sun.

I could see that the Aztecs' bloody rituals now seemed to make some kind of warped but still logical sense. But it was horrendous to think that they took this idea of personal sacrifice to such literal extremes.

But I was still curious to understand why the image of a skull appeared on the mysterious Aztec Calendar Stone and whether there was any evidence that crystal skulls might somehow have been involved in the practice of human sacrifice and this rather strange set of beliefs about the end of the world. José explained that to properly understand both the image of the skull and the calendar we should really look further into the culture of the Aztecs' predecessors, the Toltecs, the Teotihuacános and the Maya. The Aztecs were thought to have inherited much of their calendar, practices, beliefs and skull imagery from these civilizations. The calendar especially had been traced back to the ancient Mayans, who kept the most detailed records of time. But, as we had already heard, their civilization mysteriously collapsed centuries before the Aztecs arose and the ruins of their cities lay hundreds of miles further south, so we could not readily visit them from Mexico City. We could, however, visit the ruins of Tula, the Toltecs' great city, and of Teotihuacán, where the Aztecs believed the current Sun had been born.

The following day we drove out to Tula. This ruined city, dated to over 1,000 years old, was surrounded by low-lying mountains. Little of the original architecture remained. The largest still-standing monument was a low pyramid crowned with pillars that had been intricately carved to represent standing men or gods. This was known as 'the Temple of the Morning Star' or 'the Temple of the Atlantes'. Each of its pillars was carefully aligned with the heavenly bodies and this is where the Toltecs are thought to have performed a sacred ceremony every 52 years.

Every 52 years was when the ancient calendar completed a full cycle of sacred and solar years. This was a cycle of four lots of 13 years after which time the 13 months of the 260-day sacred calendar returned to their original starting position relative to the 365-days of the solar year. The end of each 52-year period was therefore a very precarious time for the Toltecs, and their Aztec descendants, as it represented one of the occasions when the current Sun was most likely to end. Accordingly, a great number of human sacrifices took place at that time. Also, every 52 years at sunset, the Aztec priests were said to have climbed to the temple on top of the 'Hill of the Star', thought perhaps to have been this same pyramid at Tula. There they would await either the end of the world or what was known as 'the start of the new fires'. They would wait in trepidation until the Pleiades constellation appeared in the sky. This was a sign that the sun would continue to shine, and so they would celebrate the birth of a new cycle of time by lighting 'the new fires'. These fires would then be passed on like an Olympic flame right across the whole empire and the original flame would be kept burning for the following 52 years.

Behind the Temple of the Atlantes was a wall, known as the *coatepantli*, or serpent wall, which had apparently once surrounded the whole pyramid. This wall was decorated with stone carvings of what looked like a series of snakes or serpents, but each with a human skull for a head (*see colour plate no. 23*). Each skull was shown with its jaws wide open, seemingly biting or swallowing the tail of the serpent in front.

The building still baffled archaeologists. It was clearly devoted to 'the Atlantes', but who they were remained a mystery, as did the reason why these wall carvings combined images of Quetzalcoatl, the original god of Mesoamerica, with the skull. Traditionally Quetzalcoatl was shown as a flying snake or rainbow-coloured feathered serpent, but this building clearly showed that there was some connection between this god, a mysterious group known as 'the Atlantes' and the image of the human skull. But what?

With these unanswered questions still playing in my mind, we set off for the ruins of the great city of Teotihuacán. This city was known to the Aztecs as 'the place where the sun had been born', or 'the place of 'the men who had the road of the gods' or 'the place where the heavens meet the Earth'. This site, only an hour away from Mexico City, was the place Eugène Boban had visited during the time he was selling crystal skulls.

For some reason I had the feeling it might contain some important clue in our search for the origin of the skulls.

Aztec legend had it that in a time of great darkness, before the current Sun, two men, Tecuciztecatl and Nanahatzin, had enabled the current Sun to shine by committing the original and ultimate sacrifice in this very city, throwing themselves off the sides of the great pyramids into the 'sacred flame'. As a result they flew up into the heavens where they became gods themselves: the sun and the moon.

The remnants of this huge city turned out to be a most impressive archaeological site. Again surrounded by low mountains, but far larger than Tula, Teotihuacán had been built on a very grand scale. The ruins of the city covered an area of around eight square miles and at their centre lay the most massive group of pyramids I had ever seen. Teotihuacán actually features the largest group of pyramids in the whole of the Americas, with three great pyramids arranged in a row, and the similarities with the Egyptian pyramids at Giza struck me almost immediately.

At its peak the city had housed around 200,000 inhabitants and the extent of its cultural and trading influence had been enormous. Traces of its artistic and cultural style could be found even in Mayan cities such as Tikal, over 600 miles away. Like the Maya, nobody knew for sure quite who the Teotihuacános really were, where they came from or what happened to them. It was also uncertain what language they spoke and how old their great city really was. Construction of the pyramids is generally thought to have started at around the time of Christ, but many have claimed they are much older. Certainly the whole city was mysteriously abandoned over 1,000 years ago, presumably some time between AD 500 and 750.

Teotihuacán had been revered by the Aztecs, who had already found it in ruins and had named the great pyramids 'the Pyramid of the Sun', 'the Pyramid of the Moon' and 'the Pyramid of Quetzalcoatl'. They had also been responsible for naming the great central 'Avenue of the Dead'.

We climbed up nearly 150 feet (45 metres) to the top of the Pyramid of the Moon, as this was said to afford the best view of the whole city. We stood on the spot where a temple had once been. The view was truly spectacular. The orderly lines of the city lay before us. To the south lay the Avenue of the Dead, with stone embankments and small pyramids all along its perfectly straight sides. Over 50 yards (45 metres) wide and with a surviving section over three miles (four kilometres) long, it stretched on ahead of us, disappearing into the distant haze (*see colour plate no. 6*). The

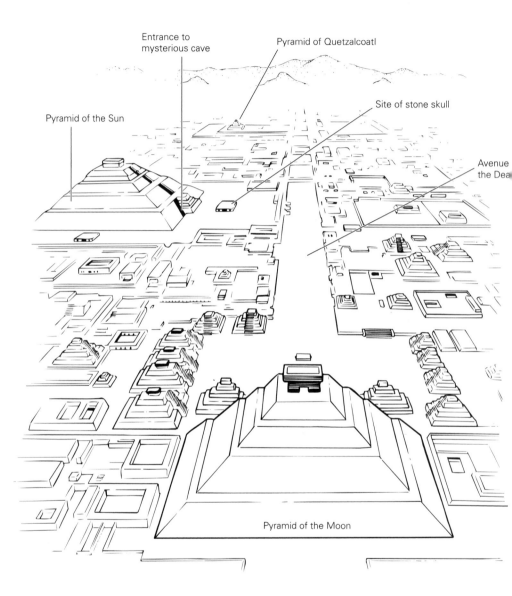

Figure 7: Reconstruction of the ancient city of Teotihuacán looking down the Avenue of the Dead

purpose of this great avenue remains a mystery. Some have even suggested that it might have been some kind of ancient runway for extra-terrestrial craft, but another, perhaps more plausible, explanation is that it had once been filled with water and functioned as some form of ancient seismograph designed to measure earthquake activity. Careful measurement of 'standing waves' appearing across still water can indicate the strength and location of earthquakes happening elsewhere around the globe and so the avenue might at one time have been used to predict earthquakes in the immediate area.[32]

The purpose of the pyramids themselves was also unknown, although they almost undoubtedly had religious and astronomical significance. To the east of the great Avenue of the Dead we could see the great towering bulk of the Pyramid of the Sun, over 700 feet (215 metres) wide at its base and over 200 feet (60 metres) high, and once also crowned with a temple. Further along the Avenue of the Dead we could also see the Pyramid of Quetzalcoatl. Whilst this was now less than 100 feet (30 metres) tall, what remains is thought to have been an early unfinished version. For this smaller pyramid is still surrounded on all sides by foundations that extend to an even greater size than the neighbouring great Pyramid of the Sun.

One of the reasons why these pyramids have always puzzled archaeologists is because their size, layout and particularly their positions relative to each other almost exactly match those of the three pyramids at Giza. The base of the Pyramid of the Sun matches to within inches that of one of these pyramids.[33] Furthermore, the Pyramid of Quetzalcoatl and the Pyramid of the Sun are both accurately aligned with each other so that if you were to run a line between their summits it would run precisely parallel to the Avenue of the Dead, whilst the smaller Pyramid of the Moon is slightly offset to the left, at the very head of this great avenue. This layout follows almost exactly the same pattern as the Giza pyramids.

Although the Teotihuacán pyramids are somewhat lower than their Egyptian equivalents, when seen from the air the only difference between these two sets of pyramids is that the Egyptian ones are at 45° to the central axis whilst in Teotihuacán they run at right angles to it. Also at Teotihuacán the Avenue of the Dead runs exactly parallel to this central axis, whilst in Egypt there is no sign of any such great avenue. None the less, if you were to lay a plan view of the pyramids of Egypt on top of a plan view of the pyramids of Teotihuacán, each drawn to the same scale, the area of each pyramid and the summit of each pyramid would almost exactly coincide. The Pyramid of Cheops would match the Pyramid of Quetzalcoatl, the Pyramid of Khafre would match the Pyramid of the Sun, and the Pyramid of Menkaure would match the Pyramid of the Moon (*see Figure 8*).

Quite what the significance of this, presumably sacred, layout is, nobody is totally sure. Recent studies of the Giza pyramids in Egypt have pointed out that this layout exactly matches the relative size and position of the three stars that make up Orion's Belt and have suggested that the ancient Egyptians may have been trying to somehow reproduce the heavens on Earth. It is quite likely therefore that the layout of the three pyramids of Teotihuacán might also have some connection with the stars and possibly the constellation of Orion, which did have its own small part to play in the complex workings of the ancient Mesoamerican calendar.

In another similarity with Egypt, it has recently been discovered that the Pyramid of the Sun, just like the Great Pyramid of Cheops, actually contains a secret mathematical code built into its dimensions. The mathematical relationship between the height of the pyramid and the length of the perimeter at its base actually contains the famous mathematical constant *pi*. (In Teotihuacán the mathematical relationship equals two times pi; in Egypt it is four times pi.) This suggests that the ancient Teotihuacános knew how to calculate the circumference of a circle, or a sphere such as the Earth, by multiplying its radius or diameter by a factor of *pi*. This implies that, at least 1,000 years before the Europeans, the Teotihuacános were not only aware that the Earth was round but could accurately measure its dimensions for use in precise scientific calculations.[34]

Indeed, it is now widely accepted that the whole layout of Teotihuacán had some deep astrological significance, as the whole city was built according to a set of incredibly accurate alignments that intimately tied the city to the movements of the planets and the stars.

The Pyramid of the Sun, for example, had probably been given this name by the Aztecs precisely because it was positioned in such a way that it functioned almost like a huge solar and astronomical clock. The eastern face of the pyramid is carefully aligned so that it receives the rays of the sun full on only at the spring and autumn equinoxes, 20 March and 22 September.[35] As Graham Hancock recently pointed out in his book *Fingerprints of the Gods*, on these days, the passing of the sun overhead also results in the progressive obliteration of a perfectly straight shadow that runs along the lowest slope of the western façade, so that this shadow disappears only and precisely at noon. This whole process, from complete

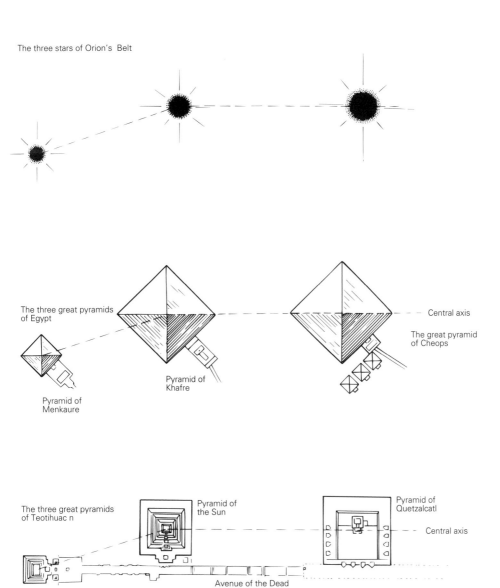

The three stars of Orion's Belt

The three great pyramids of Egypt

Central axis

The great pyramid of Cheops

Pyramid of Khafre

Pyramid of Menkaure

The three great pyramids of Teotihuacn

Pyramid of the Sun

Pyramid of Quetzalcatl

Central axis

Pyramid of the Moon

Avenue of the Dead

Figure 8

shadow to complete illumination, always takes exactly 66.6 seconds.[36] It has taken precisely this length of time every year, presumably ever since the pyramid was built, and it will continue to do so for as long as the pyramid continues to stand. In this way the ancients could check the arrival of midday at the equinoxes down to the second.

But these are not the only astronomical alignments. In every direction the city was laid out in harmony with the universe as the Teotihuacános understood it, or even, as one recent study has suggested, as a precise scale model of our solar system.[37] If the Pyramid of Quetzalcoatl were taken as representing the position of the sun, then many of the other structures spread out along the Avenue of the Dead and beyond would actually seem to indicate the precise distance of the orbits of each of the other planets from the sun. The Pyramid of the Sun, for example is the correct distance away for the position of Saturn and the Pyramid of the Moon the right distance for Uranus. This suggests that the Teotihuacános not only knew about many of the planets we did not discover until very recently, but were also able to accurately calculate their distance from the sun.

This particular study was still controversial, but the astronomical alignment that interested us the most was now very widely accepted and also involved the image of a skull. This was a huge carved stone statue of a skull that had a strangely two-dimensional appearance. It was grim and imposing, with what looked like a slot for a nose and a wide straight mouth with its red-painted tongue hanging out. The whole skull was surrounded by a circle of what looked like a deeply carved version of the rays of the sun, again all painted red (*see colour plate no. 17*). It had often been assumed that this was simply a representation of the sun god, but, as José had already pointed out, the sun god was usually represented with a full human face.

The interesting thing was where this huge image had originally been found. It had been discovered at the bottom of the western face of the Pyramid of the Sun, in the centre, along the edge of the Avenue of the Dead, pointing to a particular spot on the western horizon. In fact the whole city had been arranged along two axes: the Avenue of the Dead, and the east–west axis marked out by the direction in which the skull and the pyramid were facing.[38]

It had long been assumed that this stone skull represented only the setting of the sun and that its original location pointed towards a spot on the horizon where, on the day that the sun passed directly overhead, the sun also duly set. Given the location of Teotihuacán, the sun usually passes to the south, but in a few of the summer months it passes to the north. The days when the sun passes directly overhead are 19 May and 25 September. Indeed, it had long been believed that the Pyramid of the Sun was specifically oriented so that, as well as marking the equinoxes, it also marked these days when the sun passed directly overhead. It had long been held that on these two days the western face of the pyramid, and therefore the huge stone skull, pointed at precisely the position of the setting sun.[39]

But this theory has recently been tested in various studies by archaeo-astronomers such as Anthony Aveni of Colgate University.[40] His team observed that on the days when the sun passes directly overhead, the Pleiades make their first annual predawn appearance. They also discovered that on these two key days of the year the western face of the pyramid, and therefore this massive stone skull, was actually aligned not with the setting sun but with the precise spot where the Pleiades disappear beneath the horizon. To the ancient Teotihuacános, there was clearly some connection between the image of the skull and the Pleiades constellation.

Anthony Aveni and his team discovered that the sun does also set at this point on the horizon, but only on the night of the 12/13 August.[41] Curiously enough, this is precisely the anniversary of the start of the last Great Cycle of the ancient Mesoamerican calendar, which is understood to have started on 13 August 3114 BC. To the ancients this was 'the day the sun had been born', so perhaps this great city dated back to that time?

Another study has suggested that the great Avenue of the Dead might have been 'built to face the setting of the Pleiades at the time [Teotihuacán] was constructed'.[42] So, as Ceri and I gazed across the site, it suddenly struck me that perhaps the whole layout of Teotihuacán was like a huge clock-face, centred around the Pyramid of the Sun. The Avenue of the Dead, like one hand of a clock, pointed at where the Pleiades would have set on the southern horizon on the 12 August 3114 BC, whilst the skull beneath the Pyramid of the Sun, like the other hand of the clock, pointed at the place on the western horizon where the Pleiades set today. It is almost as though the hand of the clock pointing to the Pleiades has gradually been ticking around towards the point on the horizon the skull had always been facing. Again, another connection between the image of the skull and the star cluster of the Pleiades had been found (*see Figure 9, overleaf*).

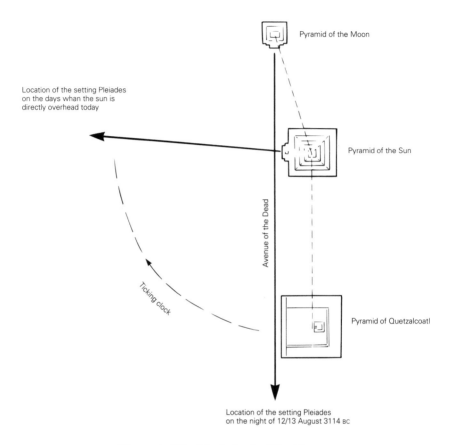

Pyramid of the Moon

Location of the setting Pleiades
on the days whan the sun is
directly overhead today

Pyramid of the Sun

Avenue of the Dead

Ticking clock

Pyramid of Quetzalcoatl

Location of the setting Pleiades
on the night of 12/13 August 3114 BC

Figure 9: The 'clock-face' of Teotihuacán

I also found myself wondering whether, if the three pyramids of Teotihuacán were taken to represent the three stars of Orion's belt, the stone
skull beneath the Pyramid of the Sun had perhaps pointed to a place in
the night sky where the Pleiades had at one time been located relative to
the three stars of Orion.

But other discoveries had also been made at the spot where this huge
stone skull had been found. As we made our way to the foot of the Pyramid of the Sun more surprises were in store. We passed by the Pyramid of
Quetzalcoatl beneath which some skeletons had recently been found.
These were thought to have been sacrificial victims and each was adorned
with a complete necklace of whole human jaws. Along the edge of the
Avenue of the Dead and around the base of the Pyramid of the Sun we
could see that archaeologists had recently begun to uncover a whole
subterranean layer of the city that had been carefully buried. A whole

labyrinth of subterranean passageways and a complete network of caves apparently surrounded the Pyramid of the Sun. But the most surprising discovery had been made in 1971.

Immediately behind the spot where the stone skull had once stood archaeologists had uncovered, quite by accident, a doorway leading right under the Pyramid of the Sun. Though we were forbidden from entering this passageway, we later learned that this 'entrance may have been the initial siting point for the east–west alignment that was so crucial in the city plan'.[43] A tunnel only seven feet (two metres) high but over 300 feet (90 metres) long leads from this entrance at the base of the western pyramid stairway right into a mysterious natural cave hidden almost directly beneath the centre of the pyramid. As we read later in *National Geographic*, 'The cave, therefore, may have been the holiest of holies – the very place where Teotihuacános believed the world was born.'[44]

This mysterious natural cave was 'of spacious dimensions, which had been artificially enlarged into a shape very similar to that of a four-leafed clover'.[45] Each of the four large chambers of the cave was about 60 feet (18 metres) in circumference. As Mesoamerican expert Dr Karl Taube of the University of California at Riverside commented, 'The Teotihuacános must have used the cave for something, because its walls were reshaped and in some places reroofed.'[46] There was also a complex system of interlocking segments of carved rock pipes, possibly a drainage system, although there was and still is certainly no sign of any water there. Only a few small, mostly broken artefacts of engraved slate and obsidian remained, as though perhaps the cave had at some time been robbed or otherwise cleared.

I wondered whether the mysterious piped technology might have had something to do with another strange discovery found at Teotihuacán. One of the uppermost layers of the Pyramid of the Sun had originally been made from the unusual material of mica. Although this had been robbed at the beginning of the twentieth century, two huge pieces of mica, each 90 feet (27 metres) square, had been found still intact beneath the normal stone floor of 'the Mica Temple' situated nearby. The puzzling thing about this discovery was that these pieces of mica, put in place well over 1,000 years ago, were of a type known naturally to exist at the nearest over 2,000 miles away. The ancient Teotihuacános, it seemed, had brought this material all the way from Brazil.[47] Archaeologists had been intrigued why they should do such a thing when the material was kept well hidden out of sight and so could hardly be considered decorative.

Today, mica is primarily used in the electronics industry, where it has a multitude of technological applications, in capacitors or as a thermal and electronic insulator. I was immediately reminded of the incredible electronic properties of the quartz crystal from which the skulls were made.

So what had the mysterious cave under the pyramid really been used for? The well known Mexican archaeologist Eduardo Matos Moctezuma commented, 'Its location and privacy suggest that it may have been one of the most sacred spots in the city, although we can't yet say what happened here,'[48] while according to *National Geographic*, the cave may have been some kind of 'oracle or meeting place for secret cults'.[49] Clearly nobody really knew for sure, but what was certain was that the entrance to this secret chamber was guarded by the image of a skull, pointing towards the Pleiades.

As we turned back to look at the site once more before leaving, I found myself casting my mind back to what José had told us in the museum. When Moctezuma began to feel a sense of foreboding about the future of the Aztec empire, he had consulted the priests, the seers who knew everything that was 'locked in the mountains'. Given the importance of Teotihuacán to the Aztecs, could those have been the man-made mountains of the pyramids? Was this the very site where the Aztec psychics had worked? Was this the secret location where the crystal skulls had once been stored?

13. THE SKULL AND THE CROSS

While we were still in Mexico City, José had told us that he had heard of the existence of another crystal skull nearby. He was not sure whether it was genuinely ancient but he would look into it for us. It sounded very strange. It was not exactly a crystal skull, but apparently made of obsidian. Obsidian is a jet black volcanic rock which was used by the Aztecs to make their sacrificial blades. In their mythology this black material was associated with the dark forces of gods such as Tezcatlipoca, who wore a dark obsidian mirror in place of his foot.

This caught our imagination. Could it be that the skull, crystal or obsidian, was a force of darkness? Our minds were still filled with the gory images left by the Aztec culture, the goddesses with necklaces of severed hearts and hands, the human skulls collected and placed on public display on skull racks, the row upon row of carved stone skulls. Was it possible that the Aztecs had used the skull as an image to terrify and subjugate their people?

This black skull was rumoured to be somewhere in Cuernavaca, an industrial town some 50 miles (80 km) south of Mexico City. We were intrigued, for we had recently heard of this place from the owner of the crystal gallery in Washington. He said he knew of a modern crystal skull which had been on sale at an international mineral fair in Tucson, Arizona, with a price-tag of $100,000 dollars! This modern skull had apparently been made in a crystal carving workshop in Cuernavaca. So modern skulls appeared to be being made not only in Germany but also here in Mexico. The gallery owner had given us the telephone number for the workshop.

Its owner, a man called Ea Orgo, was initially reluctant to reveal precisely where he worked. So he arranged instead to meet us 'under the statue of Zapata', situated on a busy traffic island on the edge of town. A complete stranger arrived and asked us to follow his motorbike. Weaving through the narrow streets we eventually arrived at the crystal workshop, which turned out to be nothing more than a wooden shed.

Ea, a slim silver-haired man, explained to us that he had long been interested in talismans and sacred objects imbued with power and meaning. He had been entranced by the Mitchell-Hedges skull ever since he had first seen it when it was being examined by Frank Dorland. Ea had shown a photograph of the skull to his head carver, Crisoforo, who said that he could never make such an object. But finally he agreed to give it a try. Using a real human skull as a model, Cris and Ea worked round the clock to get the skull made. It took an incredible amount of work, even with modern machine-powered diamond-tipped tools, and they had broken many of the skulls they had started. In the end the only skull that didn't break took them over a year to complete, with the machines running 18 hours a day, seven days a week, with the two carvers working in shifts.

This skull, which had been on sale at the mineral fair, was very much inferior to the original Mitchell-Hedges skull. Not only was it smaller, but it actually looked machine-made. The quality of the crystal, which they had imported from Brazil, was just not the same. Even Ea felt that it lacked the beauty and grace of the Mitchell-Hedges skull. Also, it had proved impossible to successfully carve the lower jaw from the same chunk of raw crystal. The jaw from the same piece of quartz as the cranium had shattered during carving and it had taken five attempts with separate pieces of crystal before the carvers were able to complete a jaw-bone, which then duly fractured for no apparent reason as soon as the skull was put on display at its first public exhibition.

It seemed the skull lacked something, some almost indefinable quality. None the less, Ea claimed even this modern copy still had some special powers. He pointed out that things do not have to be ancient to have sacred significance, although he admitted that his modern skull was nothing like as potent as the ancient original.

Ea, however, could tell us nothing more about the black obsidian skull, and as we made our way back to Mexico City, we found ourselves wondering how that had been made. Who had carved the obsidian and for what purpose? Was there a link with the Aztecs' sacrificial blade? Could crystal skulls perhaps be associated with 'the dark side'? After all, Dr Jane Walsh had been told her skull was cursed and Nick Nocerino had told us that the Gestapo had been after crystal skulls during the Second World War. The Nazis had taken the swastika, originally a Hindu symbol of the sun, and transformed it into a symbol of darkness. Had the image of the skull been similarly abused by the Aztecs? Had they used it to warn of the fate that awaited those who resisted their growing empire?

All this was playing on our minds as we ended up sitting in the lobby of our hotel back in Mexico City, waiting to hear more from José, with the constant drone of soap operas on television and lonely business travellers checking in.

The following morning José called. Despite the rumours, he had been unable to find any further information about the black skull. Whether this was because it did not exist or because it belonged to a secret cult or organization, we would probably never know, he said. He explained that the dominance of the Christian Church in Central America meant that those who still practised the ancient ways did so in secret so as not to be labelled witches and demons. However, he reassured us:

'It is too simple to say that the Aztecs created crystal skulls to terrify people and warn them about sacrifice. It is possible that a skull carved of obsidian could represent the forces of darkness, but for Mexican people there is always duality. Wherever there is darkness, lightness too can be found. You are seeing the Aztec culture only as barbaric, using the skull to terrify people, but we don't know that this was really the case. The descendants of the Aztecs, modern Mexican people, use the image of the skull in quite a different way than the tzompantli might suggest.

'In the minds of the native peoples of Central America, there was always a great duality about life and death. They were concepts that co-existed. Death was part of life.'

This completely different attitude towards death still lives on in modern Mexico. 'The Day of the Dead' celebrations are a perfect example of this. Every year on the night of 1 and 2 November the people of Mexico hold a night of festivities in honour of those who have died before them. Most people in the city dress up as skeletons or wear skull masks and parade through the streets for a night of debauched, drunken revelry. But, mostly in the countryside, those who still observe some of the old religious ways set up an altar, sometimes with real human skulls, and on

them they put all the flowers and fruits of the region. The women decorate the altars and the men are allowed to eat any meal they particularly
like, drink their favourite drink and smoke the most expensive cigarettes.
José explained:

*'For them this is a profound religious approach to death. It's about treat-
ing yourself the way you would like to be treated after you've gone.*

*'They also believe they can communicate with the spirits of the ances-
tors and relatives, who are believed to return into this physical world,
right into the house, on this particular day and talk with the living.
Some people go to the graveyard and sit on the graves of their ancestors,
so that they can communicate with them more easily.*

*'But there is nothing sinister or frightening about this. The Day of
the Dead is a celebration for all the family. Even the kids really love it,
not only because they can eat the best food, but also because it is an
opportunity to eat candy skulls. These are brightly coloured skulls made
of crystalline sugar. The large, often life-size ones carry the names of
favourite relatives who have already gone through death and the smaller skulls carry the names of the children themselves to remind them that
the same destiny awaits them. As the children eat the skulls and the
sugar dissolves in their mouths this helps the children become familiar
with death, to come to terms with it and realize that they will one day
themselves fade and disappear. It teaches them not to be afraid of death,
to see that it is really just a step into another dimension, where you can
meet once again with your ancestors, and even live a better life than the
one you have today.*

*'These attitudes amongst descendants of the Aztecs show that the skull
was not necessarily an image used to terrify and subjugate people. It was
more of an image to symbolize those who had gone before, it was the
image of the ancestors.'*

I was about to ask José whether the Day of the Dead ceremonies might
have their origins in the ancient use of crystal skulls, when he continued,
'Anyway, I have found you another skull. And this one is not made from
obsidian, it is a proper crystal skull.'

'Where is it?' I wanted to know.

'It's right here in Mexico City,' he replied. 'Its owners believe that it
dates back to before Columbus arrived in the Americas.'

Chris and I tried to find out more. After a number of calls, I found that the crystal skull had belonged to a wealthy Mexican family called the Redos. It had now been given to Norma Redo, their youngest daughter, whom I now arranged to meet. I arrived at a smart town-house in Mexico City's most exclusive area and was greeted by one of Norma's assistants. Norma ran her interior design business from her home. At the end of the hall, which was decorated with oil paintings and fresh cut flowers, was the dining-room. Here, in this airy room, bright with natural light, was where she kept her crystal skull, on the side-board, almost hidden by a huge bowl of ripe fruit.

The crystal skull was smaller than life-size, with a monkeyish face. It sat on a base of gold, dwarfed by the huge, elaborately carved golden and crystal reliquary cross that emerged triumphantly from the top of its head *(see colour plate no. 14)*. This gave the skull the most bizarre appearance. The arrangement looked all out of proportion, unbalanced. The overall effect was of a baroque extravaganza, which seemed almost out of place in Norma's elegant home.

Norma herself now entered the room. She was attractive, elegantly dressed, with shoulder-length hair and a proud expression on her face. 'So you have seen my skull?' she said. 'It's very beautiful to me.' She went over to the skull. 'It has been in the Redo family since the 1840s. I don't know if it was purchased or given to a great-grandfather of mine during the time when the government took over the properties of the Church.'

I explained to Norma that Dr Jane Walsh had a theory that most of the crystal skulls in Mexico were not actually Mexican in origin but had been made in Europe and exported to Mexico where they were then sold to wealthy tourists and unsuspecting antique dealers. The main culprit may well have been Eugène Boban. But it appeared that the reliquary cross crystal skull had come into the Redo family some 30 years before Boban had started operating in Mexico. This increased the probability that it could be genuine.

'I don't know how old the skull is, but I believe it is ancient,' said Norma. 'I do know how old the cross is.'

She picked up the skull and unscrewed the cross. I looked at it. It had a small blue jewel at its centre. Norma showed me that it had a date carved on it, which showed when it had been made: 1571. This put the cross as constructed soon after the Spanish arrived in Mexico, but gave no clues as to when the skull had been made.

I told Norma about the tests that were being planned, explaining that they would be able to prove whether her skull was genuinely ancient, whether it was made by an ancient civilization of Mexico, or was a 'fake', having been made using either the colonial technology of the Spanish or imported from Germany.

'Maybe the skull was made after Columbus, but I believe it is much older,' Norma said. 'The skull was an important symbol to the Aztecs and also to the ancient Maya.'

I asked Norma what she thought about the idea that her skull might have symbolized the forces of darkness of the Aztec empire. She thought that this was unlikely:

> 'The work that has gone into making the skull was not so that it would frighten people. There were plenty of real skulls that could be used to do that. This skull is a work of art, I believe that its purpose was sacred.
>
> 'I think a lot of the Aztec culture has been misunderstood by the Europeans. It was bad in many ways, but then you have to see what came after it, the people suffered so much from colonization.
>
> 'When the Spanish arrived, I believe that they saw that this skull was very precious to the Mexican people. When the Christians saw this skull, they saw an opportunity to show the supremacy of the new religion. They wanted to say that what the people had before, their beliefs would be transformed with the knowledge of Christ – and that's why the cross was added to transform the skull. The Christian Church did not destroy the crystal skull but put the cross in it to show the supremacy of the new religion.'

I looked once more at the skull and the cross, rising up as the triumphant gesture of the Christians who had arrived and 'conquered' the religion of the indigenous people. It reminded me of the cathedral in the main square of Mexico City that had been built on top of the original Aztec temple.

My attention was drawn towards the gold base on which the skull stood. It was like an island of gold with tiny figures carved into it. Norma pointed out John the Baptist and St Christopher and a miniature crucifixion scene at the front of the piece:

> 'There are even tiny gold skulls around these little crosses, presumably showing it is meant to represent Golgotha, where the crucifixion of Christ took place. That has to be another reason why the early Spanish

conquerors did not destroy the skull. In the Bible there is a reference to skulls at the scene of Christ's death. It was a motif the Spanish were familiar with.'

Norma said that the image of the skull was a powerful symbol also to the Catholic nations of Europe. Spanish orders of monks, such as the Franciscans and Dominicans, were fascinated by it. She explained that paintings of St Francis often show him holding a skull. She went on to say that many beautiful works of art from Mexico had ended up overseas:

'I am very fortunate that the early Spanish settlers did not take this skull back to Europe immediately after the conquest as a reliquary object, where it would have become a religious object to the Christian kingdoms in Europe. This happened to a lot of objects.'

We had certainly heard a rumour that a crystal skull is still kept in secret by the Vatican in Rome. Norma continued:

'I remember reading that the German artist Albrecht Dürer saw the artefacts that Cortés had sent back to King Charles V. Dürer said that he had never seen anything in his life that had made his heart so rejoice as the beautiful works of art that had come from this land. It is quite possible that crystal skulls were amongst those works of art.'

Was this one of the reasons why ancient crystal skulls were not more in evidence in Mexico? Perhaps they had been shipped back to Europe. I remembered the words of Mesoamerican specialist Dr John Pohl, whom we had spoken to previously. He had suggested that perhaps the reason more crystal skulls had not been found in Central America was because they had been hidden away by indigenous people when the Spanish arrived, to avoid them being coveted or destroyed by the conquerors. They had been needed for healing:

'We know today that Indian people use crystals for curing. At the time of the conquest millions of them were dying from European diseases. It makes perfect sense then that the curers would want to preserve these skulls for themselves for healing purposes. They were primary tools, primary medical tools for curing people, so they would have hidden them. They would have kept them to themselves.'

Norma likewise believed that her crystal skull had healing powers:

'I was a very normal, rational person, very scientific in my way of think-ing, but since the skull has been with me, I've started to feel different. I feel there is something magical about the skull. When I hold the skull I feel protected, I feel more energetic and stronger.

'It is true that when I am around the skull I feel really good. But it does seem to affect the body as well as the mind. It makes me feel that the oxygen is flowing round my body more easily and it makes me feel more relaxed. The clarity of quartz crystal is the clarity that you can have in your own mind, when you relax and stop feeling worried, anx-ious or afraid.

'I have a friend who believes that this skull is supposed to come together with other skulls for the purpose of giving knowledge to human-ity, very important knowledge of how we should live.'

I reminded Norma that we were trying to bring together as many crystal skulls as possible for scientific tests. Although they were not being gath-ered together to solve the mysteries of the universe, the tests should at least determine if they were genuine antiquities.

'I would like to be there,' she said.

I asked if she was prepared for the knowledge that her skull might well turn out to be a fake.

'I don't care,' she replied. 'Even if it is a reproduction or a fake it is still an important symbol, a holy symbol. It was a very important symbol to the people of this land before the Europeans arrived.'

Holding her skull so it caught the light filtering through the French windows, she continued:

'Symbols are very powerful, more powerful than words. They connect us with deep levels of truth that cannot be reached with words. It is said that they are closer to mystical experience than words are. They are a sign that we can access the realms of spirit. They can connect us with a higher awareness of our purpose, help us to be more spiritual.

'It is not just the fact that the crystal is shaped like a skull that makes it important, that makes us think of death and spirits. It is also the crystal.'

We had already heard that crystal is sacred to many indigenous people, that it is associated with light, not only in Mexico, but all over the world, and that many indigenous people have said that it comes from the heavens. Eskimo people call it 'light stones' and consider it solidified light that has come down from above. Australian aborigines also see crystal as sacred. They call it 'wild stones' and say that the throne of their great god Baiame was made of crystal and he would drop pieces broken from it down to Earth. Norma had another example:

'There is a Greek legend that tells that the gods looked down from the heavens and saw the troubles that were here on Earth. Brother had turned against brother and there were terrible wars and fighting. The gods were so saddened by what they saw. They were heartbroken. As they looked down they started to cry, and the tears began to well in their eyes, and as they fell to Earth, these tears came through the atmosphere and as they did they were transformed into pieces of quartz crystal. The tears of the gods were frozen into crystal by the cold, chill winds of mankind. So crystal was known to the ancient Greeks as "holy ice". In their view, it came to Earth as a gift from the gods, a gift that would help the people of the Earth to heal their wounds and help them to make peace with each other. Maybe the crystal skulls are something to do with this.'

She continued:

'I believe the skull is here for a purpose. I am the custodian of the skull, but it is here to benefit other people as well as myself. I feel almost as if it has something to tell me, although I am not sure what. I have spent much time with it and I want to find out what its purpose is.'

I asked Norma if she had any idea what its purpose might be.

'I don't know, but I wonder if it is like the crystal in the Greek legend, that it is here to bring the gods amongst us, to help to bring out what is positive and good in humanity, to help us to achieve peace, bringing people close together and closer to God.'

Then Norma's youngest son came into the room and I realized that I had stayed much longer than I had intended. It was time to be going. I wanted to get some maps before we headed south the next day, to the land of the Maya.

14. THE MAYA AND THE CRYSTAL SKULL

While we were still in Central America we were keen to investigate whether there might be any other evidence that the skulls might really be Mayan or even older, as Anna Mitchell-Hedges and JoAnn Parks believed.

As Ceri and I sat in a small roadside café in Mexico City with Professor José Salomez Sanchez, we asked him whether he thought this might be the case. As José put it:

> *'That's a very difficult question to answer. For one thing very little is really known about the ancient Maya. We know far less about them than we know about the Aztecs, because they had already disappeared before the Spanish arrived around 1519, so we have far fewer clear and reliable records for them, never mind their predecessors. They present us with a whole series of contradictions and unanswered questions. Although living on peasant agriculture close to the land and possessing little in the way of technical instruments and technologies such as our own, in many other respects they were an incredibly sophisticated civilization. Although they only had soft metals later in their reign and are believed to have used neither metal tools nor the wheel, they were very advanced in so many other respects.'*

As Jose explained, it is very difficult for us, with our emphasis on modern technology, to see a civilization that showed no evidence of any such technology as advanced and sophisticated. This, however, probably says more about our own blind belief in the power of technology than it does about the real achievements of ancient people such as the Maya. In fact, it is probably this apparent absence of technological development that has led many archaeologists to suggest that the ancient Maya were incapable of making objects such as the crystal skulls. It would certainly be very diffi-cult for a Stone Age people without metal instruments to carve a crystal skull, but that doesn't make it impossible. After all, the ancient Maya still managed to create one of the most advanced civilizations the world has ever known.

According to José another reason many archaeologists believe the crys-tal skulls are not Mayan is because most are more realistic to look at than traditional Mayan artwork, which was generally very stylized. But the main reason for most archaeologists' scepticism was that to his knowl-edge, no crystal skull had yet been found on any properly recorded Mayan archaeological dig.

Mayan expert Dr Karl Taube had already pointed out to us that very little crystal has been found on Mayan archaeological sites and those pieces that have been uncovered are only small items mostly dating from the very late period of the Mayan civilization.

Yet this in itself was not proof that the Mayans did not have crystal skulls, as Dr John Pohl had put it:

'I believe the reason we haven't found any crystal skulls on any properly recorded archaeological digs is because, for one thing, they would have been extremely rare, as crystal is so hard to find and manufacture. Any of those that were made would have been highly prized by the Indian people who made them.'

So did the Mayans simply not have crystal skulls, or had they hidden them from the Spanish, or had the skulls been destroyed by the European conquerors? JoAnn Parks certainly thought that her skull was at least as old as the ancient Mayan civilization and we had also heard from Anna Mitchell-Hedges that her skull was of great significance to the Maya. But was there any real evidence? We set off to find out.

We were already aware of some of the achievements of the Maya and their sudden disappearance around AD 830. Yet their true origins and destiny and the source of their great knowledge remained a mystery. Could crystal skulls have been involved? Had the Mayans made crystal skulls at the same time as they built their great cities, only to abandon them when they left? We began by looking at where the Maya might have come from to see if this would yield any clues as to where the skulls themselves had come from.

As we discovered, the origin of the Maya is a matter of considerable controversy. Today most link them with an even earlier civilization, usually known as the Olmecs, who occupied an area along the Gulf coast of Mexico from around 1200 BC. According to many archaeologists, the attributes of a complex society appeared quite suddenly among the Olmecs, although again nobody seems to understand quite why. Could crystal skulls have had something to do with their sudden rise?

However, even less is known about the Olmecs than about the Maya. It is understood that they too created well-planned urban centres with early pyramids, but unfortunately next to nothing of these remains today, as they were built of mud-bricks and have now vanished almost completely into the swampland.

What does remain are some massive carved stone heads, some as large as 10 feet (3 metres) across and weighing up 20 tons (20 tonnes) *(see black-and-white plate no. 44)*. These gargantuan heads were carved from solid basalt, a very hard and enduring igneous rock. They appear to depict helmeted warriors that held a gaze of great power. The Olmecs also left behind small pottery figurines and beautiful masks carved in jade, as well as small head-carvings.

What these artefacts show is that even in the second millennium before Christ these Mesoamerican people were capable of carving incredibly life-like heads and masks, sometimes out of the hardest of stone materials, although this by no means proves that they created any crystal skulls. Instead what interests most archaeologists about these objects is that they do not appear to have Native American characteristics. The giant heads have characteristic African features, whilst some of the little figurines have a positively oriental appearance. Other artefacts depict men with beards, something that due to the simple dictates of genetics no Native American tribe in known history has had. Still other artefacts portray human-like figures with very tall elongated heads and large slanting eyes that some consider positively alien in nature *(see black-and-white plate no. 38)*.

Despite the scant number of artefacts the Olmecs left behind, it is commonly believed that many Mayan customs, practices and beliefs date back at least to their time. Indeed, the Olmecs are now widely credited with many of the most important cultural developments throughout the whole of Mesoamerica, including the complex numbering and hiero-glyphic system used in the incredibly accurate Mayan calendar.

But where had these earliest cultures obtained their knowledge? Did it spring from within their societies or come from some early contact with outsiders, whether from across the Atlantic, the Pacific or some other source? This is one of the most heated debates of Mesoamerican archaeology.

The most common theory among present-day archaeologists is that the whole of the Native American population had its origins in Asia. At some time during or towards the end of the last Ice Age (around 10,000 BC), when sea levels were lower, travellers from Asia walked over a land or ice bridge across what is now the Bering Strait connecting eastern Russia with Alaska, and over the millennia worked their way down, populating the whole of the American continent.

Evidence used in support of this theory is that there are some apparent similarities in appearance between the people of both continents and between their ancient artwork and architecture. What interested us, however, was that there is also a tradition in the Far East of gazing into a crystal ball to see into the future. Could this be a link with a Mesoamerican use of the crystal skull?

However, it is by no means proven that there really was any ancient connection between America and Asia. It remains uncertain that the two continents were at any time joined, and the similarities in culture and physical appearance may be purely coincidental. The finding of the oldest human remains in the Americas in the northern part of the continent, often cited as supportive evidence, may actually prove nothing more than that the coldest weather acts as the best preservative.

In fact there turned out to be a whole host of theories about the origins of the Mayans and Olmecs, some more dubious than others. These included possible links with Africa, ancient Egypt, the Lost Tribes of Israel, or even Christ himself, not to mention the Phoenicians, Babylonians, Mesopotamians, Greeks or even the ancient Hindus. Other evidence suggested a connection with the legendary lost continent of Atlantis or possibly even beings from outer space. In short, almost anything seemed possible!

I asked José what he thought about all this speculation. He said that it was certainly true that many visitors to Central America had been struck by the similarity between the now crumbling Mesoamerican pyramids and the great pyramids of ancient Egypt. But did this mean there was a link between the two? The presence of obscure hieroglyphics and an apparent obsession with star gods seemed only to reinforce the similarity between these two great ancient cultures. Indeed, these similarities have led many people over the years to wonder whether at some time these two distant civilizations were somehow connected. Perhaps they traded with each other, or perhaps the Mayans were descended from the ancient Egyptians, despite the great barrier of the Atlantic Ocean in between? Certainly the coastal Africans and Egyptians were great sailors, so they may have ventured as far as Central America.

For centuries now people have considered ancient contact between the ancient Egyptians and Mesoamericans a possibility and as recently as 1970 Thor Heyerdahl, a Norwegian academic with a sense of adventure, set out to prove that even with the technology of the time such transatlantic crossings were indeed possible. Heyerdahl's voyage was spectacular. His team built a simple boat, *Ra II*, copying the designs depicted on Egyptian tomb paintings and using only the papyrus reeds available at that time. Admittedly *Ra I* had sunk, but the second boat travelled over 6,000 kilometres and arrived only 57 days later in Barbados, a mere few hundred miles from the Maya heartland in Central America. This certainly showed that it was perfectly feasible for ancient Egyptian mariners to have made just such a journey, although of course it didn't prove that they actually did.

Some even more recent evidence had added further fuel to the debate. As recently as 1996 forensic archaeologists at the University of Manchester in England were studying ancient mummies from Egyptian tombs when they made a most surprising discovery that they are still having difficulty believing themselves. In carrying out chemical analysis of the preserved corpses, scientists led by Dr Rosalie David found distinct traces of tobacco inside the hair and body tissue of some of the mummies. Similar tests on other ancient Egyptian mummies, performed by Dr S. Balabanova of the Institute for Anthropology and Human Genetics in Munich, also found traces of tobacco and, of all things, cocaine. Both of these plants are native only to the American continent and until then it had been generally accepted that they had not found their way across the Atlantic until after Christopher Columbus. However, stronger evidence of pre-Columbian connections between the Americas and ancient Egypt would be hard to find.

As we discovered, however, many archaeologists are sceptical about this, pointing out that the last of the great Egyptian pyramids at Giza are thought to have been built around 2500 BC, probably at least 1,000 years before the Olmecs even arose, never mind the Maya. So where are these pyramid-building skills supposed to have disappeared to in the intervening period? They also note that whilst the Egyptian pyramids rise to a point on top and all seem to have served as tombs, Mesoamerican pyramids are flat-topped, generally with a temple at the summit, and only occasionally appear to have served as tombs. In any case, to date there seemed to be no evidence that the ancient Egyptians were ever in possession of any kind of crystal skull.

So where did this bring us? Over the years a whole cast of explorers, archaeologists, anthropologists and assorted eccentrics have made a name for themselves with competing theories of who the Mayans were and where they came from. But this just brought forth even more possible origins for the crystal skulls. And our attempt to solve these mysteries was seriously hindered by the fact that much of the native Mesoamerican culture had been destroyed by the Spanish.

However, as José assured us, as well as the few scant records kept by the early Spanish settlers, there are still the remains of many of the great Mayan cities themselves. Maybe these would yield some clues.

The great ceremonial cities of the Maya lay undisturbed in the jungles for hundreds of years even after the arrival of the Europeans. For when the Spanish first arrived in Central America they quickly abandoned their first attempted conquest of the Yucatán, instead heading further north to more temperate climes, driven on by rumours of great treasures of gold in the still thriving Aztec cities of central Mexico. Meanwhile, hidden deep in the jungle, many of the great Mayan architectural sites were able to escape destruction. It was not until the eighteenth century, with the discovery of Palenque, probably the most beautiful of Mayan cities, that the Western world even knew of the Mayan civilization.

Apparently Cortés had passed within 70 miles of Palenque, but it was not until 1773 that the city was eventually discovered by Friar Ordóñez, a canon who lived in nearby Ciudad Real in Chiapas. Like Mitchell-Hedges over 100 years later, Ordóñez had heard rumours that a splendid city lay buried somewhere deep in the jungle and, after his poor parishioners had carried him nearly 70 miles through the undergrowth, he finally discovered it, half-ruined, tucked away at the foot of fine jungle-clad hills. He named the tranquil ruins 'Great City of Serpents', after a symbol that seemed to have been of great importance to the city's original inhabitants.[1]

Immediately the speculation began as to what had inspired construction of such a vast city, with its magnificent pyramids, temples, palaces and towers. Most archaeologists today believe that Palenque was built by local Mayans some time between AD 600 and 800, but Friar Ordóñez himself had his own theories, inspired by a book written by the Quiché Maya, an important Mayan group, themselves. This book had actually been burned by the Bishop of Chiapas, Nuñes de la Vega, back in 1691, but Ordóñez had managed to obtain a copy of part of it that the Bishop himself had made before committing the rest to the flames.

According to Ordóñez, the Mayans' own book claimed that Palenque had been built by people who came from the Atlantic. They were led by a long-robed leader, Pacal Votan, who had supposedly actually written the book and whose symbol was the serpent. This is in fact an important symbol throughout Mesoamerica, particularly amongst the Maya on the Yucatán Peninsula. It was often used as a sign of Kukulcan, one of the Mayan gods who bears a striking resemblance to the great Aztec god Quetzalcoatl, whose name means 'rainbow-coloured feathered serpent'. As with Quetzalcoatl, it is again unclear whether this character was a god, a man, or a series of famous leaders, but he is widely credited in native mythology as the founder of the whole of Mesoamerican civilization.

Votan and his followers had apparently come from a land called Valum Chivim. They came in peace and the locals accepted their leadership, allowing them to marry their daughters. The book also said that Votan made four trips back to his old homelands across the Atlantic. Ordóñez thought that Pacal Votan had been a Phoenician sailor and that Valum Chivim was actually the Phoenician city of Tripoli, now in the Lebanon, and not that far from Egypt. He based this belief on a legend that said Votan had visited a great city where a temple was under construction which would reach right up to heaven, but would also lead to a break-down of communication. Bishop Nuñes thought the town referred to was Babylon and the temple was the biblical Tower of Babel, whose fall was due to a great confusion of languages. Interestingly, if this was true, the temple was probably one of the great ziggurats of Mesopotamia, which were stepped pyramids with crowning temples, just like the great temple pyramids of Palenque.[2]

There was one aspect of this story, however, that was of particular interest to us. For according to Friar Ordóñez the old Quiché Mayan book also said that during their original journey by sea to Palenque, Votan and his followers 'stopped off on the way at "the Dwelling of the Thirteen"'. Author-historians Gilbert and Cotterell interpreted this to mean 'perhaps the Canaries and another greater island, presumably either Cuba or Hispaniola'.[3] But might it not instead be a veiled reference to the 13 crystal skulls of oral legend and to their 'dwelling' somewhere between the Old World and Palenque in southern Mexico, perhaps even at Lubaantun?

Just as intriguingly, according to the original Mayan book, Votan had placed a secret treasure in a 'dark, subterranean' building. We speculated whether that treasure could have been a crystal skull. It was said that the Bishop himself had searched high and low for it, in order to destroy it, but although he did discover a few stone beads, clay jars and other manuscripts, which he burned along with the original book of Votan, it seems that the real treasure was never discovered. Was it possible that the Bishop had searched in vain because the crystal skull had already been removed and hidden in Lubaantun or some other place? Or was it still waiting to be discovered somewhere in or around Palenque? We, of course, were itching to find out.

Saying our last goodbyes to José, we headed back out to the airport to fly south and check out some of the remnants of the ancient Mayan civilization for ourselves.

On the flight to Villahermosa, *en route* to Palenque, I read up a bit more about this mysterious Mayan city. It seems Friar Ordóñez had ordered a captain of artillery, Don Antonio del Rio, to carry out an official survey of the ruins. During his clearing and excavation work, Don Antonio developed the belief that the Americas had been visited not only by Phoenicians but also by the Egyptians, Greeks, Romans and even ancient Britons. Although his report was dismissed by the Church, it was later picked up on by an Italian, Dr Paul Cabrera, who concluded that Palenque must have been the result of an earlier visit by the Carthaginians, sailing from the Mediterranean before the First Punic War with Rome in 264 BC. Thus the first published report on the ruins espoused his belief that the Carthaginians had interbred with the natives to produce the Olmecs, whose descendants later founded Palenque.[4]

But it was not until 1845 that the ideas later espoused by Frederick Mitchell-Hedges were to find their first expression in the work of the Frenchman the Abbé Brasseur de Bourbourg. This man took the step of learning Nahuatl, one of the main languages of the Mexican people, as well as Cakchiquel and Quiché, two of the languages of the Mayan descendants who still inhabit this area today. This allowed him to understand the handful of ancient manuscripts that had escaped the flames of the early settlers and that he had managed to find languishing in monastery and convent libraries. One of these manuscripts, which he found in Madrid and so came to be known as the *Madrid Codex*, is still the largest known surviving Mayan manuscript in the world. In this book of hieroglyphs de Bourbourg found some support for the myths that he claimed he had heard from the local Mayan people.

De Bourbourg put forward the revolutionary theory that a great island continent known as Atlantis had once existed somewhere in the Atlantic Ocean, between the Central American coast and the coastlines of Europe and Africa *(see Figure 10)*. He believed that civilization had actually begun there and not in the Middle East, as is still commonly supposed. According to de Bourbourg the Maya were descended from the survivors of this lost continent, said to have been destroyed by a great cataclysm or series of cataclysms, and that it was these survivors who had actually brought civilization both to Central America and ancient Egypt.

Immediately we wondered whether the 'Dwelling of the Thirteen' might actually be this lost continent? Could the crystal skulls really be from Atlantis? At first this idea seemed quite unbelievable. Indeed, most archaeologists dismiss Atlantis as pure fantasy. As we would later discover, how-ever, the idea that this great island civilization did once exist is not entirely without support from other sources. But in the meantime,

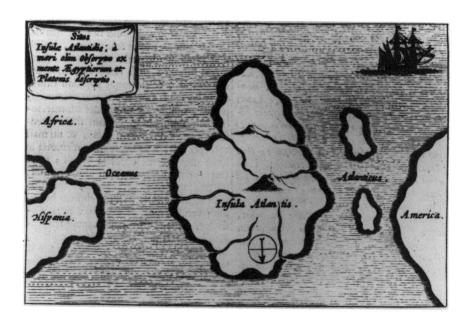

Figure 10: Fanciful seventeenth-century map of Atlantis (with north at the bottom)

our first question was whether or not the ancient Mayans really did possess crystal skulls.

Nothing had prepared us for the beauty of Palenque. Set amongst low, forested hills, it turned out to be a surprisingly small site, with a palace, various temple pyramids and assorted other buildings. When we arrived, the white limestone palaces and towering pyramids were shrouded in early morning mist, the green foliage of the rainforest, its wild tangled heights, a brilliant backdrop to the orderly arrangement of the buildings below. Colourful toucans and hummingbirds darted through the nearby greenery. There was a deeply harmonious atmosphere.

To stand in the middle of Palenque is to contemplate the achievements of an incredible civilization. The palace, with its still plastered walls, showed a king on a jaguar throne being crowned with the plumes of the famous quetzal bird. In some places the colour of the wall paint was still visible. There were corridors and courtyards and, rising up from the palace, a tall and unusually square astronomy tower from where the ancients used to gaze out upon the stars.

In the bright morning sunshine we climbed up the steps of the tallest pyramid, known as 'the Temple of the Inscriptions' on account of the elegant stone carvings and colourful frescoes that had once adorned the walls of the small temple at its summit. It was in this very temple that a discovery had been made that turned out to be one of the greatest finds of New World archaeology.

In 1949 Mexican archaeologist Alberto Ruz had been standing in this small temple when he noticed that a stone slab on the floor had some holes in it plugged with stone stoppers. When the stoppers were removed, the holes allowed the slab to be lifted. Underneath was a narrow staircase leading deep inside the pyramid.

We made our way down into the damp, cold, dimly lit interior (*see colour plate no. 19*). The stairway had originally been filled with rubble, which it took Alberto Ruz and his team three years to clear. What looked like offerings of jade, shell and pottery had been found amongst the debris. Then, half-way down, the stairway changed direction, though still leading downwards. In the next section were the skeletal remains of six young men and then, at the end of a short passageway and at a level even below the base of the pyramid, was a massive stone slab which looked like a doorway. Upon prising this slab open Ruz's team made the most remarkable find.

We had now descended hundreds of steps and were deep beneath the temple in the middle of the pyramid, where Ruz had found a chamber 10 yards (nine metres) long and nearly eight yards (seven metres) high. As we could still see, the walls of this chamber were painted deep red and decorated with stucco relief figures of men in ancient decorative costume, now thought to represent the Nine Lords of the Night in Mayan mythology. The chamber had turned out to be an undisturbed royal tomb. At its centre was a massive stone sarcophagus in which lay the remains of a Mayan king, now generally thought to have been a particularly highly respected king of Palenque whose name was Sun Lord Pacal. By deciphering the hieroglyphs left behind, it has been discovered that he ascended to the throne at the age of 12 and died in AD 683 at the ripe old age of 80.

It seems that the skeletons found outside the tomb were the bones of the king's attendants, who were sacrificed so that they could accompany their master after death, much as was the practice in ancient Egypt on the death of a pharaoh. Also much like the design of ancient Egyptian pyramid tombs, a small shaft or tube, known as a 'psychoduct', was built into the fabric of the pyramid. It led from inside the tomb chamber right up the stairs and out of the floor of the temple above. As with the similar Egyptian design, this is thought to have been provided to enable the spirit of the dead king to make its way back up to the heavens after death, although, according to Mayan cosmology, only after it had confronted and defeated the Lords of the Underworld.

Inside the tomb were found more of what were presumed to be offerings – two carved jade figures and two beautifully moulded and highly realistic stucco heads. Inside the sarcophagus were even more treasures. The king's skeleton was adorned with jade and mother-of-pearl earspools, he wore necklaces of jade beads, his fingers were covered in jade rings, a large jade was placed in each hand and another was placed in his mouth. This practice was also carried out in ancient China, where, as in Mesoamerica, jade was associated with eternal life. Perhaps most beautiful of all, the dead king wore an exquisite mosaic death mask. This was his portrait, complete with large nose and sloping forehead, the skin fashioned from jade and the eyes from white shell with deep black obsidian pupils.

So here again was evidence, as with the Olmecs, that the ancient Maya had been able to make elaborately crafted representations of the human head, sometimes from the hardest of stone materials. Indeed, the stucco

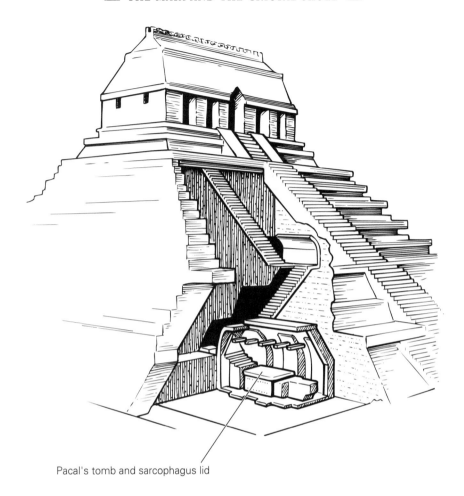

Pacal's tomb and sarcophagus lid

Figure 11: Cross-section of the Temple of the Inscriptions at Palenque, show-ing the location of Pacal's tomb and sarcophagus lid

heads, many of which have now been found at Palenque, are stunningly anatomically accurate, just like the Mitchell-Hedges crystal skull *(see black-and-white plate no. 43)*.

The problem with assuming that the Mayans could also therefore have made crystal skulls is that stucco is very soft and easily moulded by hand. The jade mask would have to have been carved, but it was very stylized and not exactly anatomically accurate. What is more, most of the artefacts found here, as at most other Mayan sites, were carved from jade, not crystal. According to most archaeologists, this was the material most highly prized by the Mayans. For us, then, although the objects

Alberto Ruz found in Pacal's tomb were both beautiful and in many respects similar to the crystal skull said to have been found at Lubaantun, we were no nearer to solving the mystery.

But what has interested most archaeologists has been the elaborately carved lid on Pacal's sarcophagus. For it is in these carvings that many believe lie the greatest clues as to the real origins of the ancient Maya.

We peered through the heavy metal bars that now protected the tomb. The great sarcophagus lid of Palenque was huge, one massive slab of magnolia-coloured limestone, weighing around five tons (five tonnes) and measuring over 12 × 7 feet (3.5 × 2 metres). It is now widely believed that King Pacal designed this and his own tomb in the final years of his reign, beginning construction around AD 675. Certainly the sarcophagus was constructed first and then the rest of the tomb, pyramid and crowning temple built around it. This could be the only explanation, as the lid of the sarcophagus is too big to fit through the tiny door into its chamber. It remains to this day impossible to remove the lid and get it up the narrow staircase without knocking the whole pyramid down! Again, this is a feature in common with the pyramid tombs of ancient Egypt.

The sarcophagus lid is very intricately carved, featuring a Mayan figure curled in an almost foetal position and surrounded by all sorts of fancy designs, figures and an intricate border, all of which seem almost to breathe with symbolism. There is a great lightness to the design, giving the appearance that the central figure is almost floating, surrounded by a flourish of swirling symbols *(see Figure 12)*. Ever since its discovery, it seemed that this lid had sparked lively and often heated debate. Just who was this figure, what on Earth was he doing and what did all the various symbols mean? And so Alberto Ruz's discovery had led to even more theories about the origins of the ancient Maya.

Probably the most controversial of these was put forward in the 1960s by the Swiss writer Erich von Däniken in his famous book *Chariots of the Gods?* [5] Von Däniken amassed examples from all over the world in support of his theory that primitive peoples had in ancient times been visited by intelligent life from other planets and that this was in fact the catalyst for the emergence of civilization. He proposed that, given that there are literally billions of stars in the universe, there is every probability that somewhere there are human-like creatures at a more advanced stage of evolution than ourselves. Such beings would certainly have been considered akin to gods by ancient primitive peoples.

Figure 12: Detail of the sarcophagus lid of Pacal at Palenque

Von Däniken claimed that the lid of Pacal provided strong support for his hypothesis. He believed that the figure hunched at the centre of the lid was actually an astronaut at the controls of his spaceship as it took off:

'*Today any child would identify this vehicle as a rocket. It is pointed at the front, then changes to strangely grooved indentations like inlet ports, widens out and terminates at the tail in a darting flame. The crouching being himself is manipulating a number of undefinable controls and has the heel of his left foot on a kind of pedal. His clothing is appropriate; short trousers with a broad belt, a jacket with a modern Japanese opening at the neck and closely fitting bands at arms and legs ... the complicated headgear ... with the usual indentations and tubes, and something like antennae on top. Our space traveller – for he is clearly depicted as one – is not only bent forward tensely, he is also looking intently at an apparatus hanging in front of his face. The astronaut's front seat is separated by struts from the rear portion of the vehicle, in which symmetrically arranged boxes, circles, points and spirals can be seen...*

Could primitive imagination have produced anything so remarkably similar to a modern astronaut in his rocket? Those strange markings at the foot of the drawing [of the lid] can only be an indication of the flames and gases coming from the propulsion unit.'[6]

Some have even speculated that the Maya's sudden disappearance was because they departed in the spaceships of these alien visitors and that the skeleton in the tomb of Pacal is actually the remains of one of these early extra-terrestrials who did not manage to make it back home! However implausible this may seem, von Däniken's ideas certainly caught the public's imagination and his book proved to be an international bestseller. It is also true to say that the skeleton found in the tomb was far taller than any other Mayan remains so far found. The Maya were somewhat obsessed with 'sky gods' and were certainly great watchers of the stars. Many of the images around the border of the lid of Pacal are now recognized as representing the sun, the moon, the planets and certain constellations, and many Mayan buildings are carefully aligned with the planets and the stars.

Of course none of this was sufficient evidence for us to accept von Däniken's wild alien visitation theory, or to suggest that such early space travellers might have instructed the ancient Maya with the aid of any crystal skulls! But it was interesting to note that it did not seem to be in any way inconsistent with the original legend of the skulls or with what Joshua Shapiro had told us about their real origins.

Many archaeologists, however, are unhappy not only about extra-terrestrial visitation theories but also about suggestions that the Mayan culture was affected by any kind of external influence, even from else-where on Earth. They believe, perhaps quite rightly, that the Maya were perfectly capable of creating an advanced civilization entirely on their own. A leading Mayan expert we consulted, Dr Linda Schele, argues that any theory of external influence takes attention away from the real achievements of the Maya, and robs them and their descendants of their rightful heritage. Reacting against centuries of claims that the Mayans were not intelligent enough to create such an advanced civilization by themselves, she sees such theories as implicitly racist, as perpetuating cultural imperialism and the myth of intellectual superiority in the West.

If nothing else, however, von Däniken's theories do at least highlight how little we really know about ancient people such as the Maya and how they developed as they did. Perhaps this is why so many wild theories abound.

Whatever the true origins of the ancient Maya, Dr Linda Schele certainly has a more plausible interpretation of the great lid of Palenque than von Däniken. Her reading is based on the most recent advances in decoding the Mayans' cryptic hieroglyphs. From this work, it is now widely accepted that the Maya believed in a form of parallel worlds or universes: the underworld, or place of the dead, the upper world or heavens, the place of the celestial gods and ancestors, and the middle world, our own familiar physical world. The ancient Maya symbolized these worlds and the connections between them as a tree, usually the ceiba tree, which represented the sacred 'Tree of Life'. Its roots reached down into the underworld, whilst its branches reached up into the heavens.[7]

According to Linda Schele, the great lid of Palenque actually shows King Pacal at the point of death, and tells us much about the ancient Mayans' attitude towards death and their belief in these other worlds or dimensions. At the top right-hand corner of the sarcophagus lid is a 'sky-band', a sign for daytime. In the opposite corner is the sign for darkness and night. Through the centre of the carving runs the Tree of Life, indicated by a cross, topped by the celestial bird, a symbol of the heavenly realms. Two square-nosed serpents form the branches of the tree, growing from sacrificial bowls. These serpents are mirrored by two skeletal serpents who rise up from the underworld, their jaws open, awaiting the king at this moment of his descent into the underworld where death awaits him. Dr Schele believes this represents the sun at the point of sunset, as it descends below the horizon into the underworld carrying the dead king with it. For, she claims, the Maya believed that just as the sun passed below the horizon so the dead king would travel below our earthly horizon to the underworld, where, just like the sun, he would continue his life after death. Thus the king is also shown in a foetal position because although he is dying in the middle world he is also being reborn into the underworld.

But the story doesn't end there. What happened to the king after his descent into the underworld is also indicated by the layout of the tomb itself. For the Temple of the Inscriptions was built so that the east–west axis of the tomb is carefully aligned with another temple, the Temple of the Cross. If you draw a line between these two and beyond the whole configuration, it is aligned with a particular point on the horizon. This is the point the sun reaches at one of the most significant alignments of the solar year, its southernmost point, the winter solstice. As it sinks below the horizon it comes into direct line with the centre of the tomb where Pacal is buried. As the sun falls into darkness, so Pacal falls into the darkness of the underworld. As the sun will rise again, to make its journey northwards, so Pacal will rise again and travel northwards, taking up residence in the northern sky, near to the North Star. Thus the story of a king's death and rebirth was not confined to the tomb but stretched out across the whole city of Palenque, because the whole universe was full of symbolic meaning for the Mayan people.

More and more of these patterns of sacred geometry are emerging as the new science of 'archaeo-astronomy' gathers momentum. It is becoming increasingly clear that the practice of aligning buildings with the heavenly bodies for deeply spiritual reasons was widespread among the Maya. In fact it seems there was no accident in any aspect of their building design. Here again we see parallels with the ancient Egyptians.

Yet another interpretation of the sarcophagus lid of Palenque is given by authors Gilbert and Cotterell in their discussion of the prophecies of the Maya.[8] They suggest that it represents four of the Mayans' great gods. The figure at the centre of the lid is the goddess of water, Chalchuihtlicue, who clasps the leaf of a lily in her hand, and the other symbols reveal some of the other great gods: Ehecatl, the god of wind, Tonatiuh, the sun god, and Tlaloc, the god of thunder, celestial fire, lightning and rain. They believe that these four gods represent each of the different elements and also the different ages of mankind. For, like the Aztecs, the Maya also believed there had been several previous 'worlds' or eras before our own, each of which had been destroyed by a different element of the Earth.

The apparently abstract patterns that decorate the sides of the sarcophagus lid are said to be a coded pattern which can be deciphered to reveal more of the gods of Mayan mythology. Gilbert and Cotterell claim that the designs across the whole sarcophagus lid, when taken together, represent an abbreviated history of mankind, showing the destruction of previous worlds, and offer a coded message, a warning, from the great ruler Pacal, of the devastating events that await us in the very near future.

But whatever the real meaning of the lid of Palenque, and whatever the real origins of the Mayans, the question to which we still needed an answer was whether there was any evidence that the Mayans really did make the crystal skull, or were in possession of any crystal skulls handed down to them by their forefathers, whoever they may have been.

Emerging into the sunlight, we came back down the Temple of the Inscriptions and continued our explorations of Palenque.

The Temple of Inscriptions was situated at one end of a row of three similar temple pyramids. In the next pyramid, as recently as 1995, a woman's tomb had been found, probably that of a queen, perhaps Pacal's partner. At the other end of the row was a temple pyramid we had overlooked on first entering the site. This pyramid was still half covered in greenery as it had only been partially reclaimed from the rainforest. Most tourists are too eager to climb up the Temple of Inscriptions even to notice this half-excavated temple right on the edge of the current site. It looked somewhat dilapidated and did not even feature on the map of the site we had originally purchased. But we thought we might like to climb it all the same.

When we reached the top we were in for a surprise. There at the top of the 52 steps and just at the entrance to the temple was a magnificently carved stone skull. It was carved into the white limestone of the temple wall and measured about 18" (45 cm) in diameter *(see colour plate no.18)*. It appeared to be guarding what looked like a shrine.

At once we recalled the skull we had seen at Tikal, the original skull we had nicknamed 'the Skull of Destiny', as it had introduced us to the riddle of the crystal skulls and set us on our quest. This skull was similar, but considerably more beautiful. It was raised up from the surface of the temple wall in shallow relief, an artistic style that is particularly characteristic of the decorative work of Palenque. The skull at Tikal had been darkened by the growth of lichen, its features slowly starting to crumble and distort. Exposure to the damp of the rainforest had taken its toll. But the features of this skull at Palenque were well preserved and still clearly defined. On the Tikal skull it had been difficult to tell, but this skull definitely had a missing jaw. Both of these skulls were carved at the top of a row of steps leading into an enclosure that looked like a shrine. But whilst the decaying skull at Tikal guarded a shrine half-way up a somewhat smaller and more obscure pyramid, this skull appeared to be the crowning feature of this pyramid, positioned right at the entrance to the shrine on top.

We were curious to know why archaeologists appeared to have ignored these skulls. Why had they had not captured their imaginations and why, particularly in the light of what is said in the book of Votan, had this pyramid never, it appeared, been thoroughly searched? What great treasures might it hold, perhaps even a crystal skull? However, it soon became apparent why no one had excavated this pyramid. As we discovered, there appeared to be no means of accessing its inner depths. There was no sign of any stone stoppers, like those found by Alberto Ruz. The shrine inside the temple was completely bare and gave no further hint as to what its function might have been.

Looking for further clues, we searched through all the buildings of Palenque, through warrens of undercover corridors still intact, through the remains of the ceremonial square within the palace complex, through outbuildings with their distinctive upturned V-shaped arches, down steps and up still more pyramids. But, just as we had found at Tikal, there was but one solitary wall-mounted image of a skull protecting the entrance to a mysterious shrine.

These skulls raised many questions. What was their significance? What were these shrines they seemed to be protecting? What was their purpose? Where they places of contemplation, of worship or of human sacrifice? Had they perhaps at one time contained crystal skulls? The elaborate carvings and shrines certainly demonstrated that the Mayans were interested in skulls. But why? And would any answers to that question provide enough evidence to prove that they knew of crystal skulls?

We didn't seem to be any nearer to an answer, but there was certainly no shortage of skull imagery in ancient Mayan culture. Another of the ancient manuscripts the Abbé Brasseur de Bourbourg found turned out to be probably the single most important surviving document of Mayan mythology, for it is nothing less than their equivalent of our Old Testament. This is the famous *Popol Vuh*, or 'Council Book', containing the epic holy creation story or, as Dr Linda Schele put it, 'the alien odyssey' of the Quiché Maya.

Although the original hieroglyphic manuscript no longer survived, the *Popol Vuh* had been copied into Spanish at some time during the sixteenth century. Even its first page hinted at rich mystery and intrigue:

> The Popol Vuh, *as it is called, cannot be seen anymore…*
> *The original book, written long ago, once existed but is now hidden from the searcher and from the thinker…*[9]

In an early part of this mythical creation story, the image of a skull plays an important role as a symbol of forbidden knowledge. Like the biblical story of Adam and Eve in the Garden of Eden, the Mayan story features a young woman tempted by fruit growing on a tree. In the Mayan version, this is not an apple tree but a calabash tree. The fruit this tree bears, when dried and hollowed out, actually looks curiously like a human skull.

The story begins when the lords of the Mayans' underworld, the gods of death, call another important god, the god of maize and therefore a symbol of life, to do battle with them. The gods of death kill the god of life and place his head in a tree which becomes heavy with calabash fruit. This 'skull' fruit is left as a warning to everyone not to mess with the great lords of death, who tell everyone to stay away from the tree, here again echoing the biblical story. But:

> 'The daughter called Xquic [actually one of the daughters of the lords of death] heard how the formerly barren tree gave forth fruit.
> 'She was curious and wished to see it. When she saw the tree full of fruit, she said to herself: "I shall not go without tasting one of these fruits. I am sure I shall not die."
> 'She was thinking this when the skull that was placed in the fork of the tree said: "Do you really want of this fruit with all your heart?"
> ' "Yes, I want it," the maiden said.'[10]

The skull in the tree then spits in the girl's hand and she becomes pregnant. The skull then speaks to her again:

'[This] is just a sign that I have given you, my saliva, my spittle. This, my head, has nothing on it, just bone, nothing of meat. It's just the same with the head of a great lord; it's just the flesh that makes his face look good. And when he dies, people get frightened by his bones. After that, his son is like his saliva, his spittle, in his being, whether it be the son of a lord or the son of a craftsman and orator. The father does not disappear, but goes on being fulfilled.'[11]

Could the stone skulls at Tikal and Palenque, or indeed the crystal skulls, represent this original skull (or fruit) and thereby the forbidden fruit of the tree of knowledge? This skull was certainly able to speak, but what did it all mean?

However, the story continues. The maiden eventually gives birth to twin sons, Hunahpu and Xbalanque, who are the great heroes of much of Mayan mythology. These twins go on to confront the gods of death. They make an epic journey to the underworld during which the lords of death succeed in killing Hunahpu, who has his head bitten off by a vampire bat. The twins then trick the lords of death by substituting the head with a vegetable until they can restore the real head. So could the stone, or crystal, skulls represent this severed head of Hunahpu? Again, though, if so, what did it mean?

But these were by no means the only images of the skull in ancient Mayan mythology. The ancient Maya believed in an underworld, a place of death and fear, known as Xibalba. This was a terrible place ruled over by the powerful lords of death. Xibalba is actually derived from the word *xib* which means 'fear', 'terror' or 'trembling with fright'. We had already seen a series of carved bones found at Tikal which illustrate the journey at the threshold of death *(see Figure 13)*.

Figure 13: The Mayan journey to the underworld as shown on carved bones found at Tikal

The metaphor for life and death was a river journey. The bones show a king seated in the middle of a canoe. He holds his hand to his head in a gesture that suggests his impending death. He is accompanied by animal companions: a dog, a parrot, a spider monkey and an iguana. The boat is paddled by two old gods, Stingray Paddler and Jaguar Paddler. The second pair of bones shows the canoe sinking underwater as the king departs to the underworld, for the Maya also thought the underworld could be reached through water or caves.

The Mayans believed that when you died your soul travelled to the underworld, facing terrible trials along the way. The similarities with medieval Christian mythology are striking, particularly with the description of Hell contained in the work of the Italian poet Dante, writing around AD 1300. Both feature a river journey to the underworld accompanied by a dog. In the medieval Christian version the dog is there to torment lost souls, however, whilst in the Mayan version it assists people on their journey. But again, like Dante, the Maya believed that the underworld had nine levels, what Dante called the 'Nine Hells'. In Mayan mythology, if the deceased passed through these successfully, they had the chance to join once again with their ancestors, who lived in the skies.

But the underworld was also a place populated with old toothless gods who were named after the various causes of death such as old age, sacrifice and war, and the image of the skull also often appeared in connection with one or other of these gods. A pottery figurine has even been found showing that one of the gods of death in the *Popol Vuh* story himself had a skull for a head, and one that looks surprisingly like the stone skull at Tikal (*see Figure 14, overleaf*).

The best known of the death gods was often called Yum Cimih, but precisely what name he went under depended on which of the over 30 known Mayan languages was being used, so he is now often simply referred to as 'God A'. He was the mightiest of the lords of death and is also often depicted with a skull for a head, frequently, it appears, without a lower jaw. So it may have been that the stone, or crystal, skulls may actually represent one of these gods of death.

But strangely, in these images, the gods of death are shown as somewhat comic figures. 'God A', for example, is usually depicted with a potbelly and scrawny limbs (*see Figure 15, overleaf*). He was also often known as Cizim, 'The Flatulent One', and many elaborate scrolls in Mayan art indicate a foul smell emanating from him! So, even though the gods of death are often depicted using skull imagery, these were not figures to fear.

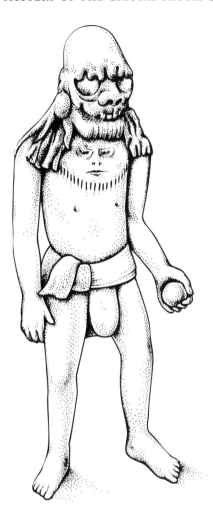

Figure 14: Death god ball player

Instead they were viewed almost with affection. We were most surprised to think that the stone skulls at Palenque and Tikal, set grandly on their pyramid-top shrines, let alone the crystal skulls, might represent nothing more elaborate or terrifying than some comic, fat-bellied, farting god!

However, it was becoming increasingly clear that neither the art of the Maya nor their mythical stories were supposed to be taken literally. They had to be viewed on a symbolic level.

We thought about this and decided that, on a deeper level, the mythology was actually there to inform the ancient Maya about life and death, about what to expect, and how to think and behave in response. It was

Figure 15: Death 'God A'

full of meaning by which people could make sense of their lives. Encoded in all their stories are rich metaphors from which we can extract meaning, providing a richness and texture which we may even apply to our own lives today.

The skull in the tree in the *Popol Vuh* legend, for example, has a deeper symbolic meaning. A woman is tempted to taste the fruit of the tree of life and knowledge, to live by her own choices. She bites into the fruit, or rather the skull. So here the skull is not just a symbol of death, but also a symbol of life. For though the skull is the result of the god of death's actions it is also the physical remains of the god of life. It is ripe with possibilities, the source of new life and knowledge. But it is eaten. So, in this sense, the very act of living is to die, to die to the choices that you can no longer make, the opportunities past, like the fruit consumed, discarded and never to be offered again.

As Mayan expert Dr Karl Taube had already explained:

'Throughout Mesoamerica it was believed that without death you cannot have life. Every time you eat something you're killing something to live. And also you have to give something back to death. If you don't give anything back to Mother Earth no more life can come out. So it's like a constant dialogue between these two opposites. But they're not separate, they're always interdependent.'

Indeed, as Linda Schele had informed us:

'In almost all Mayan languages, and most Mesoamerican languages even today, the word for "skull" is almost indistinguishable from the word for "bone", and the word for "bone", which is bak*, is exactly the same as the word for "seed".'*

Bak is also curiously enough the Mayan name for Palenque. Palenque is only the Spanish name and means nothing more interesting than 'fence'. The Mayan name, however, meaning 'skull', 'bone' or 'seed', has led Linda Schele to suggest that the stone skull at Palenque may actually have had a very ordinary, everyday function. She suggests that it may have been nothing more than the ancient Mayan equivalent of a roadsign. Rather than warning people of their own imminent death or performing any other strange and elaborate function, it simply let them know the name of the town they were visiting.

That this beautifully carved skull, staring out across the city from its temple-top setting, should be something as humdrum as a roadsign rather offended our romantic sensibilities! Surely there had to be more to it than that?

Indeed, there may well be more to this place name than at first appears. For words can sometimes provide a key to unlocking deep philosophical concepts which reveal rich cultural attitudes. The Mayan language itself reveals a very different conception of skulls and bones from that with which we are familiar. To us skulls and bones are a reminder of our own delicate mortality and human frailty. We tend to think of them as 'out of sight' and therefore, thankfully, 'out of mind'. But to the Mayans, skulls and bones, like seeds, are the very structuring principles of life. They give form to our human existence just as the seed gives life to the plant. Flesh grows on our bones just as leaves grow on a plant. By using the same word for all of these concepts, the Maya remind us that each has an active, life-giving role. And thus, for the Maya, the potential for life exists in the very face of death, and the skull was a symbol not only of death, but also of life, rebirth and regeneration.

We learned that the influence of this belief can still be seen today amongst the modern descendants of the Quiché Maya who live near Lake Atitlán in the Guatemalan highlands. Each year they preserve the maize seed corn to replant it. These special grains are called 'little skulls', because every year they are symbolically replanting the skull of the maize god and starting the cycle of resurrection over again.

The duality of life and death, as well as being contained within the image of the skull in the *Popol Vuh* tree, is also neatly encapsulated within the idea of twins, one of the most enduring mythical concepts throughout Mesoamerica. Twins represent a structuring principle, the dual forces that infuse all life. This has some similarity with the Chinese principle of yin and yang, a duality of twinned, unified but mutually opposing opposites, seen as an essence which runs through all things.

But for us, there was even more to the story of the *Popol Vuh* twins than that. For, after defeating the lords of death, they go on to find their father, who is buried on the ball court. He can only be revived if he can name all the parts of the face that he once had. But he can only manage to get as far as mouth, nose and eyes, the most distinctive features of a skull. So the twins leave him on the ball court, but they promise that he will be honoured and remembered. Then they are freed from the power of the lords of death, their spirits can soar up to join the ancestors in the skies above and they become the sun and the moon.

The Maya placed great emphasis on remembering and revering the ancestors. As Mayan expert Dr David Pendergast had already told us:

> 'It was believed that the dead were in some way part of the living, that the people are linked to the past. They believed they were somehow protected by their ancestors, and that they could derive knowledge from them, at least in some indirect sense, if not in a direct way. And so the crystal skull and other skull representations can be seen as part of a very long tradition of keeping the ancestors close by.'

The Maya often kept the remains of their ancestors, usually buried beneath their houses. In some cases even the real heads, or rather the real skulls, of important ancestors were kept nearby, 'communed with' and seen as a source of great knowledge. If this was done with real skulls, we reasoned, then why not crystal skulls?

For the ancient Maya death was not something to be afraid of. Fear of death was to be overcome, and this could be done through a profound and deep understanding that life and death are mutually interdependent. The two are fundamentally interrelated, like the twins themselves, like the plant and the seed, like the united but opposing forces that run through all things. The Mayans knew that to die was to be reborn.

Again, I wondered whether the crystal skulls had anything to do with this belief, their transparent nature somehow symbolizing that death itself is not final but is something we can transcend. But for the Maya it went further than that. As the story of the hero twins shows, they believed that through reconnecting with the ancestors, they could somehow triumph over death itself and ultimately ascend to the highest heavens.

Anna Mitchell-Hedges had been told that her crystal skull represented the head of an ancient priest. Could it be that the skulls carved in stone or crystal represented much-revered ancestors with whom the Maya wished to reconnect?

The ancient Maya certainly attributed incredible powers to their ancestors, especially those believed to date back to the beginning of time. This could be seen in their description of the original writers of the *Popol Vuh*:

> *'They knew whether war would occur; everything they saw was clear to them. Whether there would be death, or whether there would be famine, or whether quarrels would occur, they knew for certain, since there was a place to see it ... [perhaps a crystal skull?]*
>
> *They saw, and could see instantly far, they succeeded in knowing all that there is in the World. When they looked, instantly they saw all around them and they contemplated in turn the arch of the heaven and the round face of the Earth. The things hidden, they saw all, without first having to move; at once they saw the World ... great was their wisdom.'*[12]

This extract reveals that the Maya were aware that the Earth was round many years before we in the West. An earlier part of the book tells that the divinatory gifts of the ancestors were taken away from their descendants by the gods who created them. For, according to the legend, the early people could see too far:

> *'Such were their gifts that the gods became uneasy, the gods then breathed upon their vision like a mirror and their vision was clouded, they were then able only to see what was nearby...'*[13]

This first part of the *Popol Vuh* also describes the dawn of time and the origins of humanity. The action begins when 12 gods get together and conceive the emergence of the Earth from water. Several attempts are made to make humans, but all fail until the humans recognize and understand their role, which is 'to name the name of their creators, to praise them and to be their providers and nurturers'.

Thus the *Popol Vuh* story spoke about the purpose of humanity. The gods had created humanity to reflect their own glory. The purpose of the people therefore was to give something back to the gods and to the forces of nature in recognition of this gift of life. They needed to honour the gods and serve them with 'good customs', both through remembering their own origins, and through prayer and sacrifice.

We had occasion to think of this relationship between man and nature as we travelled on to the ancient Mayan city of Yaxchilán, about 100 miles south of Palenque.

Our journey to Yaxchilán was a sobering experience. But it was neither the many armed road-blocks we encountered along the way nor the hair-raising boat journey across the Usamacinta river that bothered us. It was something else, something far more important.

For Palenque today stands in a fast receding jungle which is sadly and all too quickly being felled by local people and timber companies alike to make way for intensive agriculture and cattle-ranching. Although the rainforest immediately adjacent to the site is still intact, each year more and more trees in the adjoining forest are coming under the axe. As demand for Mexican beef grows, modern descendants of the ancient Maya find themselves forced off the land by rich landowners, as traditional subsistence farming is replaced by large cattle ranches. The greed of large landowners hungry for fast profits has made many of the indigenous people homeless. They, like the trees, are being cleared away in the name of progress.

This has led to the recent uprisings in the state of Chiapas as peasant farmers join forces to resist landowners who threaten the way of life they have enjoyed for millennia. The army roadblocks we met were designed to quell this unrest.

We were horrified when we opened a copy of *National Geographic* we had with us.[14] In it we found an aerial photograph of the surrounding area taken by a NASA satellite. We were shocked to find that the terrible decimation of the surrounding rainforest was clearly visible even from outer space. Just east and south of Palenque snakes the Usamacinta river, dividing Mexico from Guatemala. Even from thousands of miles above the Earth this border was vividly clear. The satellite picture showed the exact contours of the river because the Guatemalan side was a rich deep green, whilst the Mexican side was a pale empty yellow. This was because the Guatemalan side of the river was still rich with trees and vegetation, as yet untouched by the ravages of the chainsaw. But on the Mexican side there were only the stumps of trees, with field after field of nothing but grass, all newly created.

Gazing across the hillside today on what must have once been one of the most beautiful landscapes in the world, we saw only too many blackened stumps and branches, the charred remains of virgin forest. Under the leaden sky, the occasional lone ceiba tree, still alive, its trunk tall and solid after hundreds of years of growth, stood in solitary isolation. There was something mournful about these trees, as if they were left alone to grieve for the forest now gone.

I thought about the purpose of humanity being to give something back to the gods and the forces of nature and wondered what we were giving back with our plundering of the rainforests of Central America. What had happened to the reciprocal relationship the ancient Maya believed we were supposed to have with the gods and the forces of the natural world?

The ancient Maya, we had learned, would give back to the gods of the Earth by making an offering, through ritual, re-enactment, ceremony and sacrifice. They also believed they could strengthen their relationship with the gods by remembering and somehow connecting with their ancestors. The ancestors, like the earliest people, were seen as a source of the knowledge necessary to see not only into the past but also into the future. So, by giving something back to the gods and to the earliest ancestors, the Maya believed they could temporarily regain the psychic powers of their earliest ancestors. It seemed that skulls, and quite possibly even crystal skulls, were somehow involved in this process.

As Dr Linda Schele had told us, 'Blood was the mortar of Mayan religious practice.' For what more precious gift could be given than blood, the precious substance of life that assures existence? Again we could see parallels with Christian mythology. Christ sacrificed himself, giving of his blood, and at communion Christians partake of that sacrifice, drinking Christ's blood in the form of wine. In the Mayan practice of blood offering, however, blood was often ritually drawn from different parts of the body – from the tongue, the earlobes and even the genitals. These sacrificial rituals were reserved only for royalty, the priesthood and those of the highest nobility, and careful preparations, including privations of the body and soul, were necessary. Those making sacrifice separated themselves from the physical world through fasting and abstinence. The sweat lodge, a ritual steam bath, was often undertaken as a means of purification. Once purified and prepared, the participant hoped for the desired result of the sacrifice – the vision. And this is where a skull seemed to have come in, linking the vision seeker with the ancestors and the realm of sacred knowledge.

In Yaxchilán we were able to see in graphic detail stone carvings of this practice of blood-letting. The town had once been the site of some very fine carved limestone lintels, dating to around AD 725–770, though many of these have now been removed to the British Museum. Lintel 17 *(see Figure 16)* shows a royal male known as Bird Jaguar poised ready to pierce his penis with a long perforator. A sumptuously dressed woman,

Figure 16: Lintel 17 from Yaxchilán showing Bird Jaguar about to pierce his penis and Lady Balam-Ix piercing her tongue

Lady Balam-Ix, one of his wives, sits on her knees before him. They appear calm, dignified, absorbed in their activities. Lady Balam-Ix pulls a rope through her tongue, in a practice characteristic of female blood sacrifice. The blood which flows from the wound is collected on paper swabs that are placed in bowls then burned as offerings to the gods. Interestingly, Bird Jaguar is wearing a head-dress that features some kind of skull and skeletal serpent. Indeed, most of the other lintels in the series also depict the same skull and serpent head-dress. It seems that this was the ritual attire for those seeking vision.

Another feature of the ritual was the appearance of the vision serpent. This, it seems, was a representation of the spirit. Spirit is represented in many of the world's main religions as energy, movement, as a dynamic principle. Here the serpent represents this shifting energy.

The vision serpent can best be seen in Lintel 25 from Yaxchilán *(see Figure 17)*. This lintel shows Lady Xoc kneeling, wearing the obligatory skull and skeletal serpent head-dress and holding in her left hand the artefacts used in ritual blood sacrifice. In front of her we see the huge undulating body of the vision serpent, with large goggle eyes and scrolls of blood pouring from its mouth. The serpent wears the mask of Tlaloc, the god of water who was also linked with sacrifice and fertility. As the British Museum guidebook describes it:

'The sacrificial offering of blood conjures up a visionary manifestation of Yat-Balam, founding ancestor of the dynasty of Yaxchilán ... this ancestral spirit emerges from the gaping front jaws of a huge double-headed [vision] serpent rearing above Lady Xoc. Now alone, she gazes upward at the apparition she has brought forth. In her left hand she bears a blood-letting bowl containing other instruments of sacrifice, a sting-ray spine and an obsidian lancet.' [15]

But what the guidebook fails to mention is what Lady Xoc appears to be holding in her right hand. Either held in her hand or somehow suspended just above her right wrist we could clearly see a human skull, perhaps even a crystal one. Indeed, it seemed that the apparition of the vision serpent, from whose mouth the image of the great ancestor was appearing, was actually emerging from the skull itself. Whilst we could not be entirely sure from the drawing that the serpent was not also, or even instead, emerging from the bowl of blood on the ground, this beautifully carved lintel certainly appeared to depict an ancient Mayan seeing a vision

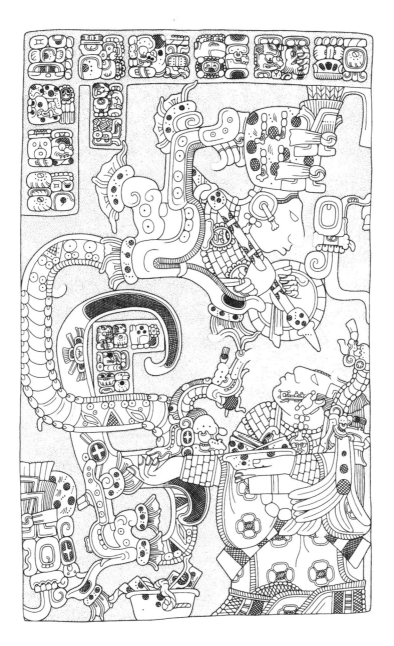

*Figure 17: Lintel 25 from Yaxchilán showing Lady Xoc
having a vision emerging from a skull*

emerging from a skull, and quite possibly a crystal skull at that. Also, the fact that this skull appears at waist height indicates that it was in the middle world, in normal waking reality.

We were amazed. This notion of visions emerging from a skull was certainly consistent with everything we had seen or heard about the various crystal skulls we had visited, with Carole Wilson's channelling of information from the Mitchell-Hedges skull, and with Nick Nocerino's and others' claims that the crystal skulls could still present people with visions. At the very least the crystal skulls were commonly believed to be able to facilitate a change in consciousness in the onlooker and all those who have worked with them on a regular basis today claim they can bring about visions. Perhaps Lintel 25 from Yaxchilán was a picture of Lady Xoc, all those years ago, using a crystal skull to see into other dimensions. I suspect we shall never know for sure.

But what was now clear was that the image of the skull was important to the ancient Maya. They had a completely different attitude towards death and it seemed that the skull was also associated with their quest for vision. But, as we were to discover, this was not all the skull meant to the Maya.

15. THE SKULL AND THE ANCIENT CALENDAR

For the early Maya self-sacrifice and the image of the skull seem to have been related mostly with the quest for vision and a desire to reconnect with the ancestors, who were imbued with divine wisdom and an ability to see all things. But it seems that later the Maya became involved in other forms of ritual and sacrifice that were sometimes far less pleasant than mere penis piercing and tongue blood-letting, and again the image of the skull seems to have been involved.

Archaeologists believe the later, Toltec-dominated Maya, like the Toltecs themselves, placed far greater emphasis on the practice of human sacrifice. There is some dispute amongst archaeologists as to whether the Mayans were willing or unwilling victims of this. Many believe that the practice of self-sacrifice, which appeared to have started quite voluntarily amongst the early Maya, later became corrupted and was imposed involuntarily by the Toltecs, who came to dominate what was left of early Mayan culture after the Classic Maya disappeared. What does seem very strange is that, whether voluntary or involuntary, it was generally the healthiest young males, the potential co-creators of healthy future generations, that were the main victims of human sacrifice. Some have joked that this may be why the Mayan civilization didn't last – but there again, it wouldn't explain why they disappeared quite so suddenly.

Some of the best known Mayan stone carvings of skulls are to be found at Chichen Itzá, the largest and most famous Mayan city in the Yucatán. This has the greatest number of skull-related images of any Mayan site, images that were created during the last decadent phase of Toltec-dominated Mayan history, an era of full-scale human sacrifice. One of these carvings is found along the edge of the ball court. It seems that all Meso-american cities featured a ball court where a ritual ball game was played out, apparently in symbolic re-enactment of the struggle of the great hero twins of the *Popol Vuh* legend. According to most archaeologists, the ancient Mesoamericans took their version of this game even more seriously than do today's football fans. For it is widely believed that once the game was over one of the teams was sacrificed by being decapitated. Whether this was the losing or the winning team remains uncertain. Many Mayan descendants today do say, however, that this whole theory is a load of euro-centric, anti-native, racist propaganda perpetuated since the days of the early Spanish arrival in Central America, and they may well be correct.

What we do know for sure is that on the walls that surround the ball court at Chichen Itzá there is a stone-carved bas-relief that depicts two groups of contenders and in the centre a ball with a skull on it, with blood spurting from its mouth *(see Figure 18)*. This is assumed to symbolize the fate that awaits the sacrificed team. To the right of the skull-ball kneels a figure, presumably one of the players, who has been decapitated and has streams of blood, represented by snakes,coming from his neck. On the other side of the skull-ball stands another player, a knife in one hand and the disembodied head in the other. All the figures wear elaborate costumes, presumably the ritual attire associated with the game, some featuring skulls emerging from serpents, worn on the waistband, or *palma* as it was known. Again, this presumably indicated the fate that awaited one or other team.

Next to the ball court at Chichen Itzá lies a large stone platform decorated on all sides with row upon row of stone-carved skulls *(see colour plate no. 21)*. Like the skull racks used by the Aztecs, these stone platforms were known as *tzompantli* and certainly the one at Chichen Itzá, lying close to the ball court, is thought to have been used as a repository for the decapitated heads of the sacrificed players.

But it is not entirely clear what the purpose of such sacrifice was. Some have suggested that for the Maya, as for the Aztecs, the blood from the sacrificial victim helped nourish the sun, and certainly the timing and significance of the game do seem to have been related to the movements of the sun. For it is only on a particular day of the year that the sun's rays pass through the stone circle through which the players also had to pass the skull-ball.

But we should not let the Mayans' occasional bouts of brutality fool us into thinking they were unintelligent, for they certainly were not. The

Figure 18: Stone carvings of sacrificial victims of the ball game on the ball court at Chichen Itzá

Mayans are generally thought to have been a peace-loving people and even the practice of human sacrifice, if it did occur after the ball game, had far more to it than that.

Not far from the ball court and stone *tzompantli* at Chichen Itzá is to be found a great round astronomical observatory, or 'Caracol' *(see colour plate no. 20)*. The striking thing about this observatory is that it looks just like a modern one. As von Däniken correctly put it:

> *'The circular edifice rises far above the jungle on three terraces; inside it a spiral staircase leads to the uppermost observation post; in the dome there are hatches and openings directed at the stars and giving an impressive picture of the firmament at night.'* [1]

Von Däniken is also correct in noticing that 'the observation posts in the observatory at Chichen Itzá' are 'not directed at the brightest stars', nor even at any known position of the sun. For it is now widely believed that this observatory was used primarily for tracking the movements of the planet Venus. Indeed, the shafts from the observatory point not only up at the stars but also down to the nearby ball court, and so both the timing of the game and the symbolic significance of what happened to the souls of the sacrificial victims were related not only to the movements of the sun but also the stars and planets, Venus in particular. It seems that the victims' souls were seen as ascending into the highest heavens, just like the hero twins of legend.

Quite whether any crystal skulls were involved in the practice of human sacrifice, however, remained unclear. But we did discover another, and perhaps more likely, connection between crystal skulls, the ancient Mayans' use of skull imagery and their ancient calendar.

As the observatory at Chichen Itzá had indicated, the ancient Maya were, above all, experts in astronomy, mathematics and calendrics. They had a very different view of the world from our own and had a very complex idea of their place in the universe. They were great psychics and seers, and whilst they were obsessed with ritual, sacrifice and death, they were also incredibly scientific in their stargazing, mathematical and calendrical activities. The Mayan cosmos was a universe not only of great and terrifying gods, but also of accurate mathematical measurement and highly precise calendrics all based on the movements of the planets and the stars, and all geared towards one single aim – predicting the future.

The ancient Maya were quite literally religiously obsessed with numbers, mathematics and timekeeping. One of their most remarkable achievements was their use of 'zero'. This concept enabled them to handle large numbers with ease in a way that was never achieved even by their contemporaries in Europe, never mind the great ancient civilizations of Europe such as the Greeks and Romans. Indeed, the Mayans' expertise in mathematics was such that they are now widely credited with having invented the concept of zero, on which, incidentally, our modern computers are based. These use a binary system of mathematics in which all operations, no matter how complex, are broken down into the numbers one and zero.

To the ancient Maya numbers were not just abstract concepts used for accounting or measuring quantity. Instead each number was thought to possess a quality or spirit of its own, a quality that mirrored and celebrated the animating processes that go on in the world of spirits. To the Maya, numbers were manifestations of the spirits, the gods and the energies of the universe, and their prime function was for use in the highly complicated world of Mayan calendrics.

For the Mayans were in possession of a calendrical system far more complex and accurate than our own. It was a system whose primary purpose was prophecy and prediction. So it not only told them what day it was, but also what would happen on any particular day – and it was stunningly accurate. Based on the movements of the planets and stars, it could not only predict solar and lunar eclipses that the Mayans could actually see, but also eclipses that might be happening well out of sight on the other side of the world. The calendar was so sophisticated that it even accurately predicted eclipses that have happened recently, over 1,000 years after the collapse of the Mayan civilization. In fact it is now widely believed that the Maya were even able to predict the collapse of their own civilization and the subsequent arrival of the Europeans in Central America.

The Mayan calendar also stretched back in time to well before their own civilization arose. Some Mayan hieroglyphs record dates even as far back as 400 million years ago.[2] The Maya considered their calendar a gift from the earliest people who could see everything. It was nothing less than a gift from the gods.

The actual system was based on the movements of the sun, the moon, the planets and the stars, and especially on the movements of the planet Venus and the Pleiades constellation. For the Mayans, it seemed, had knowledge about the universe that modern astronomers are only just beginning to grasp, and concepts of time and space that modern physicists are only just beginning to 'discover'.

Unlike our Gregorian calendar, which simply numbers the days in linear or chronological order, in terms of how many days, months and years before or after Christ, the Mayans had around 17 different types of calendar, 17 different ways of deciding which day it was. Almost all of these different calendars related to a different planet, star or constellation. What day it was on a particular calendar therefore told you where that particular planet or star was on that day in relation to the Earth. So, rather than being simple linear calendars, each was cyclical in nature, and all the calendars together formed a complex set of concentric and interlocking circles or spheres, just like the movements of the planets round the Earth. The name of each day told you not only when but also where you were on each of the different 'cycles of time', therefore what day it was showed where the Earth was in relation to other bodies in the universe.

In our modern view of the world, time and space are two completely different dimensions, but in the Mayan view there was no such distinction. Time and space were inextricably linked. Like the hero twins, or life and death, they were simply different aspects of the same dimension. This is a difficult concept for us to grasp, but is useful in helping us understand the cyclical nature of Mayan calendrics and how they believed they were able to see into the future.

Perhaps fortunately for us, in day-to-day life the Maya tended to use only three of their basic calendars: the 365-day solar calendar, or 'vague year', the 260-day sacred or divinatory calendar, usually known as the *tzolkin*, and the incredibly long 'Long Count'. The solar calendar was probably the most secular and is the one we can most easily relate to, as it is the most similar to our calendar year. It recorded the approximately 365-day cycle of the Earth around the sun, though it was divided into 18 months, each 20 days long, leaving five days left over, which were generally regarded as 'inauspicious' or, roughly speaking, 'unlucky' days.

The number of days of this solar calendar are embodied in stone in the great pyramid, or 'El Castillo', at Chichen Itzá. This has precisely the right number of steps to correspond with the number of days in a solar year. On four of its sides it has 91 steps, adding up to 364, and the crowning temple on top brings the total to 365. This pyramid also marks the spring and autumn equinoxes, when a great serpent's shadow, presumably representing Kukulcan or Quetzalcoatl, appears undulating down its steps.

How the 260-day sacred calendar, or *tzolkin*, related to the solar calendar can best be understood by the analogy of interlocking cogs on two separate wheels. Unlike the other calendars, the sacred calendar does not seem to relate directly to the movement of any known planet or star. It has been suggested that this is in fact a summary, an interpretation of the combined meaning of the movements of all the universal bodies added together. This would certainly explain why it was often referred to as 'the cycle of cycles' (*see Figure 19*).

But whatever the underlying principle of the *tzolkin*, its primary purpose was to give meaning to each of the days and to tell people what they should do on any given day. For each day also had a particular meaning, including whether or not it was a good day or bad day, a lucky day or an unlucky day. This is slightly oversimplifying it, but the point is that the configuration of the planets and stars on any particular day had a significance that conferred upon the day its own specific characteristics. The day on which you were born was highly significant as it determined your role in life, whether you would become, say, a craftsman, orator or priest. The *tzolkin* also told people what kind of day it would be in everyday life and advised them accordingly. Thus the sacred calendar dictated the cycle of rituals and ceremonies required on each day throughout the sacred year.

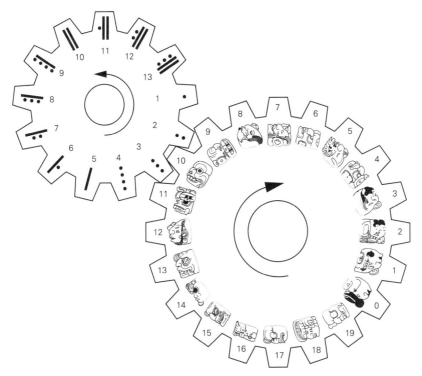

Figure 19: Cog wheels illustrating the days and months of the 260-day sacred Mayan calendar

One particularly important occasion was the end of any 52-year period, or Calendar Round, the day on which both the 365 days of the solar calendar and the 260 days of the sacred calendar completed an entire cycle and each returned to the same start day. On this day the ancient Maya carried out a ceremony known as 'the start of the new fires'. This was a highly sacred and important ceremony as the ancient Maya believed that at the end of each Calendar Round, there was the possibility of the world ending if the new fires were not started and the accompanying ceremonies were not performed properly.

Author-historians Adrian Gilbert and Maurice Cotterell have suggested that the crystal skulls may have had an important function to play in the start of the new fires ceremony. In their book *The Mayan Prophecies*, they suggest that the unusual optical properties of the crystal skulls may have been used as an integral part of the ceremonies that marked the start of the new fires.[3] Given that the Mitchell-Hedges skull is known to be capable of starting a fire itself from sunlight, this struck us as perfectly possible. Gilbert and Cotterell suggested the mysterious chac-mool fig-urines, such as the one at Chichen Itzá *(see colour plate no. 31)*, might also have been involved.

Adrian Gilbert suggests that when the right day came, the crystal skull may have been placed either on top of one of the pyramids or on the flat-topped receptacle held on the belly of the famous chac-mool figurine at Chichen Itzá and other similar sites. When the sun rose to a particular point, at midday, its rays would have struck the back of the skull's head at just the right angle to be focused into a beam of light coming out of the skull's mouth, a beam of sufficient intensity to start the new fires.

Like the crystal skulls, no one really knows what these mysterious chac-mool figurines were actually used for. They are often thought to represent Kukulcan or Quetzalcoatl, and most archaeologists believe they were used to hold the still-beating hearts torn out during human sacrifice cere-monies. Given that the real Mayan descendants we later spoke to believed no such sacrifices really took place, but were invented by the Spanish sim-ply to discredit their traditions and label the natives as ignorant savages only worthy of slaughtering, then this alternative function of holding crystal skulls may well have been be the case.

The sixteenth-century chronicler Diego de Landa reported the ancient fire ceremonies in some detail and his account also raises the possibility that a crystal skull may have been involved. In his book *The Relacion* he states that:

> *'They set their banners on top of the temple and below in the court set each of them his "idols" on leaves of trees brought for this purpose; then making the new fire they began to burn their incense at many points and make offerings.'*[4]

Whether or not a crystal skull was really involved in marking the end of each Calendar Round, we did come across another Mayan use of skull imagery in calendrics that also appeared to relate to the crystal skulls.

The Mayans believed what kind of day it was was determined by which of the gods or 'day lords' was represented on that day of the calen-dar. In the Mayan view of the world, the gods and the days were not real-ly separate entities at all, and the same word was used to describe both the god and the day.

Indeed, the lack of distinction between science, religion and mathe-matics in the Mayan world view was such that gods were not only used to describe which day it was, but different gods were also associated with different numbers. Thus each of the gods of the upper realms was not only a day-name but also represented a number, and vice versa. Mayan mathematics was so sacred to its ancient practitioners that gods, numbers, days, and in some cases even months and years, were all seen as different aspects of the same spiritual essence.

Trying, with some effort, to get our heads around this, we turned our attention to the sacred Mayan 260-day calendar. We found that the divine year, just like the Aztec sacred year, was made up of 13 months that were each 20 days long. Yet again, we seemed to be coming across the sacred number 13. As well as 13 crystal skulls, there are 13 gods in the Mayans' upper world, the very gods who were believed to rule over the days; in fact, the very gods who were believed to rule over time itself.

One of these gods was the great lord of death, 'God A' himself. He represented the number 10, or *lahun* in Mayan, meaning 'to be destroyed, or abandoned, or completion'. What surprised us was that in the sacred Mayan calendar, the god of death and the number 10 were usually represented by a fleshless human skull, complete with a detachable lower jaw, just like the Mitchell-Hedges crystal skull.

The Mayans actually had at least two different systems of numbering, much as we have both the Arabic numbering system and occasionally use the old Roman numerals. The most frequently used, and some believe the more secular of the two, was the 'bar and dot' system. Here, the number zero was represented by an oval, or saucer-shaped figure, that many compare to a shell, a seed, an egg or even a symbolic image of the cosmos. Like these objects it represents a potentiality. Unsown, the seed remains a seed and unfertilized, the egg remains an egg. But sown or fertilized, when combined with the energy of complementary forces each is transformed, it becomes alive, capable of recreating itself again and again. Thus whilst it is nothing it also contains infinite possibility. In the same way, the number zero, combined with other numbers, makes the infinite possible.

The Mayans believed that this combining of complementary energies was the principle of all life, indeed, the principle through which all life was first created. Zero is the void out of which the totality of the cosmos was created, the nothingness out of which everything else unfolds. It signifies infinite potential. Zero exists in relationship with every other number and combination of numbers. Alone, it is nothing, but combined with other numbers, a symbolic marriage occurs that can lead to an almost infinite number of possibilities. The other numbers with which it is combined in turn therefore also contain the spirit of nothing. Thus zero represents the ultimate power of transformation. The power to create the infinite out of nothingness and ultimately transform it back again to nothing.

In the Mayan bar and dot system of numbering, the other numbers are represented quite simply as follows: one was represented by a dot, two by adding another dot alongside, three by a row of three dots side by side, four by a row of four dots, five by a straight line, six by a line with a dot above, seven by a line with two dots above, and so on up to 10, represented by two lines one above the other, and so on up to 20, represented by a zero symbol with a dot above *(see Figure 20)*.

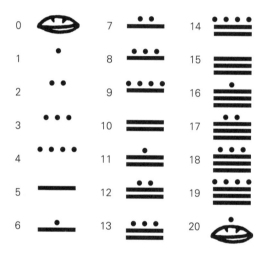

Figure 20: The Mayan 'bar and dot' numbering system

But the Mayans' other system of numbering, generally considered the more sacred of the two, was the 'head-variant' system. Here the 13 numbers from zero to 12 were each represented by a hieroglyph showing the head of one of the 13 gods of the upper world. In this numbering system, for example, the god of zero, Mi, is shown with his hand over his jaw. Dr Linda Schele has suggested that this may also represent a particularly unpleasant form of sacrifice in which one's lower jaw was removed. The absence of the lower jaw in this hieroglyph certainly suggests that 'zero' was unable to speak.

But the most interesting number for us in our investigation of crystal skulls was 10, *lahun*, often represented by the hieroglyph of a fleshless

0. mi	5. ho	10. lahun	15. holahun
1. hun	6. uac	11. buluc	16. uaclahun
2. ca	7. uuc	12. lahca	17. uuclahun
3. ox	8. uaxac	13. oxlahun	18. uaxaclahun
4. can	9. bolon	14. canlahun	19. bolonlahun

Figure 21: The Mayan 'head-variant' system, showing the number 10, lahun, as fleshless human skull with detachable jaw

human skull, complete with a detachable jaw *(see Figure 21)*. This god was known as the patron god of numbers. Furthermore, as one of the 20 day-names, he appeared 13 times in each sacred calendar year.

Whilst the highly sacred head-variant system comprised only the heads of the 13 gods, day-names or numbers, the Mayans were still able to use it to count well above the number 13. They needed to do this, if for no other reason than their sacred calendar was comprised of months that were actually 20 days long. Indeed, their whole numerical system was based on counting to 20. It was a vigesimal system. In much the same way that our modern numerical system is a decimal system, based on counting up to 10 and then repeating the pattern of one to nine, their system was based on counting up to 20 and then repeating the numbers one to 19.

The Mayans used the detachable lower jaw from the head glyph for 10 to convert lower numbers to higher numbers, in much the same way as we use the figure 1 to convert, say, 3 to 13, thereby giving a total of 20 numbers, including the god for zero.

So the skull, whilst representing the nothingness of death, also contained a potentiality. Like our number 10, its lower jaw could be used to transform mathematical possibilities. It could be used to convert lower numbers to higher numbers.

And so it seemed that the symbolic point of the image of a skull with a detachable lower jaw was that it represented a means of transition from a lower level to a higher level. Like death itself, it offered the possibility of moving from a lower level of normal everyday waking reality, or consciousness, to higher levels of consciousness. For the Maya believed there were higher levels of thought and consciousness in the universe, their upper world, the domain of the gods. And the skull represented the means by which they could get there.

Here it is worth remembering that it was only after they had symbolically defeated death, only after they had overcome their fear of death and reunited with their ancestors, that the great hero twins of the *Popol Vuh* were able to defeat the lower worlds of death and ascend into the highest heavens. Indeed, Hunahpu was said to have battled specifically with the god of zero on the way. So, by defeating the 'nothingness' of death the hero twin is able to ascend beyond the nine levels of the underworld and achieve the 10 of death, the aspect of death that contains the power to transform the lower numbers, or levels of consciousness and existence, into the higher numbers, or higher levels of consciousness of the upper world.

Thus, the symbol of a skull with a detachable jaw, which represents both the god of death and the number 10 in the Mayan head-variant system of numbering, is also a symbol of the power of transition to the higher levels, to the higher levels of consciousness above and beyond the simple lower and human worlds. The skull is the image that enables you to escape from the lower physical world and join the world of the gods, the spirits, and the ancestors, to see above and beyond and into the nature of all things. It therefore, presumably also allows you to see into both the past and the future.

Suddenly, it seemed we had an explanation as to why the maker of the Mitchell-Hedges skull would have gone to the trouble of creating a separate jaw-bone. The Mitchell-Hedges crystal skull may well have had something to do with the number 10 of the Mayans' sacred head-variant system of numbering, used by the Mayan priesthood to count the days, and a powerful symbol of transformation. Take away the jaw and we have a direct reference to zero, to nothing, to death, but also to potentiality; add the jaw and we have the number 10 that takes us beyond the nine levels of the underworld to the great beyond where the heavenly realms begin.

Could this somehow relate to the legend of the singing skulls? Once the skulls were complete with a jaw-bone they were transformed, as symbolized by the number 13, they were no longer earth-bound, connected with the lower-world, but were connected with the heavenly realms. No longer governed by physical laws, but by the limitless possibilities of the spirit world, this connection with the heavens made them complete and enabled them to 'sing'.

It also seemed that the image of the skull might refer back to primordial history. It appeared to be a symbolic reminder of the 12 other gods of Mayan legend who created the Earth, and of the incredible psychic powers of the first ancestors. What we wondered was whether, as well as working on a symbolic level, Mayan numbers also referred back to actual events. Could it be that the other heads of the counting system related back to the creation of all 13 original crystal skulls? Were these head-variant numbers a sign that there were 12 other crystal skulls, the one with the detachable jaw-bone being number 10 in a series of 13?

Certainly it was clear that the image of a skull, particularly one with a detachable jaw, was an integral part of the ancient Mayan calendrical system, but was this really a crystal skull, and if so what did it mean? Why was it that the ancient Maya had a day, as well as a god, named 'death'? Was this perhaps the day on which the sacred calendar told the ancient Maya to use a crystal skull? I was curious to find out.

We had already learned that the calendar was so important to the ancient Maya that on each of their carved stelae and alongside each of their beautiful works of art, they had left complex hieroglyphic inscriptions giving incredibly detailed and accurate dates as to when exactly the event depicted had, or would, occur. So I looked again at the picture of Lady Xoc from Yaxchilán apparently seeing a vision emerging from what looked like a crystal skull. The date for this event was quite clearly given as '9.13.17.15.12.5 eb 15 mac' on the Mayan calendar, which translated as AD 28 October 709. But the original Mayan date did not seem to bear any clear relation to the day-names we had just learned about. Then I realized that I had forgotten about another integral part of the Mayan calendar – the all-important Long Count.

Only the last two numbers on Long Count inscriptions (in this case 5 eb and 15 mac) related to the short 260-day sacred and 365-day solar cycles. The other numbers on the Long Count were concerned with far longer periods, up to several thousand years, which actually relate to the movements of the planet Venus. But this Long Count is not only concerned with the regular cycle of the planet Venus around the Earth, which takes on average 584 days, but also with its overall cycle in relation to the Earth's own axis of rotation, a cycle which takes place over a period of thousands of years. The regular cycles of the planet Venus around the Earth, normal Venusian years, show marginal fluctuations in duration between 581 and 587 days. Whilst these fluctuations in themselves were of some interest to the Mayans, they were actually far more interested in the reason behind these small variations, which was that there are actually very small, almost imperceptible, shifts in the relationship between the plane of rotation of the planet Venus and the rotational axis of the Earth itself. Until very recently our own astronomers had not even noticed this, but the Maya were absolutely obsessed with this overall 'Great Cycle of Venus', the relationship between the plane of axis of the regular cycles of Venus and the rotational axis of the Earth itself. All their calendrical dates were ultimately related to this Great Cycle, which they tracked back into history well before their own time, and even accurately predicted well into the future, well beyond the date at which their own civilization so mysteriously collapsed.

The many Long Count dates the Maya left behind on their great monuments have now been translated into our own Gregorian calendar dates by expert Mayanists such as Eric Thompson[5] and an incredible pattern has emerged. For it has now been established that the original start date on this Venusian calendar, the day 'zero' on the Mayan Long Count, corresponds to our Gregorian date of 13 August 3114 BC. This was when the bright planet of Venus first appeared over the Earth's horizon, signifying the birth of the current cosmos. One surprising thing is that the night before, the setting sun would have precisely aligned with the stone skull of Teotihuacán, so perhaps this really was the date when that great city was founded?

Another interesting thing about these Great Cycles of Venus is that again the image of the skull is involved. The ancient Mayan manuscript known as the *Codex Copsi* shows different aspects of Venus (*see Figure 22, overleaf*). As Dr Karl Taube explained:

'The planet is personified in these images and its head is shown as a skull with goggly eyes. Venus is shown spearing particular individuals which represent different things that are threatened by particular aspects of Venus. On the top [right], for example, we see the goddess of water, Chalchiuhtlicue, being speared. This tells the reader that something terrible is going to happen to water at a particular time, perhaps a drought. Down below is the maize god being speared, quite probably referring to the destruction of the maize crop. And so with these Venus cycles the ancient Maya were able to foretell, or at least thought they were able to foretell, what would happen each time Venus "died".'

For the Maya, like the Aztecs, also believed that the world has been created and destroyed several times. They believed that they inhabited the 'Fourth World', or 'Fourth Sun'. For the Maya, it was not only humans that the gods had made several times, but entire previous worlds, or epochs of time, each ruled over by a different god. But each of these worlds had been destroyed by one cataclysm or another.

According to most ancient Mayan accounts, the first world was destroyed by fire from the skies, perhaps referring to volcanic or meteorite activity, the second world was destroyed by the sun, presumably meaning drought, and the third world by water, presumably meaning floods and perhaps coinciding with the Biblical reference to the great deluge in the story of Noah and the Ark.

But the really interesting thing is that although the precise cause for the end of each world varies slightly in different accounts, unlike the Aztecs, the Maya were able to give very precise dates as to when each of these worlds had been destroyed. For the end of each of these previous worlds coincided with the end of each of the previous Great Cycles of Venus.

The start and nature of the current age is well recorded in Mayan manuscripts, the start date being 13 August 3114 BC. All of the Long Count

Figure 22: A section of the ancient Mayan Codex Copsi *showing the Venus god, with a skull for a head, spearing various other gods; thought to represent the destruction of previous worlds*

calendar dates relate back to this date of 'zero' – the last time the calendar was 'reset'. Most Mayan codices refer to the current generation of humans as the 'people of maize', the people who occupy the fourth and quite probably final epoch of humanity. Before the present generation was created, there was a time of great darkness. The newly created people, who are described as being both black and white, left the place of origin known as Tulan. For this was the night when the first people waited anxiously before the first dawn for the sun to rise. Then they saw 'Venus the star which was the guide and herald of the sun, and feeling very happy they burned their incense.'[6]

Current astronomical information does indicate that on the morning of 13 August 3114 BC the Venus 'star' would indeed have preceded the sun. Furthermore, it has also been calculated that the Pleiades would have crossed the meridian of the night sky just before dawn, just before Venus would for the first time in its 1,366,560-day Long Count cycle actually precede the sun. And so many believe the ancient Maya would also have seen the Pleiades as the great herald of Venus. Just as Venus announced the dawning of the sun over the new and current era, so it would have been the Pleiades which in turn announced the dawning of the current Great Cycle of Venus.

The Pleiades were strongly associated with the greatest of Mayan sky gods, known as Itzamna. He was seen as the head of the Mayan pantheon, and many believe he was the prototype of the later Kukulcan or the Aztec god Quetzalcoatl, the founder of all of the civilizations of Central America. Itzamna ruled the heavens and was also the god of what the Maya believed was the all-important Earth's axis.

The interesting thing about this god is that there also appears to have been some kind of connection between him and the image of a skull, quite possibly a crystal skull.

We came across a link between this god of the Earth's axis and the image of a skull and were immediately reminded of 'the voice of the skull' speaking through Carole Wilson, predicting that the Earth would soon shift from its axis. When we consulted Mesoamerican expert Dr Karl Taube, he showed us a painting on the side of an ancient Mayan vase *(see black-and-white plate no. 45)*. Karl commented:

'What we see here is Itzamna, the god of the world's axis, sitting in front of a package. And what this package seems to be is an open sacred bundle containing a skull inside. It could well be that many of these sacred bundles contain skulls, not necessarily actual human skulls, but skulls carved in rare materials.

'It could well be that one of these skull-like figures is what they put inside these sacred bundles, as a secret item of treasure... Some of the material they probably kept inside these bundles would be ashes of revered ancestors, jade carvings and perhaps even crystal skulls.'

As Karl explained, the ancient Maya had what they called 'sacred bundles'. These were bundles in which they put their most sacred objects, objects believed to date back to the beginning of time itself, to the very start of creation, to the very earliest people. These objects were highly secret. Only a few select people of noble lineage were allowed access to them. These were known as the 'god-bearers' as they were the only ones who were allowed to look after the sacred objects and to carry them around. Each tribe carried these objects safely concealed within their bundles from place to place as they migrated.

This is a practice still carried out today by some Mayan descendants in the highlands of Guatemala and also by the Pueblo and other Plains Indians of North America. The Pueblo call them 'clan bundles' and, like the Maya, are known to have carried out 'bundle ceremonies'. During these ceremonies the Plains Indians are thought to have used their sacred bundles to locate more buffalo or bring rain. Like the Maya, they believed that the sacred objects, or information, could only be extracted from the bundle in the right way and by the right person at the right time. If it was done in the wrong way, or by the wrong person at the wrong time, the Maya believed that the world might end. For because the objects went right back to the origins, to the ancestors, they were sources of great and fertile power, but they were also associated with death.

I wondered whether this image of Itzamna sitting in front of what seemed to be a crystal skull actually showed him inputting rather than extracting information. After all, why should the god of all gods need to extract information from anywhere? And the idea of a god inputting information into a crystal skull would certainly be more consistent with the original legend of the crystal skulls, which said they were containers of great knowledge.

But what might this information have been? Could it have had anything to do with the passage of the Great Cycles of time? The Mayans believed that there had been great death and destruction at the end of each of the previous worlds and, as we discovered, the date for the end of the current world has now been finally decoded. This date is definite and alarmingly soon. It translates into our Gregorian calendar as just before sunset, Central American time, 21 December 2012!

Quite what will actually happen on that day none of us knows for sure. But certainly the ancient Maya accurately predicted every solar and lunar eclipse. We also know, from modern computer-aided astronomical calculations, that, as the ancient Mayan calendar predicts, just before sunset on 21 December 2012 Venus will indeed sink below the western horizon and at the same time the Pleiades will rise above the horizon in the east. Symbolically speaking, we will see the death of Venus and the birth of the

Pleiades. In Mayan terminology the current world, or Great Cycle of time, lorded over by Venus, will end. The current age, epoch or 'Sun' will die. The question for the Maya at the end of each cycle was whether or not a new world would begin.

The Mayans' concept of Great Cycles of time that came to an abrupt end may seem fanciful, but their belief that previous worlds had been destroyed is now supported by scientific evidence. Scientists at Cambridge University, led by Simon Conway Morris, Professor of Evolutionary Palaeobiology, have recently uncovered evidence from the fossil record that 'life seems to have been inscribed, erased and written again four or five times since the Cambrian period'.[7] What they have found is that at several different epochs of history life has flourished and then been almost instantaneously wiped from the face of the Earth. Each time this has happened has been followed by a period of millions of years when the Earth has been devoid of all life.

Whether another of these periods really is imminent we shall probably have to wait and see, but clearly the image of the skull was intimately involved in the Mayans making these predictions. Was this some of the secret knowledge that the crystal skulls were said to contain? We wondered whether perhaps the skulls had a message for humanity that was connected to this prophecy in some way?

In the meantime, however, all we could do was to continue our investigation to find out where the crystal skulls had really come from. It was time to turn to the scientific tests which were now due to take place at the British Museum.

Figure 23, overleaf: The sky at sunset in Central America on 21 December 2012, showing the death of Venus and the birth of the Pleiades

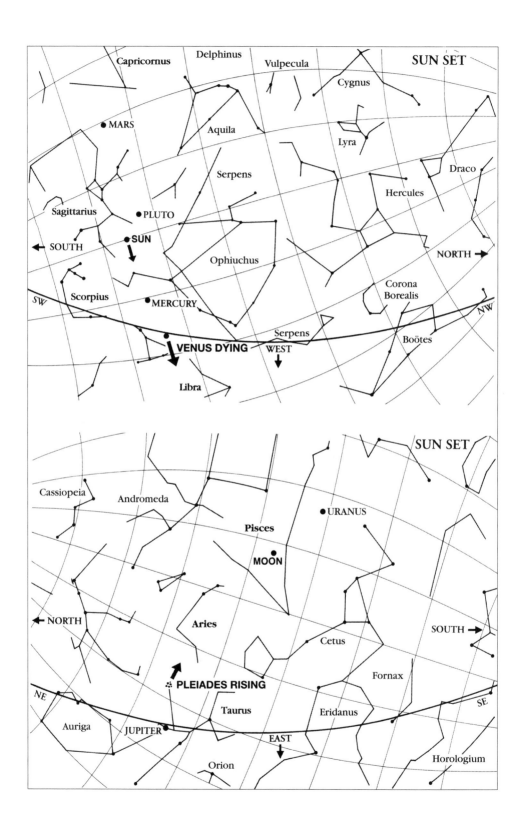

16. THE BRITISH MUSEUM TESTS

Back in Britain, Ceri and I sat down and reviewed where we had got to in our investigation of the origins and purpose of the crystal skulls. Clearly the image of the skull had been important to the ancient Maya. It was associated with their quest for vision, it was an integral part of their sacred numbering system and calendar, it was linked with the god of Venus, the god of the Earth's axis and even the Mayans' prophecies about the end of the world.

We had also discovered that the Mayans not only produced highly stylized works of art like most of the crystal skulls, but also highly realistic ones, akin even to the Mitchell-Hedges skull. Indeed, we had found evidence to suggest that far from being simple peasants incapable of making anatomically accurate crystal skulls, the ancient Mayans had mathematical, astronomical and calendrical skills to rival, and even surpass, our own. But we still had no firm evidence that the ancient Maya really were in possession of any crystal skulls.

While there was some evidence to suggest that the ancient Mayans could have produced crystal skulls, there was also evidence that they could have been created by the later Aztecs and Mixtecs of central and highland Mexico. These people were known to have carved some beautiful objects from crystal and were prolific in their use of skull imagery. Most archaeologists seemed to be of the view that if the crystal skulls were of ancient Mesoamerican origin then they were more likely to have come from either of these two later cultures than from the Mayans. Yet again, some archaeologists doubted that the crystal skulls were of Central American origin at all. They believed them to be nothing more than modern fakes.

Whatever their origins, we were certainly hearing of more and more crystal skulls. Josh Shapiro had told us that he knew of three life-size skulls that belonged to Joke (pronounced 'Hoka') Van Dieten, a woman who lived in Florida. One of these was called 'The Jesuit' on account of its purported connection with the Jesuits of Italy and possibly even St Francis of Assisi. Another was said to have come from Russia and Joke believed it to be over 1,000 years old. But the one that interested Josh the most was called 'E.T.' on account of its decisively non-human looking features and its supposed 'extra-terrestrial origins'. However, Josh admitted that he had no absolute proof about where any of these crystal skulls had really come from.

Indeed, he warned that we must be wary as there were now several modern crystal skulls around that had been recently manufactured not only in Germany and Mexico, as we had discovered, but also in Brazil! Though these were generally nothing like as beautifully crafted as the really ancient crystal skulls and carried little or no 'psychic energy', some people were now trying to pass them off as the genuine article.

Nick Nocerino had told us that he believed that there were now a number of fake skulls on the market. He explained that when he had first started looking into crystal skulls there had been very few around. 'But now,' he said, 'there seem to be more and more, and the majority of these are recently made fakes. They're showing up all over the place.'

Nick said that a man called Damien Quinn was importing crystal skulls from Brazil into the USA on a regular basis. Quinn himself made no claim for the ancient origin of the skulls he sold, but he could obviously not give the same guarantee for the people he sold them to. As Nick had been keen to point out, there was nothing to stop people buying skulls then burying them, digging them up and claiming that they were ancient artefacts.

Meantime there were rumours of other skulls in South America. Sammy Mitchell-Hedges had been contacted by a family in Argentina who claimed to have a crystal skull just like hers, but they would not allow her to pass on their details for fear of robbery if the information became public. Apparently there was another crystal skull in the northern part of Peru that was held by the Campa people, living quietly in the jungle. According to this rumour the skull was made of a single piece of clear quartz, but the crystal contained blue inclusions both in the eyes and on the top of the head. We were of course reminded of Carole Wilson channelling that a blue crystal skull would soon be found somewhere in South America, but again there was no conclusive evidence.

We had now heard of several roughly life-sized crystal skulls from our researches. Many of these skulls were known to be modern and others we suspected were so. But the legend had said that there were 13 genuinely ancient original crystal skulls.

By now preparations for the tests at the British Museum were well underway. We were hopeful that they would come up with some definite answers to our questions. Were any of the crystal skulls genuinely ancient sacred objects with a mysterious past or were they all the product of modern technology, made simply for profit? It appeared that the only way to find out was to investigate them within the confines of a controlled environment and to subject them to a series of rigorous scientific tests. It was just these kind of tests that the British Museum was now preparing to run.

With the guidance of Dr Jane Walsh, the British Museum now planned to bring together as many crystal skulls as practically possible alongside their own large crystal skull and the Smithsonian skull. The skulls would then be subjected to tests at the British Museum's research laboratory in London, tucked away behind the museum near Russell Square, under the auspices of the enthusiastic Dr Ian Freestone, a scientist who was accustomed to the practices of dating antiquities.

The British Museum was particularly keen to know about the true origins of their own skull. If Dr Jane Walsh's theory were correct, and the British Museum skull were found to be a modern fake, it would be a startling revelation. After all, it had been kept and displayed in one of the world's leading museums for a whole century, having fooled the museum establishment and the public alike.

But what of the skulls that were in private collections? If the owners agreed, these skulls could also be tested, which would reveal whether they too were the victims of unscrupulous dealers, con-artists or tricksters, or whether their skulls were genuine artefacts.

I was surprised that the owners were prepared to take the risk of finding that their skulls might well be fake. It struck me that they were taking a big risk. Each had a lot to lose if their skull were found not to be ancient. Norma Redo, owner of the reliquary cross skull, risked finding out that the precious family heirloom that had been handed down the generations was nothing more than a cheap fake. Perhaps the situation was potentially even more devastating for Nick Nocerino. He had put his reputation on the line as a 'crystal skull expert' by putting Sha Na Ra forward for tests. If Sha Na Ra were not found to be at least as old as the Aztecs, then Nick was in trouble. A crystal skull 'expert' unable to determine the origin of his own skull would have little credibility. As for JoAnn Parks, she might have the most to lose of all. Max had given her a new life. She toured around with him and had become a regular TV personality, appearing along with her crystal skull. How might she take the news that Max was nothing more than an imitation and that she had been the victim of a hoax? She was currently involved taking Max on a lecture tour to different US cities, but managed to fit a visit to the British Museum into her busy schedule. Norma Redo planned to tie her visit to the British Museum with a visit to two of her sons, who were at school in Britain. The date for the tests was duly set for only a few weeks away.

As we got further into discussions about exactly what the tests would involve, it became apparent that they might not be as straightforward as we would have liked. Dr Freestone explained that there were several problems when dealing with crystal artefacts. First, there was the fact that it is impossible to date crystal. Each piece of crystal could have been formed perhaps billions of years ago and carved at any time since. Neither could anything be achieved by analysing samples taken from the surface of the crystal. As we had seen with the Parisian skull, which had not been submitted for these tests, any examples of, say, metal on the surface could easily have got there well after the skull was first made. As the scientists at Hewlett-Packard had found, the best way to find out when the crystal was carved was by looking for toolmarks.

The technique is to establish what tools were used by examining the markings that were left on the surface of the crystal. This test is known as 'useware analysis'. With the crystal skulls, the idea was to take small moulds from each, so as not to damage the original. These silicon moulds would then need to be coated with a thin layer of gold so that they could be looked at under a scanning electron microscope. This would reveal if there were any signs of 'modern' tool marks.

By 'modern' the scientists meant any kind of tool marks that looked as though they might have been made with the assistance of the jeweller's wheel. Since around the fourteenth century, craftspeople in Europe have used such wheels. Nowadays they are made of metal and coated in diamonds or other hard abrasive materials, which helps speed up the process of carving hard gems and other materials such as crystal. They are now powered electronically, but used to be powered by hand or foot. In fact, as Margaret Sax, the British Museum's useware analysis specialist, informed us, the ancient Sumerians, who preceded the Babylonians in Mesopotamia, are known to have used the wheel for stone carving as long ago as 2000 BC. But the same is not thought to be true of the Native Americans.

According to Dr Jane Walsh and the British Museum laboratory staff, the jeweller's wheel was not introduced to the Americas until after the arrival of Christopher Columbus in 1492. The ancient Olmecs certainly knew about the wheel itself, as an ancient artefact with wheels was found at Tres Zapotes on the Gulf coast of Mexico earlier this century, but this object, thought to date back to at least 200 BC, is thought to have been nothing more than a child's toy. Jane Walsh and the British Museum did not appear to be aware of any evidence that the ancient Mesoamericans used the wheel for any other purpose. Indeed, as Elizabeth Carmichael pointed out, the early Spanish chroniclers quite specifically stated that the locals used hand carving to make their incredible objects in jade, obsidian and crystal.

Of course the early Spanish conquerors may have wished to paint a picture of the natives as primitive people, even savages, to excuse their brutal treatment of them. This is, however, unlikely to have included their descriptions of the natives' stone-working techniques. And so the British Museum assumed that before the Europeans arrived, the ancient Mesoamericans did not use the jeweller's wheel and carved their artefacts entirely by hand.

To the naked eye it is usually impossible to tell the difference between a piece of crystal carved by hand and a piece carved with a jeweller's wheel. But under the intense magnification of the electron microscope, if an object has been carved by wheel this shows up as tiny 'parallel' scratch marks across the surface of the crystal, whilst a hand-carved object displays a more 'random' pattern of scratches.

The museum scientists now had access to the crystal skull known to have been carved with the assistance of a wheel in Germany as recently as 1993 with which to compare the minute scratches on the surface of the other crystal skulls. They knew that under intense magnification the German crystal skull would show the parallel grooves on its surface that would demonstrate that it was carved with modern tools. Hans-Jürgen Henn, the owner of the skull, was quite happy for the museum to use it as a benchmark against which to compare the others. If the other skulls showed similar parallel scratch marks or grooves, there could be little doubt that they were of modern manufacture.

But what was also needed was an ancient crystal artefact from Central America against which to test this theory. It was believed that such an artefact would show the more random pattern of scratch marks created when an object is made without using a jeweller's wheel. But an ancient Mesoamerican artefact was needed to prove this point. A benchmark of the antiquarian methods of carving would be necessary to make the tests properly scientifically valid. The question was, where was such a piece of definitely ancient and presumably hand-carved piece of crystal known to be Central American going to come from?

The problem was that large pieces of crystal from properly recorded archaeological digs in Central America were extremely rare. So how were we to find our benchmark? As we pondered this question, the possibility of obtaining a crystal artefact from Mesoamerica that was known to be ancient seemed remote. So we were anxious to hear from Dr Freestone whether there were any alternative tests, besides usewear analysis, that he could carry out.

Dr Freestone explained that there was another test that could be carried out. He said that the crystal itself could give us information about where it had originally come from. If this were known, it would help establish when the skulls might have been carved. If the skulls were found to have been made of crystal originating in Central America, that would indicate more strongly that they were made by indigenous people. If they were found to be made of European or Brazilian crystal, we could fairly safely make the assumption that they were modern. Jane Walsh suspected that the British Museum crystal skull might be made from Brazilian crystal rather than crystal from Central America. Archaeologists generally believe that crystal from Brazil was not imported into ancient Central America before the Europeans arrived (despite what we had previously heard about massive slabs of mica apparently having been transported from Brazil to the ancient city of Teotihuacán). However, as we had already discovered, crystal had been imported from Brazil to Europe for use by carvers in towns such as Idar-Oberstein in Germany.

Examination of the source of the crystal appeared a useful way of determining the origins of the skulls. As Dr Freestone explained, there were several techniques that could be used here. All were to do with studying the tiny bubbles, or 'inclusions', as they are known, of other material that are often trapped inside the crystal at the time of its formation. These other materials, such as 'greenstone', often get caught inside minute pockets in the crystal and it is possible to analyse both the size and shape of these pockets, and their contents, usually a combination of solids, liquids and sometimes air, in order to find out where the crystal originally came from. Ideally, the precise chemical composition of these impurities is analysed, but as they are trapped within the crystal, this usually involves damaging the object under study.

The most advanced and sophisticated way around this problem is a technique known as 'laser raman spectroscopy'. This involves firing a laser at the inclusions in the crystal and because each element heats up at a different rate, computer analysis of the movement observed within the inclusions can be used to work out exactly which chemicals are present. When Nick Nocerino heard about this test, he said, 'The British Museum had better be careful with my skull. I heard a rumour that government scientists in Brazil tried to extract information from a crystal skull by firing lasers at it and it just blew up! So they'd better not try anything like that on mine!'

Fortunately for Nick, laser raman spectroscopy requires very expensive equipment that the British Museum does not have and could not afford to hire in.

The next best alternative is a technique known as 'X-ray diffraction analysis'. This involves obtaining a tiny sample from any inclusion that appears near the surface of the crystal and subjecting it to a high-radiation bombardment of X-rays. This provides X-ray photographs displaying a particular pattern of diffraction. Because each element has a different atomic structure, or shape, from any other, it diffracts X-rays in its own distinctive way. The resulting pattern of diffraction therefore can be used to work out exactly which chemicals are present and therefore where the crystal comes from. This technique sounds impressive, but the problem is that it does involve slightly damaging the object under study.

In fact in the event of the tests it transpired that the only technique for establishing where a piece of crystal came from that was both affordable and could be properly guaranteed not to damage the skulls in any way was the vague art of 'videomicroscopy'. This is simply a question of pointing a videomicroscope – a microscope with a video recorder attached – at the inclusions and then asking an expert geologist to give an opinion as to where the crystal comes from, based on the size, shape and any colouring of the pockets of inclusions. This struck us as rather unscientific. Could any expert really know where in the world a piece of crystal came from just by looking at it under a microscope, without in any way analysing its chemical contents?

So we spoke to Professor Andrew Rankin, the British Museum's consultant geologist at the University of Kingston in London, who was due to help with the tests. We were most disappointed to learn from him that when the museum had talked of determining where the crystal had come from to make the crystal skulls, what was really meant was where *geologically* speaking, rather than *geographically* speaking. In other words, Professor Rankin would be able to give his opinion as to roughly at what temperature and under what pressure a piece of crystal had been formed and what other minerals might have been present in the area of growth. He could not say for sure whether a piece had definitely come from Brazil or Central America. However, some geological types of crystal are more common in Brazil and others more common in Central America, so he could 'hazard a guess' as to which of these geographical locations the crystal had originally come from. The problem was that there are sometimes more similarities between crystal from different areas than differences. The same types of crystal can be found in vastly different geographical regions. So we could not be sure exactly where any piece of crystal came from and it would be impossible to gain a truly accurate picture of whether the skulls were ancient or modern by analysing the crystal itself. But we could get a pretty good idea.

We now had several of the crystal skulls lined up and ready for testing, but so far it seemed that the tests were not likely to prove definitive, as we still lacked the necessary comparative object to make the usewear analysis scientifically verifiable, and testing the crystal itself looked as though it would not provide the hard geographical evidence we required.

We were beginning to wonder how we were going to get to the truth about the skulls when Dr Jane Walsh came up with a solution. She had discovered the object that we needed to verify the usewear analysis tests: a genuinely ancient and large crystal artefact discovered on an archaeological dig in Mexico.

This object, known as 'the crystal goblet from Tomb No.7 at Monte Albán' was tucked away in an obscure little museum in central Mexico. Not only was the goblet of great interest scientifically, but the more we heard about it, the more fascinating it sounded in its own right.

The place of its discovery, Monte Albán, lies near the beautiful town of Oaxaca in highland Mexico, to the south of the former Aztec empire and to the north of the ancient Mayan territories. Believed to date back to at least 500 BC, the archaeological site is situated on a flat plateau at the top of Monte Albán, or 'White Mountain', and is unusual in that when the original city was built the whole of the top of the mountain had first to be removed.

Archaeologists believe the city was built by the Zapotecs, a somewhat obscure civilization who populated this region at around the same time as the early Maya further south. Little is known about them, though Monte Albán contains evidence that they too possessed a form of hieroglyphic writing. Generally regarded as the earliest known writing in Mexico, it has not yet been decoded. There is also evidence to suggest that the Zapotecs possessed an earlier version of the Mayans' famous calendar and dot-and-bar numbering system, and may even have invented it. But little or nothing is left of them today, apart from some mysterious stone carvings of 'dancers'. No one is sure that they really are dancers, but, like the even more ancient Olmec carvings on the Gulf coast, they do appear to show what look like Negro people and bearded Caucasian figures and so provide more evidence that the people of Central America were once visited by peoples from either across the Atlantic or elsewhere *(see Figure 24)*.

It is believed that Monte Albán was ultimately abandoned by the Zapotecs and in its later years became home to the Mixtecs, who arose in highland Mexico just after the collapse of the ancient Maya and before the rise of the Aztecs. Again, little is known about them except that they were highly skilled craftspeople and were particularly renowned for their many pottery figures of skulls in various guises *(see black-and-white plate section)*. Craftspeople were apparently the highest strata of Mixtec society and later the Mixtecs were absorbed into Aztec society as craftsmen-slaves.

But the Mixtecs, it seems, were also great stargazers. One of the most prominent features of Monte Albán is the J-shaped astronomical observatory. It appears that the city was built in this strange location precisely to take advantage of the high place and clear skies to gaze at the stars while remaining almost unseen from the surrounding countryside. Whether the

Figure 24: Some of the bearded Caucasian 'dancers' found at Olmec sites such as La Venta and at Monte Albán

Zapotecs or Mixtecs built the observatory is unknown, but whoever it was clearly had aspirations that extended right out into the heavens.

The discovery at Monte Albán that interested the British Museum, however, took place back in the 1930s, when a young Spanish archaeologist named Alfonso Caso was excavating the ruins. Caso, now widely regarded as the founder of modern Mexican archaeology, discovered that just below ground level, all around the site, below what looked like mere mounds of grass, lay buried dozens of small burial chambers or tombs. It seemed that these dated back to the Mixtec period of occupation. The tombs were painted red, the colour of the womb. Inside were huge earthenware pots containing human skeletons, many of them coiled into the obligatory foetal position. Each tomb also contained various small artefacts, bits of jade or pottery, which were given to the occupants to accompany them on their journey into a new life after death.

The most remarkable discoveries were made in the rather unimaginatively titled 'Tomb No.7'. Although only around six feet (two metres) wide by nine feet (three metres) long, it was filled with all manner of strange and beautiful objects, many made of solid gold. It was a veritable hoard of buried treasure, with ornate jewellery, exquisitely carved pottery and precious stones in abundance. Alongside the skeletal remains of the still unidentified inhabitant of this small treasure-chamber, Alfonso Caso found a small crystal lip-plug, crystal ear-spools and crystal beads, all believed to have been associated with the astronomer caste in ancient Mesoamerica. But most impressive of all was a large and beautifully crafted object that looked like a goblet or drinking vessel, made from pure, clear and flawless solid rock crystal.

The goblet had been sealed in its tomb for over 1,000 years. The theory was that it would have been made using techniques which showed no evidence of the jeweller's wheel. If it did show markings of the jeweller's wheel then the archaeologists had got it wrong about the ancient Mesoamericans' technical capabilities. Either way, it was known to have been made before the Spanish arrived in the Americas and had been identified as an ancient artefact.

With the tests now less than a few weeks away, was it going to be possible to get this almost priceless object to the British Museum's research laboratory in London in time for the tests? Museums are known for their cumbersome bureaucracy. Inter-museum loans are a complex business which require incredibly detailed paperwork – understandably, as on more than one occasion, objects not properly accounted for have been known to disappear without trace. There was little time to persuade the Mexican authorities to agree to take this fragile object from its home in highland Mexico and fly it half-way round the world only to be subjected to scientific tests. Yet if the Mexicans decided against the loan, the tests on the crystal skulls would be invalid.

There was a flurry of activity to ensure that the goblet could make the trip to London. Both the British Museum and the National Archaeological Institute of Mexico (INAH) put in a tremendous effort to speed the goblet to Britain. Museum committees met, lawyers were called in and contracts drawn up, and insurance was put in place. The goblet was valued at over three million dollars, placed in a specially made box and, under a cloak of great secrecy and security, flown over the Atlantic, accompanied by the Mexican museum's keeper, Arturo Oliveros, who arrived at the British Museum's research laboratory in a security van.

The British Museum skull had been removed from its display case and cleaned, and was waiting in the museum safe, along with the German skull and the Smithsonian skull. The private owners were flying in. All was ready for the tests to begin.

As we arrived at the British Museum laboratory on the day of the tests, we felt a real sense of anticipation. At last it seemed that we had the chance to find out the truth about the crystal skulls. We would find out how old they were and solve the mystery. At least after the tests we would know if any of the crystal skulls were genuinely ancient or whether they had all been made using European technology sometime during the last 500 years.

The atmosphere in the British Museum research laboratory that morning was one of expectancy. As we looked on, a visual feast unfolded on the old wooden benches of the now somewhat dilapidated laboratory. One by one the crystal skulls were carefully removed from their packing cases. Max came out of his brand new vanity case, Sha Na Ra out of his travelling case and the Smithsonian skull out of a huge specially constructed wooden box, while Norma's skull had been carried wrapped only in a headscarf. The crystal goblet was the finishing touch. They were all roughly arranged in a small grouping on the table top and the differences in size, style and shape were immediately obvious. The arrangement was stunning. There was the gargantuan, and some would say 'cursed', Smithsonian skull with its heavy clouded features and wry-looking smile; the stylized but still beautiful and almost transparent British Museum skull;

the smooth lines of the modern 'hi-tech' looking German skull with its silver-grey transparent crystal; the cloudy and simple features of Max the 'healing' skull, said to have originally belonged to a Guatemalan shaman; and the still dirty, rough-tooth, primitive features of Sha Na Ra, the skull that had shown Nick Nocerino so many images over the years. Alongside these was the reliquary cross skull, skewered beneath its crowning crucifix; and beside that the beautiful crystal goblet that looked just as I would imagine the Holy Grail. British Museum employees from other sections of the research lab couldn't resist squeezing into the room to look on the extraordinary spectacle of the crystal skulls that had gathered there (*see colour plates 25 and 26*).

Then the tests began. Margaret Sax began the process of cleaning the surface of the skulls, starting with giving Max's teeth a good clean as JoAnn looked on protectively. She then began making small moulds of parts of each skull. I watched as she took a sample cast from Max. The idea was to make casts of the areas of each skull that had required the most detailed carving, particularly around the eyes and teeth. Moulds were also taken from the smoother areas on the very top of each skull so that the workmanship on the different parts of the skulls could be compared. Later these moulds would be scanned under the electron microscope where the intense magnification would reveal any tool markings used to create the skulls.

Although the usewear analysis was likely to be the most effective test, the British Museum was also interested in an analysis of the geological source of the crystal. After Margaret Sax had finished with each skull it was handed on to Dr Andrew Rankin, who began looking at it through his videomicroscope. The microscope showed an enhanced image of the inclusions within each piece of crystal. I watched as Dr Rankin scanned the reliquary cross skull. He was extracting as much information as possible from visual comparisons of the types of crystal that the skulls had been carved from.

We would have to wait two days before the results of the tests would be available.

As we waited for the results we were on tenterhooks. We had been pursing the truth about the skulls for so long and now, at last, we were going to know. What was the museum going to find? Had Nick Nocerino, JoAnn Parks and Norma Redo travelled all the way to Britain only to find that their precious skulls were modern fakes, or were they about to receive confirmation of their authenticity? What about the skulls belonging to the Smithsonian and the British Museum? Had the experts been duped or were these skulls authentic?

We crowded into the British Museum research laboratory again to get the results. A member of staff from the museum started going through the skulls one at a time, starting with the British Museum's own skull. We were somewhat disappointed to learn that traces of wheel markings had been found on its teeth. This meant that it would now be considered 'post-Columbian', the assumption being that it had been made using so-called 'European technology' either in Europe or in Central America some time after the arrival of the Europeans in 1492. It turned out that the Smithsonian skull also showed evidence of wheel markings.

As for the source of the crystal used to make these skulls, as far as the British Museum skull was concerned, the geological evidence seemed to support the notion that it was not ancient. Dr Andrew Rankin thought that the crystal might have come from Brazil. He was unable to say where the crystal used to make the Smithsonian skull had come from, but Dr Jane Walsh appeared very satisfied with the results, presumably concluding that her theory about Eugène Boban was correct: that Boban had obtained at the very least the British Museum skull in Europe towards the end of the end of the nineteenth century, where it had been made using crystal imported from Brazil.

It seemed that two skulls had been shown to be 'fakes', but what of the others? Norma Redo had been philosophical about her skull. She said that it would 'still mean the same' to her if it was found to be modern. However, the tests on the reliquary cross skull appeared to give strangely contradictory evidence. Margaret Sax had found evidence of both types of workmanship on this skull. It seemed that the detail of the teeth had been produced with a wheel and also the area on the top of the skull where the cross had been added. But the rest of the skull had definitely been hand-carved and displayed markings that were, considered 'characteristic of pre-Columbian work'. This piece appeared to have been originally carved by hand, presumably by pre-Columbian Mesoamericans, and then later the teeth were retouched by wheel.

According to Dr Rankin, the reliquary cross skull was made from a largish piece of crystal, of the size normally only found in Brazil. Curiously though, he found the type of crystal from which it was made looked almost exactly the same as that used to make the crystal goblet of Monte Albán, known to be over 1,000 years old, and presumably made of crystal from Central America. The 1571 hallmark on the crucifix on top of the skull was thought to be genuine, so the skull itself had presumably been made sometime before this date. So here indeed was what appeared to be a genuinely ancient crystal skull made in Central America at some time before, or possibly immediately after, the Spanish conquest. Its teeth, it seemed, had been retouched at around the same time as the early European conquerors had drilled a hole in its head to add the crucifix.

But what were the results for the other skulls? Nick Nocerino and JoAnn and Carl Parks looked tense with expectation. We were all waiting to hear the truth about their skulls, Max and Sha Na Ra. But the British Museum representative simply stated, 'I'm afraid we are unable to comment on the other two skulls.'

We were taken aback. The British Museum representative sounded very embarrassed and added that strict orders had been given from above, apparently instructing all staff 'not to comment'.

What was going on? What was it about Max and Sha Na Ra that couldn't be made public? Had the museum discovered that these skulls were genuinely ancient? But why could they not say so? Had they discovered some important information too sensitive for public consumption? Had the skulls been made by aliens or something? Or were they such obvious modern fakes the museum was simply afraid to admit it?

I pressed the point further and was told that it was museum policy not to do any tests on privately owned artefacts. But this didn't make any sense. The museum had been preparing for these tests for almost six months and knew that some of the skulls belonged to private owners. Certainly Dr Jane Walsh had stated in her own research report that she hoped to borrow skulls both from museums *and private collectors* for the purpose of scientific examination and to make the findings public.[1]

In any case, the reliquary cross skull quite obviously belonged to 'a private collector,' the aristocratic Norma Redo, and yet the museum had duly commented on her skull.

Nick Nocerino and JoAnn Parks left the museum disgruntled and went back to their hotel. We arranged to meet them later to discuss the day's proceedings. Then it suddenly occurred to me that perhaps, having found their own large skull and the Smithsonian skull to be modern, the British Museum had discovered these other two skulls to be the same, but was afraid to comment for fear of some sort of legal reprisal from the owners. I spoke to the museum's representative and asked whether they would be able to let us know the results if we could get some written guarantee from the owners that there would be no comeback against them whatever their comments. But I was told this wouldn't make any difference.

Regardless, I spoke to the skulls' owners. They both said that, having come all this way, they too were determined to get to the truth about their skulls, even if the tests should prove them to be modern. So both JoAnn Parks and Nick Nocerino duly signed written affidavits. In these documents the owners guaranteed not to argue with the results of the tests, whatever they might be, and guaranteed not to take any action, legal or otherwise, against the British Museum or the BBC, whatever comments they made or whatever results they published about Max or Sha Na Ra. These documents were hand-delivered to the British Museum, but their representative still refused to comment, now adding, to our surprise, that no tests had actually been done on either of the skulls in question.

But JoAnn and I had actually watched while a plastic mould was taken from Max and Nick said he had seen Sha Na Ra being examined under the video microscope. Surely the scientists would not have scanned and recorded the inclusions in the crystal or taken such moulds and then never analysed the results? But the museum representative now said they could not release any results because they had not carried out any tests on these two skulls. And they point blank refused to give any reason for not doing so.

It just didn't make any sense and we tried hard to think of a reason. I could think of only one other possibility. I remembered that while the moulds were being taken two days earlier, some of the skulls' keepers and the museum staff had been chatting to each other and I had overheard Jane Walsh talking to Nick Nocerino. She had asked him where he had got his skull from. Nick had produced a map and proceeded to explain that he had dug up Sha Na Ra while doing some psychic archaeology up the Rio Bravo river. Jane Walsh had enquired whether this was a museum-sponsored dig, to which Nick had replied, 'Hell, no!'

Dr Walsh had pressed him further. 'Was it an official government dig?'

'Hell, no!' Nick exclaimed once again. 'You don't find nothing on those digs!'

Perhaps this conversation had had something to do with it. I know Jane Walsh did not seem pleased at the time and had said something about how the Smithsonian and the British Museum would not want to have anything to do with any 'illegal' archaeological artefacts. However Nick had explained that in Mexico in the 1950s private digs were not considered illegal and that had seemed to be the end of it. But understandably, in archaeological circles, 'illegal' digs are anathema. If digs are not properly recorded, historical 'facts' become very difficult to verify and so archaeologists' jobs become even more difficult. Sensitivity on the subject is further heightened by the number of artefacts in the great museums of the world whose ownership is hotly disputed. Understandably again, the countries from which many of the exhibits have been taken claim that at one stage or another their treasures were 'looted'. So museums these days now try to steer well clear of any further such controversy.

But the 'illegal dig' theory still didn't seem to make sense in explaining the museum's refusal to comment on Max and Sha Na Ra. JoAnn had told the British Museum only what she knew for sure about Max, that she got him from a Tibetan Buddhist healer who said he had been given the skull by a Guatemalan shaman. She had said nothing to the British Museum to suggest that Max might have come from any sort of dig, illegal or otherwise. The Smithsonian skull and perhaps the British Museum skull could have had 'illegal' origins, and yet the museum had tested and commented on these. And when I put the question of whether worries about 'illegal' origins had anything to do with the museum's silence, I was simply told that the British Museum did not have to give any reason why it had chosen not to comment.

But why not? We were even more intrigued. JoAnn Parks was convinced that the museum had something to hide, that the scientists had found something they did not want the public to know about. But what could this be? Had they, like Hewlett-Packard with the Mitchell-Hedges skull, been unable to find any kind of tool marks whatsoever, no sign of either wheel or hand carving? If so, the implications would certainly be phenomenal. It would imply that these two skulls were not man-made at all, but had some kind of strange, perhaps unearthly, origin. Had the museum been frightened off in some way? Or could the scientists have found that these two crystal skulls really were some kind of store of important and ancient information? But this seemed very unlikely.

Alternatively, had the museum experts perhaps found some more down-to-earth results that they just did not like or were not prepared to accept, because they challenged the conventional views held by archaeologists? Had they found that the skulls had been made by hand from the same type of crystal and as long ago as the crystal goblet? But, if so, why were they not prepared to say so?

It was time for the skull owners to make their way home. JoAnn and Carl were disappointed at not finding out the scientific facts about Max. Nick was cynical. 'The problem is that the archaeologists and the scientists just don't want to upset the applecart,' he said. 'They have their opinions on things and they don't want them challenged. They like the way things are. There is a whole lot more to those skulls than they will ever know, or at least admit to.'

As I looked at Max and Sha Na Ra being carefully packed back into their carry cases, I remembered the original legend of the skulls. This had said that information would only be forthcoming from the skulls when they were *all* gathered together, not just a handful like this gathered only for scientific tests. It had also said that knowledge would only be revealed when mankind was ready for it, apparently to prevent the information the skulls contained from being abused. Could that perhaps be it? Could it be that perhaps we were just not ready to hear the truth about the skulls, not sufficiently 'evolved' and 'developed', as the legend had said?

I thought about how we had put our trust in the scientists to provide the answers, but these had not been forthcoming. Indeed, it struck me that our approach to the questions posed by the riddle of the skulls was typical of the way our whole society responds to so many of the mysteries with which we are faced: we look to science to provide all the answers. Maybe this is just not possible.

As I looked again at Max the whole situation suddenly seemed quite comic and I found myself reminded of Douglas Adams' science-fiction comedy *The Hitchhiker's Guide to the Galaxy*. In this story one of the most powerful and brilliant computers ever invented is asked to come up with an answer to 'the mystery of life, the universe, and everything'. The computer is duly fed with all the data it is possible to collect and then spends years and years completing the task. Finally it comes up with an answer: '42'! That's when everyone realizes they may not have asked the right question...

Had we asked the right question about the crystal skulls? We had believed the scientific tests were going to prove the origins of the skulls once and for all. But now we were none the wiser. The skull owners had gone home puzzled and we ourselves were bewildered. What had stopped the British Museum from producing the much needed answers?

Some time later I put in a call to another eminent Mesoamerican expert, Professor Michael D. Coe of Yale University. When I told him about the British Museum tests I was greatly taken aback by his reply. According to him the scientists we had been relying on at the British

Museum may not have been asking the right questions at all.

Professor Coe told us that evidence of wheel markings on a crystal skull, such as those found on the British Museum and Smithsonian skulls, did not in any way prove that these skulls were modern. He explained that although it had long been accepted by the archaeological establishment that no pre-Columbian civilization had used the rotary wheel, new evidence contradicted this belief. Apparently some obsidian ear-spools had now been found that were wafer-thin, perfectly and absolutely circular and could only have been made using rotary carving equipment. These ear-spools were definitely known to date back to the Aztec/Mixtec period. So even the British Museum and Smithsonian skulls might not have been 'modern' after all.

Michael Coe added:

'People who sit in scientific laboratories don't know the full range of the culture they're dealing with. We really don't know half as much about these early cultures as we think we do. People need to re-examine their beliefs.'

In his opinion, the British Museum tests didn't prove anything. Indeed, this view was further reinforced by other Mesoamerican experts, such as Dr John Pohl of UCLA.

Only one thing seemed certain. The scientists had let us down. For whatever political or other reasons, it appeared that perhaps they had not even asked the right questions, let alone provided us with the answers.

How were we going to continue our investigation? We were very disappointed. It felt as if we had been so close to finding out where the skulls had really come from. What could we do now? Somehow it didn't feel right to give up our investigation completely. We just couldn't. There had to be an answer. But the question was, how were we going to find it?

17. THE FORENSIC

Now the British Museum tests had failed us it occurred to us that we needed to broaden the nature of our investigation. There were, after all, other areas that we had not explored, avenues that we had rejected. Perhaps now was the time to look at these again.

When we had first spoken to Dr Jane Walsh at the Smithsonian, scientists at the museum had suggested that if any of the skulls were highly anatomically accurate, then the chances were that they had probably been modelled on an actual individual. If this were the case then it might be possible to reconstruct that person's face and their racial characteristics, if nothing else, would help determine where, and therefore possibly also when, the skull had been made.

As only one of the crystal skulls had fitted the description of 'anatomically accurate', we had not previously followed up on this test. But now it occurred to us that any information we could uncover about one skull might help us to determine the history of at least some, if not all of the others.

The skull in question was the Mitchell-Hedges. We had put aside investigating this skull when Anna expressed her reluctance to get it tested at the British Museum, telling us that 'he has been through all that before' at Hewlett-Packard. In many respects the Mitchell-Hedges skull was already the most interesting, as this was the skull on which the Hewlett-Packard team had been unable to find any trace of tool marks. But with the forensic tests, Anna's skull would not need to be involved in any intrusive tests, as it was standard practice amongst forensic experts to work with photographic images.

It now seemed that this type of test could yield some important results. If the facial characteristics were of a Caucasian racial variety, then the skull had probably been made in Europe at some time, or if it had been made in the Americas then it would have to have been made at some time after the European conquest. If, on the other hand, the reconstructed face were of any other type of racial variety, then it could safely be assumed that the skull had probably been made by the group of people whose facial characteristics the skull displayed. If the reconstructed face showed Negroid characteristics, for example, then the skull had in all likelihood been made somewhere in Africa. If the reconstructed face displayed Mongoloid features, then it had probably been made either somewhere in Asia or by Native Americans.

This suggestion was obviously based on the assumption that it is very unlikely that someone, say, in Europe would have had, say, a Native American person to hand as a model from which to carve a crystal skull. Whilst not impossible, such a scenario is certainly improbable. The proposed test was also based on the assumption that the racial characteristics would be prominent enough for any forensic scientist to be able to tell the origins of the model. This could, of course, prove to be difficult, not only due to slight discrepancies from the original model that might have been made by the carver, but also because far greater physical variety exists within rather that between racial groups. None the less we felt such a test would certainly provide a pretty good clue as to whether the Mitchell-Hedges skull was made in Europe or in Mesoamerica. It felt as if we were engaged in a sort of archaeological 'whodunit', looking for whoever was responsible for making the skull.

While Ceri pursued another avenue of research, I spoke to Richard Neave, medical and forensic artist at the University of Manchester's Department of Art and Medicine. Richard is the UK's leading specialist in facial reconstruction. Much of his day-to-day work is on behalf of the police, investigating murder and missing persons cases. On some occasions, the only piece of evidence is the decomposing body or just the skeleton of some unidentified victim. In these cases Richard's services are required. For over 25 years now it has been his job to reconstruct the original face of a person from their skeletal remains.

I visited Richard Neave at his studio in Manchester. His workshop, tucked away in a far corner of one of those vast institutional buildings, was an extraordinary place. The first thing I noticed as I walked in was a full-size skeleton hanging from a stand, and all around the room, right up to ceiling level, the shelves were lined with various body parts. There were dismembered hands and arms that looked as though they had been freshly chopped from the body. In one area the shelves were lined with row upon row of human skulls, of various shapes and sizes, that looked curiously like an Aztec skull rack. And in the middle of the room was what looked at first glance to be a skull speared on the end of a stick with its decaying flesh rotting off. I was relieved to discover that the precise opposite was happening. The 'decomposing flesh' was really nothing more than red-brown clay which was being added to the skull to build up a full picture of its original inhabitant and in fact most of the skulls, like all of the 'dismembered' body parts, were really just highly realistic wax replicas.

None the less, I was unable to stop myself from asking Richard how it felt to be surrounded by so much death. Richard explained that a lot of people saw it that way, but in fact he was surrounded by the very stuff of life. In much of his work he was helping to promote life by providing teaching materials for medical students. Even his forensic work for the police served an important function for the living. It was vital that accident and murder victims be identified, if for no other reason than to allow family, friends and relatives to understand what happened. This also helped them to grieve properly and to allow loved ones to rest.

I presented Richard with our problem. There was a skull we wanted identified, not a real skull, but a crystal one. He was intrigued and wanted to know more. But, as I explained, I could not tell him anything else about it, or where it was thought to have come from, in case it influenced his judgement. Richard said that he was quite used to this. He was also required to work 'in the dark' on police cases for similar reasons. His only concern was that if the crystal skull he was given was already a copy of a real one, it might be too stylized or poor in its workmanship for him to properly identify the individual it had been copied from. But he was prepared to give it a try.

Ideally, he wanted the original skull to work from and to make a three-dimensional facial reconstruction out of clay. But the original was still in Canada. Time and money did not allow us to get hold of it. Besides which, Anna was concerned that it might get damaged *en route* or during the process of taking a mould or adding clay to it. However, Richard was also used to working from good photos, ideally taken from all angles and at equal distances from the original. Fortunately as we had foreseen this possibility earlier I had arrived complete with just such a set of photos.

As I pulled out the photos, Richard's eyes lit up. 'It's so beautiful and so anatomically accurate.' He was so impressed with the accuracy of the skull he agreed to reconstruct an approximation of the face while I waited.

The technique itself was simple, but relied on the skills and knowledge of the artist. Richard carefully placed the various photos of the skull beneath tracing paper and proceeded to draw right in front of me. He talked me through what he was doing as his pencil moved swiftly but skilfully across the tracing paper, teasing out the shape of the face that lay beneath.

As Richard began drawing I asked him whether it might be possible to determine what sex the skull was as well as its racial group. He answered:

'Quite possibly. On a real skull there are certain features which are associated with a male or female skull and it's a matter of whether the maker of this skull has actually put these fairly discrete features in or not.

'But it looks as though this skull has been copied from an actual skull. Though it doesn't have every single tiny feature of a real skull, it includes almost all of the fine detail one would expect from a living original and it is certainly a good deal more accurate than one would expect if there had been no actual original specimen to copy it from. So the chances are it's, er ... that it's going to speak for itself.

'The proportions are very important. The mandible is rounded at the front and that tends to be associated with the female. The supercirial ridges over the eye here, they are very, very smooth, and that is another female feature. And the face itself has the sort of proportions that one might associate more with a female than a male skull. Female skulls tend to have bigger orbits in relation to the rest of the face than a male skull, and that's what we're tending to see here. So, as I say, it's a matter of ... what actually comes out of the skull. It will tell us in its own good time.'

I watched in amazement at Richard's skill and workmanship as the original face on the Mitchell-Hedges crystal skull slowly emerged right in front of me. As Richard continued to add the flesh over the skull and the image of the face gradually became clear, he explained:

'What we've got here is a face with a broad, gently hooked nose, high cheekbones, a fairly wide mouth with thick lips, a very strong solid jaw and a very powerful bone structure. It has large, gently slanting eyes and overall a sort of smallish, rounded, wide sort of a face.

'It's definitely not a European face. I would say that this face is in keeping with the facial characteristics of the indigenous population of the Americas, the American Indian peoples. It's hard to say exactly which area. It's certainly not dissimilar to the faces of the people I've seen from Central or South America, although I wouldn't want to rule out the North American Indian population either.

'The hair and eyebrows I cannot be absolutely sure about. A skull can give us no direct information about these, so we have to make assumptions here based on the other information we're getting about the type of face the skull originally had. And of course the other thing we don't know is the age. There are none of the usual features which give us some kind of indication as to what age this person was – as though this is some sort of an ageless kind of a skull. But there we have it. That's as far as we can go. But I would be absolutely certain that this skull is not European and it looks to me to be the face of a woman belonging to the indigenous population of the Americas.'

The face that emerged certainly looked to me to be that of a Native American woman *(see black-and-white plate no. 46)*. In fact it looked just like the faces I had seen in Central America.

So at last we had some definitive scientific information about the Mitchell-Hedges skull, independent of Anna and Frederick Mitchell-Hedges. In fact it transpired that similar tests had also been done in America in 1986. Anna Mitchell-Hedges had loaned the skull to Frank Dorland for further research and he in turn had loaned a plaster cast of it, together with various photographs, to a forensic artist who worked for the New York Police Department. This man, Detective Frank J. Domingo, had drawn a reconstruction of the face which was almost identical to the face Richard Neave had drawn *(see black-and-white plate no. 47)*. Interestingly enough, this was the same face that Frank Dorland claimed to have had presented to him by the crystal skull itself when he was in deep meditation.

But these were not the only forensic scientists to have worked with the skull at one time or another. One man who had studied it, although he had not had the opportunity to reconstruct its face, was Dr Clyde C. Snow of the State Coroner's Office in Oklahoma City, one of the foremost forensic scientists in the whole of North America. He normally works on human rights violation cases and had recently had the unfortunate task of identifying the remains of thousands of Native American peoples executed by various government agencies during the early 1980s and only just excavated from their mass graves in various parts of Guatemala.

In the case of the Mitchell-Hedges crystal skull, Dr Snow and his colleague Betty Pat Gatliff had actually handled a plaster cast made of the skull[1] and had noticed something else unusual about it. When I spoke to Dr Snow on the telephone he explained that one of the most striking features about the skull was that, although it was indeed incredibly anatomically accurate, it seemed to have been modelled on no ordinary Native American woman. In particular, the teeth, though rendered to an incredible degree of accuracy and detail, were 'not of any human variety'. Dr Snow explained that the molars were 'X-shaped'.

The molars in all races have natural indentations in them which give them a rough or ridged feel. These indentations look like a 'plus sign' (+) running across the chewing surface. The strange thing about the Mitchell-Hedges skull was that the indentations were running across the surface of the teeth at a completely different angle, giving them an 'X-shaped appearance' (X). Given the skull's overall degree of anatomical accuracy and the fact that it even included such apparently minor detail, Dr Snow felt that this was unlikely to be a mistake on the carver's part. After all, why go to such great lengths to be so precise and yet make such a silly 'mistake'? The only problem with this analysis was that it meant the original model cannot have been quite human – or at least not from any human race we know of today.

We were now even more puzzled. Was the skull really modelled on the face of some 'alien'? Surely this was not possible. Or was this perhaps evidence of some ancient race of human beings now extinct? Again, this all seemed so unlikely. But with the refusal of the British Museum to comment on Max or Sha Na Ra, this was the only evidence we had to go on.

As I looked again at the face that Richard had drawn, I wondered who this beautiful woman really was. Anna Mitchell-Hedges had said the skull was modelled on the head of a priest, but it was now beginning to look more like a priestess. Frank Dorland, meanwhile, was convinced that the face he had seen was that of a pre-Mayan princess.

What was now almost without question was that the Mitchell-Hedges skull showed the distinct features of a Native American. Here was the most exquisite of all the crystal skulls with a clear connection with the Americas. At the very least this particular crystal skull did not appear to have been put together in the workshops of Europe. I wondered for a moment whether the whole 'made in Germany' argument about the origins of the skulls might not have been a subtle form of archaeological colonialism, suggesting that the peoples of Central America had not had the ability to produce the skulls themselves, as well as undermining their status as possible sacred objects. Was it another way of down-grading the artistic achievements of the Mexican people?

I looked again at the beautiful features of the mysterious woman. Where in the Americas had she really originated? While she may have been Mayan, she could also have been Chinook, Sioux or Cherokee, or from any number of other tribes in North, South or Central America. How could we find out?

18. THE CRYSTAL ENTITY

In the meantime, while Chris had been to see the forensic artist, I had been visiting 'Professor Brainstorm'. His real name is Harry Oldfield and he is a scientist who has conducted a great deal of research into crystal and has been coming up with some very controversial results. He is definitely outside the mainstream, but I wondered whether he might be able to suggest a new means of getting to the truth about the skulls. Although I was not too hopeful, I felt we had nothing to lose. One way or another, we were determined to get to the bottom of the mystery of the crystal skulls.

I arrived at Harry Oldfield's 'electro-crystal therapy' centre in Ruislip, north-west London, to find the surgery of the 1930s semi-detached house was packed with people holding boxes wired up to themselves. Harry was using electrically charged crystals to help heal people who had been written off by the medical profession. Although I was sceptical about the healing power of crystals, I had now heard from all the owners of crystal skulls in private collections that their skulls had the power to heal. So was it possible that the skulls could work directly to affect the human body? I was very resistant to the idea of crystal, let alone crystal skulls, having any healing powers whatsoever. Maybe the reason that I didn't believe that crystals could heal was because I thought of them as just stones, to which my attitude had at best been indifferent.

I tended to agree with academic Dr Linda Schele who called the crystal skulls the 'relics of the twentieth century'. She likened them to the relics of dead saints sold during the medieval period for their healing powers. Undoubtedly, many of these relics were fake. But people really believed that they could heal. Certainly, when people believe that something will make them better, it often does. This 'placebo effect' has been well documented and I had always assumed that this was the only effect that the crystal skulls could actually have.

But I had by now come across some research which challenged my preconceptions. One scientific study into the possible healing effects of crystals had been carried out in the USA by C. Norman Shealy and described in his book *Miracles Do Happen*.[1] Shealy looked at the effect of crystals on depression. A sample of 141 chronically depressed patients was given either a piece of glass or a piece of quartz to wear around their neck. The subjects were not told which they were wearing. After two weeks, 85 per cent of all the participants reported an improvement, in all likelihood a 'placebo effect'. But six months later, only 28 per cent of those who were wearing glass reported any continued improvement, whereas 80 per cent of those who were using crystal were still claiming that they could feel its benefits. So, at least for depression, crystal seemed to have more than just a placebo effect. But what of the claims that crystals can heal physical conditions?

Harry Oldfield says he has used the healing power of crystal to successfully treat a diverse range of ailments from cancer and heart disease to arthritis. He greeted me with a vigorous handshake. He was schoolboyish in appearance despite being in his mid-40s. He explained that his interest in crystals had come via a rather circuitous route.

As a science teacher at a busy London comprehensive school, Harry was always dreaming up ways of getting his students to share his passion for science. One day he introduced an aura photography camera into the classroom.

The aura camera photographs the electro-magnetic energy ring around the body, displaying it in a range of colours using the technique known as 'Kirlian photography', invented behind the Iron Curtain during the 1930s. Eastern philosophy and alternative medical practice recognize that the body is made of different energy centres through which electromagnetic energy flows. But this idea is still dismissed by most scientists in the West. I was reminded, however, of Dorland's theory that subtle energy is produced by the body and can be affected by contact with crystal. Exactly the same theory is the foundation of Harry Oldfield's work.

Back in his classroom, Harry's students used Kirlian photography techniques and began to notice subtle differences between the energy fields of those who were going down with 'flu and those who were not. Harry recognized the potential of Kirlian photography as a diagnostic tool and developed a video version, which he called PIP, or 'poly contrast interface' photography, and which could also show disturbances in the energy field. These disturbances would occur before the physical symptoms of an illness presented themselves. The different patterns would indicate the exact location of a health problem.

Although Harry initially worked closely with the medical profession, he found medical practitioners less keen when he became interested in treatment as well as diagnosis. Harry had been diagnosing illness then referring patients on for hospital treatment, but he felt that conventional medical treatment for diseases such as cancer was often misguided. He considered the standard 'cut and burn' approach often too harsh for the body and so he set out to find a gentler way of healing.

Harry began to develop a machine that would work with the body's own natural energy frequencies. He spent some time working on it, but felt there was something missing. It was a friend who suggested that he might use crystals. Harry began experimenting and found that they were indeed the missing piece of the jigsaw puzzle.

Harry now uses electricity to stimulate crystals and to send a pulse into the patient's body. He says that crystals can be stimulated by hand, but even the best crystal therapists can not be on top form all the time. Harry believes that, when stimulated by quartz crystal, the body uses its own electrical forces to heal. He sees his work as 'rebalancing' the body, and likens himself to a piano tuner 'with a Steinway piano which has gone out of tune'. The crystals are like a tuning device. As Harry says, 'All I do is tweak the strings, tweak some a little bit further, relax some and leave others alone because they are OK.'

Harry explained that using crystal for healing was not new, but had been practised by Native Americans for millennia. He claimed that he had also made a discovery which he thought confirmed the traditional Native American belief that crystal was not an inanimate object, but contained a living presence.

Harry went on to describe this discovery, which had occurred whilst he was working with his video imaging system. One day, his camera had been recording changes in the energy field of a patient when his eye had been drawn to the crystal that the woman was holding. A strange white ether-like substance seemed to be emerging from it. Invisible to the naked eye, it was clearly visible on the video imaging system. It moved up from the surface of the crystal, looking like a snake emerging from a basket.

'Good God, look at that!' Harry exclaimed, whereupon the 'presence' vanished. Harry now calls this 'the crystal entity', the being that lives within the crystal. Since first catching sight of the elusive creature, he has seen it numerous times and even has several video recordings of it.

I didn't want to believe any of this, but Harry invited me to witness it for myself. I sat down and he selected a large piece of crystal for me. Apparently the entity cannot be seen in all crystals. I held the crystal while Harry got the camera running. I watched the screen, which showed my hand holding the crystal. After a few moments had passed, with the crystal lying flat on the palm of my hand, I could see a strange snake-like form seeming to emerge from the crystal. Although nothing was visible when I glanced at the crystal in my hand, when I looked at the screen I could see a white, semi-transparent form, almost like a wisp of smoke.

As I looked on transfixed, I thought of the ancient Mayan carving which showed Lady Xoc looking at a vision serpent seen emerging from a skull. Was this what she had been looking at? Was this a vision serpent? Had this electronic device enabled us to actually see what normally could only be seen in an altered state of consciousness? Or was it just some elaborate form of video trickery?

I moved my hand slightly, and whatever it was I had been looking at disappeared from view, seeming almost to dart back into the crystal.

'They like the heat of the human hand, but they don't like movement,' said Harry, excitedly.

I put the crystal down. What was I doing here? Had I been conned or had I really seen an 'entity' inside a piece of crystal?

Harry was speaking animatedly. He was clearly thrilled by his discovery. 'They are out there looking for alien life forms when we have them right here,' he said. 'This is a life form like no other on the planet. It is not carbon based.'

Had Harry identified a non carbon-based life form or was it wild imaginings? As I left the privet hedges and rose-bushes of Ruislip behind, I was undecided. Did Native Americans really believe that crystal was in some way alive? It seemed so weird. I thought back to Star Johnsen-Moser and her encounter with the 'presence' inside the crystal skull. Was this what the crystal entity was? Surely this was just the stuff of science-fiction fantasy?

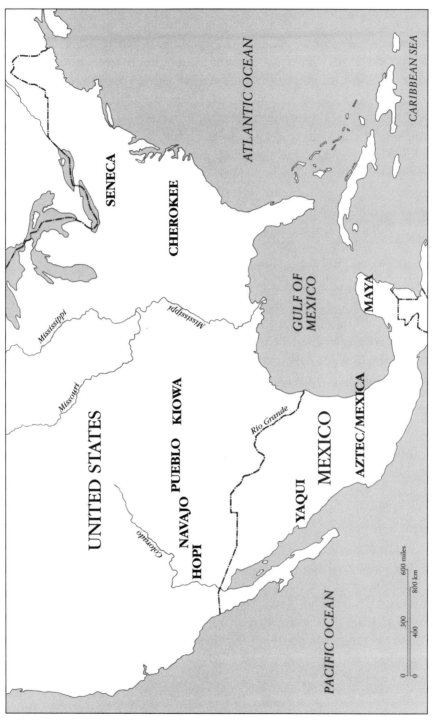

Figure 25: Some of the traditional tribal territories of the USA and Central America

19. THE SKULL PEOPLE

The night after I had visited Harry Oldfield and Chris had told me about the results of the forensic tests, I had a vivid and somewhat puzzling dream. In the dream I was walking alone across a vast grassy plain. It was evening, the light was fading. Then I saw some people in the distance. It was a group of Native Americans, dressed in traditional clothing. They were seated in a circle and there was a great seriousness about the gathering. As I got nearer to them an old man got up and walked towards me.

'You are here to help us,' he said gently.

I was quite taken aback. 'Sorry,' I said. 'I think you must have the wrong person.'

And then I woke up.

At the time I had simply dismissed this. It just didn't seem to make any sense at all.

A few days later we got a telephone call from my cousin Gerry, who lives in Albuquerque, New Mexico. He knew that we had been researching into the mystery of the crystal skulls and he was ringing excitedly to tell us that he had spoken to someone at his work about our interest. They had told him they had heard a rumour that a group of local Navajo tribespeople actually had a crystal skull.

We realized that so far our research into the skulls had been undertaken only in consultation with archaeologists, skull owners and scientists. We had not talked to any Native American people about the skulls at all. I began to wonder whether this might have been a serious omission.

If Native Americans used crystal for healing, as Harry Oldfield had suggested, then perhaps they also used crystal skulls? The forensic test had shown the face of a Native American woman on the Mitchell-Hedges skull. Was it perhaps in North America, not Central America, as we had thought, that the skulls had their origin?

We spoke to the colleague and he explained that he had heard this rumour from a friend, who had heard it from a friend etc., etc., so he was not even sure whether there was any truth in it. The problem was that it was considered very sacred to these people and so they generally tried to keep it a secret. The only way we were likely to be able to find out any more would be if we were to actually come out to New Mexico and try asking around on the various Navajo reservations for ourselves.

It was certainly a long shot, but it had to be worth a try. So we booked a ticket and within the week were heading out to New Mexico. We hired a car and, after visiting Gerry, were off driving around the Four Corners area of New Mexico, Arizona, Colorado and Utah trying to find more clues as to the whereabouts of the Navajo crystal skull.

The desert landscape was truly beautiful, with stretches of road that at times seemed to run for hundreds of miles between any signs of human habitation.

Our first proper lead on the Navajo crystal skull came in the Navajo reservation of Monument Valley, with its amazing landscape of flat desert interspersed with the great towering blocks of deep red sandstone mesas rising up with their sheer vertical cliffs and flat tops that have featured in so many Westerns. We had struck up a conversation with a young Navajo who ran a horse-riding ranch there and he told us we could speak to Emerson, a medicine man who lived nearby, or to the chief of the Canoncito Ban branch of Navajo, who lived further south near Albuquerque.

We met Emerson in a diner in the rather ugly town of Gallup between Monument Valley and Albuquerque. He was quite stockily built, had black hair, and wore sunglasses. He had a blunt manner and thought long before speaking. He was a practising shaman, a Native American medicine man who worked on behalf of his Navajo tribe in the Window Rock area of Arizona. Although he was not able to tell us whether the Navajo had any crystal skulls, he did explain that the use of crystals for healing was very common amongst the Navajo tribes of the southern USA. But it was difficult to put into words exactly how the crystal worked:

'It's real hard to explain, to even tell you how it happens, because it happens through the power of the Spirit, and for a human being to explain

something that happens through the power of the Spirit, I just cannot explain it. But it works, it really works, and it's as simple as that. Our people do use crystals like that and people do recover due to the power of crystal.'

Emerson's ability to use this power, he said, was God-given; he was simply 'administering the power that Great Spirit has given'.

Emerson uses crystal as a diagnostic as well as a healing tool. As he explained, 'Generally crystals are used at night, when you can see things in the dark with the crystal.' When someone is sick, Emerson said he is able to use 'the spirit of crystal' to examine the body:

'It's like an X-ray into somebody's body. It's a way of being able to look inside the person and see what is wrong with them. But it's better than a medical X-ray because you can see the whole person. You can see in three-dimensions instead of just two, and you can see the whole person, including their soul. It's not like a still photograph, it's moving and it's in full 3-D. You can even look inside yourself and the crystal will show you the bad spirit to help you to heal yourself, to purify yourself. I cannot tell you exactly how it works, but it does, and once you have seen it, once you have seen that bad spirit even inside yourself, well, then you believe it, then you know it to be true.'

Emerson, like Harry Oldfield, had no doubts about the healing powers of crystal. But unlike Harry, Emerson used it to transform his own powers of perception, to enable him to see in quite a different way from usual.

After we left Emerson, we drove out to the Canoncito reservation and asked around for directions to the chief's house. We finally arrived at his small mobile home, surrounded by a cluster of others, on a desperately barren hillside. The chief was not what I expected at all. Instead of the huge stern character pictured in so many Westerns, he was a petite figure of a man with a thin face, with high, chiselled cheekbones and a warm, friendly, almost knowing smile (*see black-and-white plate no. 51*). You could quite clearly see all of the bones that made up his fine features, almost as though he himself were nothing more than a skull, a living and animated one, covered only in a thin layer of finely weathered and slightly sun-wrinkled skin.

His name was Leon Secatero, and he preferred to be called the 'spiritual leader' rather than the 'chief' of his small band of Canoncito Indians.

He seemed not the least surprised or upset by our unexpected visit. However, when we told him we were looking for a crystal skull we had heard was somewhere in the area, he appeared somewhat surprised, a little flustered and a bit unsure what to say next. He said that the crystal skulls were very important and very sacred to his people, so sacred in fact that he was not really permitted to speak of such things publicly. 'Only the very holiest of holy ones are allowed to know where the crystal skulls are and to have access to them. In our tradition we do not use them openly,' he said. 'The skull cannot be brought out from its hiding-place deep in the mountains. Only the shaman who looks after the skull knows where it is.'

It was clearly something he was not free to talk about. But, he said, we could come back in a few days, and he would let us know whether or not he could tell us any more.

So while we were in the area we took the opportunity to see some of the ancient archaeological sites of the region. We visited the ancient Anasazi cliff dwellings at Mesa Verde, with whole stone-built houses carved deep into the caves under the steep cliffside, and the largest ancient ruins in the area, at Chaco Canyon, accessible only after a 26-mile drive on a simple dirt track crossing rough desert and dried-up river beds (*see black-and-white plate no. 49*). The impressive stone buildings we saw were built by the Anasazi people well over 1,000 years ago. They were all abandoned around AD 1100, well before the arrival of Christopher Columbus in the Americas, but no one really knows quite how far back the earliest ones date.

Anasazi means simply 'the ancient ones'. Little is known about these people, except that they are thought to be the early ancestors of today's Pueblo and possibly Hopi and Navajo peoples of the same region. They are also known to have had at least trading links with the Aztecs and possibly the Mayans, thousands of miles further south. The evidence for this is that the ancient Mesoamericans made many objects out of turquoise, which could only have come from this region. Also, in some of the ancient Anasazi ruins macaw feathers have been discovered dating back to at least AD 1000. This beautifully coloured parrot can only be found in the jungles of southern Mexico and further south. The latest theory is that the people of this area and the Aztecs even had a common origin. The 'place of the seven caves' referred to in Aztec legend is now held to be near Durango in southern Colorado.

The Anasazi were also great astronomers. Many of their buildings and works of art were carefully aligned for astronomical observation and prediction. At Chaco Canyon, for example, spiral figures are carved into one of the great rock faces. Great slits in an adjoining rock mean that the rays of the sun pass through the centre of the spiral only on the summer solstice and two shafts of light form on either side of the spiral only at the winter solstice, so that the whole rocky outcrop functions as a sort of natural clock.

Like the Maya, the Anasazi believed in other worlds. Their ceremonial 'kivas', circular buildings half sunk into the ground, were considered the doorway into the other dimensions. It is understood that these doorways only opened when the planets were at the correct position in the sky as indicated by precisely aligned openings around the edge of the kiva.

The question as to why these ancient people were so interested in the movements of the planets and the stars was still playing on our minds as we returned to Leon Secatero's house.

When we arrived, Leon's grandchildren were playing outside. Leon greeted us and invited us into his home. He had been preparing for a tribal meeting the following day. He said he had now consulted with the other tribal elders and the spirits. He explained that although it was tribal tradition not to speak of the skulls, the Navajo elders had also spoken of a time when the people of the Earth would all 'learn to speak the same language'. As Leon told us, 'They spoke of a time when the grandchildren of the white people would come and ask the Native Americans to share their knowledge and wisdom, and show them how we could save the Earth from destruction.' This was why he had decided to tell us more about the skulls.

Leon began by explaining that the Navajo were a fiercely independent, nomadic people. He said that when the Spanish first arrived in the area, his people, the Canoncito, were known to them as 'the skull people'. He said that as the chief elder of his small tribe it was his responsibility to be the record-keeper for his people and that he was responsible for keeping the history of his people alive. He still had an old map of the original territories to which his people belonged when the Spanish first arrived in the area at the beginning of the seventeenth century. We asked him if these were the lands that his people had then owned and he replied simply, 'In our tradition we do not believe that anyone owns the land. The land does not belong to the people. It is the other way round. The people belong to the land. And our people belong to this land, the land of the skull.'

He then proceeded to produce a copy of the old map and we could quite clearly see what he meant. The aerial view of the traditional tribal lands of the Canoncito quite accurately reproduced the side profile of a skull stretched out across a vast expanse of desert.

Leon pointed to a mountain on the map and explained that to his people this was the 'ear of the skull'. This mountain is traditionally sacred to all of the Navajo people, who, as we later discovered, quite widely refer to it as 'the sacred crystal mountain'. Leon then pointed to a large area of low-lying land that looked like some kind of canyon and explained that his people call this area 'the eye of the skull' or 'the eye of the Holy One'. He pointed to his home and to the tiny area of land to which his people had now been restricted, and explained that this area represented to his people 'the mouth of the skull' or 'the mouth of the Holy One'.

Leon did, however, ask us to keep the details of this map to ourselves, explaining that his people would not want anyone to try to look for any crystal skulls. He said that the white people had taken enough from his people over the years and he would not want anyone trying to take their holiest objects away from them now. He told us he could perfectly understand that people were curious about the crystal skulls, but pleaded, 'Please do not try to go looking for them.' Such things were best left alone:

'People do not really need to see the skull, they just need to know that it exists and that it is there. Please let it be good enough for you just to know that it is there. Take comfort in knowing that it is there and that it is fulfilling its purpose and that it is being looked after carefully. Leave it to be like the mountains, the trees, the wind and the rain.'

He added that when crystal skulls are put in glass cases in museums, they 'lose all their powers'.

Then he went on to say he would like to tell us a story that he had heard from his grandfather. It was said that his people had once found a beautiful object made of quartz crystal. It was 'like a modern gadget':

'When it was properly activated it gave off beams of light, like laser beams, in all directions. But in the 1600s the Spanish arrived looking for gold. The Canoncito people had no gold, but they knew the Spanish wanted something and were willing to help the strangers. So one of the young boys from the tribe took this gadget from the cave in which it was

kept and he placed it before the Spanish, because he thought this was what they were looking for and what they wanted. But they were not impressed, so he tried to show them how it worked and so he started to activate it. Then beams of light shot out of it so brightly that they were visible in the daylight. Panicking, the Spanish opened fire on both the object and the boy. Then they rode off and left the boy bleeding to death and the crystal object shattered into tiny pieces.'

For the Canoncito Navajo this was a brutal and sobering lesson. For this was when they came to realize that what the white people did not understand, they would try to destroy. The Canoncito people themselves were almost completely destroyed. Like millions of other Native Americans, those who were not killed intentionally by the European settlers died of the new diseases they brought with them. Smallpox and cholera alone are estimated to have killed around 10 million people over the years in North and Central America, and those few Native Americans who did survive were herded into smaller and smaller reservations with few life-supporting capabilities. Though Leon's Canoncito Ban were weakened to a point almost beyond endurance, they had still survived in the face of incredible adversity. This experience had made them wary of outsiders.

'But now,' Leon said, 'it is time to make the traditions of my people known.'

He started by describing the origins of his people. It was from 'the eye of the skull' that they had originated, emerging from caves deep underground after a great deluge. They returned there every year to perform some of their sacred ceremonies.

As tactfully as possible, Chris pointed out that we had heard from anthropologists and archaeologists that all of the Native American peoples had originally walked from Asia to North America across a land bridge that was said to have spanned the Bering Strait between present-day north-eastern Russia and Alaska until around 10,000 years ago. Was this not therefore where his people had come from? Leon replied that this was also what he had been taught at school, but that his elders had assured him otherwise. He said he suspected the anthropologists might have their own reasons for suggesting that the indigenous people were no more native to these lands than the early white settlers, but that his people had their own history and that they had actually been on the continent 'since the very beginning of time'.

Leon said that because his elders had told him that there would come a time when his people would be needed to help the 'white grandchildren', he had decided that if we were interested, we would be welcome to join his people's annual pilgrimage to their place of origin. He said that never before had this sacred ceremony been open to anyone beyond the immediate tribe, apart from the occasional representative from one of the neighbouring Apache, Pueblo or Hopi Indians. But this year, particularly as he was now having difficulty in keeping the younger members even of his own tribe interested in their traditions and origins, we would be welcome to accompany them if we liked.

We were very excited about being invited to the ceremony. So a few days later we were back at Leon's house to rendezvous for the gathering. Thirty or so people were already there, making themselves comfortable on the colourful Navajo blanket covered sofas or busying themselves in the kitchen preparing provisions for the journey. The journey to the 'place of the origins' was going to be a long one through the desert and we would be passing over some very rough terrain, so we were advised to leave our hire car behind. Instead Leon offered us a lift on the back of his four-wheel drive pick-up truck, as unfortunately the cabin was already full of his extended family.

After what seemed like hours of a very bumpy and dusty ride across rough barren landscape that had an almost lunar feel to it, we passed behind a great flat-topped mountain before arriving at a deserted encampment.

Chris and I erected our tent to face the stunning views across the desert. We were just starting to unpack when a young woman came over to us. 'The old people want to know why your tent is facing north,' she said with a knowing smile. We looked around in surprise and saw that all the other tents were facing in another direction. Rather sheepishly, we took the tent down and reassembled it to face east, ready to greet the sun and the new day.

As the others were setting up camp, I went for a walk. The light was fading across the canyons and bushes of the desert landscape and the mountains in the distance were a soft blue. It was such a vast and beautiful country. The landscape stretched before me, untamed and wild for as far as the eye could see. I thought of the neat fields of England. Where was our wilderness? It seemed we had always seen nature as something savage, untamed and threatening. Back home our untamed country had been mythologized, almost demonized as a dark and dangerous place, at least until the last of our great forests had been felled several hundred years ago. It seemed that what we could not control we feared – simple things like wild places, wild animals and what we thought of as wild, untamed people. Perhaps it was our own animal natures that scared us the most.

I began to wonder whether the appeal of the skull was the fact that it was the repository of the brain. Was it our belief in the supremacy of the human mind that lent the crystal skulls such a power? After all, throughout Western history it seems that the intellect has always been valued more highly than the physical aspects of life, almost as if the body were secondary. Our school system has always championed the mind. And as we have accepted this hierarchy within ourselves, so it seems we have come to accept a form of hierarchy in all things. We have come to believe all things can be divided, separated, evaluated and judged according to their value only to ourselves.

It struck me that our search for the truth about the crystal skulls had been affected by this hierarchical, judgemental thinking. Reason had dictated. We had wanted to classify and categorize the skulls, divide them up according to age, size and value. We had been preoccupied with the question of whether they were ancient or modern, genuine or fake. While these were worthwhile questions, they may not have helped us to understand the skulls any better. In fact they may well have distracted us from actually getting to the truth about them. Could it be that what we needed was to start seeing the crystal skulls with a new perspective?

At that moment, I noticed something catching the last rays of sunlight and shining it back into my eyes. I stumbled down the loose rock of the hillside and was surprised to find, emerging quite naturally from a thick seam beneath the earth, a huge chunk of crystal. All around me were similar chunks of pure quartz, just lying there quite naturally on the ground.

Immediately I picked up a piece to take it back to camp with me, but then I had a sense that everything had to be left exactly as it was. I put the crystal back and returned to the camp.

The warm orange glow of a fire greeted me. A huge pot of lamb stew was bubbling over an open fire. I helped the women prepare the Navajo 'fry bread', a delicious unleavened bread that would accompany the stew. The women played an equal role in running the traditional Navajo society. As one of the young women proceeded to tell me, their tribal culture was not built on a hierarchical system. She said that in her society no one was seen as better than any one else. Each person was believed to be able to contribute to the culture as a whole. That was why they always stood or sat in a circle – no person was considered above or below any other.

One of the older women lamented the lack of involvement of young people, their lack of interest in 'the old ways'. 'If we are not careful, these ways will die with us,' she said. 'The young forget that without the wisdom of the previous generations, the present one may not have survived.'

Navajo women are often spiritual leaders and it was a woman in her sixties who 'communed with the spirits' at dawn the following day. Wearing the traditional long skirt, her hair tied back in a neat 'Navajo style' bun, she took her place at the centre of a clearing in the middle of the camp. Everyone sat in a circle around her, colourful hand-made blankets protecting them from the early morning desert chill. The woman at the centre sat with her eyes closed, went into a trance and began speaking with the spirits in Navajo.

I was expecting to hear some deep words of wisdom from the spirits, who instead began by asking everyone to 'clean up their act' in the most simple and practical way. It transpired that the spirits were unhappy about the disposable nature of modern life, the rubbish that was generated by our disposable paper plates, cutlery and cups. Apparently they did not like to see things used only once and then thrown away. They preferred the old ways, where people took only what they needed and threw nothing away. Although unexpected, this was a stern reminder about how easy it is to be unthinking about our environment. It suddenly struck me how our own everyday actions are contributing to the thoughtless use of the Earth's natural resources. It was a reminder of the importance of considering the implications of all actions, no matter how small they may seem.

After the spirits had had their say, our cheeks were daubed with fine white clay. This was to show the spirits in the canyon that we walked in the land of the living, not the dead. And then, each carrying a small sprig taken from the few local trees, we began a long walk in silence across open countryside towards the sacred canyon.

A soft breeze blew the clouds on the horizon. The youngest woman went first, followed by her elders in single file, and this pattern was repeated with the men behind. As a sign of respect to the spirits the men were all required to wear headbands and the women long dresses and turquoise jewellery. The Navajo believe that turquoise facilitates communication with the spirits.

Along with other North American tribes such as the Hopi, as well as the Maya and Aztecs of Central America, the Navajo believe that a previous world was destroyed by a great flood. As Leon had told us, the survivors retreated underground until the waters had subsided and it was in the canyon we were visiting that the first people had emerged after the flood. So, every year, this walk was done to honour those first people and all those who had followed and would hopefully continue to follow.

Before entering the canyon, pollen, a symbol for the Navajo of fruitfulness and the continuity of life, was sprinkled on the ground as an offering and prayers of thanksgiving were said. The sun was high as we walked to the place, deep in the canyon, where ancient carvings on the walls depict the history of the Navajo people. These petroglyphs, as they are called, are like the pages of an ancient book, telling a story, with pictures, that unfolds across pages of stone. Etched into the surface of the rocks was a creation story, depicting a myriad of life forms, animals, birds, insects and what looked like amoeba. Some of the creatures were familiar, some no longer exist, while others were part human, part something else. These strange, alien-looking beings were what the Navajo thought of as gods from the sky (*see black-and-white plate no. 50*).

It occurred to me that the petroglyphs were an example of the way in which stones have traditionally been used as a medium for a message. Their enduring quality was chosen for the 10 commandments given to Moses. Likewise, the Hopi have an ancient, detailed, although incomplete set of instructions carved into tablets of stone. It seemed that rocks, stones and crystals have often been chosen for messages that need to be conveyed over vast periods of time, for they can endure as no other substance. As I looked at the beautiful stone carvings on the Navajo canyon wall, I wondered what message we were leaving for future generations. Leon had told us that Native Americans have a saying that the implications of any action should be considered by the consequences it will have for the next seven generations to come. I wondered how far we in the world today consider the implications of our actions?

We left our fresh sprigs off the branches of the trees at the bottom of the canyon as an offering to the spirits of the ancestors that had gone before, and as we stood beneath the ancient petroglyphs, prayers were said in Navajo and sacred blessings were made for the continuation of the tribe and the whole of humanity on the Earth. Then, as we made our way, in solemn silence still, back out of the canyon, a beautiful half-rainbow appeared in the sky.

That evening back at the camp a large fire was built and everyone sat around it, tired but peaceful after the ceremonies. The sky was clear and the stars shone brightly above. Gazing up at the huge starry expanse, we found ourselves wondering who the mysterious figures were we had seen carved on the rocks. The Navajo had spoken of them as gods from the skies. Were these perhaps alien beings?

We were still sitting by the fireside after most of the others had crept off to bed. Leon came over and, looking up at the stars, said:

> *'A Navajo word that you heard a lot today in the prayers was* sohodizin. *It means the radiance that comes from the stars. It means that all of life, all of creation, comes from the stars.*
>
> *'The Earth is spinning through space, like a spaceship. And spinning past us, sometimes less than 50 light years away, are supernovae that could completely destroy the Earth. And the only controls we have on this ship are the crystal skulls. They are part of a crystal matrix that links us on this Earth with the rest of the universe.'*

He said that the original crystal skulls had been made 'by the Holy Ones'. But later on, other skulls had also been made by people. These crystal skulls, he said, had been 'crafted using human hair'. The people had used their own hair to carve and polish them over the years. He said that to his people hair was sacred:

> *'Hair is like the antenna to the soul. It contains information. The whole history of your life is recorded in your hair. So when we use hair to polish a crystal skull, it passes on that information to the skull and so the skull contains all the history and all the wisdom of those who carved and polished it using their own hair.'*

According to the Navajo understanding, the skulls made by the Holy Ones were 'like a template, a prototype for the whole of humanity'. They 'contained the essence of mankind, like a blueprint'. Leon said that 'for all things there is a blueprint', that 'there is another level on which things exist that is invisible to the naked eye'. But it is 'on this level that all things were first made'. This other dimension contains all the 'dimensions and definitions for all things, for all species and even for mankind':

'In this dimension is contained information that is intrinsically linked to all species. Each species of animal has a prototype in this dimension that contains information that relates to its physical and material characteristics. Biologists have called the processes that go on in this invisible dimension "fields". Each species of animal has a field of information around it that is not visible but is essential to each life form. The crystal skulls are like this field that the biologists talk about, but given a physical form.'

It seemed the skulls represent not only the norm of the mental, material and physical information necessary for humanity, but they also represent the ideal. Leon continued:

'The skulls are like a map of our human potential. They set our limitations, they define what we are and what we are able to become. The skulls contain the very paradigm of our human capabilities. They define our limits, of how we are and what we will be in the world.

'As long as the skulls stay where they are, mankind will continue to walk this Earth. They are there to help humanity to steer the right course, to help the mountains remain intact, the rivers and the streams, and even to ensure that the continents stay in their current place. If the crystal skulls go through changes, then so will humankind.

'These sacred objects exist alongside us, in parallel to us and to our human development. They contain the set of original instructions for the whole of humanity, they set our limitations, they define what we are and what we are able to become.

'The crystal skulls, like us, exist in the mind of the Great Spirit, that you call "God". We, like the crystal skulls, were once created in the mind of these beings from another dimension. The crystal skulls are what they used as a template to bring us into our physical and material form. And so we are all invisibly linked to this original act of creation, whether we like it or not.'

I said to Leon that I was not totally sure what he meant. I had always understood human development to be a result of our DNA and the process of evolution. But Leon answered gently:

'You will soon begin to understand. What I can tell you does not mean that DNA and evolution do not also have their part to play. You in the West have not yet seen the bigger picture, but it will come in time.

'The skulls are lots of different things at the same time. It is hard to explain. They function in a way that is both subtle and essential to our well-being. You have heard of the call of the wild? It is the sound of nature that only animals can hear. It is a powerful sound that draws them back to their true nature. This is the sound of the crystal skulls. We live in a vast ocean of sound and vibration. Sound surrounds us, but it is across this vast ocean that the sound of the crystal skulls can travel. The sound they make is the unheard sound, a sound that cannot be heard with the ordinary human ear. We can hear it only with our "inner ear". It is the unheard sound of creation. Without this sound nothing could live, for it is this sound that animates everything. A leaf unfurling in the spring makes this sound. It is the sound that happens at the moment of conception, when new life is born. It is the very same sound that was made when the Earth came into existence and when we ourselves were given our current human form. It is this same sound of creation that is also within us and it is a beautiful sound.

'If you really think about it, we are all made up of sound. Everything is just a vibration, constantly moving and changing. Our own minds, our very consciousness is vibration. Crystal is a vibration. It is a particular type of vibration that sings to our spirit. It comes through the silence and although we can't hear it with our ears, we can hear it with our hearts. This is why the skulls are sometimes called "the singing skulls". Their song is of the joy of creation, the wonder of existence. They remind us that we have come into being, that we are part of the miracle of creation, and this sound can help us steer the right course through space and time.

'Every human being has a connection with the crystal skulls, for the unheard sound of creation also vibrates from the crystal skull to your own skull and it is already in your thoughts. It is part of an unseen force that holds your life together. It is a vibration that is woven into everything. It is a tone that is always going to be with you. It is the gift of creation that has manifest your human form and provided you, and each and every one of us, with knowledge, abilities and talents. It has given you life to enjoy. The crystal skull emits a certain tone so that you may realize your resonance with the sound of creation. The wisdom of the skulls becomes available when you open yourself to this mystery and let the sound come in.'

I wasn't sure that I had completely understood what Leon had been saying, but I was moved by the poetry of his words. It seemed such a different way of looking at the world. As I gazed at the dying embers of the fire
glowing against the darkness, I thought about how the crystal skulls were
here to remind us about the awe and beauty of creation. It seemed so
straightforward, so deeply inspiring. I thought back to our previous
research into the crystal skulls. We had been obsessed with getting a
'rational' and scientific explanation. Unwavering in attempts to slot the
skulls into an archaeological framework, we had seen them only in terms
of their construction date, the tools used in their manufacture and where
they were from. Now, it seemed that their significance could never be
determined under a microscope, however powerful. Their importance
went beyond anything that could currently be examined in a science lab.

Just as our quest for the truth about the skulls had been limited by our
scientific framework, was it not true that our whole view of the world had
been undermined by our Western 'rational' way of looking at things, by
our view of the whole of creation as merely a collection of simple biologi-
cal, chemical, mechanical and certainly purely physical objects and
processes? Had we somehow robbed creation of its mystery, of its poetry
and beauty? It suddenly occurred to me that perhaps we had actually
managed to cut ourselves off from the very mysteries of life itself.

Chris asked Leon if he could explain a little more about what he had
been saying earlier about how mankind had been created by 'beings from
other dimensions', but he said simply, 'It is not yet time for you to know
any more. It is now time to sleep. When the right time comes you will
find out more.'

The following morning we were relieved to find that there was someone
else at the gathering with sufficient room in the cabin of their pick-up
truck to give us a more comfortable lift back to our car. Besides which, it
was starting to rain, much to Leon's delight. It was confirmation that the
ceremonies had been done correctly when they were followed by a down-
pour. This came as a sharp reminder that we were in harsh desert terrain
frequently devoid of water.

Patricio Domínguez ushered us into his pick-up truck. He was in his
early 40s, wore sandals and had a long ponytail of dark hair (*see black-
and-white plate no. 48*). Patricio turned out to be quite a character. He
described himself as a 'spiritual adviser' to his people, but he was also an
electronic engineer. He was a member of the Pueblo tribe, a Spanish word

which means simply 'the people'. He told us he was actually a direct descendant of 'the last few remnants of three different tribes known as the Tiwa, the Piro and the Manso' who had lived in the area now close to the US border with Mexico until most of his ancestors were wiped out by the Spanish during the Pueblo revolt around 200 years ago.

Patricio lived with his wife and family on a reservation near Albuquerque, but, as he put it, he had 'a foot in both worlds'. One foot was in the indigenous world, as he spent around half of his time practising and studying native beliefs and traditions, but the other foot was firmly in the modern world in his job as an electronic engineer designing, maintaining and repairing computers, televisions and other electronic devices for a company in Albuquerque. Patricio was a very knowledgeable and highly entertaining man complete with a lively sense of humour. He described himself as being like 'a bridge between cultures' or 'worlds', or more jokingly as a 'techno-shaman'.

Although Patricio said the Pueblo themselves had no crystal skulls, he seemed to know an awful lot about them. He too had heard of the legend that there were 13 original ancient skulls and that one day they would come back together again to reveal their knowledge. He explained that the crystal skulls contain so much knowledge in such a tiny space that they are like human cells or computer microchips, that they are 'whole living libraries of information'.

Patricio was well aware that scientists were working towards extracting the information from the skulls. He said that there were huge vistas of knowledge within the skulls and that they had a permanent memory bank which had been created at the molecular level:

'Think how many molecules even the tiniest piece of crystal contains and you start to get the idea. For example, think of the dust particles that you see in a shaft of light. Normally we cannot see these particles at all. In normal light there appears to be nothing whatsoever there, but as soon as you open the doorway and allow a flood of light to come in, you start to see millions upon millions of these tiny little particles suspended in the air. If you imagine a similar scenario going on inside the crystal skull, that we see nothing until we look in the right way, when we open the doorway of the mind and allow the right focus of a beam of mental light, then if you imagine that each of those tiny particles contained within the crystal skull is a tiny piece of knowledge and those particles are filling the entire room, like stars on a bright clear, starry night, it is just like that inside the skulls.*

'But there is more to it than that, because you see, the crystal skulls really are multi-faceted. You must realize that the crystal skulls are actually living depositories of knowledge. Though they are made of crystal they have their own sense of consciousness. They have a sentience within themselves and they were constructed in a very special way using psychic forces. We think of crystal as dead matter but it is really more like a living plasma that has a relationship directly with our own thoughts and with, if you like, the mind of God. In fact that's really something to do with how they were formed. The original crystal skulls were not really chiselled or sanded into shape, as some people believe, they were, if you like, "molten" into shape by psychic forces so that they actually describe and define the thoughts and mental processes of we human beings. They were shaped by the consciousness of those earliest people or beings that actually put them together using their own particular psychic potentialities.'

Listening to all this, sitting in the cab squashed up between Patricio and Ceri, I must admit I was beginning to wonder if I really was talking to someone who had 'one foot firmly in the modern world'. I had expected to hear from Patricio a more down-to-earth explanation of the crystal skulls than we had just heard from Leon. So I asked him, 'Do you really, then, go along with this idea that the skulls, and indeed we human beings ourselves, were created "in the minds of beings from other dimensions", as Leon was telling us last night?'

I added that I had great difficulty believing in the existence of other, non-physical dimensions at all, let alone that beings from them may have had something to do with the origins of the human race itself.

To this Patricio replied quite simply:

'Why not? When you think about it, in our minds we have created beings that exist in another dimension quite separate from ourselves. What do you think computer viruses are? You are not going to tell me computer viruses don't exist and yet what are they? We cannot see them, we cannot touch them and yet their effects on our world are very real. Just because they do not exist in our physical world, but instead in the parallel reality of the electronic computer world, does not reduce their ability to wreak havoc and destruction in our real, physical human world. They exist in a completely separate reality from ours, in the virtual computer world, and yet how were they created? They were originally created in our own minds. The whole virtual reality of the electronic

computer world was devised and created by scientists, by the workings of the human mind in our own physical world.

'Of course even the virtual world of computers has an interface with our real physical world, in the form of hardware. Without the hardware the software of computer programs and viruses simply would cease to exist. The living, working mechanisms of the software, such as the viruses, which incidentally can reproduce and replicate themselves and go on living for a time quite happily, without any further assistance from us, still had to be created in the first place, and this was done by us human beings. To these computer viruses we are "beings from another world that created them and their world". Without our assistance they would simply not have come into existence or would soon simply cease to exist.

'And so we can also look at the crystal skulls as, if you like, the hardware. Without the hardware of the original creation of the crystal skulls we, as the software, would quite simply never have come into existence. And without the continued good maintenance and goodwill of our creators, we, like computer viruses in a virtual world which is no longer being properly maintained or having its power supply turned on, would quite simply soon cease to exist.'

By this stage my mind was boggling with trying to take in all these new ideas that seemed to be being fired at me from all directions. It was fast becoming clear that the Native Americans had a completely different view not only of the crystal skulls, but also of the whole world and indeed the universe, from our own 'normal' or Western world view.

I explained to Patricio that I was having great difficulty in trying to understand the whole Native American approach to reality. He tried to reassure me that although there were some fundamental differences between the Native American and Western world views, the findings of our own Western physicists now seemed to be converging with the traditional Native American view of reality. He pointed out that most of our own physicists now reject the traditional Western view that objects are just solid matter in favour of the view that atoms are part of a vast sea of energy particles. He said they would probably find no objection to the notion that the crystal skulls were made up of vibrations, or waves of energy capable of communicating with ourselves. He added jokingly, 'Those guys are so close behind us now that they are almost knocking on our back door.'

But I was still a little confused. So, as Patricio dropped us off back at our car, he said he would be more than happy to try to explain all this if we would like to come and visit him at his office the following day.

20. THE KNOWLEDGE

As we entered Patricio's office the following afternoon, we felt as though we had walked into the laboratory of some nutty professor. Circuit boards, bits of electronic equipment and various technical diagrams seemed to almost completely line the walls. There were bits of paper and stray pieces of electronic technology everywhere. The room was obviously a veritable hive of technical and intellectual activity.

Patricio welcomed us in, sat us down with a cup of coffee and then proceeded quite amiably to try to lecture us on the differences between our own 'normal' Western materialist way of looking at the world and that of the indigenous people.

He explained that we in the Western world tend only to see the world, indeed the universe, as a collection of physical parts, usually thought to function together like the different parts of a machine. We see all these parts, whether different planets or different people, as essentially separate from each other and related only physically, though this includes electrically or chemically, within the strict confines of time and space. We see everything as inhabiting only physical dimensions which we can see, or otherwise accurately record with the help of technical instruments.

As we see everything as separate in time and space, an event which happened, say, in one particular place and at one particular time in the past exists for us only in that particular time and place. It cannot have any kind of effect on anything which happened before and it can only affect things which have happened since by means of its physical proximity to them in both time and space.

As Patricio explained:

'Take as an example, an ant crushed underfoot by a peasant farmer on a piece of land, say, in Central America 4,000 years ago. According to our traditional Western way of looking at the world, this event would have no effect whatsoever on anything that had happened before and would have precious little effect on anything that has happened since. The ant would die, the peasant farmer would probably not even notice it, and the effect on the land would be nothing more than to add a mere milligram of dead material that over time would decompose and become a very small part of the soil. Beyond that, in both space and time, the consequences of this event would be so negligible, so insignificant, as to be to all intents and purposes only worth completely ignoring.'

He explained that in the Native American world view, on the other hand, everything is sacred. This goes for both living material and inorganic material. Everything that exists, no matter how large or how small, is a part of the whole, a part of the sacred essence of all existence. Nothing is separate from anything else. Everything is a part of creation. Whilst individual things may have a physical existence that makes them appear separate according to our concepts of time and space, the very concepts of physical dimension and of separate time and space are themselves really just an illusion:

'We like to think of ourselves as separate both from each other and from the rest of the world, but we are not. Our physical existence is only one level of the greater reality, which has many layers, many dimensions, and many paths through which everything is connected and through which everything is both a part and a parcel of the one great whole. All that really exists is part of the sacred act of creation. Everything we perceive as separate things in their own separate times and places, even we ourselves, everything is really an essential part of the sacred act of creation itself.'

Patricio explained that this is something we normally cannot see because we are limited by the constraints of the five-sense physical world, but our physical world is only one of many worlds, only one of the many dimensions of creation, only one of the many threads through which all things are connected to each other.

'Indeed, according to much of Native American philosophy, time and space are not really separate entities at all. They only appear as separate because of the lens through which we perceive things, the lens which we call the physical or material world. In a sense, the crystal skulls are like another type of lens that helps us to see the full wonder of creation.

'All things have a sense of consciousness and of memory. All things are connected, if not on the physical level then at least on this other non-physical level, where all things are truly connected to one another and to the whole.

'So in the Native American view of the world things do not just exist in one particular place and in one particular time. They do not exist only in this one physical dimension of ours. There are other levels of reality, other dimensions, in which something which exists or an event which happens can actually have a subtle but unmistakable effect on other things and other events which may be far removed in both time and space, or which may be happening in these other non-physical and hence non-visible dimensions.'

'But the things which exist and the events which happen in these other dimensions, and the effects which they can have on our physical world, do not necessarily obey the simple laws of our physical dimension and so cannot be understood by our simple twentieth-century laws of physics.

'In this sense, there is, quite literally, more to the world, more to the universe, more to creation, than meets the eye, and we simple physical people, lesser mortals if you like, are often unable to perceive, let alone understand, quite what goes on in these "other worlds" or "dimensions of the spirit".'

Patricio took the example of the ant crushed underfoot once again:

'In the Native American view of the world this seemingly insignificant event, far removed from us in both time and space, may still have some subtle but unmistakable effects that go far beyond the minor effects of the event itself within the boundaries of our simple physical world. Whilst we may not be able to readily perceive them, the events going on in the other worlds or dimensions of the spirit world may actually have had something to do with why the ant was trodden on in the first place, and the effects of its being trodden on may have influenced events in these other worlds which we cannot perceive but which in turn may actually still be having some impact on us today.

'The ant is perhaps not a particularly good example, but the point is that the effects of this simple event that we can actually perceive happening in our simple physical and material world, in this case almost negligible ones, are not the only effects that this event may have had and may still be having in the other dimensions of reality, the other layers of creation.

'Just because we may be far separated from an event by the simple mechanics of time and space does not mean that something which happened in a distant time and place in the past, or which may in fact happen in a distant time or place in the future, is without its effects on us now, just because we are not consciously aware of any of its direct physical influences. All aspects of creation have their effects, no matter how imperceptibly small, on all other aspects of creation. We are all part of the whole. We all have links, many of them through dimensions we do not yet understand, and so all parts of the universe, or of creation, are related in some sense to one another. In this sense at least, everything is living. On some level, all things have some sense of consciousness and memory. And, through the greater consciousness and memory of creation, in a sense each little part of creation also contains the whole. The crystal skulls can help us understand this better.'

Thinking hard about all this, it struck me that much Native American philosophy at first seems to make no sense at all from a contemporary Western viewpoint. We tend to believe that our own particular view of reality is the only one. This was probably one of the reasons why the Western world had always been so keen to suppress or destroy Native American ways of seeing. Their alternative viewpoint had been seen as a direct threat to the status quo and therefore something to be afraid of or destroyed. As we had learned, this is a process which began with the massacre of millions of Native Americans immediately after the arrival of the Europeans in the Americas just over 500 years ago, with the offer of forced conversion to Christianity and the Western world view or death. The massacres continued right through the Indian Wars in the USA at the end of the nineteenth century and seemed to be finding fresh impetus in some parts of South and Central America even today. We had already heard that whilst some Native Americans died of diseases introduced quite accidentally, many others were, and still are being, killed quite intentionally, whether by the sword, the gun, or through diseases introduced with the very intention of wiping them out.

Leon had told us that in the United States, the great land of freedom itself, many Native American religious practices and ceremonies were quite literally banned by law until as recently as 1978. Apparently even today many herbs and plants traditionally used by native medicine men and known to have beneficial therapeutic effects are categorized by the US Surgeon General's Office as 'poison' and marked, somewhat ironically, with a skull and crossed bones.

Patricio suggested, however, that the traditional Western scientific, mechanistic, materialistic and purely physical world view was now looking a little less sure of itself. As he had mentioned the previous day, recent scientific discoveries, particularly in the field of quantum physics, have started to pose fundamental questions about how the universe really works, questions which simply cannot be explained by the traditional laws of mechanistic physics, as originally defined by Sir Isaac Newton and later refined by Albert Einstein.

Patricio suggested we look into this area further and, as we discovered, many of the recent findings of scientific research cannot be explained according to the usual rules of chronological time. Others cannot be explained according to our usual assumption that the parts are somehow separate from the whole, while others challenge our usual belief that inanimate objects have no non-physical relationship to each other and no sense of themselves or the whole situation of which they are a part.

Until very recently, scientists largely concerned themselves with explaining the world at the level that is larger than the atom. Quantum physicists, on the other hand, dedicate their lives to studying how the world works at the sub-atomic level. It is in this area that the traditional Western laws of physics are proving largely unable to explain what is going on.

Indeed, as Patricio had already hinted, it seems that the observations that have now been made by our quantum physicists are, for the most part, actually better explained according to the traditional Native American view of the world than according to the traditional Newtonian view.

As we discovered, one of the earliest cracks in our Western world view actually appeared quite by accident when scientists were experimenting with modern holographic image technology and accidentally dropped one of the holographic images they had so carefully prepared. It fell to the floor and shattered into tiny pieces. At first the experimenters were simply annoyed that they had managed to break an object which was the result of so many years' work and so much money invested in developing the necessary technology. But the discovery they made as a result of this accident was ultimately far more interesting.

Holographic image technology is a relatively recent development. A holographic image is a three-dimensional image 'encrypted' into a special kind of glass. The resulting image is unusual in that, although it is etched onto a two-dimensional surface, it appears to the human eye, if viewed from the right angle and under laser light, as three-dimensional. By some ironic coincidence, or as if by some as yet unknown hand of fate, one of the first images reproduced in this way was that of a human skull. It may also be more than coincidence that many people claim to have seen what look like three-dimensional holographic images within the crystal skulls themselves.

A holographic image works by using laser light, or 'uni-directional' light, rather than normal light, which is 'multi-directional'. In a laser beam of light the 'photons', or individual separate particles of light, are all moving in exactly the same direction, instead of being scattered around and bouncing off things in all directions, as photons normally do. In standard photography these particles of multi-directional light pass through the lens from all angles and are concentrated onto photographic paper which is covered in chemicals which are sensitive to the light they are receiving and so change their shade or colour accordingly. In the holographic technique, on the other hand, the object being copied or 'holographed' is kept in total darkness and a laser light is fired at it. The laser beam is actually split so that one half is bounced off the object and the other half off a mirror. The photons are bounced back, half of them off the contours of the object and the other half off the totally flat surface of the mirror, so that all the particles come back together as they hit the holographic plate of glass, which is sensitive to light particles. The molecules within the glass then change their shade or colour accordingly and the resulting image, when lit by a 'whole' laser beam, is a three-dimensional one.

This in itself is a mysterious enough process that suggests that in some way the particles of light bouncing off the object can somehow 'communicate' this to the particles of light that have simply bounced off the flat surface of the mirror. But this interpretation is highly debatable and the 'normal' laws of physics can also be used to explain the process.

But the discovery that shook the scientists was what happens when a holographic plate of glass is broken. For, instead of breaking into individual pieces that have to be put back together again, rather like a jigsaw puzzle, before we can see the whole picture, each of the resulting pieces, however small, is still capable of showing the whole image.[1] According to the traditional laws of physics, this just isn't possible. Every single molecule in the piece of glass would have had to instantaneously change its appearance without any direct physical reason why it should do so. These results imply that at some deeper and perhaps non-physical level even the simple, non-living, inorganic molecules of a piece of glass somehow 'know' their role, that they have a sense of 'consciousness', a sense of their own condition and how it fits in with the whole. It also implies that there has to be some kind of collective 'memory' and means of communication amongst the molecules of glass. Otherwise, how would the individual molecules know in what form to regroup?

There are in fact many other examples in nature where the small parts of a system appear to contain the whole – or at least contain vital information about the whole. In many cases the information contained in each part is actually necessary either to create or to vitally change the whole.

One example is genetic information. Inside each and every individual cell in the human body, or in a plant or animal for that matter, are molecules of DNA which actually contain the pattern, the blueprint or template if you like, of the whole. This genetic information somehow communicates to each and every tiny living cell the information about what it should become, whether it should grow into, say, a bit of skin on the left big toe, a bit of muscle tissue on the right thumb, a brain cell within the outer cortex of the brain or muscle tissue that makes up the hind leg of, say, a frog. Each living cell is potentially capable of growing into anything it likes, but it needs to understand its place in the whole in order to grow into a healthy part of it.

This is in fact thought to be the precise problem that gives rise to cancer or cancerous growths in the body. Cancer cells are ones that seem to have somehow forgotten their purpose and do not know what to become. They do appear to contain the essential genetic information, but do not, for some reason, successfully use, translate or understand it. Such cells are not in and of themselves necessarily harmful, but because they do not function as part of the whole, they tend to interfere with other parts of the body in a way that is often fatal.

Leon Secatero had already compared our DNA to the crystal skulls, rather to our surprise:

'Like DNA, the crystal skulls are like a set of directions, a blueprint, or a template if you like, for the role of humanity within the universe.

'They are a template not only for our physical bodies, but for our whole selves. Just like the DNA within each and every living cell in our bodies, within each and every one of us lies information about the whole of creation. Like "mirrors to our own souls" the crystal skulls can help us to find this information and teach us what it is to be truly human. Like the individual cells of the human body, which have the physical potential to become anything they like, on a less physical level we, too, as individuals, have the potential to become anything we like. But, just like the physical cells of the human body, we need to have and understand information about the whole, in order to "grow" into a healthy part of it.

'The crystal skulls can help us to see the whole picture, they can help us to see our total potential and also our own limitations. Like the DNA inside each and every living cell, the crystal skulls present us with information about where we have come from and what we should be. They show us where we are going and present us with the full image of what we are able to become. Like cancer cells, we can choose to ignore this message and grow out of place and out of step with the whole. But the crystal skulls can help us to see what we should become on all levels, both physical and spiritual, in order for us to know how to grow for the good of the whole. So we can take the image of the whole they present to us and grow into a full and healthy part of it. In short, the crystal skulls show us our potential to be fully enlightened and spiritual beings who function fully and effectively as part of creation as a whole.'

In time-honoured fashion physical scientists have tried to explain how individual cells in the body know what to become by analysing only the smaller 'building blocks' of DNA information they contain. This mechanistic way of looking at things has at least managed to explain how genetic information is passed from parent to child and how, when an individual body cell divides during growth, exactly the same genetic information about the whole person is passed on to the newly born cell.

But what the traditional physical scientists have failed to explain is how any individual living cell in the human body 'knows' where it is in the whole.

As Patricio told us:

'By the same token, the physical scientists have so far failed to explain how we as individual human beings fit in to the whole of creation. They have provided us with their model of the universe, as a collection of largely inanimate and certainly separate and purely physical "things" that have a purely mechanistic and functional relationship with each other. Like the different parts of a machine, the behaviour of all things is dictated entirely by the basic laws of physics and chemistry discovered so far, and all strictly bound within the limitations of time and space. But deep down in our hearts I think each and every one of us knows there is more to it than that.'

I was certainly beginning to think so myself. However, here it may be helpful to know that some quantum physicists have recently begun to question the whole idea that all things are in turn made up only of smaller separate 'things' with no inherent memory, consciousness or purpose of their own. The beginnings of this debate actually started some time ago with what is often known in the scientists' trade jargon as the 'wave-particle' debate.

Traditionally, scientists have believed that everything is in turn made up of only smaller and smaller things, i.e. particles, that have a purely physical, materialistic or mechanistic relationship to each other. Quite early on in the history of physics, however, it began to be noticed that certain phenomena could not be explained this way – radio, for example. A radio message from, say, London to New York, could not be due to any physical particle actually making the journey itself, instantaneously, but could be explained as a 'wave' of energy or information crossing the Atlantic. What we now understand to happen is that particles in London are being electronically 'excited' so that they move around and vibrate at a particular frequency against the particles next to them. This process is repeated, spreading out like ripples on a pond, with the resulting electro-magnetic vibrations being felt, say, on the other side of the Atlantic.

Interestingly, Leon Secatero actually compared the way the crystal skulls work with the way a radio works. According to him they transmit their 'unheard sound of creation' in effectively the same manner. This is why, he claimed, no matter where we are in the world, we are able to receive their message. We don't have to be in the physical presence of a crystal skull to hear it.

Until very recently, conventional physicists have recognized only two basic concepts: particles of matter on the one hand and waves of energy on the other. These, they believed, could explain the workings of the whole universe. The effects of both were deemed to be entirely predictable and observable, and determined purely by physical mechanistic processes. But there have always been some phenomena which do not fit easily into this mode. The most obvious example is light. Light sometimes acts as though it is made up of separate and individual particles of matter. For example it cannot pass through most objects which get in its way. But at other times it acts as though it is a 'wave' of energy or information, with no physical substance of its own. It can, for instance, move through other physical objects, so long as they are made of matter that is transparent.

One famous experiment, known as the 'single photon interference experiment', even implies that single particles of light, known as photons, not only act like waves and like individual particles simultaneously, but also that they can communicate with each other over time as well as through space.[2]

But light was considered one of the few exceptions to the rule until sub-atomic particles began to be studied in more detail. At the sub-atomic level, the traditional distinction between the wave and the particle disappears. Things cannot be explained as just one or the other, they can only be understood as *both*. In a sense, matter *is* energy, energy *is* matter, 'things' are also 'waves of information' and so effectively, 'information' or 'energy' is the essence of all 'things'. At the sub-atomic level at least, these very concepts themselves are ultimately not separate at all.

Findings such as these have now begun to divide the scientific community. On the one hand there are those who seem quite happy with the concept that things can be both 'matter' and 'energy', both 'objects' and 'information', at one and the same time. But on the other hand there are those who see this as a ludicrous contradiction, a logical impossibility.

One such person is Professor David Deutsch of Oxford University, a leading expert in the field of quantum mechanics. According to him, and many others like him, the reason why individual particles behave also as though they are part of a wave of energy or information is really because of the existence of 'parallel universes'! According to this eminent professor of physics:

'We are not actually seeing particles and waves at the same time. The results of the single photon interference experiment are actually due to the influence of particles which exist in parallel universes. The photons in our experiment are actually interacting with these other photons in these other universes which we simply cannot see.'[3]

Although at first Professor Deutsch's words sound somewhat metaphysical, in actual fact his interpretation is completely in line with quantum physicists' latest theory of how the universe works. As he himself puts it:

'In fact, the classical laws of physics just aren't true. In fact, the quantum laws of mechanics are actually a true description of nature.'[4]

The essence of quantum mechanics is the principle of 'uncertainty'. Everything is made up of 'uncertain' particles of 'uncertain' location. As quantum physicists often put it, 'An individual particle, at any one moment, has as much probability of being in any one place as in any other.' This has always struck me as being a bit like admitting you don't really know what is going on. But, as Professor Deutsch has explained it:

'Quantum mechanics is basically a theory of many parallel universes. Some of these universes are very like our own and some are very un-like our own. The nearby universes differ from ours by, say, only one photon, whilst the other, more distant universes are completely different from ours.'[5]

In a sense, every universe has an equal chance of physically happening, but what we see is only one of the great myriad of possible universes. According to David Deutsch, 'In a sense each and every particle exists in its own separate universe, but these universes interfere with each other to produce the pattern of the universe that we can actually see or perceive.' Professor Deutsch concludes, 'Reality does not consist of just a single universe.'[6] We are, however, confined to only one of its dimensions.

The parallels with the Native American view of the world and with the ideas we had heard from the keepers and 'channellers' of the crystal skulls were striking. Native Americans have long believed that we inhabit only one dimension of reality, that there are other non-physical dimensions. They also believe that things can exist both in one physical place and time, like a particle, *and* have influence elsewhere simultaneously, like a wave. According to this view, as Leon and Patricio both told us, the presence of the crystal skulls can be felt everywhere simultaneously and they can help us to communicate with these other levels of reality that our modern physicists are only just beginning to discover. Indeed, we were beginning to come to the conclusion that the Native American understanding of how the universe really works is one step ahead of our own modern scientists.

Native Americans, for example, believe that it is possible on some level to communicate with inanimate physical objects, such as the crystal skulls, as well as with other living and non-living things. They also believe that such communications can open doorways into the other worlds of the spirits, or the 'parallel dimensions' now referred to by our physicists, and can actually enable us to transcend the boundaries of time and space.

Once again recent scientific experiments at the sub-atomic level suggest that this might be the case. Another recent quantum physics experiment, for example, suggests that it may indeed be possible for the human mind to communicate directly with inanimate objects, at least at the level of sub-atomic particles. This was carried out in 1989 by Wayne Itano and his colleagues at the National Institute of Standards and Technology in Boulder, Colorado, and reported by Dr Fred Alan Wolf in his book *The Dreaming Universe*.[7] It involved the scientists watching some 5,000 beryllium atoms confined in a magnetic field and then exposed to radio waves of energy. To help us understand this experiment Fred Alan Wolf uses the analogy of watching a pot of water as you bring it to the boil. Briefly, the experiment proved the old adage that a watched pot never boils. The more often the scientists observed the process, the longer it took for the beryllium atoms to 'boil'. This effect could not be explained by the process of 'looking' – which was done by means of a laser beam – as this actually added energy to the system, thus heating the atoms up rather than cooling them down. According to Dr Wolf, the results were caused by 'the observer effect'. The observer effect says that 'the more a quantum mechanical system is observed in a particular state, the more likely it is that it will remain in that state'. This principle is now widely recognized in the area of quantum physics research.

According to Dr Wolf, what matters is the *intent* of the observer. For the object or system to remain in its initial state, the observer must have the intent of seeing it in its initial state. If, on the other hand, the observer intends to see the pot boiling, it will boil.[8]

Whilst Dr Wolf does point out that it is important to realize that 'intent' is distinct from 'intention' or mere 'expectation', in that the appropriate action must also be involved, the important thing for us here was that it had now been experimentally proven that the workings of the human mind can have a direct effect on the behaviour of sub-atomic particles, or 'quantum systems'. And so some kind of interaction or communication is possible between inanimate objects and the human mind.

Our thoughts are capable of influencing the things around us in a way that cannot be explained by the traditional laws of physics.

It seems that the atoms themselves are, in some way, 'aware' that they are being observed and change their condition or behaviour accordingly. This phenomenon suggests that even sub-atomic particles have some kind of 'consciousness', or sense of 'awareness' of what is going on around them. This is what Native Americans have referred to as 'the mind of molecules', and it seems that this awareness extends to some kind of relationship between themselves and the inner workings of the human mind.

Indeed, if we view the crystal skulls as 'quantum systems' (i.e. both particles of matter and waves of energy simultaneously, or particles that exist in more than one parallel universe), the idea that they can somehow interact or communicate with the human mind and affect our consciousness starts to make a lot more sense. After all, if it has been shown that the workings of the human mind can profoundly affect the behaviour and condition of inanimate objects, or atomic particles such as beryllium atoms, then why should the reverse not also be the case?

But the keepers of the crystal skulls and many Native Americans say there is more to it than that. They believe that communication between the human mind and the crystal skulls is not only possible but can also enable us to escape the confines of our own purely physical dimension and transcend the boundaries of time and space. So, with the help of the crystal skulls, we can communicate not only with the past but also the future. Once again, the latest experiments in quantum physics suggest that this could actually be the case. The idea of communicating through time may indeed prove to be more than just science fiction.

Einstein's theory of relativity states that nothing in the universe can travel faster than the speed of light. The reason for this is that if it did then it would effectively be travelling backwards in time. For time, like everything else, is relative. In the case of time it is relative to your speed, or the rate at which you are travelling through space. The faster you travel through space, the slower you travel through time. Indeed, many modern physicists now consider time and space to be different aspects of the same dimension, what they call the 'time-space continuum'. This is exactly what the ancient Mayans believed. Interestingly, it is also the same concept that we heard mentioned by 'the voice of the skull' speaking through Carole Wilson. Physicists have concluded that time and space are related because by travelling fast enough through space it is actually possible to 'warp' time.

Whilst this may at first sound a bit far-fetched, it has actually been tested many times, in a famous experiment that relies, perhaps more than coincidentally, on a piece of quartz crystal. Einstein said that because nothing in the universe travels faster than the speed of light, if you could travel at the speed of light time would seem to stand still. The example is often given of an astronaut travelling across the universe at nearly the speed of light. According to Einstein's law he could travel for what on Earth would be many, many years, but when he arrived back he would hardly have aged at all, and the clock on his spaceship would hardly have moved.

Of course, Einstein's theory has proved impossible to test in precisely this form, but it has been tested in a more down-to-earth way. In 1971 scientists from Hewlett-Packard set two atomic clocks, based on the precise electrical oscillations of a piece of quartz crystal, to zero.[9] One remained in the lab whilst the other was flown right around the world on a jumbo jet. Of course the speed at which a jumbo jet travels is nothing like the speed of light, but it was the best they could do at the time. The idea was to see whether there would be any difference at all in the amount of time that had elapsed on each of these phenomenally accurate clocks.

Believe it or not, the clock which had been flying for many hours, even at a speed of only around 600 mph (965 km/h) did show less time had elapsed than the other clock when it got back home. The effect was tiny, only a fraction of a second, but none the less it was precisely in line with Einstein's mathematical predictions. This experiment has been repeated many times and with many variations since then, and always the results are consistent with the idea that if you were to multiply this effect right up to the speed of light, time would indeed stand entirely still.

But by the same token, Einstein's theory also says that if you could travel faster than the speed of light, time would appear to travel backwards. Or, put another way, you would actually travel backwards in time. Whilst no one has yet been able to find a way of making a human being do this, the same can no longer be said for sub-atomic particles. As recently as 1995, Professor Günter Nimtz carried out a sub-atomic experiment at the University of Cologne in Germany.[10] His experiment involved splitting in two a microwave signal containing a message. One half of this signal was sent through air and so travelled, like all microwave signals, precisely at the speed of light. This signal arrived at its destination at precisely the same moment as it was sent, as is common to all microwave signals. But for the other half of the signal Nimtz tried something different. Across its path he placed what is called a 'quantum barrier'. This is an electronic barrier whose purpose is to prevent the transmission of all sub-atomic particles, including microwave signals. The idea was to block all transmission of the signal along this path. In fact, precisely the opposite happened.

In practice, the microwave signal which was sent across the quantum barrier actually travelled at 4.7 times the speed of light and was received *before* it had even been sent. Although over such a short distance the effect observed was minuscule, a mere fraction of a second, the results were still earth-shattering. As Nimtz himself pointed out, if you could build a quantum barrier that stretched from one side of the universe to the other, any message you sent by this route would go faster than the speed of light and would actually travel backwards in time. It would arrive at the other side of the universe way before you had even sent it!

Physicists are still arguing about the result of Nimtz's experiment. Some dispute that it was really 'information' that was sent. In fact the 'message' was a recording of Mozart's 40th Symphony, which I think most people would consider 'information'. Whilst the debate continues, there is certainly now no dispute that *something* can travel backwards in time.

The emerging consensus seems to be that the effect is due to 'quantum tunnelling'. The idea is that stray sub-atomic particles can in fact 'tunnel' through a quantum barrier in such a way that they come out of the 'time tunnel' before they went in. This theory is a little too complex to go into in detail here, but it relies on the idea that the precise position of an 'uncertain' quantum particle is determined as much by its future position as by its past, that there are 'imaginary waves of probability' about the precise position of any particle, or rather 'quantum system', which travel backwards in time as well as forwards. And so, in a sense, the present is determined as much by the future as by the past.

This concept would not have been at all strange to the ancient Mesoamericans, nor for that matter would it be to many Native Americans today. The ancient Maya and many other Native American tribes represented time as a circle, and Native Americans have apparently long believed that time is cyclical in nature, rather than a straight line from past to future, as we in the West tend to envisage it. Therefore they believe communications through or across time are possible. As Patricio aptly put it:

> *'The Western world thought the Earth was flat until only around 500 years ago, until they discovered America, and realized that the Earth is*

round. It is a shame that it seems to be taking Western scientists about another 500 years to realize that time is also not flat. It too is really a great cycle.'

We weren't sure quite what Patricio meant by this, but it certainly did seem that once again, even when it comes to the very basic concept of time itself, our modern physicists are only just beginning to 'discover' knowledge that the ancient Native Americans have known for perhaps thousands of years.

By now the idea that through the crystal skulls we could receive messages from the future as well as from the past was beginning to sound a lot less like science fiction and a lot more like reality.

But how might the crystal skulls be involved in the process of sending information through time and space? Nick Nocerino believed that this has something to do with the fact that the Earth itself is made up largely of quartz crystal. He had referred to the existence of some sort of living entity, perhaps a form of quartz crystal, that is buried deep in the centre of the Earth. Again we found that even this idea is no longer totally dismissed by our own scientific establishment.

Given that no one has been able to drill deeper into the Earth's crust than about seven miles (12 km), no one knows for sure what the centre of the Earth is really made of. From the evidence of volcanic activity it is certainly the case that just below the solid outer crust there is a layer of molten rock, which we see as lava during volcanic eruptions. It was long believed that due to the intense heat and pressure exerted by the weight of the Earth's rock itself, this liquid matter extended right to the centre of the Earth and got hotter and more liquid towards the centre. But as recently as 1996, this idea was challenged.

Two French geologists working near Paris devised an experiment which replicated the conditions of intense heat and pressure found inside the centre of the Earth.[11] Doctors Poirier and Le Mouel squeezed some lava material between two diamond-protected vices and heated it up using laser technology to the estimated 5,000°C found at the centre of the Earth. What resulted was a battle between the forces of pressure and temperature. The outermost thin crust did solidify, just like the Earth's crust, and due to the phenomenal temperature, the next innermost part of the material melted and became molten liquid, just like the lava or mantle just beneath the Earth's crust. But right at the very centre of this boiling mass, the material solidified into a crystalline structure. What seemed to be happening was that the lava that makes up the inner Earth is a mixture of iron and silicon, and for the iron component temperature was the winner over pressure and so it melted and 'floated' to the outer area of the core. But for silicon, pressure won out over temperature and so it solidified, forming a very hard and very solid crystal right in the centre.

Recent studies of earthquakes have led other scientists to similar conclusions. Lars Stixrude of the University of Göttingen and Ronald Cohen of the Carnegie Institution have been studying the fact that over the last 10 years earthquake reverberations around the world have been discovered to be anisotropic, just like quartz crystals. They realized that the high, fairly constant temperatures and low gravity at the very centre of the Earth are actually ideal for growing crystals. In 1995, they published their new theory that the very innermost core of the Earth is in fact a very large and very solid crystal some 744 miles (1,200 km) across![12]

Assuming this turns out to be the case, as Patricio put it,

> *'This means that the Earth itself actually has the very properties necessary to receive radio waves, microwaves or other electronic information from right across the universe, perhaps even travelling backwards through time. In a sense we could think of the Earth itself as effectively the biggest radar receiver in the world, capable of picking up messages both from the past and from the future.'*

Certainly Native Americans have long believed that the crystal skulls form part of a natural 'energy grid' which surrounds the whole of the planet and connects all things to each other. They believe this grid, which is often referred to as Grandmother Spider's web, is vital to maintaining the natural balance of the Earth. And, as Patricio suggested, perhaps it also has a role to play in communications?

Certainly quantum physicists have recently discovered what they call 'superstrings', an all-pervading web-like structure believed to connect all things in the universe to each other at some imperceptible level. Connecting all energy and matter, these infinitesimally delicate subatomic linkages are thought to give structure to the whole. After hearing what Patricio had to say, we wondered whether this was the same 'energy grid' as 'Grandmother Spider's web'.

We had also come across a recent scientific study[13] which suggested that the universe might be made up of a huge crystalline matrix. A team of scientists from Germany, Russia, Estonia, Spain and the United States had presented the theory that a regular crystalline honeycomb of voids and galaxies exists, with galaxies clustered in a regular and three-dimensional lattice structure, and the pattern repeating itself every 391 million light years, just like the basic underlying (although obviously far smaller) structure of a piece of quartz crystal.

We had also heard that, recently, scientists have discovered an 'unheard sound'. This is a low-level background noise of radiation, a tiny pulse of radiating energy that is thought to remain constant wherever you are in the universe. Scientists consider this to be the after-effects, an echo if you will, of the original 'Big Bang' that is believed to have created the universe. We wondered whether this might be the mysterious 'unheard sound of creation' that Leon had said the skulls could 'help us hear'.

We put these questions to Patricio, but he immediately cautioned us:

'You must not make the same mistakes as the physicists. They are learning some things of "the knowledge", but they do not understand. For all their intellectual capabilities they insist on hearing only what they want to hear and still continue to miss the main point. They insist on thinking that they are separate from everything else, that the rest of the world is somehow "out there" and that we can do what we want "out there" and it will not affect us.

'The skulls are here to help us to change our own state of consciousness, to teach us that the world, indeed the universe, is a living, almost breathing, spiritual entity. Everything has a soul. The world is not just some collection of "superstrings" which are there for us to manipulate and control. The universe is a sacred living and spiritual being. And we are part of that creature, part of its essence, part and parcel of that living and sacred whole. We must learn to respect all things, both the living and what we think of as dead. For it will soon be time for us to fulfil our greater function and take up our rightful place in the greater consciousness of all things.'

We didn't know what to say. Patricio was clearly concerned at the way our modern science had misinterpreted so much. So we decided not to press the point.

It was obvious from everything Patricio had already told us that the Native Americans had knowledge about the workings of the universe that our modern scientists were only just beginning to grasp. We couldn't help wondering whether any of this knowledge might have been gleaned from the crystal skulls?

I found myself deep in thought about the Native Americans' completely different view of the world and the implications for our own world view. What if it turned out that we in the West had got it all completely wrong and it was really the keepers of the crystal skulls, the indigenous people of the world, such as the Native Americans and other tribes now largely destroyed, who had been right all along?

I was just contemplating this potentially great loss to humanity when Patricio interrupted my thoughts.

'I'll let you in on a secret,' he said. 'I've been invited to attend a sacred gathering of indigenous elders and wisdom-keepers in Guatemala in a few weeks' time.' This gathering, he said, had been called in accordance with the ancient prophecies. 'They'll be discussing the knowledge of the crystal skulls, the ancient calendar and the other great prophecies about the future.'

Of course we wanted to know more. Patricio explained that many Native American tribes have similar prophecies about the crystal skulls and one of these is that before the crystal skulls can come together the people must come together first to prepare for the knowledge that is going to come out.

Patricio explained that the gathering itself had been predicted by the ancient Maya in their sacred divinatory calendar. They had a prophecy which they shared with several other Native American tribes, such as the Hopi of North America and the Almara and Kalaway, descendants of the ancient Inca, from Peru in South America. Patricio explained that he was most familiar with the Hopi version, which said that, when the time was right, 'the People of the Centre will bring together the Eagle of the North and the Condor of the South, and that all of the peoples shall become one like the fingers of a hand'. This meant that the Maya of Central America would call together and reunite the people of North America and the people of South America and that all of the people would come together in Central America 'to prepare for the knowledge that would be reawakened at the end of the age'. This knowledge, Patricio calmly informed us, was closely connected with the crystal skulls:

'The Maya are regarded by many of the other native tribes not only as "the keepers of the skulls" but also as "the keepers of time". They were

entrusted not only with preserving the knowledge of the crystal skulls, but also with being "the keepers of the days", the "day-keepers" or "keepers of time". They were given the burden of looking after many of the skulls, of counting the days and being the callers to each of the other tribes. It was their task, entrusted to them many thousands of years ago, to mark the passing of the days and to inform the other tribes when the right time had arrived.

'According to these Mayan day-keepers, who still practise the old ways, the time is fast approaching when it will be necessary for the knowledge of the skulls to go out into the world. And the time for the people to start coming together and preparing for the knowledge to go out is now. That is why the gathering has been called at this time. The gathering will take place in accordance with the prophecies of our ancestors and in keeping with the ancient calendar, which the Mayan day-keepers have kept sacred and secret all this time.'

According to Patricio, such a gathering of all the tribes had not taken place for many thousands of years, '5,126, to be precise'. Much of the knowledge that would be discussed had been kept secret for over 500 years, maintained by the few remaining survivors of the ancient Mayan civilization who had kept the 'sacred flame' of knowledge alive all this time, but hidden, for fear of persecution and the resulting loss of their ancient wisdom and ways.

We were dying to find out more. Patricio informed us that the gathering had been called by a man called Don Alejandro Cirilo Oxlaj Peres, a Mayan priest now in his late sixties and a direct descendant of the ancient Mayan priesthood. He was a diviner and shaman who lived in a remote village in the Guatemalan highlands, one of a long line of Mayan 'day-keepers' who had handed down the knowledge from one generation to the next. Don Alejandro himself had spent six years preparing for the gathering. During this time, he had travelled around the Americas visiting the people who needed to attend.

Perhaps one of the strangest things Patricio told us was that before Don Alejandro left his own country to find these people physically, he had apparently already located them 'psychically' in his dreams, in the 'dreamtime' or the other dimensions of the world of dreams. Whilst we found this a little hard to understand, let alone believe, Patricio explained that this was how he himself had become involved. He had known nothing of the gathering only a few months before. But one day he answered a knock at his front door to find a small man on his doorstep. This was Don Alejandro. Patricio had never met or even heard of him before, but the old Mayan priest proceeded to tell him about the gathering and how important it was that he attend. For Patricio was not only expected to attend, but had also been nominated as the organizer of the whole delegation from North America. Eventually he was persuaded to fulfil both of these tasks but, try as he did, he remained unable to find anyone who might have passed on his contact details to the old man from Guatemala.

Patricio said that if we wanted to know more about the crystal skulls we would have to attend the gathering in Guatemala ourselves, but that he would first have to clear this with the other indigenous elders. He said this might take him some time, so as we finally left his small office we gave him the details of where we would be over the next few days, so he could let us know if he was able to get permission for us to attend the great gathering.

21. THE SPIRIT OF THE SKULLS

While waiting to hear from Patricio, we drove across the New Mexico desert to Santa Fe. We were visiting Jamie Sams, the world's best-selling Native American author, who lives nearby. Jamie is a mixture of Cherokee, Seneca, Scottish and French ancestry. She also spent a large part of her earlier life as an apprentice to a medicine man in Mexico who was 'part Mayan, part Aztec and part Yaqui mix', and to two grandmothers from the Kiowa tribe. We had contacted Jamie on a friend's recommendation. She had established the Native American Tribal Traditions Trust and had written numerous books on Native American philosophy and spirituality, including *The Thirteen Original Clan Mothers*,[1] which made reference to the 13 crystal skulls.

When I had contacted Jamie I had explained what had happened at the British Museum and told her that Chris and I had not got as much information from the scientific perspective as we would have liked and were now seeing whether we could find more information about the skulls from other sources. Jamie said that although she had mentioned the crystal skulls in her book, that had been all she was permitted to reveal about these sacred objects at that time. But her teachers had spoken of a time, at the end of the century, when the teachings she had been given could be shared. She had also been told that two people would come from overseas asking for knowledge about the skulls and that they were to be entrusted with the teachings of her grandmothers. This is why she had invited us to come and stay at her home.

Jamie lived in a typical sand-coloured, Pueblo-style home that seemed almost to blend into the landscape. When we arrived we soon found out that Jamie had a wonderful down-to-earth quality and a deep, raucous laugh. We told her some of what we had heard from Leon, Emerson and Patricio, and Jamie explained to us that the teachings of Native Americans involved looking at the world quite differently. They required us to see what was familiar in a new, sometimes, unexpected way. In order to do this we would have to put aside the familiar, the safe and the known and take a leap into the unknown. 'This territory will at first seem unfamiliar,' she warned, 'and you will probably find that some of the things that you take for granted are not as they seem.'

We talked about the British Museum tests and how we had been trying to get to the truth about the skulls. Jamie pointed out, 'The problem is that you want to pin a label on the crystal skulls, but you will find that there is no label that will stick.'

She was right, I did want a neat category to put the skulls into. I still liked the idea of being able to explain them, sum them up. But so far, it had not been possible.

Jamie continued:

'The thing about the crystal skulls is that there is not one simple explanation of them. They operate, function, exist on many different levels at the same time. There are really many different ways of looking at them and understanding them. They are multi-dimensional. To understand them properly, you are going to have to leave behind your idea that there is only the one truth, the one simple answer and the one explanation. You no longer need to narrow things down, but broaden them out, to start looking at the skulls in a new way.

'Our way is not the way of textbooks and libraries, experts or specialists, our way is a living philosophy. You might call it a religion, but it is more than that, more than going to church once a week or saying prayers. It is more about a way of life and a deep connection with the Earth. Before I answer any of your questions, it would be helpful for you to understand with your heart a little more about the ways of indigenous people. That will also help you understand the crystal skulls, and that goes for both of you.

'The Western world has been seduced by the pursuit of what you call "objective" facts and knowledge. Yet this objective knowledge is known only with the mind. It has been cut off from the heart. Without a connection with the heart, "facts" can be manipulated and used cruelly. For us, knowledge is not something that is known only with the mind. For

us, true knowledge is not something that you read about in a book or that someone else tells you, but comes from what you directly experience for yourself. The truths we learn are not "objective" facts but come to us from the rich experience of life, for truths are what we know with our hearts as well as our minds.'

I wasn't at all sure what Jamie meant about understanding truth with the heart but she promised that she would tell us more the following day.

The next morning Jamie suggested that we go out to the countryside where we could better understand the skulls. As we were driving along the freeway, heading north towards Colorado, Jamie explained that one of the features of the crystal skulls was that they could teach us about transformation. They represented positive change that could occur on the physical, emotional and spiritual levels. As we passed yellow pueblo houses decorated with lines of vibrant red chillies drying in the autumn sunshine, Jamie told us there was a church she wanted us to see along the way. It was a small sandstone church called Santuario de Chimayo, which the local Pueblo people had been forced to build over their own sacred site by a wealthy Spanish landowner in 1816.

In the cool interior was a magnificent altar showing the local Indians in soft rich colours. As we gazed up at the altar, my attention was drawn to the solid wooden cross at the centre. Then Jamie said:

'When you started out looking into the crystal skulls, you were relying on science. You wanted the British Museum to tell you which of the skulls were genuine and which were fakes. You know, at the end of the day it really does not matter, in the same way that it does not matter whether the piece of wood we see in front of us here is actually from the real cross. It is a symbol. That is what matters.'

We took a seat in the centre of the church. It was pleasantly cool after the heat outside. Jamie continued:

'Quartz crystal, though, unlike the cross, has its own particular and unusual qualities that can quite literally connect us with the workings of the spirit world.

'There is actually only a very thin membrane, like tracing paper, separating this physical world of ours from the world of the spirits. The fact that the crystal skulls are made of quartz crystal represents the clarity of

the membrane that exists between worlds, the physical world and the spirit world.

'Indigenous people all over the world have long believed that quartz crystal can provide an access point into this spiritual dimension. Like my own teachers, and shamans or "dreamers" the world over, some people are able to use the crystal skulls to transit the different dimensions, to go from the physical world into the non-physical world and find answers or make changes or perform healings which can also affect us back in our ordinary physical world. In a sense, they are able to bend the known physical laws of this three-dimensional, physical world we call reality. That world is actually just as "real" as this one, although most people are totally unaware of this fact. But that world is going on right alongside our normal three-dimensional physical world, only there all the things that have happened and will be happening are all going on, simultaneously. This is what we Native Americans mean when we say that the ancestors are still walking with us in this world. Indeed, there are certain places on this Earth where the membrane between worlds is very thin, like some places in Guatemala, where the visible and the invisible worlds almost collide.

'Mostly, we can only perceive events and things as going on in one particular time and one particular place, within the usual strict limitations of our simple physical world. But in that other world, in this non-physical reality of the spirit-world, or what the aborigines call "the dreamtime", is where many of the answers and solutions to the problems of this physical world can actually be found.'

I asked Jamie if the main point of the skulls was to access other realms. She said that this was only one of the qualities of the crystal skulls. As we looked up at the cross, Jamie commented that the crystal skull also had a similar function to the Christian cross. I had always thought of the cross as a negative image associated with death, but Jamie saw it in quite a different way:

'It is a symbol that during pain and suffering, at the time of the darkest reaches of the human soul, there can be transformation of that suffering. From suffering comes love and compassion. Within our hearts we have the power to transform darkness into light, to transcend, to move beyond the confines of our ordinary, egotistical selves into our ultimate being.

'The cross is the symbol of the Christian faith in immortal life, just as the crystal skulls are the same symbol of the immortality of the human spirit. The skulls represent the Native American faith in the intangible force that all religions call God, the Creator, the Maker, and we call the Great Mystery or Great Spirit.'

An elderly Hispanic couple sitting at the front of the church got up, their footsteps echoing as they went into a side room. Jamie continued:

'If you fear the cross, you are separating yourself from the power it offers as a symbol. It is the same for people who see the image of the skull as an image of death and are afraid. It is all part of the way that people see themselves as separate. They have put a distance between themselves and death so that they no longer see that it is an essential part of life. When they are cut off from this they are cut off from the knowledge that only when we are aware of death are we free to fully appreciate life.

'Like the cross, the crystal skull is a symbol of transformation. It is an image of death that is transparent. It shows us that death is not a place of darkness and gloom but a place of crystal clarity and illumination.'

'So you are saying that we don't die?' I asked.

'That's right. We don't die, we transform. Although our physical body will no longer exist, our spirit body lives on. It is eternal. The crystal skull shows us that death is not the end, it is not final, but, like the crystal, we can see through it. To die is to move beyond physicality and into a new way of being. It is a new beginning, for birth and death are part of a continuum, part of a constant cycle of renewal and rebirth.

'The crystal skulls symbolize transformation on many levels. For not only is the skull a symbol of the transformation we can experience in physical death, but it is a symbol of the transformation that is available to us in life. If we see that to die physically is not the end, then we can see that all the other "endings" we fear in our lives are new beginnings. Fear of death makes us want to cling to things for security. We want things to stay the same, even when our habits are not doing us any good. Our fear of change is at root a fear of death. Once we no longer fear death we are able to see that all changes in our lives are part of the constant cycle of death and rebirth. Each moment, as something in us dies, something else can be reborn.'

I thought about how science had failed us. Was there not a sense in which our old ideas had to 'die' in order for new ones to come in? Did we need a new way of looking at the world – not just as individuals, but as a whole culture? Had not the narrow parameters of our own investigation held us back? While I recognized the many benefits scientific analysis has given us as a culture, I now also began to realize that it would only ever offer a partial picture, a limited window on life. We had to learn when to let go of what was no longer working, let it 'die' and allow a new awareness, a new understanding, to emerge.

'Have a look in the Room of Miracles,' urged Jamie.

I walked through to a small room at the back of the church. Amidst the flickering light of the candles were displayed hundreds of photographs, trinkets, lucky charms, even a pair of old crutches. There were letters, some typed, some handwritten, now yellowing with age. They came from people filled with gratitude for the healing they had received from the 'miracle church'. I watched the elderly couple as they knelt down on the floor and prayed. There was a circular hole in the foundations of the church and sand was visible through it. At the end of her prayers, the woman scooped a little of the sand up and placed it in a bag. She crossed herself as her husband helped her up and they left the room.

It seemed that the real focus of the church lay not in the altar, impressive though it was, but in this side room. For here were the 'healing sands' that lay beneath the building. I reached down and ran a few coarse grains through my fingers. They were the tiny particles of thousands of broken down pieces of quartz crystal. Just as the crystal skulls were believed to have healing powers, so too were these fragments of quartz. These tiny bits of crystal seemed almost to be rising up through the foundations of the church.

I asked Jamie whether she believed in the healing power of quartz crystal. She said that, according to her teachers, the Earth was 40 per cent quartz crystal and the healing power of quartz was that it could help bring the mind and body back into harmony with the Earth.

As we left the church, Jamie explained that the land on which it had been built had a particularly sacred significance to the people who had lived in these lands thousands of years before. She said it was a common practice amongst the early Christian settlers to build their churches right on top of the indigenous people's sacred sites. But before the church had been built people would commune directly with the spirit of the place.

'The problem with the church is that it has mediated spiritual experience. It is the priest who is seen as having the connection with God, what we call Great Mystery. Before we had the priests, our connection was direct. But when Christianity came, it all had to be done through the church, through the priests who became the authority on God and the experts on the spirit. Only they knew best. Only they were seen as the official recipients of God's word. They now conduct and supervise our contact with spirit. Yet what has really happened is that many people have now lost their own direct connection with Great Mystery.

'Over time, the simple, natural connection with Spirit is experienced by fewer and fewer people. When we cut ourselves off from God or Great Mystery, we lose awareness of the sustaining relationship with Spirit that is there for us. This relationship with Spirit that has the power to transform and enrich our existence then simply fades away. Yet without this vital connection in our lives we can become impoverished beyond measure. Many of the problems our societies are now facing are a direct result of the many ways that we have cut ourselves off, severed our connections not only spiritually, but all our connections with all other living things. What has happened is that people think of themselves as separate from what is around them. They fail to see the connections between themselves and others. This separateness is an illusion, and in this illusion lies much of the grief and suffering of humanity.'

We walked around the church, through the tall aspens whose leaves were beginning to turn to the yellow-gold of autumn. Jamie continued:

'It is our greatest illusion that we are separate. Like the Maya, the Cherokee and Seneca also call the world we live in "the Fourth World". But what we call it is "the Fourth World of Separation". For we live in a period of history that is a great lesson in the many different forms that separation can take. For 65,000 years we have lived in this cycle of history. It is during this period of time that people have wanted to rule others. This has been accomplished through conquest, through rules and regulations, through the class system, through governments and religion. All types of separation began during this period.

'My people's prophecies always predicted that during this period of history people would come to see themselves as separate not only from each other, but also as separate from the Earth. They said that during this period we would see an increased desire in people to rule over each other

and across the natural world. And so separation has now become the main organizing principle through which people now understand the world and by which they live their lives. For now we think only of "self" and "other". We think only of "us" and "them". We see every other person and every other thing as somehow separate from ourselves. When we look at others this way we stop seeing the connections between ourselves and our fellow human beings and other living things. And so, because we see them as somehow separate, somehow "other" than ourselves, we start to treat other people and other things less favourably than we would treat ourselves.

'While our individuality and our uniqueness should be celebrated, it should not become a way of thinking that separates us from others, that makes us think that we are better than others. It is this current way of thinking that our people call "the mind of separation".'

Again, I was reminded of the comments about 'separation' we had heard from Carole Wilson when she was 'channelling' the Mitchell-Hedges skull.

The windswept landscape of northern New Mexico now stood before us. The blue peaks of the Rocky Mountains were in the distance. We had arrived at Jamie's small plot of land. It had once been farmland, but was now left wild as a sanctuary for birds and animals, for the wolf, the fox and the deer to roam. The only sign of human habitation was the tipi that Jamie had put up for use during ceremonies. We walked up the hillside to a place where the tracks of a wolf were still visible, imprinted on the damp earth. The air was cool and fresh. Two ravens flew above us, gliding and playing on the breeze.

'So where exactly is this mind of separation leading us?' I asked.

'Good question. The mind of separation has led to all forms of oppression, to conquest, to class systems and so on. It is now leading even to a breakdown of whole families and communities. For this mind of separation refuses to see the connections between all people, to see that we are brother and sister, to see that we are all equal, to see that we are all the same people. This mind of separation has led to much destruction, to the Spanish Inquisition, the Nazi Holocaust and the near total genocide of indigenous people in this land. But we are all the same people, the same race, the human race.

'One of the consequences of the mind of separation is that it has led people to see the natural world as something out there that is separate from

THE SPIRIT OF THE SKULLS

themselves. People have lost contact with the earth, forgetting that she is a living being, and that we only have life because she has given it to us.'

As we walked down towards the stream that snaked through the wet grasslands, I recalled the legends I had heard about the Earth. There was the Aztec myth that tells that the world is a woman who was slain by a monster. From her body ran rivers which are her blood, grass which is her skin, trees her hair. The Cherokee talk of the Earth as a fertile woman whose breasts give corn, beans and squash and whose tears became rivers of fresh water. The Kogi of South America have a similar myth. To native people it is Mother Earth who gives us life, who nourishes us, provides us with food, clothing and shelter. Jamie continued:

'What needs to be remembered is that all living things have only one mother, Mother Earth. We are all connected with her and with each other. The crystal skulls are here to help us to reawaken our sense of connection with all life.'

As we wandered along the edge of the stream and I gazed across at the plains and mountains in the distance, Jamie said:

'We have been taught by the white man that God is separate from us, that he has to be worshipped in the church, that contact with God is not possible except through organized religion, through the church, mediated through the priest. Yet for my people, this is religion. This beautiful place where we are now is our church. God is what we call Great Mystery. It is all around us, in every tree, leaf, mountain and cloud.'

Jamie picked up a pebble from the stream and handed it to me.

'This stone has spirit within it. It is animated with the consciousness of the Creator. It is living. The spirit can be seen in everything, every bird that sings, every animal that walks upon the earth and every child that laughs. For Great Mystery is within us also. There is no separation, we are one with all of creation, we are one with God. That is one of the first teachings of the crystal skull.'

Jamie walked back across the land, but I felt compelled to stay just a few moments longer. I sat down by the stream and looked at the small grey pebble in my hand. Before now, stones had hardly figured in my aware-ness. They had always seemed totally irrelevant to me. As it was, crystal had only caught my attention because of the crystal skulls. I had never thought of stones as having any sort of significance. Yet the idea that this small inanimate object might be somehow alive with spirit filled me with wonder. I had a sense of the aliveness of all that was around me. I realized that there was a consciousness, an experience of being alive that was expe-rienced by trees, plants, even stones. It was an awareness, very different from the one that I normally had, but none the less meaningful.

I felt very moved by Jamie's teachings. I realized that to contemplate the consciousness of what is around us is to enter into a much deeper awareness of the connections between ourselves and all things, an aware-ness that offers a far richer and deeper sense of what it is to be alive than the one that we, or at least I, normally experience. Jamie had said this was part of the message of the crystal skulls.

Later, as we drove back through town, I thought about how easy it is to lose touch with this message, how easy it is to feel disconnected from the natural world when we are surrounded by ugly buildings, dirty streets and endless advertising hoardings. Where in our crowded, noisy, utilitari-an cities are there places to contemplate our connection with the natural world? I wondered how many people in today's modern society had picked up a stone and contemplated its intelligence and design, had thought about the life force that it contained. How many people had the time to look at the flowers coming into blossom or the leaves falling from the trees? How many people had the chance to watch a butterfly stretch out its wings or to listen to a bird in song? Our frenetic modern daily lives mean these moments of connecting with nature are all too rare.

Jamie said the Hopi believe that people exist upon this Earth to reflect back to the world its beauty. They say that every time we appreciate the beauty of a flower or the magnificence of a tree these living beings increase their beauty. By being appreciated, they actually become more beautiful. It seemed so simple, and yet how many of us were living this way today, living this beautiful, simple philosophy of appreciation, a phi-losophy that applies both to the natural world and to each other?

I began to wonder how were we appreciating the animals? It is known that more species of animal and bird have died out in the last 100 years than in the last 10,000 years, since the last Ice Age. Was that how we appreciated our fellow creatures, by destroying them? I remembered an old Native American saying: 'Only after the last tree has been cut down, only after the last river has been poisoned, only after the last fish has been caught, only then will we realize that we cannot eat money.' Perhaps this was only what was to be expected from our current way of looking at the world, our collective 'mind of separation'. Perhaps it was by seeing the other creatures of the world as separate from ourselves that we were allowing them to perish. Native American Chief Seattle had also said over 100 years ago, 'If the beasts were gone, man would die of a great loneliness of spirit.' Was this, I wondered, where the mind of separation was leading us, to a death from our own thoughts and actions in the world, or perhaps to a death caused simply by our own desire for separation from the natural world?

As Jamie put it:

'The problem with the Western world view is the way it has separated people from nature. It sees nature as inanimate, and does not see its soul. There is a loneliness that comes from being cut off from nature, from the stars, the animals and the plants. This separation means that many are cut off from the joy that is inherent in the natural world.'

The more I thought about this idea of separation, the more I could see that it permeated all aspects of our existence. Many people, myself included, have become cut off from the forces and cycles of nature. And what seems to be happening is that as we lose awareness of the natural world, we have also become separated from a sense of completeness within ourselves. We seem constantly to reach outside ourselves to compensate for this separation, this sense of loneliness. We look to relationships, to work, to money to make us feel complete as we search to plug the gaps in our lives created by this sense of separation within ourselves. Yet so often, even when we get what we thought we wanted, the job or the car or perhaps the relationship we hungered after, it still somehow doesn't seem like enough.

As we sped along the highway, I looked at the bright lights of the advertising hoardings, their glossy images appealing to us to buy this product or that. It struck me that they relied totally on our sense of separation, on the idea that there was something missing in our lives and that their product would somehow make us feel complete. Was our own investigation into the crystal skulls a search that would make us feel more complete?

Certainly our investigation had begun to show us that there were some great limitations in the 'normal' lives we thought we had been leading.

Perhaps what was missing was the knowledge of our own spiritual nature and of our connection with all other things.

We finally arrived back at Jamie's house very late in the evening. We sat in her kitchen, having a last cup of hot chocolate before retiring to bed. As we watched the moon through the window softly illuminating the contours of the landscape, Jamie left us with a few final words:

'The crystal skulls will only come back together when the family of humanity has been united, when we can meet together without hostility, defensiveness and distrust, when we meet together with our hearts united. This can be done. See how often people will rush to save another when they see their life endangered, with no thought to their own safety. We each of us have this same quality within us. It is a place where our individual egos are put aside, where the ego steps back and takes its place alongside our true loving and compassionate nature. We have to call on this true nature now. It is the time to reach inside and find that impulse, that generosity of spirit, that deep caring for others, to bring it to the fore.

'Remember one of the most important things the crystal skulls can teach us is that we are all spiritual beings in physical bodies. They show us that our physical world is not really separate from the dimensions of the spirit world. For the crystal skulls can provide us with an access point into these other dimensions of the world of the spirits, where we can begin to see our connections with all other things. The crystal skulls show us that we need to awaken to this knowledge, that we need to wake up to our connection with each other and with this Mother Earth that sustains us, and that we need to start to repair and celebrate these connections in our lives.'

All we were ready to do then, however, was to crawl into bed.

22. THE KEEPER OF THE DAYS

The next day we rang Patricio Domínguez to see whether we would be permitted to attend the great gathering in Guatemala, now less than two weeks away. He still wasn't sure, but he had spoken to one of the Mayan priests, shamans or 'day-keepers', Hunbatz Men. Hunbatz, who lived on the Yucatán Peninsula, near Chichen Itzá in southern Mexico, was a member of one of the families that had been entrusted with certain sacred information when the Spanish had first arrived in Central America and given the responsibility of keeping it secret so that it would not be abused or destroyed.

But, said Patricio, Hunbatz Men would be prepared to talk to us if we could come and meet him in Mexico in the next few days. 'Who knows,' said Patricio, 'he might even agree to you attending the gathering.'

Although we were currently over 1,000 miles away, this seemed like an opportunity not to be missed, so we rang the airport and a few days later found ourselves at the ancient Mayan ruins of Tulum, on the Caribbean coast of Mexico, where we had arranged to meet Hunbatz.

Tulum was beautiful, with old pyramids and temples slowly crumbling off small limestone cliffs into the clear blue sea (*see colour plate no. 22*). We met Hunbatz Men at the entrance to the site. Dressed entirely in a white outfit, traditional of the Maya, with a small red sash around his waist, he was quite a short, somewhat rounded figure of a man, with straight, greying hair. He had a wide face with quite prominent features, a lofty brow, a wide, slightly beaked nose with flaring nostrils, and thick lips, almost like a male version of the face on the Mitchell-Hedges' skull.

I also found myself reminded of the ancient carved stone heads of the Olmec that had been found buried along the Gulf coast.

Hunbatz's voice was quiet but firm and its low notes were somehow gently soothing. He explained that even Spanish was not his native tongue and that he had some difficulty making himself clear in English. Hunbatz explained that over 500 years ago his family had been entrusted with keeping safe a small part of the ancient wisdom tradition and that he was the contemporary holder of the lineage, 'although now, because it is time, I can begin to share these secrets with you'. He said:

> 'The eyes of modern civilization see only a short span of time. To the Western mind 500 years seems a long time. But 500 years is nothing in the eyes of the Maya.
>
> 'It is written in time and in the memory of the Indian peoples that our sun will rise again. My ancestors, the Itzas [a group of Maya who lived in Yucatán], made a prophecy, that the knowledge of the Maya will come back again.
>
> 'It is prophesied that we will re-establish our culture, its arts, its science, its mathematics and its religion, because all of this is based on the cosmic knowledge, the knowledge we have been given by our ancestors. It is said that the Mayan knowledge will come forward again and today we are already beginning to see how that knowledge is coming back. We will soon be having our first gathering in Guatemala and this is part of our prophecies – that the people are going to try to understand the Mayan civilization.
>
> 'Because today's humanity, it is in an endangered position. Because the current culture that they bring to us, the European people, it is not good for humanity. And we can see the bad things about the common culture. We don't have respect today for many things that exist, like the wind, the clouds, the rivers, anything. We don't have respect for humanity. Because in that common culture it's not good, because they don't know how ... they didn't include, they didn't include the respect for everything. It is for this reason that we are once again uniting and beginning to speak again. Because the Maya, they had and they understood the cosmic culture, and in that there exists a respect for everything that exists.'

I was about to ask Hunbatz what he knew about the crystal skulls, but he continued:

'The prophecy of the Itzas is that they are going to come back again, the knowledge of the Itzas, because it is the cosmic knowledge. We are now beginning to do our ceremonies, but in the future we will do many more ceremonies, because they are now beginning to come back again, and people will come to be open and to try to understand the cosmic culture of the Maya people. And the skulls are coming to help us because this is part of the prophecies. This is part of what the people need, and the skulls will come to be re-established in the original place. And some time soon the Maya are going to deposit the skulls ... because they need to be back in their original place. They need to be back in their place at the top of the pyramids.

'And again the Mayan priests are going to pray again and work with that crystal, because only in that way is going to come the way that that positive energy is going to work from the sacred centre, and then that energy is going to expand to the other sacred centres, and then later to all the whole world. So the skulls, they need to come back to their original places, because in that way it's going to be easier, the work for the whole of humanity.

It is part of the prophecy that people are going to have the skulls in many different places, but soon they are going to bring them back to the sacred places, to these pyramids, and then later they are going to appear.'

I was intrigued, wondering what Hunbatz meant by 'the work for the whole of humanity', and also what he meant by 'later they are going to appear' – did 'they' mean more crystal skulls, or the Mayans' ancestors, or what? Hunbatz continued:

'And this is part of the prophecy that this is going to happen, for this is part of the prophecy of the Mayan people, the Itzas who now live in Mexico and the other Maya who now live in many different countries.

'And with the skulls it is now going to be easy, the big change, the big change for the whole of humanity ... for the big change of the knowledge, for the knowledge for the Age of the Light. But we are going to need everybody, and I pray to Hunab Ku [the original god of creation who the Mayans believe lies at the very centre of the universe]. It is now time and so I pray to Hunab Ku that this will now be happening.'

We listened in fascination to what Hunbatz was saying, but I found myself still wanting to know more about the crystal skulls. So I asked him to explain a little more specifically about where the crystal skulls came from and what they really meant. Hunbatz explained:

'Long time ago, in the area of the Maya, Itzamna, he gave us the knowledge. Itzamna, he gave us the knowledge how we need to understand the skulls, he gave us the education how we need to work with the skulls and he showed us how to work with the skulls in the sacred places like Tulum and Chichen Itzá and many other places in the area of the Maya. Itzamna, he gave us the education how we need to understand the skulls. Because the crystal skull in Maya, it has some sacred connection with God. Because, for the Maya, the name of God it is Hunab Ku. We Maya believe that our skull, it has some connection with the sacred proportions given to us by Hunab Ku. Because we need to understand that all of the proportions we have in every place in our face, in our head and in our body, it has some connection with the sacred proportions of God. But there is something else, because the crystal skull in Maya, the name of the crystal it is lembal and it means "light", "knowledge" and it has something to do with our sacred connection with God.

'In many places, in many centres, in many sacred centres like the ones of the Maya we have worked with the skull. We have worked with the skulls for many, many thousands of years. And Itzamna, he also gave us the education and the indication how we need to make more other skulls for ourselves, because there will come a time when we need to have the skulls not only in the sacred centres of the Maya, but in many other sacred centres around the world. Because now, as it is predicted, the rest of humanity begins to take an interest in the skulls.

'As it was prophesied, the rest of humanity, it began to take the skulls from our sacred centres and then they were sleeping for a while. But now it is good to send us back the skulls for our sacred centres, because we need the skulls to activate each sacred centre in all of the areas of the Maya. Because now it is necessary for all of humanity to wake up. Let them give us the skulls to re-establish them in our sacred centres, because that's another part of the prophecy. We need the skulls again to establish in our sacred pyramids ... and then the others will come. The crystal skulls they're going to begin to give lembal again, they're going to begin to give the light, the knowledge again to humanity. And then humanity is going to begin to wake up again, and not only in the area of the Maya, it's going to be in many places around the world. Like even in

Stonehenge. We need also to establish a crystal skull there. Because it is now going to begin, the right energy, the right energy for all these places, because Itzamna, he shows us how we need to modulate that part of the energy of the creation. But first the original crystal skulls we need again.'

I asked Hunbatz again if he could explain where the crystal skulls had originally come from. He answered, rather esoterically:

'We Maya, we know we are from the Earth, but we also understand that part of ourselves belongs to the sky, part of ourselves belongs to the cosmos, and it belongs to some other law outside of this beautiful dimension. For the Maya, we understand that at the same time as we are from the Earth, in the sky we have more family. And the word we use to understand the family we have there is the mishule. *Mishule, it means our brothers and sisters outside of this beautiful Earth.*

'A very long time ago we, the Maya, we have communication with every other race in the world and we have communication with every other race outside of the world. And that's why we, the Maya, most of the time we make identification with the people of the air. And that's the reason why we have many symbols, many of the symbols in our inscriptions are the symbols of something which exists in the air, like the symbol of Kukulcan or Quetzalcoatl, it is the symbol of the flying serpent.

'We only have a few symbols that explain about the cosmos, few of them, but those few symbols usually make a combination, they are a combination of a symbol of the Earth and another symbol of the air or the sky. And this is because we know that every change in the Mother Earth, it is because of some change that is also happening up there, and it is connecting, and the change it is also going up and it is coming down. So that is why we, the Maya, we have more respect for all of the manifestations of life. Because it does not really matter where it came from, because we are all one family. And that is why for the mishulas, *the* mishule, *that's our brothers and sisters up there [pointing to the sky], that's why we need to pray for them sometimes, because we understand that they pray for us sometimes, and that's the good relationship that we had a long, long time ago with all of the manifestations of life.'*

I was intrigued as to what Hunbatz meant by 'our brothers and sisters outside of this beautiful Earth' but this was all he would say. So I asked him if he could explain more about the skulls and the ancient Mayan calendar. He said the calendar been left by the earliest ancestors 'to help us to understand the cosmic timetable of the universe':

'For the Mayan civilization, for us, all of the bodies in the sky, we need to understand that each of the bodies in the sky, they have something to teach us. Like the sun, the four movements of the sun, even in the two equinoxes and the two solstices, the sun, it has something to teach us. Like why is the reason they need to happen. We need to understand what are the changes that make the sun and the Mother Earth move each time when we have the two solstices and two equinoxes.

'And our sister moon, it has a noted education to give to us. We need to understand each of the four divisions of the moon and each of its four faces. Each time, like the full moon, it has something that can affect the air and at the same time this has an effect on the humans. And then there are the other planets, like Venus, like Mars, like the constellations, each of them has something to give to us, something to teach us. That is one of the reasons that the Maya, we create our own 17 calendars, to help us know more about the sky and the movements that are in the heavens.

'But now, in this modern day, they do not understand very much about time, because they do not even use the correct calendar. They have made and they use their own personal calendar. But the Maya, our calendar, it is the cosmic calendar. Each of our calendars is for something, it means something. It is to measure some of the main bodies in the sky and that is one of the big differences. The calendar and the astronomy of the Maya are still to do with the original mind of Hunab Ku, to do with the original cosmic energy force.'

I asked Hunbatz if he could explain more about the 'cycles of time':

'One of the huge calendars of the Maya is approximately 26,000 of your solar years. And that calendar is the calendar to indicate when the Earth Mother is going to make the big changes. Because, this land many times it was under the water. And this is going to happen again, because that is part of the natural cycle of the universe.

'The Earth has its own natural cycle, just like a human. The cycle of the human, from when we are born to when we die, is naturally around 100 years, or two Baktun. *No human can be born, grow, live, mature and die naturally in only one year, nor can they much outlive their naturally given period. They need to process the whole cycle. And the process*

of change in Mother Earth is similar, but it is a far more accurately allotted and longer cycle. We understand and you need to understand the workings of that Earth process. For the Maya, we know that that process of change in the Mother Earth is around 26,000 of your years, 26,000 of the circles of our Earth around our fellow sun.

'But one of the big problems today is that the modern world thinks it is separate from this process. The dangerous situation we are now in is that the people do not understand that the Mother Earth is now in for this very big change. People are now doing all the wrong things to help with this process. People are now testing the atomic bombs, making a lot of pollution in the sky, cutting all the trees, taking all the oil from the Mother Earth. And that's a very big mistake that they're making, because today there is ignorance in every place, and even more in the richer countries. So people are now helping to accelerate the process of the natural change in the Mother Earth and people don't realize what they are doing.

'And the work we're going to do now, the Maya are now beginning to do some work, to give everyone this information. Because the information from the skulls can help the human beings to wake up and then begin to see the mistakes they're making on the Mother Earth. Because what we need now is more respect for the Mother Earth, because with the respect we can begin to understand the process of the Mother Earth, the normal changes of the Mother Earth.

'And we need the skulls because humanity now it must wake up. Because if humanity does not wake up then we will kill the Mother Earth and there is nowhere else we can live. This is the only place we have that can support us. But people in America and in Britain they are now destroying the jungles, even as far away as Brazil. But even though Brazil is a long way from the United States it does not mean that the Earth changes we accelerate there are not going to affect the United States. And because they are killing the trees in Brazil now the trees in the Mayan area are also beginning to die. Because all the trees in the world they can communicate. The Maya, we say, don't kill any tree because if you kill any tree you are killing your family. When you kill a tree it is like killing your own brother or sister. In that way, the Maya, we believe in the trees. But the trees are only one part of the Mother. The trees are for the Maya the skin of our mother, and the oil it is the blood, and the rivers they are her sweat, her perspiration. But the mistakes today they are accelerating her life and now it is not good because the big change is coming.'

I found myself worryingly reminded of the Mayan calendar's prediction that the current Great Cycle of time will end on 21 December 2012. But I was also still curious to know where the crystal skulls had really come from, so I asked Hunbatz again:

> 'My ancestors, the Itzas, the Mayan Itzas, they brought with them the crystal skulls. And they made the construction of many of the great sacred centres, like in Chichen Itzá, and here in Tulum, Cobá and in Petén, all of them. And we came to understand the skulls through the teachings of the Itzas, the Maya learnt about the skulls from the Itzas, and they became known as the great Mayan Itzas, and they explained to us all about the crystal skulls.'

'But,' I asked, 'where did the Itzas come from?'

> 'My ancestors, the Itzas, they came from Atlantis, and it is they who gave us the knowledge how to understand the skulls, and they taught us of Itzamna and the workings of the universe. You say in English "Atlantis", but in Maya we say Atlantiha, that's in the Mayan language.
> 'The Itzas they told us about the place where they came from and they explained that in that place, the place of water, they told us how they ate the knowledge, the knowledge of the stones, the knowledge they had of the crystals, the knowledge they brought with them in the crystal skulls. And in that place they told us that there is more information about the crystals and more knowledge about the skulls. They have inside them, the crystal skulls, access to those places. And so we believe that many other crystal skulls still exist in that place, the place you call Atlantis. Because as I explained to you in the beginning, the crystal skulls will be needed in every sacred centre, because they are an essential part of these sacred centres, they are a very part of these pyramids. The Itzas explained to us that there exist many other crystal skulls, like the ones that exist here in the area of the Maya, where there are many sacred centres here, but there are many other sacred centres all over Mother Earth.'

So, according to this direct descendant of the ancient Maya, the crystal skulls really had come from Atlantis, after all. But, on this note, Hunbatz explained that he must now go as he had nothing more to tell us 'at this time'.

23. THE LOST CIVILIZATION

We walked along the white sandy beach near Tulum, watching the first stars appearing in the night sky, the waves crashing on the shore. As we looked out across the blue ocean of the Gulf of Mexico I wondered about Atlantis, that mythical paradise island that had shimmered in the human imagination down the centuries like some long-lost jewel.

The crystal skulls seemed to have been associated with this lost kingdom ever since the Mitchell-Hedges made their controversial discovery back in the 1920s. Frederick Mitchell-Hedges himself had devoted much of his life to trying to prove that Atlantis really did exist. He believed it was the cradle of civilization and was originally located somewhere in the Atlantic Ocean along this very coast. He was also of the view that his crystal skull had originally come from this great civilization. Even the Abbé Brasseur de Bourbourg before him, way back in the seventeenth century, had been convinced that this was where the Maya had really come from.

Conventional wisdom held Atlantis to be nothing more than a myth. But Hunbatz Men had now told us that according to the oral traditions of his people the Mayans' earliest ancestors had come from Atlantis, bringing the crystal skulls with them. As Chris and I gazed out across the azure blue ocean, I found myself wondering whether the remains of that lost civilization might really lie somewhere buried beneath those waves.

My mind went back to a meeting we had had with another Native American earlier in our journey. This was Paula Gunn-Allen, Professor of English at the University of California in Los Angeles and one of the world's leading specialists in Native American literature and mythology.

Professor Gunn-Allen herself is of Laguna Pueblo and Sioux heritage. She is also a poet, mystic, novelist and writer, 'depending on what hat I am wearing', as she put it. She has a razor-sharp mind and excellent sense of humour, and she is particularly unusual for an academic in that she takes the idea of Atlantis quite seriously.

Professor Gunn-Allen told us that Atlantis has long been part of the oral history of Native American peoples. Just like the Maya, the Laguna Pueblo have many legends about this lost civilization, as do the Seneca and several other tribes, such as the Cherokee. But, as Professor Gunn-Allen put it:

> 'People put their trust in the written word. They think that oral history and legends are unreliable sources of information. But when stories are passed on in an oral tradition great care is taken to preserve the integrity of the information. These stories were not just "make-believe", but the histories of whole nations. It was no less true just because it was never written down.'

As she pointed out, written records in the West only take us back as far as ancient Greece, Rome, Egypt and Mesopotamia, whereas the oral traditions of many native peoples take us back much further than that. The legends of the Seneca people, for instance, speak of 'stories to tell "the children of the Earth" about the worlds before the written histories of the "Two-leggeds" even began'.

There are also remarkable similarities between the mythologies of many continents. The general outline of the story of Atlantis can be found in South America, for example, and even amongst the writings of the ancient Sumerians of Mesopotamia, who lived in what is now the Middle East.

But perhaps the earliest known written reference to Atlantis itself is to be found in Europe, in the writings of the famous Greek philosopher Plato, writing around 350 BC. In his book *Timaeus*, Plato recounts that Solon, the great lawgiver of Athens, had travelled through Egypt and talked to a priest at a place called Sais. The priest said that compared with the Egyptians, the Greeks had only scant knowledge of the great events of history that had shaped their culture:

> 'You [Athenian Greeks] remember only one deluge though there have been many... You and your fellow citizens are descended from the few

*survivors that remained, but you know nothing about it because so
many succeeding generations left no record in writing.'*[1]

He then goes on to explain that there had once been a great island continent in the middle of the Atlantic:

*'There was an island opposite the strait which you call ... "The Pillars of
Hercules" [the Greeks' name for the Strait of Gibraltar], an island larger
than Libya and Asia combined; from it travellers could in those days
reach the other islands, and from them the whole opposite continent
which surrounds what can truly be called the ocean.'*[2]

The incredible thing about this ancient Greek account is that it strongly
suggests that the ancient Egyptians knew of the American continent,
regardless of whether or not the Atlantean civilization to which it also
refers really did exist. But Plato's story goes on to explain how powerful
the Atlantean civilization was:

*'On this island of Atlantis had arisen a powerful and remarkable
dynasty of kings, who ruled the whole island, and many islands as well
and parts of the continent [i.e. America?]; in addition it controlled,
within the strait [i.e. within the Mediterranean] Libya up to the borders
of Egypt and Europe as far as Tyrrhenia [Tuscany in Italy!]'*[3]

It seems this ancient civilization had dominion over rather a large territory, including parts of both America and Europe. Indeed, the Atlanteans
were keen to extend this territory even further eastward:

*'Our records tell how your city [Athens] checked [this] great power which
arrogantly advanced from its base in the Atlantic Ocean to attack the
cities of Europe and Asia. For in those days the Atlantic was navigable.'*[4]

And then the great war came to rather an abrupt end:

*'At a later time there were earthquakes and floods of extraordinary vio-
lence, and in a single dreadful day and night all your [Athenian] fighting men were swallowed up by the earth, and the island of Atlantis was
similarly swallowed by the sea and vanished; this is why the sea in that
area is to this day [sometime prior to 350 BC] impassable to navigation,*

which is hindered by mud just below the surface, the remains of the sunken island.'[5]

Some archaeologists have suggested that what Plato was referring to was really the Minoan civilization on what is today the Greek island of Crete. This island is certainly thought to have been hit by a massive tidal wave around 1400 BC, caused by a volcanic eruption on the nearby island of Santorini. But it is actually located in the middle of the Mediterranean Sea, rather than in the Atlantic 'opposite the strait which you call ' "The Pillars of Hercules" '.

Furthermore, another of Plato's books, *Critias*, explains that 9,000 years have elapsed since these events took place. If so, then they must have happened at the latest around 9500 BC, well before the generally accepted start dates for either the Greek or Egyptian civilizations, let alone the Minoans of Crete. Even ancient Egypt is not thought to have founded anything that could be considered a civilization until 3000 or 4000 BC at the earliest. So the precise location of the legendary Atlantis has remained a mystery.

There is, however, other supporting evidence for the idea that Atlantis did exist, or at least that a whole continent did once exist somewhere in the Atlantic Ocean between Europe and the Americas. For several ancient maps have been found which show not only what look like the present coastlines of the American continent, as well as Africa and Europe, but also another continent in between.[6]

The most famous of these maps, known as the Piri Reis map, was found in 1929 in the old Imperial Library at Constantinople, now Istanbul, and dated to AD 1513 at the latest, but the accompanying notes explained that it had been compiled from several other source maps, some of them dating back 'to the fourth century BC or earlier'.[7] These source maps in turn are thought to have dated back to 'even older sources', probably originating in 'the furthest antiquity'. According to Professor Hapgood of Keene College, New Hampshire, who studied the original map, there was 'irrefutable evidence that the Earth had been comprehensively mapped before 4000 BC by a hitherto unknown and undiscovered civilization which had achieved a high level of technological advancement' and whose 'accurate information' was then 'passed down from people to people' over the years.[8] Hapgood stated:

'We have evidence that [these maps] were collected and studied in the great library of Alexandria [in ancient Egypt and] … were passed on, perhaps by the Minoans and Phoenicians, who were, for a thousand years and more, the greatest sailors of the ancient world.'[9]

But who were the originators of these maps? What was the 'hitherto unknown and undiscovered civilization which had achieved a high level of technological advancement'? Could it perhaps have been the legendary Atlanteans who were drawing 'accurate' and 'comprehensive' maps from their base in the Atlantic Ocean?

What is curious about the Piri Reis map is that it shows the coastline of a continent in the southern Atlantic, which recent studies suggest may represent the 'subglacial topography' of present day Antarctica,[10] although it is clearly thousands of miles north of the current location of Antarctica and the continent shown is completely free of ice. Given that the whole of the Antarctic, both land and sea, is covered in ice, most of it over a mile thick, and that the continent was not officially discovered until 1818, this finding is bizarre.

Some scholars, such as Hapgood, have tried to argue that what the Piri Reis map shows is really Antarctica, but that since the map was first drawn the continent itself has actually moved thousands of miles further south due to a massive displacement of the Earth's crust. Another alternative, that the originators of the map were trying to draw Antarctica but simply got its location wrong, cannot explain why the continent shown is completely free of ice, unless of course global temperatures prior to 4000 BC were considerably higher than they are today. Certainly Greenpeace recently managed to sail a ship through a new sea channel which has opened up in the Antarctic ice as a result of global warming, so perhaps something similar happened at some time in the past?.

However, perhaps a more plausible explanation is that the continent shown is not really Antarctica at all, but some other continent, which has now disappeared. Whichever is the case, the mysterious land mass was clearly capable of supporting a human population and could quite possibly have been the legendary Atlantis.

Its location, however, would be difficult to fit with Plato's description of Atlantis being positioned opposite the Pillars of Hercules. Indeed, many have suggested that Atlantis may have been situated in the middle of the north Atlantic, not the south. The problem, of course, for most archaeologists over the years has not been any absence of written records, but an apparent lack of any hard and fast physical evidence. If this civilization had really existed and had sunk as recently as around 10,000 BC, why are there no physical remains of it today? Indeed, the middle of the Atlantic is actually one of the deepest parts of the ocean in the world.

In his book *The Secret of Atlantis*,[11] German author Otto Muck has attempted to answer this question. Muck points out that, like the pieces of a jigsaw puzzle, the eastern coastline of South America and the west coast of Africa fit together almost perfectly and in keeping with the now widely accepted geological theory of plate tectonics. However, the coastlines of North and Central America and Europe do not fit together at all. There appears to be a chunk missing. Muck suggests that this could perhaps be due to the absence of Atlantis, now lost deep beneath the waves.

Most geologists would argue that the movement of the American continental plates away from the African and European plates occurred several millions of years ago and not during, say, the last 12,000 years, but Muck even has an answer to this. He points out that it is widely accepted that glaciers in Europe advanced almost as far south as London during the last Ice Age. This would not have been possible if the present warm air and ocean currents of the Gulf Stream that cross the Atlantic today had been able to oppose them. So something must have been blocking the Gulf Stream during the last Ice Age. Muck suggests that this was Atlantis, now lost beneath the waves as a result of a catastrophic asteroid collision that struck the continent and created today's deep hole in the middle of the Atlantic Ocean.

Whether or not there is any truth in this story, it certainly fits Plato's description more closely.

But perhaps the middle of the Atlantic, whether north or south, was not really the most likely location of Atlantis anyway. Perhaps it lay far nearer to the coast of either Europe or America.

Some writers have certainly found connections between the ancient Mesoamericans and Atlantis. In the nineteenth century the American Ignatius Donnelly, in his book *Atlantis the Ante-diluvian World*,[12] found circumstantial evidence of a link between Atlantis and Central America through analysing similarities in words and language:

'According to the traditions of the Phoenicians, the Gardens of the Hesperides were in the remote west. Atlas lived in these gardens. Atlas, as we have seen, was king of Atlantis... Atlas was described in Greek

mythology as "an enormous giant, who stood upon the western confines of the earth, and supported the heavens on his shoulders, in a region of the west where the sun continued to shine after he had set upon Greece"…

'Look at it! An "Atlas" mountain on the shores of Africa; an "Atlan" town on the shores of America; the "Atlantes" living along the north and west coast of Africa; and "Aztec" people from "Aztlan" in Central America; an ocean rolling between the two worlds called "Atlantic"; a mythological deity called "Atlas" holding the world on his shoulders; and an immemorial tradition of an island called "Atlantis".'[13]

I remembered 'the building of the Atlantes' in the pre-Aztec city of Tula, near Mexico City, its walls decorated with stone-carved skulls. We had also heard that today's highland Maya of Guatemala have named their great lake 'Atitlán'. Like Donnelly, I couldn't stop myself asking, 'Can all these things be an accident?'

Could it be, as Hunbatz Men had suggested, that Atlantis was really located somewhere quite close to the Central American coast? Certainly there is a whole string of islands in what is now the Caribbean Sea. Frederick Mitchell-Hedges had already identified the Bay Islands off the coast of Belize and Honduras as a possible outpost of the original Atlantean civilization, and some, such as Gilbert and Cotterell, have suggested that perhaps the Caribbean islands were at one time the peaks, plateaus and mountains of a larger land mass or series of larger islands. Certainly many of these islands, as well as much of the eastern coastline of Central America, are today surrounded by very shallow waters, particularly that area known as the Great Bahama Bank, to the north of Cuba.

Gilbert and Cotterell have pointed out that the date Plato gives for the great Atlantean cataclysm, around 9500 BC, actually corresponds very closely with the date that is widely believed to mark the end of the last Ice Age.[14] It is also generally accepted that during the last Ice Age the ice caps were much larger, resulting in lower sea levels. Much of the world's water would have been held frozen as ice within glaciers and the ice caps, and so islands and coastlands would have been far more extensive at that time than they are today. As the last Ice Age ended, ice caps and glaciers started to melt and sea levels to rise. The main cities of the Atlantean civilization would probably have been concentrated around the coast and would have been the first areas to disappear underwater.

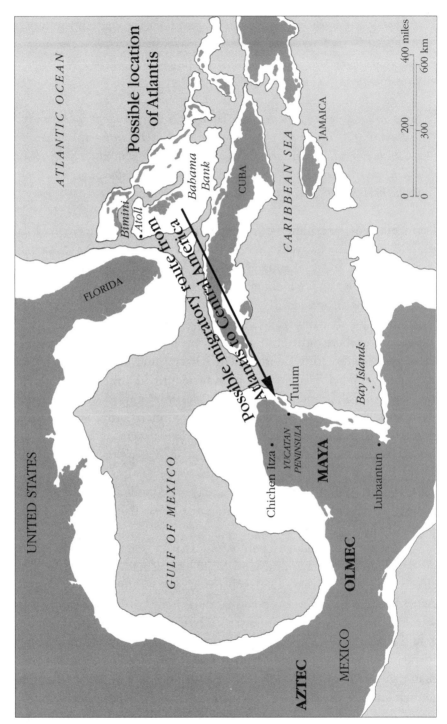

Figure 26: Area of shallow waters around the Central American and Caribbean coast, showing possible location of Atlantis

The theory is that refugees from Atlantis were able to escape by boat to the larger and higher land mass of Central America, bringing with them their culture, practices and beliefs, and perhaps, as Hunbatz had said, the crystal skulls. Once in Mesoamerica this handful of survivors may have interbred with the local people to create the Olmecs, Mayans and possibly Teotihuacános, Toltecs and even Aztecs. Thus many believe that the ancient Maya, and perhaps several other Mesoamerican tribes, may really have their origins in Atlantis, just as Hunbatz had said.

As Paula Gunn-Allen had told us, there was no denying the great prevalence throughout the Americas of myths and legends about 'wise men' or civilizing people who had come from the eastern sea. Many South American tribes, including the ancient Inca of Peru, spoke of a legendary figure, usually known as 'Viracocha', who had arrived from the seas to the east following a great deluge. This legendary wise and knowledgeable figure bore remarkable similarities to the Mayan figure of Kukulcan and the Aztecs' Quetzalcoatl, the great 'rainbow-coloured feathered serpent'. Though in many Mayan and Aztec versions of this story the great teacher came originally from the skies, almost all versions agree that, having imparted their knowledge and founded great civilizations, this legendary character and his companions sailed off again across the seas to the east. These great gods of Mesoamerican culture were figures of great 'light', learning and knowledge, akin to divine or higher beings. I wondered whether perhaps they could have been inhabitants of Atlantis who had visited the Americas either before or just after their own great civilization collapsed.

But had such travellers ever brought any crystal skulls with them? Certainly it was Professor Gunn-Allen's opinion, based on her personal experience with a crystal skull, that they did originate in Atlantis. She told us she had channelled information from the Mitchell-Hedges skull at Anna Mitchell-Hedges' home in Ontario back in 1987. I had been somewhat surprised that an academic would be interested in channelling at all, let alone have tried it out for herself, and at the time I had not taken what she said too seriously, but it now came back to me in the light of what we had heard from Hunbatz.

Like Carole Wilson, Paula Gunn-Allen believes that through entering a trance-like state she has been able to communicate with the 'mind' of the skull and to 'speak' its words. She cautioned, 'You never know when you're channelling if you're making it up or if it is truthful and accurate,' but nevertheless she told us of her experience:

'I channelled the skull, who told me that her name was "Gentian", which is the name of a flower, a healing plant that grows in the cold Alpine regions of western Europe.'

This seemed particularly appropriate to me as I had always felt there was an 'icy' quality to the Mitchell-Hedges skull. Interestingly, as I discovered a few months later from an article in a newspaper,[15] this particular plant is now one of the world's most threatened species, specifically because the glaciers around it are melting due to global warming.

According to Paula Gunn-Allen, Gentian is female:

'Contrary to what most of the owners say, the skulls are all female. They represent a feminine wisdom. By "feminine wisdom" I don't mean something that men don't have, but qualities that have traditionally been more highly developed in women, that is, the more intuitive side, the less hierarchical, competitive ways of thinking and behaving.'

In her opinion, interest in the skulls is surfacing now because this is a time when we are beginning to return to a more female-based form of society. As she put it, 'It is the time of the return of the grandmothers. It is the end of patriarchy.'

She then told us what she had channelled about how the crystal skulls had 'come into being':

'The crystal skulls were made by females. I'll call them people though I think they are not humans like we are, I think they're a different kind of human. [Gentian] told me that they lived for a very long time, hundreds of years, and they came from some place that had collapsed, what people call Atlantis. I saw them walking across this vast space that has no plants, not even lichen, no moss, nothing. My impression was that it was the floor of the ocean. Certainly it wasn't land as we know it. Eventually they came up an incline and then they were on the Yucatán Peninsula in Mexico, which, as you know, is not far from where Mitchell-Hedges found the skull in the 1920s.'

She described the advanced knowledge that the Atlanteans had:

'These people developed these tremendous disciplines. They knew about movement, the body and balanced emotion. Through discipline

they could imbue their bodies with knowledge and wisdom, and then they abstracted themselves, their awareness, from these bodies and slowly the process of petrification took place so they became like rocks, like stones. They left behind in their bones every iota of cosmic knowledge spread throughout the entire universe, not our galaxy alone but many, and through many time frames, including the one that we're presently occupying.'

Gunn-Allen was unsure exactly how many skulls had been made in this way, although she felt sure that their creators had left their remains, their bodies and their crystalline skulls, in a cavern under the mountains, west of the coast of what is now Belize. She believed the skulls to be 'communication devices':

'What they are is transceivers. What they enable you to do is to talk with the other quadrants of the galaxy. You might think of them as like telephones that get you connected with Galactic Central and enable you to stay in touch with other parts of the consciousness, civilizations if you will, that are beyond our little bitty modern world.'

This knowledge of the wider cosmic connections between the Earth and other planets had been 'held by indigenous people from Africa to Tibet through to Siberia', according to Paula Gunn-Allen, but had been inaccessible to the Western world for thousands of years.

That great knowledge from the past had been hidden from us was an idea we had already encountered when we had met psychic channeller Carole Wilson and had heard 'the voice of the skull' talking about Atlantis and great discoveries that were yet to come. Again, we had not taken this too seriously at the time, but now we were beginning to keep more of an open mind.

The information Carole had channelled from the skull is that it was once part of the 'great crystal of Atlantis'. According to 'the voice of the skull' 'the minds of many' are stored within it and those minds became 'locked within the crystal skull during the fall of Atlantis'.

As Carole explained it:

'What happened was that the beings placed the essence of their minds within the crystal. They saw that their home would soon be destroyed and wished to preserve their knowledge for use in the future. First of all

they thought to hide the knowledge just within one place, but then
decided that it was too dangerous and it was better to distribute the
knowledge in different receptacles.'

For Carole, the crystal skulls are a form of remembering that which has
been forgotten, and this is especially important now. She urged us particularly to remember some of the other words the skull had spoken:
'Because of the disasters upon this planet, you will be needed to call upon
your reincarnational memories to heal, to counsel, to guide and to love a
world gone mad.'

Carole believes that some of these 'reincarnational memories' are of
Atlantis and that we need to know what really happened so that we can
avoid the same catastrophe again. This echoed Nick Nocerino's view that
the skulls were reminding us about past events so that we could learn
from the mistakes of the past and not allow them to happen again.

Carole had urged us to read the writings of Edgar Cayce, one of the
world's best-known psychics, for he too had channelled information
about Atlantis. Cayce (1877–1945) was a photographer by trade but was
renowned as 'the Sleeping Prophet'. He had accidentally discovered the
ability to diagnose illness and prescribe accurate treatment while in a
deep trance state, and also channelled information about the past and the
future. According to Cayce, Atlantis did exist, but was inundated by
water and destroyed as a result of a great environmental cataclysm. He
described the migration of its handful of survivors:

> *'Then, with the leavings of the civilisation of Atlantis, Iltar – with a*
> *group of followers that had been of the house of Atlan, the followers*
> *of the worship of the ONE – with some ten individuals – left this land of*
> *Poseidia, and came westward, entering what would now be a portion*
> *of [the] Yucatán. And there began, with the activities of the people there,*
> *the development into a civilisation that rose much in the same manner*
> *as that which had been in the Atlantean land...'* [16]

Could this group have been the 'Itzas' that Hunbatz had referred to, led
possibly by the great 'Itzamna', who helped found the Mayan civilization
on the Yucatán Peninsula?

According to Cayce, the survivors brought records of their earlier history and these were still to be found in three places:

'The records ... are stored in three places in the earth as it stands today: in the sunken portion of Atlantis, or Poseida, where a portion of the temples may yet be discovered under the slime of ages of sea water – near what is known as Bimini off the coast of Florida.' [17]

We had already heard 'the voice of the skull' mention Bimini. Cayce had made the prediction on 28 June 1940 that the temples off the coast of Bimini would be discovered in 1968–9, but the importance of the find might not at first be realized.

I was amazed to discover that it was precisely in this area, on one corner of the Bermuda Triangle, in 1968, that a group of divers led by a Dr Manson Valentine did in fact discover something completely unexpected beneath the waves, in only 20–30 feet (6–9 metres) of water.[18] What they found were massive stone blocks, some as large as 15 feet (4.5 metres) in diameter and weighing around 25 tons (25 tonnes) apiece. Whilst controversy still rages over whether these might be naturally occurring rock formations, one of the most peculiar things is that each block is of almost exactly the same dimensions. While some appear to have been rounded off by the action of sea water, they had originally been 'fashioned' into almost perfect squares, with accurate right angles on each corner. They also seem to have been carefully arranged in what looks like a man-made sea wall completely surrounding the small island of Bimini, as if they had been built as a massive defence against the encroaching waves.

Cayce also said that further evidence of Atlantis would be found 'in the temple records that were in Egypt ... also the records that were carried to what is now Yucatán, in America, where these stones (which they know so little about) are now'.[19] I couldn't help wondering whether 'these stones' might be crystal skulls, perhaps some skulls lying still undiscovered somewhere on the Yucatán Peninsula?

But what of the temple records in Egypt? We later spoke to a British psychic, Ann Walker, who had recently made a trip to Egypt in search of these very records. In her book *The Stone of the Plough*,[20] she puts forward her belief that ancient Egypt, just like the ancient civilizations of Mesoamerica, was actually founded by the Atlanteans, who were instrumental in the design and building of the pyramids in both places. Certainly, much of the archaeological evidence suggests that rather than developing slowly and painfully, as is normally the case with human societies, the civilization of ancient Egypt, just like that of the Olmecs and the later Maya and Aztecs, emerged as if all at once, fully formed.

Indeed, even in ancient Mesopotamia, amongst the Sumerians, who built a civilization in the Middle East that is believed to have immediately preceded the ancient Egyptians, there is a legend of 'wise beings' who had emerged from the seas in remote pre-history. These strange amphibious beings, like men crossed with fish, but 'endowed with reason', had given the people the knowledge necessary to found their civilization. Were these perhaps the Atlanteans that Ann Walker was so convinced had brought civilization to the Middle East and to Egypt?

Ann believes these bearers of world civilization also carried records from Atlantis and that these may have included one or more crystal skulls. With the help of her 'spirit guide', she now believes that she knows exactly where these records are stored. Like Cayce, she thinks they lie in a 'Hall of Records' buried beneath the paws of the Sphinx. Interestingly, this very site has now been earmarked by the Egyptian government for excavation. Ann believes that a crystal skull will be unearthed in the process, unequivocally revealing the vital role the crystal skulls have played in shaping our human destiny, even in the West. Whether or not she is right, we shall just have to wait and see.

But if Atlantis really did exist, what had led to its final downfall? According to the information Cayce channelled, there was a 'breaking up of the land owing to the misapplication of the divine laws upon those things of nature or of the earth'[21] and it seems that crystal, if not crystal skulls, was involved in this process.

According to Cayce, the Atlanteans' original use of crystal was strictly sacred:

'In the Atlantean land ... among the household of a priest – a princess of royal blood – [was] one that had supervision of that stone upon which the light of heaven shone, for the blessings of man – that brought the divinations to the people as to their relationship to the godly forces as might find expression.'[22]

Although Cayce did not refer directly to crystal skulls, I couldn't help wondering whether 'that stone' might be a covert reference to them. Indeed, as I read on it became clear that certainly crystal, whether or not it was fashioned into a skull, had a very important role to play in Atlantis. For, according to Cayce, the Atlanteans originally used crystal as a means of divine communication, just as Hunbatz said was the function of the crystal skulls, but later the power of the crystals became corrupted:

'Developed originally as a means of spiritual communication between the finite and the infinite, the huge reflective crystals were first known as Tuaoi *Stone. [But] later, as its use was improved upon over the centuries, it expanded to become a generator of power and energy radiating across the land without wires. Then it became known as the* Firestone, *or the* Great Crystals.*'* [23]

Cayce described a people who learned how to manipulate their environment through harnessing the power of crystal. In an account which sounds like something straight out of science fiction, he goes on to describe these 'Great Crystals':

'Set in the Temple of the Sun in Poseidia, the Firestone was the central power station of the country... Above the stone was a dome which could be rolled back for exposure to the sun. The concentration and magnification of the sun's rays through many prisms was of tremendous intensity. So powerful was it that it could be regenerated and transmitted throughout the land in invisible beams similar to radio waves. Its energy was used to power ships at sea, aircraft and even pleasure vehicles. ...Cities and towns received their power from the same source.' [24]

Everything Cayce said seemed to corroborate what we had heard from Carole Wilson about a civilization with 'advanced minds'. The society he described even seemed to have some curious parallels with our own. His account also appeared to back up what Professor Gunn-Allen had said about the Atlanteans manipulating their longevity and their own bodies:

'The human body could even be rejuvenated through the moderate application of the rays from the crystals, and man often rejuvenated himself.' [25]

But, according to Cayce, it was specifically through the abuse of the power of quartz crystal that the Atlanteans sowed the seeds of their own undoing:

'Yet by mis-application the Firestone [or crystal] could be and was turned to destructive uses [and this] contributed to the cause of the second catastrophe. The rays combined with other electrical forces to start many fires deep within the earth, and volcanic eruptions were precipitated from nature's powerful storehouse of energy.' [26]

He added:

'The first breaking up of the land [was] when there was the use of those influences that are again being discovered – that may be of use for benefits in communications, transportation, etc, or turned into destructive forces.' [27]

Cayce had been writing back in the 1940s when the 'benefits' of crystal were being explored primarily for military purposes. But now quartz is found in almost every electrical appliance, I wondered whether the Atlanteans might have been using a more advanced form of the very same crystal technologies that are so widespread today?

Native American Seneca legend also describes how Atlantis was destroyed due to an abuse of the power of quartz crystal. In her book *Other Council Fires Were Here Before Ours,*[28] Seneca elder Grandmother Twylah Nitsch describes this legend. According to the Seneca, Atlantis was originally part of a great continent known as 'Turtle Island', which actually included all the countries of the world before they became separated by the process that scientists now recognize as continental drift. This process is normally assumed to take place very slowly over millions of years, but the legend suggests that it can also take place far more quickly and that it was during one of these great 'Earth changes' or movements that Atlantis was destroyed.

According to the Seneca, during the time of Turtle Island, all five races of the world occupied the same land mass, each with their own area. The white race, known as the 'Gagans', occupied what was then Atlantis, in the north east of the island. This race was blessed with great creative talents:

'Marvels … poured forth from [their] brilliant minds. They discovered cures for all the human diseases and found ways to restore their physical bodies [to] health by using the colors of the light from Grandfather Sun.' [29]

In what sounds like an extraordinary parallel to today, the white people 'developed curious things, which they called machines, to do their work for them. We called these curious forms Makes Work Easy for Two-leggeds.'[30] Initially this was not done in a way that was damaging to the Earth. There were no roads or mines. But as time went on, things began to change. Because they did not share their medicine with the other four races, the gagans started to live much longer than them and this gave them a feeling of great superiority. It was then that they decided to enslave the other races.

The new medicine of the Gagans was white and the colour white consequently took on a host of new associations. The Gagans believed that it was strong and clean, and that anything which was not white and pristine was destructive. Soon their fear of dirt, dust, soil and sand began to destroy their sense of belonging to Mother Earth. They moved to all-white encampments made of marble and crystal, and created plants and trees which would not shed their leaves or flowers. This brought to my mind plastic plants in modern office blocks and shopping malls. The Gagans became known as *Aga Oheda*, or the 'Afraid of Dirts', by the other races, who were only allowed into the encampment as servants, singers or dancers to amuse the Gagans during feast days.

So great became the Gagans' fear of infection by anything that was not white that they began to cover the Earth's surface with a white substance, known as 'Hard-Like-Rock Snow'. This 'rock-hard white robe' destroyed plants and animals in its wake. At the same time, the Afraid of Dirts began to exploit the properties of crystal:

> *'The Afraid of Dirts medicine people found a way to melt ... Crystal ... and to mix their fluid bodies with ores found on the Earth Mother. [The 'Crystal People'] were being melted and therefore, murdered, in order to aid the Afraid of Dirts Tribe in their desire to harness the Earth Mother's natural forces.*[31]

Extracting ores from the Earth created great caverns. There was no balance in the frenzy with which the resources of Turtle Island were being used up without being replaced. Again, I was struck by some of the similarities with what is happening today. Were we not taking the Earth's resources, chopping down forests, mining and taking from the Earth? Were we not slowly covering the planet, not only with the white substance of concrete, but also with roads that were eating up greater and greater areas of countryside? We wondered, was this legend really talking about the past or was it a prophecy describing the present world and our immediate future?

As the story moved towards its conclusion, the Earth Mother looked on with deep sadness at the fate that awaited her children:

'The Two-leggeds who are my children have always been given free will. It was their choice to destroy the roots that kept them connected to the abundance that was their natural legacy. The waters of the tides of change will purify the damage done this day, but the legacy of their wanton destruction will be felt in the coming worlds and will be inherited by all future generations.' [32]

And so, according to Seneca legend, just as told in the Mayan calendar, the Third World of Water was destroyed by flood. The lakes in our current world are there as reminders.

The story ends with the statement:

'The flooding will continue across Turtle Island every time the sacred bonds of life and equality are broken by the Two-leggeds. It is time to call all the Medicine Stones together, because they are the Record Keepers of the true history of our journeys together. There, high on Sacred Mountain, the truth of the coming worlds will be revealed to The Faithful through the records of the Stone People.' [33]

Again I wondered whether the 'medicine stones' might be a reference to the crystal skulls, which have kept the records not only of Atlantis but also of previous worlds. Might these 'medicine stones' really be here to remind us of the terrible events of the past so that we can learn from our mistakes and not let such catastrophes happen again? If 'the flooding will continue ... every time the sacred bonds of life and equality are broken', might there really be some truth in the ancient Mayan calendar and in what Hunbatz Men had said about the possibility that our world might also soon come to an end?

We had been surprised enough to hear from Hunbatz and other sources that Atlantis might really have existed and that at least some of the crystal skulls might have come from this source, but this was nothing compared to what we were about to hear when we got back to the USA.

24. THE ANCIENT ONES

We had to fly to Arizona the next day because we had arranged to meet a metis Cherokee medicine man whose name was Harley SwiftDeer. We had heard that this man was renowned as a source of great knowledge and wisdom about the crystal skulls. It was said that he was one of the few people who knew the original legend in full and that the knowledge he had went far beyond only the Native American tradition. His teachings apparently showed that the skulls were part of a truly global history, part of a hidden legacy of all the people of the Earth that had, until now, been kept highly secret. Harley was, however, apparently now prepared to 'share with all the children of the Earth' this 'true story of our own human history'.

We knew very little about this man except that he was considered a highly controversial figure within the Native American community. As far as we could tell this was largely on account of his extremely contentious decision to share with the world the secret teachings and history of his people. According to his many assistants, these teachings had never been spoken of before outside the sacred teaching lodges of the indigenous people. What Harley had agreed to tell us was normally reserved only for those members of the Cherokee and other indigenous tribes who had undergone full 'shamanic initiation', for those who honoured the traditions of the forefathers and who 'walked the sacred path of true knowledge' and lived their lives according to the original teachings of the very first ancestors.

We had already heard that the sharing of sacred knowledge has long been a controversial issue for Native American peoples, many of whom feel that the Europeans have taken an awful lot from them already and now want to plunder the last vestiges of their sacred traditions. Indeed, this issue has deeply divided some native communities. On the one hand there are those who want to keep the ancient traditions and teachings private and therefore intact and uncorrupted. On the other hand, an increasing number are of the opinion that it is now time to share their sacred knowledge in the hope that it may benefit the whole of humanity. Harley's assistants explained to us that Harley was in the latter category.

But we were warned that some of these teachings were not for the faint-hearted. They were only for those who were ready to hear, for those who could accept what at first might appear to be somewhat crazy and certainly controversial. They were only for those who could listen with an open mind and for those able to really listen but without judgement. It was explained to us that the teachings we were about to hear might just shock those who were not yet ready to hear. For the history of the Cherokee and some of the other indigenous people, what they considered the true telling of history, contained information that could be deeply un-settling to those who were unfamiliar with the native world view or to those who were not prepared to accept that the history they had always been taught might actually be wrong. For 'the true teachings' contained whole concepts that we might not previously have even considered, ideas that might sound highly implausible or disturbingly unfamiliar, ideas that might not before ever have entered our consciousness. We were told that in order to hear these properly we would need to put aside the familiar, the safe and the known and take a leap into the unknown, to enter a new and strange territory, where we might well discover that many of the things we had always taken for granted were really not as they seemed.

We had learned all this through Harley's assistants, as he had himself been a somewhat elusive figure who had not been available to answer any of our telephone enquiries. We had been told that his view was that if we were serious about the knowledge of the crystal skulls then we would have to come and meet him for ourselves at his 'teaching and healing practice' in a suburb of Phoenix, Arizona.

As we arrived in Phoenix we were greeted by the unexpected sight of bright green, neatly manicured lawns in the midst of an arid desert landscape. The whole place had the feel of an upmarket holiday resort, but lacking the beach. As we drove through the town, I wondered what this controversial man was going to be like and, more to the point, what exactly was he going to tell us?

Harley SwiftDeer had already agreed to be interviewed and filmed. Chris and I both thought that a shot of this genuine Cherokee shaman outlined in semi-profile against the brilliant red rocks of the desert would be stunning, suggesting a wisdom of ancient timelessness as beautiful as the haunting desert landscape itself. The sun would be setting behind him, its golden rays catching the angular structure of his serene, intelligent face, his dark eyes, intense with wisdom and compassion, and his long black hair streaming behind him in the wind.

When we finally arrived at Harley's practice, our first surprise was the low concrete office buildings, which looked more like the headquarters of an international firm. It was certainly not the sort of place where we had expected to find an indigenous elder and shaman. The clinical atmosphere of the buildings, the hum of air conditioning and the white office interiors struck me as more befitting a modern hospital than the working environment of an indigenous medicine man.

We were greeted rather formally by one of Harley's assistants, Jan, a woman in her mid 40s, who whisked us into one of the plush offices to discuss our filming plans. She seemed to have forgotten that we wanted to shoot in the desert. 'Oh, but Harley has dressed up all smart today and is wearing a Western suit especially for the occasion,' she said. This was not exactly the image we had in mind...

I was anxious to meet the man himself, so we were now taken through to wait for him in a large room the size of a gymnasium. The floor was thickly carpeted and the walls lined with various certificates and photographs. I was just registering from these certificates that Harley Swift-Deer Reagan was also a member of the local gun club and a karate expert when Jan drew our attention to 'the Ark'. There, in the centre of the room, on a bright pink cloth amidst a garish arrangement of stones and crystals, was a life-size crystal skull, of somewhat crude design, with a rather more pointed face than any of the other skulls I had seen. Four lines of objects radiated out from it, apparently representing the four sacred directions. They were a jumble of artefacts, pottery and carvings of obviously Mesoamerican design, and looked to me like the sort of tourist trinkets that are for sale around the ancient sites of Mexico, although of course they may have been genuine antiquities. A small flex ran from the crystal skull, and as Jan flicked a switch, the whole arrangement was suddenly illuminated in a curiously tacky manner.

'It's a modern skull, isn't it?' I asked.

'How did you know?' Jan replied. 'Yes, Harley has found a wonderful carver in Brazil, in Minas Gerais province, where a lot of very fine crystal comes from.'

It transpired that Harley had got the crystal from Damien Quinn, who Nick Nocerino had told us about.

I looked up to find Harley himself had entered the room and now stood before me. 'Howdy!' he said, hand outstretched and sporting a large grin. His accent was pure Texas. I was most surprised to see a man with blue eyes, pale skin and curly grey hair, dressed in a Stetson and wearing a full cowboy outfit, complete with bootlace tie and cowboy boots. He looked to be in his late sixties, was over six feet tall and appeared of decidedly European ancestry. I found myself wondering whether he was really Native American at all.

It transpired that the word 'metis' means 'part' Cherokee and that actually Harley was part Irish, hence the 'Reagan' in his full name. His grandfather was an Irish settler who had taken a Cherokee bride and the story he was about to tell us had been told to him by his Cherokee grandmother when he was still a young boy.

Harley began by taking a seat, lighting a cigarette and regaling us with tales of his work as a stuntman in Hollywood in the 1950s. He was clearly enjoying himself being the 'star' of our 'show'. The room quickly filled up with his associates and his beautiful young wife, who had come to see the interview take place. Then, whilst taking regular slugs of Dr Pepper™ and availing himself of a chain of cigarettes, Harley began to tell us the 'true story' of the crystal skulls, at quite astonishing speed, so that it was actually quite hard for us to take it all in at the time.

'I am the heyoehkah *or war chief of the Twisted Hairs Society's council of elders. That's who I'm speaking for as a Twisted Hairs and as a member of their council of elders.*

'I'd like now to tell you the story of the legend of the crystal skulls, that we call "the singing skulls" and of the Ark of Osiriaconwiya.

'The legend starts in the way of the Twisted Hairs, for they are the storytellers.'

Amongst Native Americans the tradition of storytelling is the means through which the sacred traditions and the history of the people are passed on from one generation to the next. According to the Cherokee, the

Twisted Hairs are people who represent a very ancient tradition of story-telling that goes back thousands of years. As Harley went on to explain:

'The Twisted Hairs include members of over 400 different tribes that represent all of North, South and Central America.

'These were, and are, men and women that would travel all the way from the furthest tip of South America all the way up to the furthest reaches of North America to pass on the sacred teachings.

'Long ago, North, South and Central America, along with the continents that are now called New Zealand and Australia, were all of one land mass, they were all one continent, known to our people as "Turtle Island".'

This, as we had discovered, is actually a very common belief amongst many Native American tribes. But Harley continued:

'The elders of the Twisted Hairs say that in the very beginning there were 12 worlds with human life. These are planets that revolve around different suns and the elders met on a planet called Osiriaconwiya. This is actually the fourth planet out from the Dog Star, Sirius. It has two suns and two moons, and they met here to discuss the plight of the "planet of the children" – and this is where we are today. This is Grandmother Earth. It is called Eheytoma *in our language, but it also represents "the planet of the children" because it is the least evolved of all those planets with human life. So we are really one of a family of 12 planets.*

'Each of the other planets took the sum total of all knowledge and they encoded this knowledge into what can best be described, in modern-day terms, as a sort of holographic image computer called a crystal skull. These are absolutely flawless, perfect crystal skulls. These skulls have moving jaws just like our skulls so they were referred to as "the singing skulls" and the entire configuration was known as "the Ark of Osiria-conwiya". Each skull represents a different planet's knowledge. The best way to think of it is, we have computers today that have huge amounts of data stored which can be accessed. All of the crystal skulls store huge amounts of information, and they can be accessed if you understand how to do so.

'Anyway, our cosmic elders took the Ark and encoded all of the knowledge of the 12 worlds with human life, which are called the "sacred 12" planets or "grandmothers", and then they brought them here and they

began to work with them and to teach the children of Grandmother Earth. These cosmic elders found a way to be able to move back and forth in their communications with the "Two-leggeds" here on Grandmother Earth.

'And this really was a most impressive and valuable gift that was given to the children of this Earth, for it was the gift of knowledge. It was the greatest gift, for it was the root from which all could develop, it was the foundation from which we all could flourish.

'And this is what originally happened and there was a period of great advancement. The elders from the other planets educated the children of this Earth and they gave them what are called "the teachings of the sacred shields".

'The elders found a way to be able to communicate with the people of this Earth from their own planets, with the assistance of two great domes, one red and the other blue, that were located beneath the ocean. And they helped the people of the Earth to build four great civilizations, the civilizations of Lemuria, Mu, Mieyhun and Atlantis. And they used the knowledge of the skulls to begin the great mystery schools, the arcane wisdom schools, and the secret medicine societies. And they began to disseminate this information. The information arrived approximately 750,000 years ago and it began to be distributed on Grandmother Earth around 250 to 300,000 years ago. To help with the teachings other skulls were created here on Earth, but though life-size, their jaws do not move. There are many more of these skulls and they are known as "the talking skulls", to separate them from "the singing skulls" of the major Ark, which represent all of the knowledge of all of the 12 worlds as well as our own.'

As Harley later explained, the Twisted Hairs Society was one of the secret medicine societies. Apparently the legend of the crystal skulls had been handed down over the generations, but had had to be kept secret from outsiders, particularly in the face of the oppression and brutality the native peoples had suffered. But the purpose of the society had always been to preserve this wisdom.

Harley continued his story:

'The skulls were kept inside a pyramid in a formation of tremendous power known as the Ark. The Ark was comprised of the 12 skulls from each of the sacred planets kept in a circle, with a thirteenth skull, the

largest, placed in the centre of this formation. This thirteenth skull rep-
resents the collective consciousness of all the worlds. It connects up the
knowledge of all the sacred planets.

  'The travelling people that first brought the Ark of the singing skulls
came to be known as "the Olmec", and then it migrated up and was
taken over in legacy by the Mayans, and then by the Aztecs, and now
this knowledge today is still held by the Twisted Hairs.'

Harley said the Ark had been kept in secret by the Olmecs somewhere
along the Gulf coast. This seemed to explain some of the mysterious references we had come across when we were in Central America – 'the
Dwelling of the Thirteen' that Abbé Brasseur de Bourbourg had spoken
about and that the mysterious founders of Palenque had visited *en route*
to Central America.

Harley said the Mayans had then looked after the Ark and that 'ultimately the Aztecs held the Ark and they kept the skulls in a place called
Teotihuacán'. As Harley was speaking, I remembered this mysterious site
just outside Mexico City. It was the place with the great pyramids
beneath which lay a great underground chamber, protected by a very
large carved stone skull, the city the Aztecs called 'the place where the
gods touched the Earth' and where they believed the sun itself had been
born. The Aztecs always associated the sun with knowledge and it now
seemed clear to me that this myth was probably a coded reference to the
birth of knowledge, the birth of illumination and power that took place
there as a result of the crystal skulls.

I also wondered once more whether it was the deep prophetic knowledge given to the Aztecs by the crystal skulls that had enabled them to
transform themselves, over less than 200 years, from landless nomadic
peasants into the largest and most powerful pre-Columbian empire the
world had ever known.

But, according to Harley SwiftDeer, the crystal skulls have to be in the
possession of those who know how to use their powers without abusing
them. Indeed, according to him, the Aztecs' demise resulted quite specifically from their abuse of the power the skulls had given them and this was
why it became necessary for the skulls to be separated:

'The Aztecs used the power of the skulls to control others, to pervert
their own power and aggrandize themselves. They were becoming so
powerful and so destructive a force that they had to be stopped. The

only force powerful enough to stop the Aztecs was the Spanish Empire. The Ark was still in its place in Teotihuacán when Cortés invaded the Americas.'

According to the legend as Harley had been told it, 'the priests who were travelling with Cortés heard about the Ark of the crystal skulls' and this information was passed back to the Pope in Rome.

'And the Catholic Pope at that time insisted, "This knowledge must be gained." He wanted the skulls more than he wanted all of the gold and all of the riches of that empire. And although at that time the Ark was hidden underground, the Spanish soldiers came and they managed to gain access to it as a result of a betrayal from within.

'But just as the Spanish were about to arrive to seize the crystal skulls, all of the jaguar-priests and eagle-warriors took the skulls and fled with them. Some were taken to the former Mayan territories, others way down into South America and others were scattered around the world.

'And so the skulls were split from each other and separated for the first time in their history here on Grandmother Earth.'

Harley told us the skulls will have to remain apart until a time arrives when their collective powers are no longer likely to be abused. He said that, sadly, the human race was still not yet quite evolved enough not to abuse the power and knowledge of the skulls. As he put it:

'The skulls have to be out there and to roam, to wander away from the other singing skulls, until such a time as we learn to share with one another, care for one another, teach one another, heal one another and live in world peace and in harmony with Grandmother Earth.

'However, as you know, that's not happening anywhere on Grand-mother Earth today, so the skulls are still meant to be out there and to roam.

'But the legend says that they will return once again back into their family, but only when this family is willing to grow up and mature and join the other family of planets in peace.

'This, then, is the legend as it was told to me by my teacher and her teacher before her since always and in the ways of the Twisted Hairs.'

With these last simple words, Harley SwiftDeer ended his extraordinary tale and we realized we had now, at last, heard the legend of the crystal skulls in its entirety.

As we took our leave, Harley reminded us once again that this was very sacred knowledge to the indigenous people. He added that although this legend had been kept secret all these years, the time was now fast approaching when it would become necessary for this sacred information to be revealed and for the knowledge of the crystal skulls to go out into the world.

As we drove back to the airport in stunned and almost total silence, I turned to Chris. 'So the crystal skulls were brought by extra-terrestrials?'

'I just don't believe it,' he said. 'You mean, we're supposed to believe that the crystal skulls were a sort of gift, like some kind of toy, given to us "children of the Earth" by aliens? I think that guy must have been having us on.'

I certainly had to agree that nothing we had heard fit into anything like a 'normal' understanding of the world or any kind of conventional view of human history.

Chris added, 'I'm not entirely convinced he was even Native American at all!'

Again I had to agree that Harley SwiftDeer been very far removed from my expectation of the wise old Native American medicine man we had been expecting. In fact, he had appeared to be the very opposite with his stetson, his gun club membership, his obvious love of Dr Pepper™ and the endless cigarettes. He was more like a gun-toting all-American cowboy, the likes of which I thought had long died out. In fact the whole scenario suddenly seemed like a huge joke.

We pulled in at the nearest diner. We needed to recover from this strange encounter before continuing our long journey back to Jamie Sam's house. But as we sat there over a cup of iced tea I realized I had been so preoccupied with the details of the character of Harley SwiftDeer that at first I had almost failed to listen to what he had been saying. And even Chris had to agree that much of what he said about the ancient Mesoamericans did seem to explain some of the enigmas we had come across in Central America.

That's it, I suddenly thought, reminding Chris that in the Native American tradition it is said that great teachings often come about through a joke or through a 'coyote', a clown-like figure who frequently turns things on their head. Such tricksters are a feature of tribal culture and are part of many mythological stories. It occurred to me that perhaps Harley SwiftDeer was just such a character. As a pale-faced, blue-eyed, gun-toting, chain-smoking joker he had certainly overturned our expectations and stereotypes completely.

But did this mean that we should totally disregard what he had said, or completely accept it, or what? I found myself thinking about the very nature of truth. Were we only to believe that which had been told to us by 'serious' authoritative sources? After all, we had already found that academics had a very delicate reputation to maintain. We had learned that the conventional experts and established institutions seemed reluctant to investigate anything that might seriously challenge the prevalent notions of history. What other reason could the British Museum have had for not revealing the results of the tests on all of the crystal skulls? If what Harley SwiftDeer had told us about extra-terrestrial visitation was true, then perhaps the skulls might really have been made in ways that we had not yet conceived of. Perhaps the British Museum had been frightened by what they had found. Perhaps it had threatened their world view.

I thought about the way in which I had previously put my trust in the experts. We had originally relied almost exclusively on the accepted wisdom. And yet we had repeatedly found that the traditional academic approach had simply failed to provide all the answers we were looking for.

I now suddenly found it strangely reassuring that Harley SwiftDeer had no particular reputation to maintain. He was not an academic who had the reputation of his department at stake. Even amongst many of those in the Native American community he was known as somewhat of a maverick.

I knew, of course, that established archaeologists would have been horrified by what he had said and I must admit I myself also had strong reservations. None the less, the possibility that the crystal skulls might have been made by extra-terrestrials was certainly most intriguing. I felt that we could not dismiss it out of hand. It was somehow important to try to keep an open mind. After all, Harley SwiftDeer's explanation certainly seemed to explain why no tool marks had been discovered on the Mitchell-Hedges skull and why the British Museum had been so reluctant to comment on Max and Sha Na Ra, as well as some of the curious anomalies we had come across in Central America.

As we headed back to Jamie Sams' house, the thought began to play in my mind as to whether she might also have heard of some extra-terrestrial connection with the crystal skulls. From my earliest conversations with Jamie, I knew that she believed that the crystal skulls had been created by 'those who had wanted to transform their wisdom into crystal so that it would not be lost, but would be contained in these libraries of stone forever'. She had also said that the skulls had been made 'using the power of light, sound and thought alone'. This had certainly suggested to me that some form of advanced technology had been involved. But was it the technology of extra-terrestrials?

Jamie had also told me that the skulls were 'a set of records that includes how the Earth Mother is related to every other heavenly body in our solar system, galaxy and universe'. At the time this had strongly indicated to me the possibility of some kind of celestial origin. But Jamie had been somewhat evasive as to the exact origins of the skulls. When she had first spoken to me on the phone she had said 'the time was not yet right' for her to tell me. But that was now many months ago. Would the time be right now?

As we arrived back at Jamie's house, my mind was still reeling from our encounter with Harley SwiftDeer. Were his words really an ancient truth or was he merely teasing us with incredulous tales?

As we sat down at the old kitchen table, I felt somewhat uncomfortable. I was anxious to hear Jamie's opinion as to whether the skulls really had any sort of connection with extra-terrestrials and was building up to asking her this question, but was nervous as to how she might react. After all, it's not exactly an everyday topic of conversation, or at least not for me it isn't. I wondered whether Jamie might just laugh at me for even having made such a suggestion. But I had also heard it said that it is often when you feel most uncomfortable about something that the most important lessons are learned and the most important questions answered.

So I began gently by asking Jamie whether she had heard anything about the Aztecs keeping crystal skulls, as Harley had said.

'As I understand it, yes, they were at one time the keepers, but they did not understand the implications of what they were supposed to be looking after,' she replied.

I pressed her a little more, asking her who else had kept crystal skulls. She explained:

'The people of Turtle Island have kept the crystal skulls for a very long time now and they have looked after them carefully.

'The skulls were kept in a lodge. This lodge was an oval structure made of stones and branches that was half underground and half above the ground. This place represented the meeting of both heaven and Earth, and the meeting of the spirit world and the physical world of ordinary mortals. According to my teachers, inside the lodge two fires were kept burning, one to represent the physical world and the other to represent the spirit world. Fire is a symbol of illumination, the illumination that we can have when the smoke of confusion clears from our minds. Fire transforms what it touches, burns away at the dead matter, creating light and warmth. It is a metaphor for the transformation that humankind needs to go through, clearing away our limitations our negative thoughts, doubts and fears.

'The skull was placed above these fires with the light shining up from beneath it and this created an ark of all the rainbow colours that spread all around and above it. This was like a microcosm of the Earth, where the aurora borealis rises above us at the North Pole, and so the rainbow rises from out of the skulls. But the rainbow is also in and around the skull. The rainbow is an integral part of it all.'

I broke in with what I was really curious to know: 'So Native American people had crystal skulls that they kept in lodges, but did the local people make the skulls?'

Jamie sat in silence for a few moments, as if I had interrupted her flow. She gazed out at the distant moon before answering softly:

'Ever since the Europeans arrived, my people have watched the white man and his ways. We have been forced to live by the white man's ways and to share his beliefs. We have watched in silence and my people have not spoken out. We have been told about God and the Church. We have been told about the course of human civilization and progress. In the classrooms we have all been taught the ways of separation and of mankind's dominion over the Earth. These are not our ways, but our people have listened in silence. For they have learned that to challenge the dominant society is to die. But now we know that the time has come. We have been silent for too long and now it is time to speak up. We know that now is the time for us to end the separation and to share the truth in our hearts.'

Looking out, I could see that the moon had begun to softly illuminate the landscape. Jamie continued:

'The view of the world that your scientists and academics have had is but one view of humanity and its history, and it is a very narrow view. From this narrow perspective, no archaeologist can truly explain the wonder of the crystal skulls. They cannot even begin to try to explain the pyramids of Teotihuacán, or even those of ancient Egypt. They have not been able to explain the huge stone blocks used by the Inca empire of Peru. They cannot answer the question of how we simple people could possibly have moved such stones. They cannot explain how our people managed to achieve the great technical precision that was needed to build these ancient sites. Nobody has been able to explain how it was done, why it is, for example, that the oldest of the pyramids was the most accurately and beautifully constructed. They cannot explain why the ancient Egyptians, or the Olmec, the Maya or the Aztecs went from being ordinary tribespeople to master builders overnight.

'I'm afraid this narrow view cannot even begin to comprehend our truths, but I will tell them, for Spirit has moved me to tell you. What I will tell you are secrets that have been kept from European people ever since they first arrived on Turtle Island, but now the time has arrived and we will speak out.'

Then to my surprise Jamie answered the very question I had been afraid to ask.

'You see, it was extra-terrestrials, as you call them, that first brought the crystal skulls. But we call them "sky gods" or "sky people". These sky people first visited the Earth at the end of the Third World of Water. The Third World of Water was a long, long time ago, before continental drift, when all of the land mass of the world was one continent known as Turtle Island.

'The sky gods have been visiting this Earth right from the very beginning and they have visited this Earth several times since. They have often been known as great teachers and were given names such as Quetzalcoatl in Central America or Viracocha in South America. They have often come at a time when humanity is struggling, or when we have been living lawless or otherwise impoverished lives. They have come as helpers, as teachers and healers, and they have tried to teach humanity

how to live in peace. It was these sky gods that helped the early people to create the wonders of the ancient world. But that is not all that they helped us with. Humanity has been transformed through its contact with these beings from the other planets within our own galaxy. They have played a key role in the development of humanity, more key than you have ever imagined.

'But what I am about to tell you takes us right back to our source. It takes us right back to our earliest ancestors. I will tell you the real story of our creation as I have heard it from my elders. In the beginning, there was peace on Earth. The people who lived back then were not Homo sapiens *as we know them today. They were like what you call Neanderthals, but we call them "Earth people". There was a golden age when Earth people and animals could communicate with each other and lived together harmoniously. There are many legends about this earliest golden era all over the world. It is the same in your Old Testament, there is the Garden of Eden. And now, if it makes you feel more comfortable, you can have your scientific proof, too. Because even your own scientists have found out that our ancestors were not aggressive carnivores as you had previously liked to think. Just recently scientists at Johns Hopkins University have looked again at the teeth in ancient skulls and they have discovered that our earliest ancestors were almost entirely vegetarian and that they did not kill other animals at all.*

'The problem was that as the Earth people started to evolve and develop, their heads started to get bigger and bigger as their brain size started to increase. This was because their brains stored all the genetic memories which grew with each generation and as their memories grew, so their heads grew also. And as their heads got bigger, so the females of the species were finding giving birth more and more difficult. Over time, the numbers of females dying in childbirth increased and the survival of the whole species was threatened.

'Now you have heard of the "missing link" in our evolutionary history that your scientists talk about and cannot explain or understand. It's that very sudden great leap forward in our human development that they have not been able to explain. They have just not been able to figure out why such a major leap happened and why it happened so incredibly quickly. Well, it is because it was precisely around the time that the Earth's population was in crisis that the sky gods, what you call "extra-terrestrials", came from the sky, from the Pleiades, from Orion, from Sirius. They came looking for a new home, here on Earth, on this beautiful blue-green planet.

'So the sky gods came and they brought with them the crystal skulls as gifts for the people of this Earth. For these crystal skulls contained all the knowledge of these people from the other planets. The skulls contained all their culture, their maths, their science, their astronomy and philosophy, it included their hopes and dreams. Everything that they were was stored in those skulls. You could say it was some gift they were offering!

'But the skulls also had another function. They were to be the template for a new species. The memories that we had been storing in our brains were then transferred into our DNA. Our brains did not have to get any bigger. The crystal skulls were a representation of the new form that we had become, the blueprint of humanity. Again, this is something that is hinted at in your book of Genesis, where it says that "the sons of Gods saw the daughters of man, and found them fair". You see, when the extra-terrestrials arrived they knew that they would not be able to live long in our atmosphere. So, just like the Earth people, the sky gods, too, they were dying. So there was an exchange. These extra-terrestrial "people from the sky" spliced the genes of the Earth people together with their own in order to help both species survive, but in a new form different from either of those that had come before.

'Although you may find this hard to believe, this is something that we now have the power to do ourselves. We will soon be able to use only one cell from one animal to create a direct replica of itself, but we are already able to splice together the genes of two animals to create whole new species. So human beings are now nearly at the same stage as our original extra-terrestrial ancestors. Though we still have far to go in many areas, not least in the respect we need to show for our own Mother Earth and an understanding of our inter-connectedness, we do already have the awesome power to create entirely new species. But our celestial ancestors were at this stage long, long ago and they also created a whole new species, a whole new form of life. But the species they created was Homo sapiens, or human beings as we now call ourselves. For only in this way, both could live, both our extra-terrestrial and pre-human ancestors, and we found a way to live together as one on this Earth.

'And the crystal skulls are the original representation of this new form that we had become. They were the original blueprint for humanity. And this is one of the many ways that the crystal skulls contain information about our origins and destiny. This is why there are indigenous people all over the world, not only from the Americas, who talk of our origins in the stars and of the ancient sky gods. The Mayans, the Sioux, *the Cherokee all say that they originated in the stars. There is a tribe in Africa, the Dogon, that has always maintained that their ancestors came from Sirius, which they said was a double star system. Nobody believed them until our telescopes became powerful enough to detect that there were in fact two stars there. Now we have discovered other planets circling stars. Soon we will have evidence of the other life forms that inhabit many of the other planets even within our own galaxy.*

'There are others who say that we come from the Earth. Both are correct. For we each have two lines of ancestry and genetic memory. In fact, that is why DNA has two strands. Originally one strand contained our Earth memories and the other those of our celestial ancestors. Scientists are now close to finding this out.

'And one of the reasons why the skulls were made of quartz is because silicon was introduced into our genetic structure by the sky gods. We were entirely a carbon-based life form. But silicon is now in our blood. So within us is a part of the whole crystalline matrix that can link us to the rest of the galaxy. Indigenous people have always known that the Earth, the sun and all the other planets are linked by an enormous web of crystalline structure. The web is made of sound and colour. The whole universe has structure and order and is connected to this web, as is Mother Earth. And again your scientists are now discovering this. This is why the crystal skulls draw people to them, because they trigger our inner knowledge, the knowledge that we are both carbon and silicon in structure. We look at the skull and we are reminded of the silicon structure that is within our fabric, within our very own being, that links us to the rest of the universe.

'My people say, "Remember your source. Remember who you are and where you have come from." And this is a message of peace for the whole of humanity. For the crystal skulls are there to show us our shared origins. For this is the heritage of all of the people of the Earth. We are all united by this common background: black, white, red, yellow and brown. All of the people of this Earth are joined at this source, in the marriage between heaven and Earth, between the seen and unseen aspects of creation.'

I was speechless. I had had enough trouble trying to accept the idea that the crystal skulls might have been brought by extra-terrestrials, let alone the idea that I was part alien myself! This was the most outrageous thing that I had ever heard! It was madness! Could we really be the product of some strange extra-terrestrial and human breeding programme? It sounded totally crazy, it was a direct affront to everything I had ever learned about our human origins. It seemed a joke – yet I recalled that that was exactly how people reacted when they first heard Darwin's theory of evolution.

Jamie could obviously recognize my disbelief and spoke again:

'Look, I'm not asking you necessarily to believe all this right now. Because you will soon come to understand. In any case, whether you believe it at this stage in history is not the point, it really doesn't matter. If nothing else, this story is important in that it will make you more aware that our past history might not be quite what you thought it was, and that, in itself, will be progress.

'Once you can see that the past history of this planet and your own origins are not what you have always thought them to be, this will help you to think more about the past, more about mankind's past and your own personal past and you will see that this increases all kinds of other possibilities. Once you have opened yourself up to this understanding you will see that your place in the world might not be what you have always thought it was and this in itself will open up possibilities not only about the past, but also about the present and the future. For if our past is different from what we have always learned, then maybe our future can and will also be very different from what it is currently determined to be. And this is, right now, the most important thing.'

Jamie's story had certainly got me thinking. After all, no one really knew for sure quite what the true history of humanity was, not even the so-called 'experts', the scientists, the archaeologists and anthropologists.

Perhaps the important information encoded into the skulls was that our true origins lay in the stars. I wondered whether this was the information that the legend had said we would one day need to know about, and if so, whether now was the right time for us to be hearing it? Why should it be so important for us to hear such information at this time? Was it really, as Jamie had suggested, just that we needed to hear a different story of who we are and where we have come from? Was it a reminder that all of humanity is united by this common origin, that we are all, as Jamie put it, both 'other' and the 'same', both from this world and from another world, and that whatever race, colour or creed, we all share this common heritage?

Our original mission had been to find out more about the crystal skulls, but in doing so it appeared that we were beginning to uncover a whole new version of human history, at odds with everything we had learned before. Much of what we held dear, that we had accepted without question throughout our lives, was being challenged and we found ourselves having to examine our beliefs. Maybe the time had come to question some of our comfortable assumptions through which we thought we had understood the workings of the world and our place in it. Was there another 'truth' that had been hidden from us all these years, an equally real, perhaps even more accurate version of human history?

25. THE GATHERING

The following morning Patricio phoned us to say that we could now attend the gathering in Guatemala. But it was starting within the next few days, so we had to set off almost immediately.

Jamie offered to give Ceri and I a lift to the airport, and my heart was almost in my throat as we sped along the highway at breakneck speed, dodging and weaving our way through the traffic. As we pelted down the freeway, Jamie explained that according to her teachers, a time would come when everything would appear to be speeding up:

'This is called "the Time of the Quickening" in our tradition, and it is said that it would come towards the end of the Fourth World of Separation and just before the beginning of the Fifth World of Peace and Illumination.

'We are now entering the Time of the Quickening. That is why it was time for me to tell you about the crystal skulls and their connection with our origins.

'Only after all of the knowledge and wisdom of the crystal skulls has found its way into all of the people's hearts will the Fifth World of Illumination truly begin.'

Jamie asked us whether we also had noticed that at this very point in history everything does seem to be speeding up. At precisely that moment we certainly had no problem agreeing with her!

It was apparently also said that at the Time of the Quickening the human race would start to become more and more obsessed with purely physical and material things, particularly with those aspects of the material world that we believed we could control. It was prophesied that we would become more and more dependent on our own physical technologies, as part of our belief, due to our 'mind of separation', that all the answers somehow lay in the world outside.

Jamie's comments suddenly reminded me of one of the things Leon Secatero had said to us when he had agreed to be filmed and recorded. As we had struggled with our tape recorder, microphone and camera leads, he had been trying to tell us that his people's prophecies also spoke of a time when technological development would come to grip our world. The prophecies said that technological advancement and material development would begin to happen at an increasingly accelerating rate, in fact too quickly for our own good. As Leon spoke he swept his hand in an upward curve to illustrate his point. He said he thought this time was now upon us, that we could now see technologies developing too quickly for our souls to keep up. He pointed to the recent developments on the Internet and with computers, the rapid rise of air as well as motor travel, and now even the experimentation with our own genetic structure and that of plants and animals. Leon said that on the physical and material front we are developing almost as far and as fast as we can. But as for our moral and spiritual development, we are falling dangerously far behind.

Leon added that technological developments were not necessarily in and of themselves a bad thing, but that we did not know how to use our physical technologies for the right ends. He said our technological advancement had to come from the right framework, from a view of the world that respects all life and that does not take from the Earth without giving something back. He said, 'Technology has to be balanced with an awareness of the Earth, and with a love and respect for all things.' The danger was that this wasn't happening, that technology and science were developing as if they were completely separate from the values that sustain life itself.

Leon also warned that if things continued the way they were going then slavery would begin to emerge again, only this time the slaves would be all of us. We would ultimately become 'slaves to our own machines'. As we sat there surrounded by all our filming equipment, I joked that this had already happened, that our cameras, microphones and personal computers were already dictating *our* lives for a start. Leon added, but quite seriously, that humanity had begun to use technology to create a totally new life form. He said that we were already beginning to feed this new being, and that we kept developing its potential, but that ultimately it had a life of its own. Once we had released this potential in the world, once we had set it in motion, we could not control where it would end up. He said it was like rolling a stone down a mountain – once we had set it in motion, it would continue to roll. We know that it must stop somewhere, but exactly where it would end up we could not foresee. His opinion was that this new 'life force', this being that would emerge from the technology we were creating, would come to be our master. Ultimately, it would live and feed off us, we would give it our flesh.

When we arrived at the airport, I realized I was beginning to understand exactly what Leon had meant. As usual, people were scurrying everywhere, trying desperately to stick to the punishing timetables the modern world so often creates for us. There was someone driving up to the terminal with one hand controlling the wheel of their car and in the other holding a telephone. There was someone walking towards the terminal with a mobile phone pressed to their ear trying desperately above the roar of the planes to reassure the person at the other end that everything was still running to schedule. And inside the terminal a whole barrage of people sat behind car-rental desks, currency kiosks, baggage and check-in points, their heads bowed to their computers, incessantly tapping in figures and credit card details to serve their new electronic masters. Suddenly it seemed as if the whole world had gone crazy servicing an onslaught of technology, that was, ironically, of our own making.

With these thoughts we made our way down what seemed like an endless corridor of strip lighting and air conditioning that extended right through the body of the first plane, through the interchange terminal and onto the next one.

We were bound for Guatemala. The time of the gathering was approaching and we wondered what we would find there. The Mayan priests and other indigenous elders were due to discuss sacred teachings and ancient knowledge that had been kept secret for hundreds of years. What might we learn from them?

In our excitement at being permitted to attend the gathering, however, we had not actually considered too carefully exactly where we were heading. It wasn't until we were sitting on board the plane heading for Guatemala City that it occurred to us that this time we would not be treading the well-worn tracks of the tourist route, but instead venturing into some of the most volatile areas of one of the most dangerous countries in the world. A civil war had been raging in Guatemala for 30 years between the US-backed military dictatorship and the indigenous people. Back in the 1960s the United Fruit Company had called in the CIA to back the unelected Guatemalan government with money, military hardware and combat training to quell the landless, and the country had been the scene of countless massacres of indigenous people and 'disappearances' of 'subversives', including the occasional foreign tourist, ever since. We were now due to head into some of the most remote areas of this troubled country, accompanied by a group of almost complete strangers, very few of whom could speak English, armed only with a tape recorder, a basic video camera and a dodgy tripod.

Our plane deposited us in Guatemala City. It was election night, the streets were busy, the atmosphere tense. Our taxi wound its way through the corrugated iron shanty streets, where the gutters seemed to glow dimly red in the neon of the street lights. Every other car we passed appeared to be a military vehicle of some sort or another with gun barrels jutting menacingly. We were relieved to reach the sanctuary of our hotel. We went straight to bed and fell asleep exhausted, only to be rudely jolted awake by the sound of gunfire. It seemed to go on and on. All our worst fears were instantly confirmed. We should never have come to such a brutal, repressive country which was once again turning its guns on innocent people. Now we were caught up in it. A military coup was being staged within minutes of our hotel on the very night of our arrival.

As we crept downstairs the following morning we found Patricio Domínguez quietly sipping his morning coffee in the calm of the hotel foyer. He was most amused when we asked him how he could remain so calm in the midst of such a terrifying situation, and we felt somewhat sheepish when he explained that what we had heard the night before was nothing more than a firework display to celebrate the end of the first round of the new democratic elections.

We decided we had to put our fears aside and try to adjust to our new surroundings. The opening ceremony of the gathering was due to take place at Tikal the following morning, and as we made our way back out to the airport and flew to Flores, the nearest airport to Tikal, Patricio explained to us a little more about the significance of the gathering.

Patricio had already told us that the Maya were known as 'the keepers of time' and that the ancient calendar that was in their keeping was a means of marking and predicting 'the events of time itself'. He now added that the Mayans were often also referred to as 'the makers of time' or 'creators of time' because they were responsible for creating the right energies necessary for the creation of new time. They gave to each new cycle its sense of continuity, its structure and the essence needed to sustain it for the next 5,126-year cycle. It was their responsibility also to make sure that knowledge of the Great Cycles was distributed amongst the different tribes, who needed to come together and share the knowledge and wisdom necessary for creating a new era at the appropriate time.

This coming together of the peoples of the Americas had been foretold in the prophecies not only of the Maya, but also of several other Native American tribes, such as the Kalawaya of South America, the Hopi and six nations of the north. It was taking place now because, according to the Mayan calendar, the current Great Cycle of time is due to run out on 21 December 2012, when a new era is due to begin. As Patricio put it:

> 'The Mayans have called us together because we only have a few years left. They have called us together to share the knowledge necessary for the new cycle to begin. It is said that all the peoples who were present at the beginning of this cycle have to come back together again at the end to share their particular areas of knowledge.'

He explained that where we are now is in a unique cosmological period, the transition between the old and new eras of time. This period is a crucial one. Apparently the transition from the old world into the new creates a time of uncertainty and although a new era will come about, exactly what form it will take and whether or not it will continue to be able to support human life is not entirely known.

According to Patricio, one of the signs that we are in this transition period is that changes will begin to happen in our environment. Weather patterns will become disrupted and extremes of temperature will be experienced. Rainfall patterns will also change, with wet areas becoming much drier and dry areas becoming wet. This is a sign that we need to take action. Patricio continued:

> 'Others call this time we are now entering "the Time of the Quickening". Recognizing this is another way of identifying the transition period we are in.
>
> 'But time is not separate from ourselves, from our own thoughts and actions and our own behaviour on this Earth. And so, in this transition

period we will all have to make some difficult choices and take some important decisions.

'Humanity has a choice about which direction to take. Right now it is as though we are standing at a fork in the road. Throughout recent human history we have taken all the wrong turnings and have lost our way, but now we have our final choice of which path to take next. Each choice has very different consequences. We can choose to go on much as we have done before, or we can choose to change. We can take a new path by changing our awareness of our role here on Mother Earth. If we don't change it is going to have very grave consequences. Most people don't realize that we only have until 2012 to get it right.

'The people who are meeting at this gathering will be working to make sure that humanity chooses the correct path and that at the end of this period of transition we have the new era that we desire, a new era for all the people of the Earth. If we get it right, we will help to ensure that the end of this world of separation will lead into the beginning of a new world of co-operation and peace. That is our intention.'

According to Patricio, the first stage of getting the crystal skulls to come back together lay in this gathering. He told us that it is vital that before the skulls can come together the people must come together to prepare themselves for the knowledge to come from the skulls. This is because, as the legend had said, that knowledge could be misused. Indeed, according to Patricio, this is what had led to the destruction of previous civilizations such as Atlantis. As he explained it:

'There is a cosmological time for everything. There is a predestined time for the skulls to come back together again, which the Mayan day-keepers know. But whether or not the knowledge that then comes from the skulls will be used for the good of all mankind or for our ultimate destruction will be determined by whether or not humanity is properly prepared.

'That, in turn, will depend on gatherings such as these. If humanity changes, as it must, and starts treating Mother Earth in the right way, then the knowledge to come from the skulls will be used for the benefit of all.'

Patricio added that hopefully the impact of this gathering and the knowledge we and others at the event would take with us would be carried out across all of the Americas and ultimately right out across the world. He also hoped that the further gatherings that would take place would be sufficient to prepare the human race for the knowledge that is to come from the skulls.

Having heard all this, by the time we arrived at Tikal we were filled with anticipation. The following morning, before dawn, we made our way along the jungle tracks to the ruined centre of the site, where the gathering was due to begin. This felt incredibly familiar; indeed, it was exactly where we had been just over a year before, when we had first heard the legend of the crystal skulls.

When we reached the Great Plaza it was eerily deserted. The sun slowly rose, but nothing else happened. Nobody arrived other than a handful of lost-looking tourists. We were beginning to wonder whether there really was going to be any sort of gathering at all, never mind the great gathering of all the tribes laid down by prophecy. Patricio tried to reassure us:

'Remember, the moment for any event to take place is already foregone, so there is no point in trying to rush it. We may fool ourselves into thinking that a particular event happens at a particular time because we have decided that's when we want it to happen, but we are only part of the story. The whole event must also want to happen before we can force it to take shape. Any truly sacred ceremony, like any other event, has its own way of drawing people to it at the appropriate time.'

After what seemed like hours of loitering aimlessly, we eventually got bored of waiting and wandered off to take photos around the archaeological site.

After a while we found the stone skull we had seen on our previous visit, about a quarter of a mile away from the Great Plaza and, as we now realized, apparently on the edge of a ball court. We were just re-examining this old moss-covered skull when we heard a beautiful sound ringing out across the treetops. Something was definitely happening, but we weren't sure quite what. The sound seemed to be coming from the Great Plaza, so we ran back through the jungle. As we got nearer we realized we had heard the very loud blowing of a conch shell in two simple tones, a high and a low, and as we got nearer still we could hear drumming, like a heartbeat, and the beautiful high-pitched tones of simple piped instruments.

As we entered the clearing we were greeted by the most wonderful sight. There, gathered at the bottom of the steps that led up to the Great

Pyramid of the Masks, were several hundred indigenous people, kneeling and praying, or playing their instruments and beating their drums. Their costumes were beautiful and so richly varied. There seemed to be people from all different kinds of tribes and all the colours of the rainbow were reflected in their attire. There were old women dressed in brightly coloured shawls, young men in pure white outfits with red sashes around their waists, young women clad in buck-skin, and old men wearing nothing but loin cloths and beautifully coloured plumed head-dresses, together with a small smattering of people dressed in jeans, T-shirts and trainers. In the centre was a very old and small man clad almost entirely in jaguar skins and wearing a feathered head-dress, and all around thick clouds of copal incense swirled up and glinted in the sunlight, its sweet-musky smell hanging heavy in the jungle air.

The old man in the centre was Don Alejandro Cirilo Oxlaj Peres (*see colour plate no. 27*). He knelt down and kissed the bottom of the steps of the pyramid and then the whole entourage turned around and made a procession across to the other side of the plaza, drums beating and feathers waving. The party halted at the bottom of the steps of the Great Pyramid of the Jaguar. Again led by the old man, they stooped down and kissed the ground, and then began the steep ascent up the 52 steps to the temple at the very top. I accompanied the group up the steps, and as my breath quickened and I could feel my heart pounding faster and faster in my chest, I began to have the most strange experience, almost like seeing flashbacks in a film.

As the group reached the top of the steps and turned to gaze out across the plaza at the Great Pyramid Temple of the Masks on the other side, I suddenly realized I had been here before. Over a year before I had stood in this same spot as the sun was going down on the ancient ruins and had, as I thought, imagined myself surrounded by these very people wearing these very same colourful costumes and performing exactly this ceremony, as I had felt they had done many times before. On both occasions I felt as if I was experiencing the past, the present and the future all rolled into one. I felt at one with everything that was around me, both physically in space and 'around' me in time. Time seemed to have stood still.

And then Don Alejandro began to speak, in broken Spanish which was later translated:

'We are here because of destiny. Because of destiny the ancient ones are returning. Now is the time that what is written in the prophecies must

be fulfilled. Because of this I am here with you. We are the messengers. But we are not the first messengers. The first messengers are the crystal skulls, the mothers and fathers of science. As the Balam *says, the Mayan prophets came and they said, "We are the ones of yesterday, we are the ones of today and we will be the ones of tomorrow."*

'The ancient people did not know how to govern themselves and so our creator sent the four prophets, the "Mia". The prophets came long ago, and they wrote the great laws and they taught all of the great science that is called "the Mayan light". These were the four lords who completed their mission and they left these great depositories here on Mother Earth. And when they were old they were great elders and said, "We are going to leave for where we have come from, now that our time has ended and our light is drawing to a close." But before they left they said, "Children, do not forget our memory. We have left you good reason and wise council. We have left you sacred knowledge. One day we will return and we will complete our mission."

'And the children said, "Where have you come from and where are you going?"

'And they answered, "We are going to go there, children, where that handful of stars are," and that way they left. "And you must cover the Earth," they said. "You must cover it in love, love one another and all other things, so that when we return we may live together as one like the colours of the rainbow, like the fingers of a hand."

'And they wrapped themselves up in shawls and they sang a song. And from then there was silence and they slept. And all the people around said, "Let the grandfathers sleep." But many hours passed and they did not get up. And then the people saw a beam of light and they went to where the grandfathers had been but they had disappeared. They had risen up into the heavens on a beam of light. But they had left behind a sign of their existence. They had left their wise words and sacred wisdom behind wrapped in a bundle. And the wisdom was kept safe until the Spanish arrived and stole the sacred bundle from us along with everything else that they took.

'But the prophecy says the elders shall return. The prophecy says now is the time of the awakening. This is your job now, to awaken. The Vale of the Nine Hells is past and the Time of Warning has now arrived. It is time to prepare for the Age of the Thirteen Heavens. The time of 12 Baktun and 13 Ahau is fast approaching, and they shall be here among you to defend Mother Earth. The prophecy says, "Let the dawn come.

Let all the people and all the creatures have peace, let all things live happily," for the love must not only be between humans, but between all living things. They said, "We are the children of the sun, we are the children of time and we are the travellers in space. May all the songs awaken, may all the dancers awaken. May all the people and all things live in peace. For you are the valleys, you are the mountains, you are the trees, you are the very air you breathe."

'And so, my brothers and sisters, I am not here to give you gold. I am not here to give you treasure. I am here to give you these words that are not mine. These are the words of our grandmothers and grandfathers, the travellers in time, our ancestors from the stars: "We are all one." We eat white food, yellow food, dark food, because these are all the colours of our mothers and fathers in the heavens. We are all one like the colours of the rainbow. We are all fed by the air, fed by the rain, fed by Grandfather Sun. Man, the animals, the birds and the trees, we are all one.

'Now is the time of the return of the grandmothers and grandfathers. Now is the time of the return of the elders. Now is the time of the return of the wise ones. And the wise ones are all of you. Now is the time to go out into the world and spread the light. The sacred flame has been kept for this purpose and now the time approaches when you will be required to love all things, to love a world that has gone crazy, to rebalance the heavens and the Earth. For the Time of Warning has come to pass and the Warriors of the Rainbow are now beginning to be born. The Vale of Tears, the Nine Hells, is over and it is time to prepare for the Thirteen Heavens. The ancestors are returning, my brothers and sisters, and we do not have long. Now is the time that the prophecies will be fulfilled.

'May all arise. May all arise. Not one or two groups will be left behind.'

And with these words Don Alejandro's arms reached up to the heavens and then down to the Earth below. The whole entourage seemed to start chanting two simple notes, a high and a low. Members of other tribes came forward and made speeches, but we could not translate them all. Each speech was punctuated by the soft sound of beautiful chanting, candles were lit and copal incense was wafted through the air. Then, as the ceremony was drawing to a close, the group solemnly carried out a salute to the 'four directions', the four cardinal points of the compass. Everyone turned to face each direction in turn and raised their arms in the air, and each time there was the loud low horn-like sound of a conch shell being blown.

All those present made their way back down the steps of the pyramid, formed a circle in the plaza and saluted the pyramids which stood at either end. I glanced around the vast circle of faces. There were people there from the far north of Canada, from the Plains of the USA, from the deserts of New Mexico, from the forests of Brazil, Ecuador and Peru. I thought of Jamie Sams' comment that the crystal skulls 'contain the knowing systems of Mother Earth'. It occurred to me that each person present also represented that system. Their experience, whether formulated under desert skies or jungle canopy, represented an unbroken tradition of a connection with the natural environment and the knowledge of living harmoniously with that environment, knowledge that we in the West had lost.

We had been looking outwards for knowledge, to the crystal skulls. Now it seemed obvious to me that there were infinite possibilities *within* ourselves that we had never explored. What potential was represented not just by the people here but by all people, each distinct and shaped by their own environment, background and culture, each unique, bearing an individual truth, but all sharing in the knowledge that they are part of a broader truth, part of this extraordinary and diverse human family.

When the ceremony had finished, we asked Don Alejandro if he could explain a little more about what he had said in his speech. We sat next to him at the top of the steps of the tallest pyramid in the city, the Pyramid of the Lost World, right next to the stone skull we had originally stumbled upon, just as the evening sunlight was turning to gold. He began by saying that Don Alejandro Cirilo Oxlaj Peres was not his real name, it was only his name in Spanish. His real Mayan name was Job Keme, or Job Cizin, which means 'Life Death'. He was given this name, like all Mayan names, because of the day on which he was born, which translated as our 2 February 1929. He said that whoever is born on that day has communication between the worlds of the living and the dead.

Don Alejandro's forefathers had been medicine men for at least seven generations and he was now the high priest of the Council of Quiché Mayan Elders, which represents 21 different Mayan regions. He said his role was to diagnose illness and interpret dream visions, and he was also the head 'day-keeper' or 'wisdom-keeper' of the sacred Mayan calendar.

We wanted to know more about where the crystal skulls had originally come from and who were the four prophets who had returned to the stars. So I asked Don Alejandro how old the skulls were and how they had been made. He replied that nobody really knew how old they were or quite how they had been made. He said we must realize that they were not made by humans, but by beings from another dimension, from another planet, from the stars. These beings, the four prophets of Mayan legend, had come from the Pleiades long ago:

'Many thousands of years ago at the start of the current age they came and they left the crystal skulls behind. They brought this knowledge to help us at a time of great need, at the Time of Warning that comes between the ages, between the old world and the new. The skulls contain great knowledge and wisdom to help us at the time which is now upon us.'

But why would they do such a thing? Don Alejandro said we must realize that we are 'all connected':

'We do not have to be apart, because we are all one. We must walk together without distinction of colour, class or belief, united like the colours of the rainbow. We need to recognize that we are all brothers and sisters. We need to respect and value this Mother Earth and our Fathers in the Heavens, Grandfather Sun, Grandmother Moon and all of the other planets in space. We are all children of the Father. This is the message that I bring to you.

'But these are not my own words that I speak. These are the words of the Mayan people and the words of the skulls. The skulls are messengers of the Mayan people. So it is not only me who is talking to you. The skulls speak to all of us and they speak better English, or Spanish, than me. The message of the Mayan people is that now is the time that the prophecies must be fulfilled.'

Don Alejandro explained that there were more than 13 crystal skulls. The Mayans originally had 13, but many others were left with other indigenous peoples around the world. According to the original teachings passed down through the council, there were originally 52 skulls in various sacred centres around the world, including many with other Native American tribes and even some in Tibet and with the aborigines of Australia. He said only the Fathers knew why there were 52, but this number, like 13, was very sacred to his people and played an important part in the Mayan calendar. He added that the skulls had helped the indigenous people keep their traditions and cultures alive through some very difficult times in the past and continue to do so today.

I asked Don Alejandro whether he or any of his colleagues had any crystal skulls themselves? He said he could not answer this question, but he could tell us a story of what happened in the past. He said that in the 1950s some of his people had shown their crystal skull to a Catholic priest in the highland Guatemalan village of Santiago, near Lake Atitlán. The priest had said the skull was the work of the devil and smashed it to pieces. 'Like the Mayan people, this is how the skulls have been abused,' said Don Alejandro, sadly.

Over the course of the gathering several different people told us that Don Alejandro and the Council of Elders themselves had at least one skull that was kept in a cave 'under the mountains' and consulted only in total secrecy. It was carefully explained to us that the skulls are considered so sacred to these people that nobody would tell us where they were, particularly given the losses and abuses in the past. It was also added that they would not want us to do anything that would encourage other people to go and look for these skulls.

So we asked Don Alejandro for more general information about the crystal skulls. He explained that they were left as something of great value, as a 'virtue' for people to gather around. They had originally been kept in the temples at the top of the great pyramids and were known to his people as 'the mothers and fathers of science' or 'the mothers and fathers of wisdom'. The skulls had been looked after by the Mayans, but 'unfortunately the Christian explorers and anthropologists, when they found the skulls in the great pyramids, they thought they were idols'. Some even thought they were Satanic:

'So they took all the values and experiences of the Mayan people and they sold them in the USA and elsewhere. So it was not just the native people who were tortured and suffered losses. The great science of the Maya was lost to the world. During the Time of the Nine Hells even that was sold.

'But for the council of elders, we see how the skulls are the mothers and fathers of science. They are the first messengers of love and peace in the whole of the world. Everything you want to know about astronomy can be understood through those skulls, and every other type of study which can be understood – archaeology, anthropology and environmental science.'

This was obviously consistent with the legend as we had first heard it and with what the various Native Americans we had met since had said. But how Don Alejandro managed to list the four subject areas I am most interested in I still do not know. He added, 'All of the knowledge and wisdom of the whole entire world, and the universe, is contained in those skulls. They have great powers, including the power of telepathy and of healing, even of psychological ills.'

But, he said, this knowledge is not just available to anyone at any time. It is not transmitted to the individual without the necessary training and it is only transmitted if it is for the right reason and at the right time:

'This knowledge is subconsciously learned. The skulls give revelations whether or not you are with them. They can carry mentally a revelation. You could be thinking about the skulls in the most quiet hours, or you could be sleeping, but your spirit and your soul are walking in space and realizing what is above. If you ask the skulls all the things that the masters spoke about, then the day after tomorrow it will come to your mind what has been spoken and that is the way that your knowledge continues to grow. That is why we Mayan people now speak. We receive education through visions, revelations and cosmic visions. This is something that very few others understand. I have spoken to many people about this. They do not know what a vision, a revelation, a cosmic vision is. They do not understand the cosmos even though they say they are the children of science.

'But there are two directions. If you want to become great by or for yourself by the skulls and you have no interest in defending the planet, just because you want to explore for your own gain, you will expend the energy of your brain in a negative way. The skulls will not talk to you and they will not make you great. But if you come in faith, even if it is only in your thoughts, and if you ask for the sacred knowledge to help and to heal this planet, and if you are interested in the sacred knowledge that the skulls have, then it will turn out well, because it is from the heart and with faith. No one will become great from the skulls unless their purpose is to heal. The skulls will only transmit knowledge if that knowledge is to be used for the good of Mother Earth and not for your own personal gain.

'But the time when that knowledge will become more widely available is fast approaching. It is prophesied that the Time of the Thirteen Heavens will soon be upon us. The Mayan prophets predicted the Time

of the Nine Hells. They prophesied a great time of darkness and for nearly 500 years we lived in the Vale of Tears. When the Spanish arrived and Western impositions began with the great hunger that was the search for gold, there was much killing.'

He explained that at that time most of his ancestors were massacred at Rio Xequijel, near Quetzaltenango, and that the river is now called *Rio Se Tino de Sangre* after the day the river ran red with blood.

'And now they have come looking for the "black gold", the oil, the gas and the minerals of our Mother Earth. And again there is much killing. This time they kill all living things with the pollution of the environment, the rivers and the streams. They kill all human beings and all living beings on Mother Earth, the animals, the insects, the birds and the trees.

'But the prophets said the Nine Hells would end between Long Count kin 1863022 and 1863023, between the days you call 16 and 17 August 1987, that the Time of Warning would come to pass and that now is the time to prepare for the Thirteen Heavens. The Thirteen Heavens will begin after sunset on 21 December in the year 2012. The next day after that is written in our Long Count calendar as 13.0.0.0.0. This number in our sacred calendar represents a new form of understanding, a new form of government, a new way of understanding each other so that we will no longer see each other with indifference and mistreat each other on this Earth. This date represents the start of the Thirteen Heavens. The date when the new world will begin. This will be the start of a new 13 Baktun period. This is what is written in the book of Chilam Balam. And, as prophesied, the skulls are here to help us all prepare for this time. The skulls are returning for the Time of Warning as the great legend said, because now is the time that what is written must be fulfilled.

'And so the Council of Elders is now meeting, guided by the prophecies and by the wisdom of the skulls, because now is the time to awaken the world. Now is the time for the people to come together. The Council has now gone public, but for 500 years we were hidden. When the Spanish arrived we took refuge in the mountains. We formed a mandate that for 500 years we would remain silent. This was during the era of suffering we call the Nine Hells. Only we knew what would happen when. But now we have come out into the open and the government will not kill us

because this is in fulfilment of the prophecies. They will now realize we have come in peace. It is time for all the governments and all the peoples now to build peace. We have no lands, no houses, no hospitals and we have no schools, but we have the wisdom that the world now needs. Did we not see when we opened the bundle over 20 years ago the hole in what you now call "the ozone layer", but no one would listen to us at that time. It was not in the prophecies for the world to listen then. But now the calendar says our knowledge must be shared with the world, for the Time of Awakening is upon us. The skulls are now here to awaken our consciousness, to help us learn to love all things. It is written in the calendar that the world will listen now, that the world will now hear the heartbeat of Mother Earth.

'And the skulls have given us a message for all of mankind. Their message is not to pollute our Mother, not to have confrontation and to stop mistreating one another on this Earth. The skulls tell us we must respect our Creator and that we must love ourselves. We must appreciate our Mother Earth, our brothers and sisters the animals, our elders the trees, and not pollute our rivers, our lakes and our oceans, so that this planet Earth may be populated again and we may once again be able to breathe. We do not have to become owners of this palace, we do not have to become owners of this Earth, because it is not ours to own. It is our mother and our father, and we are all brothers and sisters, the rocks, the plants, the animals, the wind and the rain. We don't have to be apart, because we are one. We are all living beings and we are all of one consciousness.'

As Don Alejandro spoke these words, the most extraordinary thing happened. In one beautiful, almost magical, moment a whole host of dragonflies suddenly appeared as if from nowhere. They started to fly all around him, darting here and there, their delicate wings catching the last fading rays of evening sunlight. Their rapid movements seemed to echo the very rhythm of his words, as if they were dancing or joining in with what he was saying. They completely ignored the rest of our small group huddled on the pyramid steps, instead appearing almost to merge with Don Alejandro as if they were a part of him, seeming to form a halo of golden wings all around him. We later learned that the Mayans consider the dragonfly to be one of the symbols of Kukulcan or Quetzalcoatl, whose spirit is said to be connected with the fulfilment of the calendar. As Don Alejandro opened his mouth to speak again, the dragonflies vanished almost as quickly as they had appeared.

'We must stop the pollution, the pollution even of negative thoughts and of fear. For even as we think with negative emotion, when we fear and think only of ourselves, when we stop loving, we pollute the planet and the air that we breathe. We endanger the Thirteen Heavens and the next Great Cycle of time. The skulls bring us the message that the Earth is not ours to own, it is not ours to abuse and destroy. Even the most powerful rulers must soon understand that the power is not theirs. It is not the power of people. It is the power of the children governed by the Father. The duty of the people is to respect their government, but the duty of the government is to respect all the children of the Earth. Our leaders must realize their job is only to administer, for the power is not their own. They should take care of the children and not destroy them. This Earth is only ours when we are alive but when we die it is left for our children. If we carry on as we are going, they will have no home.

'The skulls tell us we need to walk another way and it is written that the indigenous people must show the new path, how to govern so that there will be peace. The indigenous people are capable of showing how to govern the world in peace and in harmony with all living things. It is prophesied that the people will reclaim their natural rights, that the warriors of the rainbow will now return. We must all live equally and in friendship with ourselves and all living beings on Mother Earth. The skulls show us there is a way for us all to have enough food to eat, for us all to be rich and for us all to live in abundance with all other creatures on this Earth.

'You in the West have given us great science, but we have another science which you will now need. We have the mental apparatus how to learn from the skulls. The skulls show us a vision of how things could be. They show us that there is a just and natural law. You will soon understand that technology without an understanding of the Creator is destructive, but knowledge with an understanding of the Creator has no limitation at all. The skulls show us the power of creation that lies within us all. They show us the relation between all our souls. We are all related, of one and the same we are born. We can no longer be separated from each other on this Earth. We must walk together without distinction of colour, race or belief. We must walk with the other creatures for the benefit of all.'

Don Alejandro urged us to help spread the message to the whole of mankind, as the time was upon us now all to awaken:

'Listen to your heart. Mother Earth is calling to you. She is calling to every one of us through the skulls. She is calling every one of us to heal her and thereby heal ourselves. It is now time to start listening to Mother Earth and to change our way of thinking, of living and of being, before it is too late.

'We need the help of all peoples, all cultures, all religions, and all nations. We need to stop killing our brothers and sisters on this planet before it is too late. If we continue as we are going the current cycle of time will simply end. Dusk will come in 2012 and a new day will not dawn. Because if Mother Earth dies it will mean death to us all.

'Nothing in this world, nothing in this universe, is eternal. Everything has its time. A human life has its time. We individual human beings only live for so long. At some time or another we all have to die. It is the same with civilizations. They grow up from next to nothing, they mature and flourish and then they must always die. You can see the remains of these civilizations all over the Earth. Wherever you look their skeletons remain.'

The worrying thing is that Don Alejandro added that it was the same with the human race itself. We only have our allotted time. He said that it is when a species falls out of step and out of tune with nature that the end of its time on this Earth comes. 'That is the divine and natural law.'

As Don Alejandro spoke these last words the sun gently disappeared beneath the distant horizon. We wandered back through the ruined city. I felt a sense of sadness as I thought about what Don Alejandro had said. Since coming into contact with the skulls I had thought much more about what death means, but I had never once thought about the death of humanity. It had never crossed my mind that when my time was up, life might not continue for others here on Earth. The thought of the human species dying out was devastating, almost incomprehensible to me. Yet if everything was part of a cycle of death and rebirth, then Don Alejandro was surely right – humanity would one day also die. What worried me was his comments about the 'divine and natural law' that said that it would be when we lost our attunement with nature. Wasn't that what was happening now?

Later that evening, on the balcony of 'The Jungle Lodge' hotel, Ruben, an elder from the Lakota Sioux tribe, took up this theme:

'Many people who live in the cities cannot see what is happening to the Earth. It is the people who are still connected with nature in their daily lives who can see the changes that are happening to the land.

'What has been happening is that the white man has started a war against nature. The natural world has become the enemy. Pollution and poison are the weapons that are destroying whole species of animals, birds and plants.

'The people who are gathered here are seeing this destruction every day, but for many people they see it like a war in a distant country – it is sad, but it doesn't affect them. Well, pretty soon it will.'

Patricio added:

'Like I was saying to you guys earlier, we as a species are now standing at a fork in the road. If we take the proper path, we will be OK. But if we make the wrong choice, then it will have disastrous consequences for us all. That is what this period of transition is for, it is time for us to make up our minds what route to travel.

'If humanity decides to stay the same and does not start to change during this period, then the Earth as we know it will start to wane and die. This is already starting to happen. People are beginning to notice the changes in the weather, the "Earth changes" which were prophesied to start around now. What happens if we don't change is that the disruptions in the weather patterns will become more severe. This will have been caused directly by the squandering of the Earth's natural resources, leading to what scientists call "global warming". There will be droughts and floods, the global economy will collapse, there will be famine, earthquakes and widespread devastation. Ultimately, you could say that we, as a species, will be killed by our own greed. If the desire for material riches continues unabated, then it will, in the end, destroy us.'

We wanted to know how Patricio knew all this.

'It's in the prophecies,' he said simply. He explained that amongst what he considered to be the most detailed prophecies were those given to the Hopi, who are known as 'the wisdom keepers' in the same way that the Mayans are known as 'the keepers of time'. Like the Maya, the Hopi believe that the world has been created and destroyed several times before now. The Hopi also had a prophecy that 'a gourd of ashes will be poured upon the Earth'. A gourd is the same shape as the cloud of an atomic explosion and it is thought that this prophecy refers to the dropping of the first atomic bomb on Hiroshima in 1945. They were also told that later the Earth would become sick and then they should 'visit the white brother in the House of Mica which will rise in the east of the continent'. This particular prophecy came to fruition in 1991 when the Hopi elders visited the United Nations building in New York to appeal for an end to the abuses of Mother Earth. The United Nations building is 'in the east of the continent' and clad in mica. The Hopi were also given the prophecy that when the time was right the Maya would call together the tribes of North and South America to this very gathering.

'After which,' Patricio added, 'if humanity made the right choices, the indigenous people would lead the world into a new way of living once again in harmony with nature.'

'So things may change,' I said.

'That's up to each and every one of us,' replied Patricio.

As Patricio explained it, different parts of 'the original teachings' were entrusted to different tribes and so one of the purposes of the gathering was to share the prophecies of each of the tribes.

The following morning we heard indigenous elders from South America tell how their homelands had now become the final frontier of colonial expansion as the petrochemical industries and cattle ranchers moved in, precipitating the rapid destruction of the remaining rainforests. We heard how animals, birds and forests were being destroyed. A member of the Kalaway tribe from the Amazon came forward and said that one of the prophecies of his tribe predicted that a time would come when the birds would start falling from the skies and that at that time the whole world would need the help of his people. This was now happening. A particular species of bird, 'the one that flies the highest over the rainforest', had now begun to fall from the skies. This was despite the fact that the Kalaway lived hundreds of miles from the nearest centres of urban population.

As I heard how birds were dropping from the skies, killed by pollution, I remembered how miners used to take canaries into the coalmines. The sensitivity of the birds to toxic air meant the death of the bird was a warning to the miners to leave the pit. Now the death of the birds of the rainforests was a similar warning to us all.

We then boarded the old buses that would effectively become our homes over the remaining days of the gathering. As we continued our epic journey of hundreds of miles over bumpy tracks, eventually leaving the steaming lowland jungles behind and climbing slowly up into the Guatemalan highlands, we asked Patricio if he could explain to us a little more how the crystal skulls related to this transition to a new period of time. He explained that the transition is always a difficult time, fraught with dangers that the new world may not begin again at all:

'It is up to the people to create time anew and for this a new type of understanding will be required. According to the sacred Mayan calendar, a new type of consciousness will be necessary to sustain the planet for the next Great Cycle, for the next 13 Baktun, for the next 5,126 years. And this is where the crystal skulls are involved. They can help to awaken the right consciousness.'

I wanted to know more about this 'new type of consciousness'. Patricio explained:

'We are calling it a "new" consciousness, but in actual fact it's a very old one. What I mean is that people will again become aware of our living connections with the Earth. People will wake up to the fact that if the Earth dies, we also die. But it is also about the way that we relate to each other.

At some point soon, as the Mayan priests have indicated, there will be a time when humanity is prepared for the knowledge that is to come from the crystal skulls. But that time has not yet arrived. The Maya know when the right time will come for the reunion of the skulls. It is a specific time according to their ancient calendar. But the reunion of the skulls can only happen after the initial work has been accomplished and after all the people have been properly prepared.

'When that time arrives then all of the ancient skulls we know about, together with those that have not yet come to light, will be called upon and will be returned to their central location, here in Central America, and their knowledge will come forth.

'You see, the crystal skulls are complete depositories of knowledge and each skull contains a particular specialist area of information – like a living library. And the people who will in future be able to "read" the crystal skulls will only be able to extract all the knowledge from the skulls once they are all assembled together. But this will not be a problem. Since the skulls are sentient in themselves they contain not only the

knowledge that is put in each one, but also the knowledge of where each of the other skulls is.

'So when the right time arrives all of that great knowledge will once again be returned to the human race to become an integral part of humanity, after having been missing for a while, because during the intervening period the human race was simply not capable of working with and sustaining that knowledge. During the period the Maya call the Nine Hells our level of human consciousness, our moral character if you like, just wasn't sufficient to handle this type of advanced knowledge and information. That's why the beings who originally brought this knowledge stored it in these skulls in the first place. They were capable of seeing into the future and they realized that a "dark time" would come during which this knowledge had to be hidden. They could have inscribed it on tablets of stone, but that way anyone would have been able to get hold of it at any time. So instead they stored it in the particular form of crystal skulls so that this information could only be recovered at the appropriate time and not before, when it might be abused.

'Of course the knowledge that is going to come from these skulls is quite unimaginable to our current minds. But that it is definitely going to come out at a certain time is already foregone. It has been prophesied. But whether we humans then use that knowledge for good or for our own destruction is really down to our preparations, down to gatherings such as these.

'This is a wonderful thing that is now happening and I just hope that our preparations will prove sufficient to help humanity. We have made many mistakes in the past and we are making so many in the present. But our very future depends on our ability to raise our own awareness and consciousness in preparation for the new knowledge that is going to come forth in fulfilment of the prophecies.'

Over the next few days, we visited various ancient sites, including the sacred ruins of Saq Ulew near Huehuetenango, which had been 'restored' by the United Fruit Company by covering it in concrete! Then, after a sleepless night on the bus, we eventually arrived around midday at Quetzaltenango, a large town in the Guatemalan highlands.

As our bus drove up a hilltop overlooking the town we were quite shocked to see that the road was lined with armoured vehicles, tanks and personnel carriers heavily loaded with machine-gun wielding soldiers. Patricio explained that this was one of the towns that in all too recent history had been the scene of several massacres of indigenous people by the government forces. Indeed, this was the very reason that this location had been chosen for the ceremony we were about to witness, a ceremony for peace which would include the erection of a stela decorated with ancient hieroglyphs to mark the beginning of the new era. This standing stone was to mark the beginning of the Time of Warning and the Time of Awakening which was now upon us.

We joined the several hundred tribespeople who had travelled with us all the way from Tikal as they formed a large circle around the standing stone lying at the top of the lightly wooded hillside. Don Alejandro led the ceremony dressed in his ritual jaguar skins. He was joined by other Mayan elders and representatives of several other tribes as they contributed their prayers and blessings (*see colour plate no. 28*). When everyone had had their say, the stela was carefully hoisted into place and a ceremonial fire was solemnly lit in the centre of the circle beneath the newly erected stone. For this was also a ceremony to mark 'the start of the new fires'.

The material for the fire consisted of old leaves and much incense was burned. It was explained to us that during this ceremony the Mayan descendants were ritually re-enacting the moment when their ancestors had waited for the sun to rise. This was a symbol of the cycle of life and death itself, of death and rebirth, of transformation. The leaves symbolized this — they were dead, but when they were burned they gave new life, they were transformed and gave off the light and heat of the new fire.

As we stood in front of the roaring fire, many of the Maya came forward carrying sacred bundles. Each in turn held their bundle in the smoke billowing up from the fire and started to wave it over the flames. It was impossible to tell what was in these bundles, they seemed to be all sorts of shapes and sizes, but all were carefully wrapped up in layers and layers of what looked like old cloth or leather.

Then suddenly we noticed a line of rifles which appeared to be pointing straight at us. It dawned on us that around the circle of peaceful people, armed only with feathers and drums, was forming another circle, of what looked like a whole army. Whichever way we turned all we could see were soldiers with rifles and behind them armoured vehicles and even the odd tank, their barrels seemingly pointing straight at us.

We couldn't believe what we were seeing. The nightmare vision of terrible carnage we had imagined the night of our arrival suddenly looked as though it was about to happen for real and this time we were caught right in the middle of it. The government had obviously decided that this was a subversive gathering and were going to break it up the way they knew best: at gunpoint.

Two white men stepped forward from the line of soldiers and marched straight for the diminutive figure of Don Alejandro. One of them was dressed in what looked like an officer's uniform, the other in an expensive-looking suit and overcoat. They both looked very uncomfortable. One was the head of the Guatemalan military and the other was the Vice-President of Guatemala. There was silence. The tension in the air was palpable. All eyes were on Don Alejandro. He held his arms wide and began to speak:

'Let us leave behind the individualism and resentment that have separated and destroyed us. A new era of awakening is upon us. I call for a new time when we can walk together like brothers and sisters. The prophecies have said there is a time for the people to come back together and love one another. That time is now.'

With these words Don Alejandro stepped forward and embraced the head of the military. The atmosphere was electric. It was an extraordinary moment. For this was the same army that had indulged in the brutal and systematic genocide of the indigenous people.

After embracing the head of the military, Don Alejandro stepped before the Vice-President of Guatemala and opened his arms to embrace him also. The other elders turned and embraced and shook hands with the soldiers standing all around us. I knew then that we were witnessing a profound and historic moment.

In fact the 13 days of the gathering proved one of the most powerful experiences we have ever had. We became captivated by the magical atmosphere of the events, the sheer beauty of the country, and the strength, integrity, wisdom and warmth of the people we met. The events we witnessed and the words of wisdom we heard affected us deeply.

The sound of windpipes now began, followed by drumming as everyone else joined in embracing each other, shaking hands, laughing and smiling. We later learned that the two men and their surrounding army were actually there because they had been specifically invited to attend the ceremony.

Afterwards, we stood round the stela. The woods were full of people and the atmosphere was joyful. But I still could not understand how Don Alejandro could have brought himself to hug the very people who had caused the Mayans such suffering. We had watched as our companions had embraced perhaps some of the very people who had murdered some of their friends and relatives. I just couldn't have done it and I know Chris felt the same. How could these people behave with such compassion and forgiveness?

On the next leg of our journey we found ourselves sitting next to Hunbatz Men, who was one of the elders who had embraced the military. We asked him how he could have done it. Hunbatz explained that our reaction was one of fear and this fear was exactly what prevented peace. He said the crystal skulls also came into it:

'The crystal skulls teach us to expand our consciousness, to become more aware of what is around us. When your awareness increases, your sense of yourself and of other people grows. Your sense of your own relationship with other people grows too. You start to see the interconnections between you and this helps you to develop your compassion. If you think, I couldn't do that, you are allowing your pain, your hatred or your fear to trap you. Feelings of fear, hatred or pain prevent you from seeing the humanity in all, the life force, the spirit that is within all of us.

'The skulls help us to see that each living being has a spirit within them, and that each is a reflection of the Great Spirit which is within all. The Mayans, we say, "You are another myself." Each person you meet is another you, so you learn to treat them with love and respect.

'Remember the crystal skulls, remember what you have seen in Guatemala, and know that each of us is capable of this greatness, this loving compassion for all people and all things. Prove it to yourself by holding yourself to the highest standard. Let go of doubts, fears, pains and resentments. Be as the flame from a candle or the sacred flame from the sun, share your light and warmth with others. Compassion is what you have seen here. It is a shared legacy. It is for all people. Like the skulls, love is a gift to the world. Carry this in your heart always, for very soon such qualities will be needed even more than ever.'

That evening we arrived at Lake Atitlán, set beneath the towering peaks of volancoes. According to Hunbatz, this had once been a centre of learning for the ancient Mayans, who had travelled here to learn about astronomy.

The following morning we met Patricio over breakfast. He was extremely pleased with the way that the ceremonies were going. He explained that visiting the ancient sacred sites and using various traditional ceremonies was a way of reactivating those sites so that the right energies could begin to go out into the world. This was now happening. He also said that if we can successfully shift our consciousness in the right way, at the beginning of the new era we will see whole new sciences, new forms of healing, an end to the diseases and many of the problems we see today. He added:

> *'The prophecies say that at the end of this cycle and just before the begin-ning of the next, the ancient knowledge will return and that people with special gifts will begin to be born. At this time certain special psychic abilities will begin to present themselves to the world.*
>
> *'But responsibility for the new era is not only the responsibility of those with special psychic gifts but is the responsibility of us all. Each and every one of us has an active role to play in making sure that we choose the right path to follow.'*

Patricio now told us that the gathering was intended not only to facilitate the return of the ancestors' knowledge, but of the ancestors themselves:

> *'Our prayers and ceremonies are going directly to that. We are calling into the world at this time specific entities and specific beings who still have the ability to operate also in the spirit world. All we really have to do is to remind the spirits of the ancestors to return to this Earth, to remind them that it's now time to come back.*
>
> *'We have been calling to them for some time now and we are now calling to them again. You can begin to see them now and you will be able to see more of them in future as they are being born back into the physical world to carry out the new work that is needed of them now as we enter a new era here on Earth.'*

During the remainder of the gathering we heard representatives of many different tribes talking about the ancestors and their prophesied return. After one of the ceremonies, a member of the Achuar tribe from South America came forward and explained that his people shared a similar ori-gin story to the Maya. In their version, when it came time for the ances-tors to leave, they rafted down the river until they reached the sky, where they ascended to the stars of Orion and the Pleiades. This was why the Achuar had used the movement of these planets to devise their calendar, which they still use to organize their daily lives, while they await the prophesied return of the ancestors.

A member of the Yaqui tribe from the deserts of northern Mexico also came forward. He said that the ancestors had already begun to return as prophesied. He told how he was wandering alone in the desert one day when a 'craft from the heavens' had descended to Earth and he had been taken on a flight in this 'spaceship' and shown how the Earth was beginning to die. We might have expected to hear such a story from a Western urban science-fiction fan having delusions of alien abduction, but not from an elder member of an isolated desert tribe!

We were reminded of what we had already heard in Mexico City, where sightings of UFOs, which the Mexicans call *Ovnis*, are commonplace. More people there seem to have seen them than not. Mass sightings have been a prominent feature in the Mexican news over recent years. On our previous trip to Mexico City we had visited a Professor of Geology at the National University of Mexico to ask her about where she thought the crystal skulls came from. Though she asked to remain anonymous, even this respected academic told us that she had seen UFOs over Mexico City and that she would not want to rule out a possible connection with the crystal skulls.

At another of the ceremonies, a member of the Lakota Sioux from the northern US explained that one of their tribal legends had said that at the dawning of the new era on Earth, when there would at last be peace and harmony for all people and all creatures, the Great Spirit would send a white buffalo calf as a message to their people. The recessive gene necessary to create such a buffalo is generally thought to have been wiped out many centuries ago during the mass slaughter of buffalo. But apparently that very year a white buffalo calf had been born on a farm near Chicago, in fulfilment of the prophecy.

The final ceremony took place at dawn under one of the majestic volcanoes that rise up from the tranquil blue shores of Lake Atitlán. The stars were beginning to fade as we made our way down to the lakeside for the ceremony. The volcanoes on the distant shore stood silhouetted against the sky, their ancient peaks rising up like pyramids.

Don Alejandro stepped forward, joined on all sides by fellow members of the Council of Quiché Mayan Elders and representatives of many of the different tribes. Again, all of the colours of the rainbow seemed to be reflected in their attire. The Seneca of North America were represented by Jimmy Sun Wolf, the Pueblo by Patricio Domínguez and a man called Cloud Eagle, the Lakota Sioux by Ruben, Hunbatz Men represented the

Yucateca Maya, and various others represented the South American Almara, Kalaway and Achuar, to name but a few.

As the sun rose, the whole party saluted the four directions and then Don Alejandro began to speak. He explained that the ceremony to the sun was 'so that the sun might also rise in the hearts of all people, so that we might learn to live together on this Earth in peace and harmony with each other and all other things'.

Patricio spoke of a prophecy that was to make a strong and lasting impression on us. He spoke both of the legend of the crystal skulls and of the legend of the rainbow warriors. Whilst the legend of the skulls was best remembered by the Maya of Central America and the legend of the rainbow warriors by the Cree Indians of North America, they were shared in some form or another by many of the tribes and apparently formed some of the most fundamental teachings left behind by the very first people to inhabit this Earth.

Patricio then told the legend of the rainbow warriors:

'The ancestors said that light-skinned people would come out of the eastern sea in great canoes powered by huge white wings, like giant birds. The people who got off these great boats would also be like birds, but they would have two different kinds of feet. One of their feet would be like that of a dove, the other like that of an eagle. The foot of the dove would represent a beautiful new religion of love and kindness, whilst the foot of the eagle would represent greed for material wealth, technological strength and war-making ability.

'For many years the sharp foot of the eagle would dominate, for though the new people would talk much of the new religion, not all of the light-skinned people would live by it. Instead they would claw at the red nations with their eagle feet, killing, exploiting and then enslaving them.

'After offering mixed resistance to this clawing, the Indians would lose their spirit and allow themselves to be herded into small weak enclaves. This would then be the way of the world for many years. But then there would come a time when the Earth would become very sick. Because of the unrelenting greed of the new culture, the Earth would be filled with deadly liquids and metals, the air would be rendered foul with smoke and ash, and even the rains, which were intended to cleanse the Earth, would plummet in poison drops. Birds would fall from the sky, fish would turn belly up in the waters and whole forests would begin to die.

'When these things began to happen, the Indian people would be all but helpless. But then a new light would come from the east, and the Indians would begin to find their strength, their pride and their wisdom. The legend said they would also be joined by many of their light-skinned brothers and sisters, who would in fact be the reincarnate souls of the Indians who were killed or enslaved by the first light-skinned settlers. It was said that the dead souls of these first people would return in bodies of all different colours: red, white, yellow and black. Together and united, like the colours of the rainbow, these people would teach all of the peoples of the world how to have love and reverence for Mother Earth, of whose very stuff we human beings are also made.

'Under the symbol of the rainbow, all of the races and all of the religions of the world would band together to spread the great wisdom of living in harmony with each other and with all the creations of the Earth. Those who taught this way would come to be known as "the warriors of the rainbow". Although they would be warriors, they would carry with them the spirits of the ancestors, they would carry the light of knowledge in their heads and love in their hearts, and they would do no harm to any other living thing. The legend said that after a great struggle, using only the force of peace, these warriors of the rainbow would finally bring an end to the destruction and desecration of Mother Earth and that peace and plenty would then reign through a long, joyous and peaceful golden age here on Mother Earth.'

We were very moved by this and even more so as Patricio went on to explain that this legend was just as important as the legend of the crystal skulls. He said that these two legends 'had the same roots in the original knowledge left behind by the ancestors for the good of all mankind'. It was important that the legend of the rainbow warriors be fulfilled before any further great knowledge and wisdom could come forth from the crystal skulls, for only then might that knowledge be used for the good of all creation.

Don Alejandro completed the final ceremony with a short message to all present to remember these ancient prophecies. He said it was 'no longer important, it was now absolutely vital' that all those present took back with them all that they had learned at the gathering, for it was 'now time to spread these ancient teachings right across the Earth'.

As we bade Don Alejandro and the other elders goodbye before boarding our bus for the trip back to Guatemala City, Don Alejandro left us with a few personal words of farewell. He said simply, 'Now you have the keys to the future and you will publish, so that all the world will know.' At the time we had no plans to write this book, but these were his words all the same.

As our convoy of old buses drove off together for the very last time, a complete, perfect and beautiful rainbow suddenly appeared, arching right across the valley in front of us, as if lighting our path. We looked at Patricio in amazement. And he just winked.

THE FUTURE

On our return from Central America, we thought about all we had learned about the crystal skulls. The search for the truth about the skulls had opened up new vistas of knowledge, new horizons and territory. The skulls had challenged what we thought we knew about the world on many levels.

The substance of crystal itself had made us question what we had been taught about the physical world. The skulls had made us look at the relationship between ourselves and everything around us, suggesting that everything has a spirit and a life-force, that even 'inanimate' objects are fluid and alive.

The crystal skulls had invited us to explore our own way of thinking, only to reveal that what we have is but one way of perceiving the world. They had even challenged our everyday notion of reality, suggesting that unseen, subtle realms interact with our own.

The skulls had led us to Native American elders who shared their sacred teachings that the crystal skulls had been kept in Atlantis, left by beings from another planet or dimension, who would one day return. The indigenous elders spoke of our extra-terrestrial ancestors and the destruction of previous worlds. This knowledge challenged everything we knew about the history of our civilization, and offered a startlingly different perspective on our own human origins and destiny.

Arriving back home after attending the gathering in Guatemala was to see what was familiar in a new way. It was as if we had stepped outside our society for a few brief moments and so could now see it with a clarity we had hitherto never experienced. It hit us with the shock of seeing it for the very first time. What we could see was something that many people already sense. Our culture no longer knows where it is going. Science, technology and our conventional idea of 'progress' no longer seem able to provide the answers as to how we should live. Our Western civilization no longer serves its place in the whole.

Right now, our culture is deeply in denial. It is easier, in the short term, to put the problems out of our minds. On the surface, things seem OK. We still drive everywhere in our cars and fly anywhere in our planes, we still have an endless choice of products, and glossy adverts are still appearing, urging us to buy more and more. Yet every time the wheels of our civilization turn, another species of plant or animal is lost from this world. Our individual and collective pursuit of material wealth alone is ultimately suicidal because our own lifestyle is actually destroying the ecosystem of the Earth.

The crystal skulls lead us to question what type of world we are creating for our children and grandchildren. What will happen as the world gets hotter and more polluted? Will we still have clean air to breathe? Will we still have enough food to eat? What are our chances of a decent life?

Whether we believe the skulls to be ancient or modern, whether we believe, like the Native Americans, that the skulls were brought to Earth by extra-terrestrials to help humanity at a time of great need, and whether or not we believe, like the Maya, that the last Great Cycle of time will end on precisely the 21 December 2012, the fact is, if we carry on the way we are going, the world, or at least humanity as we know it, will very soon come to an end.

But we have a choice. It is not too late, but we have to act now. The skulls show us we need to develop a way of life that is in balance with the Earth and the natural forces of the universe. Every day as we go about our daily business, we must consider the consequences of all our actions. What we do matters. Even the way we think can have an effect. For, as Don Alejandro put it, 'pollution out there is also pollution within'. We need to find freedom from the stress and anxieties of modern life that pollute our minds and cut us off from our own true nature and the abundance of the natural world.

We are, each and every one of us, far more powerful than we realize and we need to wake up to our power and use it responsibly to create a better world, one without hunger, poverty and despair, one that does not champion the material above the spiritual, one that sees all of humanity taking its place in the Circle of Life.

The crystal skulls urge us to awaken. They are a form of remembering the past and creating the future. They make us aware of the life in the universe we occupy, in the trees and plants, even the rocks and stones. They remind us of the gift of life Mother Earth has given to all her children. We are all part of the great mystery that is creation.

As the Cherokee say, we have all the colours of humanity within us, the white of our bones, the yellow of our marrow, the red of our flesh, and the black of our pupils. The same soft skin covers our bones, the same warm blood runs through our veins, the same pulse beats in our hearts. Whatever our age, race or background, we are all alike, we all have that same skull within us.

Yet, more than this, the crystal skulls remind us that we are all spiritual beings in physical bodies and that we are all intimately related to all other things. The crystal skulls show us we need to honour the spirit within us and the spirit in everything around us. Only then will we be able to find peace within ourselves and celebrate our connection with all our fellow beings.

Wherever the crystal skulls really came from, they have a message: we may still have time to take up our rightful place in the universe. We may still have time to save ourselves and our planet before it is too late. Perhaps we will not heed that message. Our time will then be over and the human race will become nothing more than a skull itself. Or perhaps we will hear the message of the skulls and let the divine manifest itself through us, and humanity will then become the place where the heavens truly meet the Earth.

REFERENCES

Chapter 2: The Discovery

1 F. A. Mitchell-Hedges, *Danger, My Ally*, Elek Books Ltd, London, 1954; Little, Brown & Co., Boston, 1955; reissued Mitchell-Hedges & Honey, St Catharines, Ontario, 1995
2 Ibid., p.183
3 Ibid.
4 Ibid.
5 Ibid., p.243
6 Ibid.
7 Frank Dorland, *Holy Ice*, Galde Press Inc., St Paul, Minn., 1992, p.4
8 Ibid., pp.27–8
9 Sibley S. Morrill, *Ambrose Bierce, F. A. Mitchell-Hedges and the Crystal Skull*, Cadleon Press, London, 1972, p.13
10 Ibid.
11 Ibid.
12 Ibid.

Chapter 4: The Mystery

1 Adrian Gilbert and Maurice Cotterell, *The Mayan Prophecies*, Element Books, Shaftesbury, 1995, p.199
2 Quoted in F. A. Mitchell-Hedges, *Danger, My Ally*, Elek Books Ltd, London, 1954; Little, Brown & Co., Boston, 1955; reissued Mitchell-Hedges & Honey, St Catharines, Ontario, 1995, p.9
3 Ibid., plate section
4 Ibid., p.243
5 Ibid.
6 Ibid., p.247

7 Sibley S. Morrill, *Ambrose Bierce, F. A. Mitchell-Hedges and the Crystal Skull*, Cadleon Press, London, 1972
8 Ibid., pp.28–9
9 Quoted in Simon Welfare and John Fairley, *Arthur C. Clarke's Mysterious World*, Book Club Associates, London, 1981, p.53
10 G. M. Morant, 'A morphological comparison of two crystal skulls', *Man* XXXVI, 142–78 (July 1936), 105–7; Adrian Digby, 'Comments on the morphological comparison of two crystal skulls', ibid, 107–9
11 Digby, p.108
12 Joe Nickell and John F. Fischer, 'Crystal skull of death', *Fate* magazine, July 1984 (Part 1), pp.48–54
13 Quoted in Welfare and Fairley, op. cit., p.53
14 Mitchell-Hedges, op. cit., p.174
15 Quoted ibid., plate section
16 Welfare and Fairley, op. cit., p.53; with further details from Nickell and Fischer, op. cit., and August 1984 (Part 2), pp.81–7

Chapter 5: The Scientists

1 'History or hokum?' *Measure*, February 1971, p.10
2 F. A. Mitchell-Hedges, *Danger, My Ally*, Elek Books Ltd, London, 1954; Little, Brown & Co., Boston, 1955; reissued Mitchell-Hedges & Honey, St Catharines, Ontario, 1995, p.243
3 Adrian Digby, 'Comments on the morphological comparison of two crystal skulls', *Man* XXXVI, 142–78 (July 1936), p.108

Chapter 6: The Ancient Computer

1 Joseph Alioto, 'Introduction' to Frank Dorland, *Holy Ice: A bridge to the subconscious*, Galde Press Inc., St Paul, Minn., 1992, p.xii
2 At the time of going to press Professor Brindley's research has not yet been published.
3 Dorland, op. cit., p.17
4 Ibid., p.115
5 Ibid., p.115
6 Ibid., p.134
7 Ibid., pp.134–5
8 Ibid., p.117
9 Ibid., p.104
10 Ibid., p.112

Chapter 7: The Talking Skull

1 Brian Hadley-James, ed., *The Skull Speaks through Carole Davis*, AMHREA Publishing, Ontario, 1985
2 Lou Bergeron, 'When North flies South', *New Scientist* 2023, 30 March 1996, pp.24–8, and 'Quakes shift North Pole', *Guardian*, 21 March 1997, p.9

Chapter 8: The Curse of the Skull

1 Jane MacLaren Walsh, 'Crystal skulls and other problems or "Don't look it in the eye" ' in *Exhibiting Dilemmas: Issues of representation at the Smithsonian*, Amy Henderson and Adrienne L. Kaeppler, eds, Smithsonian Institution Press, Washington, DC, 1997
2 Ibid., p.134

Chapter 9: The Healing Skull

1 Star gave the reference J. J. Hurtak, *The Keys of Enoch*, Academy for Future Science, California, 1977

Chapter 11: The Boban Connection

1 Sandra Bowen, F. R. 'Nick' Nocerino and Joshua Shapiro, *Mysteries of the Crystal Skulls Revealed*, J & S Aquarian Networking, 1988
2 Quoted in Jane MacLaren Walsh, 'Crystal skulls and other problems or "Don't look it in the eye" ' in *Exhibiting Dilemmas: Issues of representation at the Smithsonian*, Amy Henderson and Adrienne L. Kaeppler, eds, Smithsonian Institution Press, Washington, DC, 1997, pp.123 and 125
3 Ibid., p.129
4 Ibid.,
5 Quoted ibid., p.127
6 Ibid., p.129
7 George Frederick Kunz, *The Precious Stones of Mexico*, Imprenta y Fototipia de la Secretaria de Fomento, Mexico, 1907, quoted ibid., p.121
8 Ibid.,
9 Ibid., p.131
10 Quoted ibid., p.127
11 Ibid.
12 Ibid., p.133

Chapter 12: The Aztecs and the Crystal Skull

1 De Sahagún, *A History of Ancient Mexico*, quoted in Miguel Léon-Portilla, *Aztec Image of Self & Society*, University of Utah Press, 1992, p.200
2 Ibid., p.29

3 Diego Durán, *The History of the Indies of New Spain*, 1581, quoted in Serge Gruzinski, *The Aztecs: Rise and fall of an empire*, Thames & Hudson, 1992, pp.19 and 21
4 Ibid., p.76
5 Gruzinski, p.60
6 De Sahagún, quoted ibid., p.74
7 Gruzinski, p.75
8 Durán, quoted ibid., pp.162–3
9 Michael D. Coe, *Mexico*, Thames & Hudson, p.176
10 Durán, quoted Gruzinski, op. cit., pp.163–4
11 Ibid.
12 Ibid., pp.76 and 82
13 Bernal Díaz, quoted in Coe, op. cit., p.158
14 Warwick Bray, *Everyday Life of the Aztecs*, B. T. Batsford Ltd, London, 1968
15 Gruzinski, op. cit., p.40
16 Friar Diego de Landa, *Yucatan before and after the Conquest*, trans. William Gates, Producción Editorial Dante, Merida, Mexico, 1990, quoted in Graham Hancock, *Fingerprints of the Gods*, Mandarin, 1995, p.105
17 Ibid.
18 Quoted in Coe, op. cit., p.168
19 Gruzinski, op. cit., p.97
20 Friar Diego de Landa, op. cit., quoted in Hancock, op. cit, p.121
21 Ibid.
22 Father Burgoa, quoted in Lewis Spence, *The Magic and Mystery of Mexico*, Rider, London, 1922, pp.228–9
23 Ibid.
24 Quoted in Miguel Léon-Portilla, *Aztec Thought and Culture*, University of Oklahoma Press, 1963; also in Gruzinski, op. cit., pp.130–1
25 Ibid.
26 Ibid.
27 Ibid., p.132
28 Ibid., pp.132–3
29 Ibid., p.133
30 Adela Fernandez, *Pre-hispanic Gods of Mexico*, Panorama Editorial, Mexico, 1992, quoted in Hancock, op. cit,. p.108
31 Quoted in Gruzinski, op. cit., p.130
32 Hancock, op. cit., pp.185 and 187
33 George E. Stuart, 'The timeless vision of Teotihuacan', *National Geographic* 188, no.6, December 1995, p.22
34 Hancock, op. cit., pp.191–5
35 Stuart, op. cit. p.30
36 Hancock, op. cit., p.190
37 Quoted ibid., pp.180–1
38 Stuart, op. cit., pp.12 and 15
39 *Mexico: Rough guide*, Harrap-Columbus, London, 1989, p.217; quoted in Hancock, op. cit., pp.189–90

40 Stuart, op. cit., p.15
41 Ibid.
42 Nigel Davis, *The Ancient Kingdoms of Mexico*, Penguin, London, 1990, p.67, quoted in Hancock, op. cit., p.178
43 Stuart, op. cit., p.22
44 Ibid.
45 Hancock, op. cit., p.195
46 Quoted in Stuart, op. cit., p.22
47 Hancock., op. cit., pp.188–9
48 Quoted in Stuart, op. cit., p.22
49 Ibid.

Chapter 14: The Maya and the Crystal Skull

1 Adrian G. Gilbert and Maurice M. Cotterell, *The Mayan Prophecies*, Element Books, Shaftesbury, 1995, pp.17–18
2 Ibid., p.19
3 Ibid., p.145
4 Ibid., p.19
5 Erich von Däniken, *Chariots of the Gods?* Souvenir Press, 1968
6 Ibid., p.122
7 Linda Schele and Mary Ellen Miller, *The Blood of Kings: Dynasty and ritual in Mayan art*, Thames & Hudson, London, 1992, pp.268–9
8 Gilbert and Cotterell, op. cit., pp.72–6
9 *Popul Vuh*, quoted ibid., p.76
10 *Popul Vuh*, trans. Albertina Saravia E., Editorial Piedra Santa, 1977, p.43. In the translation by Dennis Tedlock, Simon and Schuster, 1985, the head is called a bone.
11 *Popul Vuh* quoted in Karl Taube, *Aztec and Maya Myths*, British Museum Press, London, 1993, p.57
12 Quoted in Gilbert and Cotterell, op. cit., p.87
13 Ibid., p.148
14 Wilbert E. Garrett, 'La Ruta Maya', *National Geographic*, October 1989
15 Colin McEwan, *Ancient Mexico in the British Museum*, British Museum Press, 1994, p.45

Chapter 15: The Skull and the Ancient Calendar

1 Erich von Däniken, *Chariots of the Gods?* Souvenir Press, 1968, pp.123–4
2 José Arguïlles, *The Mayan Factor: Path beyond technology*, Bear & Co., Santa Fe, New Mexico, 1987, p.19
3 Adrian G. Gilbert and Maurice M. Cotterell, *The Mayan Prophecies*, Element Books, 1995, pp.141–2
4 Diego de Landa, *The Relacion*, quoted ibid, p.132
5 J. Eric S. Thompson, *The Rise and Fall of the Maya Civilisation*, The University of Oklahoma Press, 1954; Pimlico, 1993

6 *Popol Vuh,* trans. Albertina Saravia E., Editorial Piedra Santa, 1977, p.120
7 Quoted in *Guardian Online,* 19 December 1996

Chapter 16: The British Museum Tests

1 Jane MacLaren Walsh, 'Crystal skulls and other problems or "Don't look it in the eye" ' in *Exhibiting Dilemmas: Issues of representation at the Smithsonian,* Amy Henderson and Adrienne Kaeppler, eds, Smithsonian Institution Press, Washington, DC, 1997, p.134

Chapter 17: The Forensic

1 Frank Dorland, *Holy Ice,* Galde Press Inc., St Paul, Minn., 1992, p.44

Chapter 18: The Crystal Entity

1 C. Norman Shealy, *Miracles Do Happen,* Element Books, 1988

Chapter 20: The Knowledge

1 Stanislav Grof, MD, *The Holotropic Mind,* HarperSanFrancisco, 1993, pp.7–10
2 Ibid.
3 David Deutsch quoted in *Time Lords,* BBC Horizon programme, transmitted 2 December 1996
4 Ibid.
5 Ibid.
6 Ibid.
7 Dr Fred Alan Wolf, *The Dreaming Universe,* Simon and Schuster, 1994, pp.238–40
8 Ibid., p.240
9 *Time Lords,* op. cit.
10 Ibid.
11 *Le Point* 1256, 12 October 1996
12 *New Scientist,* 9 December 1995
13 'Universe may be honeycomb of huge voids', *Guardian,* February 1996

Chapter 21: The Spirit of the Skulls

1 Jamie Sams, *The Thirteen Original Clan Mothers,* HarperSanFrancisco, 1994

Chapter 23: The Lost Civilization

1 Plato, *Timaeus,* Penguin Books, London, 1965, p.36
2 Ibid., pp.37–8
3 Ibid.
4 Ibid.
5 Ibid.

6 Graham Hancock, *Fingerprints of the Gods*, Mandarin, 1995, p.5

7 Ibid., pp. 5 and 9

8 Ibid.

9 Ibid., p.9

10 Ibid., p.13

11 Otto Muck, *The Secret of Atlantis*, Collins, 1976

12 Ignatius Donnelly, *Atlantis the Ante-diluvian World*, Sidgwick & Jackson, 1950

13 Ibid., pp.132–7

14 Adrian Gilbert and Maurice Cotterell, *The Mayan Prophecies*, Element Books, Shaftesbury, 1995

15 'Meltdown', *Guardian Weekend*, 6 July 1996, pp.30–5

16 *Edgar Cayce on Atlantis*, Warner Books, 1968, p.114

17 *Atlantis: Fact or Fiction?* Association for Research and Enlightenment Press, Virginia Beach, VA, 1962, p.24

18 *Lost Cities of North and Central America*, Adventures Unimited Press, Stelle, Ill., 1992

19 *Atlantis: Fact or Fiction?* op. cit., p.24

20 Ann Walker, *The Stone of the Plough*, Element Books, Shaftesbury, 1997

21 *Atlantis: Fact or Fiction?* op. cit., p.27

22 Ibid., p.15

23 Quoted in Murry Hope, *Atlantis: Myth or Reality?* Arkana, 1991, p.298

24 Ibid.

25 Ibid.

26 Ibid., pp.298–9

27 *Atlantis: Fact or Fiction?* op. cit., p.17

28 Jamie Sams and Twylah Nitsch, *Other Council Fires Were Here Before Ours*, HarperSanFrancisco, 1991

29 Ibid., pp.68–9

30 Ibid., p.69

31 Ibid., pp.72–3

32 Ibid., p.76–8

33 Ibid., p.78

BIBLIOGRAPHY

Arguïlles, José, *The Mayan Factor: Path beyond technology*, Bear & Co., Santa Fé,
    New Mexico, 1987

Bray, Warwick, *Everyday Life of the Aztecs*, B. T. Batsford, London, 1968

Cayce, Edgar, *Edgar Cayce on Atlantis*, Warner Books, 1968

—, *Atlantis: Fact or Fiction?* ARE Press, Virginia Beach, VA, 1962

Childress, David Hatcher, *Lost Cities of North and Central America*, Adventures
    Unlimited Press, Stelle, Illinois, 1992

Coe, Michael, D., *Mexico*, Thames & Hudson, 1962

Dante, *The Divine Comedy, Vol. 1: Inferno*, Penguin Books, trans. 1971, reprinted
    1984

De Sahagún, Fray Bernardino, *A History of Ancient Mexico: 1547–1577*, trans. R.
    Bandelier, Fisk University Press, 1932

Digby, Adrian, 'Comments on the morphological comparison of two crystal skulls',
    Man XXXVI, 142–78, July 1936

Dioses del Mexico Antiguo, published by Antiguo Colegio de San Ildefonso, Mexico
    City, 1996

Donnelly, Ignatius, *Atlantis the Ante-diluvian World*, Sidgwick & Jackson, 1950

Dorland, Frank, *Holy Ice: Bridge to the subconscious*, Galde Press Inc., St Paul,
    Minn., 1992

Eliade, Mircea, *Shamanism*, first published 1964; reprinted Arkana, 1989

Fernandez, Adela, *Pre-hispanic Gods of Mexico*, Panorama Editorial, Mexico, 1987,
    1992

Gilbert, Adrian, and Cotterell, Maurice, *The Mayan Prophecies*, Element Books,
    Shaftesbury, 1995

Grof, Stanislav, *The Holotropic Mind*, HarperSanFrancisco, 1993

Gruzinski, Serge, *The Aztecs: Rise and fall of an empire*, New Horizons, Thames &
    Hudson, 1992

Guatemala, Belize & the Yucatan: A travel survival kit, Lonely Planet, 1994

Gunn-Allen, Paula, *Grandmothers of the Light*, Beacon Press, 1991

Hadley-James, Brian, ed., *The Skull Speaks through Carole Davis* (now Carole Wilson), AMHREA Publishing, Ontario, 1985
Halifax, Joan, *The Fruitful Darkness*, HarperSanFrancisco, 1993
Hancock, Graham, *Fingerprints of the Gods*, Mandarin, 1995
'History or hokum?', *Measure*, Hewlett-Packard staff magazine, February 1971
Hope, Murry, *Atlantis: Myth or Reality?* Arkana, 1991
Jung, Carl, *Man and his Symbols*, Aldus Books Ltd, 1964
Léon-Portilla, Miguel, *Aztec Image of Self & Society*, University of Utah Press, 1992
—, *Aztec Thought and Culture*, University of Oklahoma Press, 1963
McEwan, Colin, *Ancient Mexico in the British Museum*, British Museum Press, 1994
McFadden, Steven, *Profiles in Wisdom*, Bear & Co., Santa Fé, New Mexico, 1991
—, *Ancient Voices, Current Affairs*, Bear & Co., Santa Fé, New Mexico, 1992
Meadows, Kenneth, *The Medicine Way*, Element Books, Shaftesbury, 1990
Men, Hunbatz, *Secrets of Mayan Science & Religion*, Bear & Co., Santa Fé, New Mexico, 1990
Mexico: A travel survival kit, Lonely Planet, 1992
Mitchell-Hedges, F. A., *Danger, My Ally*, Elek Books, London, 1954; Little, Brown & Co., Boston, 1955; Mitchell-Hedges & Honey, St Catharines, Ontario, 1995
Moctezuma, Eduardo Matos, *The Mask of Death*, G. V. Editores, Mexico City, 1988
Morant, G. M., 'A morphological comparison of two crystal skulls', *Man*, XXXVI, 142–78, July 1936
Morrill, Sibley S., *Ambrose Bierce, F. A. Mitchell-Hedges and the Crystal Skull*, Cadleon Press, London, 1972
Muck, Otto, *The Secret of Atlantis*, Collins, 1976
Nickell, Joe, and Fischer, John F., 'Crystal skull of death', *Fate*, Part I, July 1984; Part II, August 1984
Nocerino, F. R. 'Nick', Bowen, Sandra, and Shapiro, Joshua, *Mysteries of the Crystal Skulls Revealed*, J & S Aquarian Networking, 1988
Oldfield, Harry, and Coghill, Roger, *The Dark Side of the Brain*, Element Books, Shaftesbury, 1988
Peat, F. David, *Blackfoot Physics: A journey into the Native American universe*, Fourth Estate, London, 1994
Peterson, Scott, *Native American Prophecies*, Paragon House, NY, 1990
Plato, *Timaeus*, Penguin Books, 1965
Popul Vuh, trans. Albertina Saravia E., Editorial Piedra Santa, 1977
Popul Vuh, trans. Dennis Tedlock, Simon & Schuster, 1985
Sabloff, Jeremy A., *The Cities of Ancient Mexico*, Thames & Hudson, 1989
Sams, Jamie, *The Thirteen Original Grandmothers*, HarperSanFrancisco, 1994
Sams, Jamie, and Nitsch, Twylah, *Other Council Fires Were Here Before Ours*, HarperSanFrancisco, 1991
Schele, Linda, and Miller, Mary Ellen, *The Blood of Kings: Dynasty and ritual in Mayan art*, Thames & Hudson, 1992
Shealy, Norman C., *Miracles Do Happen*, Element Books, Shaftesbury, 1988
Sheldrake, Rupert, and Fox, Matthew, *Natural Grace: Dialogues on science and spirituality*, Bloomsbury, 1996

Spence, Lewis, *The Magic and Mystery of Mexico*, Rider, London, 1922

Stuart, George E., 'The timeless vision of Teotihuacan', *National Geographic* 188, no.6, December 1995

Taube, Karl, *Aztec and Maya Myths*, British Museum Press, 1993

Thompson, J. Eric S., *The Rise and Fall of the Maya Civilisation*, University of Oklahoma Press, 1954; Pimlico, London, 1993

Von Däniken, Erich, *Chariots of the Gods?*, Souvenir Press, 1968

Walker, Ann, *The Stone of the Plough*, Element Books, 1997

Walsh, Jane MacLaren, 'Crystal skulls and other problems or "Don't look it in the eye" ', *Exhibiting Dilemmas: Issues of representation at the Smithsonian*, eds, Amy Henderson, and Adrienne L. Kaeppler, Smithsonian Institution Press, Washington, DC, 1997

Waters, Frank, *Book of the Hopi*, Penguin Books, 1963, 1978

Welfare, Simon, and Fairley, John, *Arthur C. Clarke's Mysterious World*, Book Club Associates, London, 1981

Wright, Ronald, *Stolen Continents: The Indian story*, John Murray, London, 1992

Wolf, Fred Alan, *The Dreaming Universe*, Simon & Schuster, 1994

Yenne, Bill, *The Encyclopedia of North American Indian Tribes*, Bison Books, 1986

Ywahoo, Dhyani, *Voices of our Ancestors: Cherokee teachings from the wisdom fire*, Shambala, Boston and London, 1987

FURTHER INFORMATION

Britain

The Sacred Trust
Information and courses

PO Box 603
Bath
BA1 2ZU

Tel: 01225 852615
Fax: 01225 858961
E-mail: SacredTrust@compuserve.com

Sacred Hoop Magazine
Tel/Fax: 01386 49680

USA

*The Society for Crystal Skulls
International*
Research/educational organization
Director: F. R. 'Nick' Nocerino

PO Box 302
Pinole, California 94564

Website: www.crystalskullsociety.org
E-mail: Ldyhwk13@aol.com

*Confederation of Indigenous Elders
and Priests of America*
For information about the Confederation
and their role, which is to strengthen the
traditional ways of friendship, trust and
co-operation and to promote a peaceful
future of co-existence with the Earth and
all beings.

PO Box 12340
87195
Albuquerque, New Mexico

Tel: 505-877-7618
E-mail: elders.guides@juno.com

JoAnn Parks and Max
PO Box 751261
Houston, Texas 77275-1261

Tel: 713-991-4545
Fax: 713-991-5679

Joshua Shapiro
V.J. Enterprises
Des Plaines, Illinois 60016

Tel: 847-699-8240
Fax: 847-699-9701
Website: http://www.execpc.com/vjentpr/
E-mail: rshapiro@interaccess.com

INDEX